WEYERHAEUSER ENVIRONMENTAL BOOKS

Paul S. Sutter, Editor

WEYERHAEUSER ENVIRONMENTAL BOOKS explore human relationships with natural environments in all their variety and complexity. They seek to cast new light on the ways that natural systems affect human communities, the ways that people affect the environments of which they are a part, and the ways that different cultural conceptions of nature profoundly shape our sense of the world around us. A complete list of the books in the series appears at the end of this book.

SEISMIC CITY

An Environmental History
of San Francisco's 1906 Earthquake

JOANNA L. DYL

UNIVERSITY OF WASHINGTON PRESS
Seattle and London

Seismic City is published with the assistance of a grant from the Weyerhaeuser Environmental Books Endowment, established by the Weyerhaeuser Company Foundation, members of the Weyerhaeuser family, and Janet and Jack Creighton.

University of Washington Press
www.washington.edu/uwpress

Library of Congress Cataloging-in-Publication Data
Names: Dyl, Joanna Leslie, 1973– author.
Title: Seismic city : an environmental history of San Francisco's 1906 earthquake / Joanna L. Dyl.
Description: 1st edition. | Seattle : University of Washington Press, 2017. | Includes bibliographical references and index. | Description based on print version record and CIP data provided by publisher; resource not viewed.
Identifiers: LCCN 2017007242 (print) | LCCN 2017012222 (ebook) | ISBN 9780295742472 (ebook) | ISBN 9780295742465 (hardcover : alkaline paper)
Subjects: LCSH: San Francisco (Calif.)—Environmental conditions—History—20th century. | San Francisco (Calif.)—Social conditions—20th century. | San Francisco Earthquake and Fire, Calif., 1906. | Earthquakes—Environmental aspects—California—San Francisco—History—20th century. | Natural disasters—Environmental aspects—California—San Francisco—History—20th century. | Earthquakes—Social aspects—California—San Francisco—History—20th century. | Natural disasters—Social aspects—California—San Francisco—History—20th century. | Urban ecology (Sociology)—California—San Francisco—History—20th century.
Classification: LCC GE155.C2 (ebook) | LCC GE155.C2 D95 2017 (print) | DDC 979.4/61051—dc23
LC record available at https://lccn.loc.gov/2017007242

COVER PHOTOGRAPHS: *(front)* Damaged streetcar rails and pavement, Howard Street at Fourteenth (CHS2016_2122). *(back)* Ruins along Dupont Street (CHS2016_2125). Photos courtesy of the California Historical Society.

For my dad

CONTENTS

FOREWORD

Putting the "Natural" Back into Disaster History

PAUL S. SUTTER

The great San Francisco earthquake of April 18, 1906, triggered one of the worst urban disasters in American history. In actual death toll, only the Galveston hurricane of 1900 seems to have surpassed it, though exact figures from such major disasters are often hard to come by. In popular memory, however, the San Francisco earthquake emphatically outshines all other urban disasters. What has made it so compelling? The scale and character of the destruction are part of the answer. Like Hurricane Katrina a century later, the San Francisco earthquake unfolded as a two-part disaster; the quake itself caused substantial damage and loss of life, but it was the fires, dozens of them that merged to engulf San Francisco over the following three days, that truly devastated the city. More than that, though, the distinctive character of San Francisco at the moment the earthquake occurred has made this disaster a story of lasting popular interest.

San Francisco was little more than half a century old by 1906, the product of a sustained boom with origins in two almost simultaneous 1848 events. The first was the Treaty of Guadalupe Hidalgo, signed in Mexico City on February 2, which officially ended the Mexican-American War and conveyed a vast western territory, including Mission Dolores and the tiny windswept settlement of Yerba Buena, to the United States. The second, which occurred on January 24, just a week earlier and a bit more than one hundred miles inland from what would become the city of San Francisco, was the discovery of gold by James Marshall at Sutter's Mill along the American River. Marshall's discovery triggered a massive international migration to and through the Golden Gate and into the Sierra goldfields. Over the next half century, San Francisco rapidly became one of America's largest cities and by far the biggest in the West, a city of more than 400,000 people perched at the Pacific terminus of American development. By 1906, San Francisco was an urban pot of gold at the end of the rainbow of continental expansion.

Turn-of-the-century San Francisco was also a city striving to be modern in an era of technological confidence and urban Progressivism. It had skyscrapers and a growing skyline; it boasted an increasingly sophisticated network of water, sewer, gas, and electric lines; its modern transportation system included streetcars and, distinctively, the cable cars that carried people up and down imposing hills; it prided itself on efficient urban administration and municipal services, including a modern fire department; it was an increasingly sanitary city, whose officials had fought to control the epidemiological challenges of dense urban settlement and increasingly rapid port-city connections; and it was in the process of bringing landscaped nature back into an urban fabric that had only just been wrested from sand dunes and tidal flats. San Francisco was not only a city of western destiny, then, but also a place of apparent environmental mastery. The great San Francisco earthquake of 1906 was thus something like the iceberg that undid the *Titanic* just six years later, an unsettling force of nature that shook San Franciscans' and Americans' faith in their modernity at the dawn of the American century. Indeed, the earthquake gave birth to the modern notion of "natural disaster": San Francisco, which seemed to sit outside of nature, met a force of nature that seemed to sit outside of history. Neither of these assumptions, of course, was true.

In *Seismic City*, her masterful retelling of the history of the San Francisco earthquake, Joanna Dyl both elaborates on and upsets this popular narrative of environmental mastery and undoing. As Dyl makes clear, we have been captivated by this earthquake not because it was a normal and predictable part of the city's history (which it was) but because it seemed such an aberration (which it was not). *Seismic City* is an exercise in correcting that habit of mind and a model for incorporating such hazard events into our steadier narratives of urban development. The sudden and entirely nonhuman violence of the San Francisco earthquake was certainly dramatic and destructive, but it also spawned a slow violence that flowed from latent energy held taut within the city's natural and human geography before the earthquake and that reverberated in social and cultural tremors in the decade after. Getting us to rethink just when this disaster began and ended, and how it sat at the grinding fault lines of multiple temporal scales, is one of *Seismic City*'s signature accomplishments.

Another of *Seismic City*'s achievements is its exploration of how the San Francisco earthquake was both natural and unnatural. Environmental historians have long had a conflicted relationship with so-called natural disasters. On the one hand, we are drawn to them precisely because they are moments when nonhuman forces dramatically shape human history. On the other hand, we know that such disasters are products of the human-built world and its history; they tend to uncover patterns more complicated than a universal human vulnerability in the face of fickle nature. In fact, disasters forcefully unearth our differences and divisions, revealing, reproducing, and even exacerbating social and economic inequalities. *Seismic City* effectively reconciles these two impulses. The earthquake is the epicenter of Dyl's narrative, a nonhuman part of what is often a largely human story. But *Seismic City* is a powerful urban environmental history precisely because the earthquake is, as Dyl puts it, only "one piece of evidence" in her more encompassing exploration of human-environmental relations.

The history of the San Francisco earthquake of 1906 began in geology and then proceeded with the choices made by urban residents to build a major city in such a seismic place. Those choices were not made in complete ignorance of the city's potential for disaster, for in the second half of the nineteenth century San Francisco experienced persistent trembling and frequent fire, but neither was the city designed with that potential in mind. Rather, in the midst of these portents, San Franciscans made and remade the peninsula to their liking, truncating the hills, filling the tidal flats, and building a modern, networked metropolis.

Environmental historians have long studied the terraformed and networked city, for in the made land and technologies of life support that cities require, we can see how urbanites have overcome the environmental limitations of place. One of *Seismic City*'s important insights is that the earthquake disaster in fact flowed from the vulnerabilities and failures of built systems and human achievements. The worst destruction occurred in those places where humans had done the most to remake the terrain of the city, and the fires were a product of infrastructural failures—downed electrical lines, broken gas mains, and the city's destroyed water system, which rendered the modern fire department all but useless. Not only did the earthquake reveal the structures, dependencies, and vulnerabilities of the highly engineered urban ecosystem that made concentrated human settlement possible, but the devastation that followed was a product of that ecosystem. It might be tempting to conclude, cleverly, that there was nothing natural about this disaster, but, as *Seismic City* makes clear, that conclusion would go too far. There is much about this story that is more than human, and Dyl's genius is to find the environmental dimensions in surprising places.

Influential San Franciscans responded to the destruction by attempting to reassert their social and environmental mastery. Here Dyl provides a telling case study of what scholars call "disaster capitalism," the theory that disasters serve as springboards for redevelopment that is at once profitable and inequitable. But in San Francisco, that general process ran headlong into an assortment of Progressive-era social and environmental ideologies, which in turn lent disaster capitalism a particular political ecology. San Francisco crumbled and burned just as the famed architect, Daniel H. Burnham, had crafted a City Beautiful blueprint for the city, and many hoped the extensive devastation would enable freer realization of that plan. The earthquake also came just a few years after the bubonic plague had pulsed through San Francisco, an outbreak blamed on the densely packed Chinatown, and the quake's aftermath brought renewed hopes of banishing the Chinese from the city's center. The earthquake rendered a huge percentage of the city's population homeless, and, not surprisingly, those with the fewest resources found it most difficult to rehouse themselves. Instead, they lived in tents and earthquake cottages, often in the city's parks, until wealthy San Franciscans began to call for their removal and relocation to the city's edges, fearing for the public's health and disingenuously deploying a suburban idyll as a lure. Finally, the city's power brokers used the earthquake as an excuse to take control of the streets, to rebuild San Francisco's fractured infrastructure in ways that suited them, to break unions, and to expel the remaining animal populations from the city. In short, the powerful used the pretense of the earthquake and fires to double down on their dreams of social and environmental mastery.

But what looked like environmental mastery to some felt like environmental injustice to others, and so rank-and-file San Franciscans pushed back. *Seismic City* details the complex and contingent ways in which these social and environmental tensions unfolded in the decade after the earthquake. Powerful city leaders managed to get only a portion of what they wanted. While they did push many poor and working-class residents to the edge of the city, and they broke a bitter strike by streetcar workers, the City Beautiful plan never came to fruition and Chinatown remained, albeit in modified form. Still, by the mid-1910s, city leaders were in a celebratory mood, and they threw their support behind the Panama Pacific International Exposition, designed both to memorialize the completion of the Panama Canal—another feat of modernist environmental mastery at the dawn of the American century—and to highlight the city's heroic reconstruction. But even this achievement, as Dyl reveals in a delicious irony, was built upon the unstable terrain of forgetfulness.

More than a century after the 1906 San Francisco earthquake, we live in a world of escalating urban disaster risk, and just what nature has to do with this state of affairs is getting murkier. Not only are extreme weather events increasingly artifacts of a human-inflected climate, but even some seismic hazards have taken on anthropogenic expression as humans have pried into and destabilized the subterranean world. We have indeed become geological agents, and nature as a force external to our presence on earth seems endangered. But the problem with this end-of-nature thinking is that it too easily becomes a dystopian variant of the logic of environmental mastery that drove San Francisco's creation, destruction, and re-creation. *Seismic City* is a history of how tectonic shifts undid a city, a history that accepts this traditional form of environmental causation even as it thoroughly situates the disaster in the shortcomings and inequalities of the human-built world. More than that, though, *Seismic City* is a book about the persistence in our cities of an environmental presence—in fact, many environmental presences—and the need to plan with those presences in mind, not against or in defiance of them.

ACKNOWLEDGMENTS

This book has had a long road to publication, and I have accumulated many debts along the way. This project began at Princeton University when my mentor Andrew C. Isenberg introduced me to the subject of environmental history. In addition to setting me on the path that led to this book, Drew has consistently challenged me intellectually and offered unfailing support for my career, more than once asking "What can I do?" as I have encountered various challenges. I learned a great deal about both research and teaching from Drew and other faculty in the Department of History, including Kevin Kruse, Elizabeth Lunbeck, Christine Stansell, Daniel Rodgers, and Jeremy Adelman. Ari Kelman was an initial reader of the manuscript and offered the best kinds of encouragement, including provocative questions that shaped the project's development, and he has continued to provide mentorship, support, and highly entertaining Facebook threads. Many of my graduate colleagues contributed valuable feedback and support, particularly Emily Brock, James Morton Turner, Anastasia Curwood, Jessica Salvatore, Malinda Lindquist, and the members of my writing group. I am also grateful for financial support from Princeton, the Department of History, the Graduate School, and the Program in American Studies, which funded research travel and allowed me to complete my degree without balancing a heavy teaching load. The University of California, Berkeley, also welcomed me as an Exchange Scholar for an indispensable year of research.

I have been lucky to teach at several excellent institutions with supportive colleagues and smart, engaged students. My time in the Department of History at the University of South Florida allowed me to develop as a scholar and teacher, and I would like to thank my colleagues there—particularly Frances Ramos, Steve Prince, Julia Irwin,

Tamara Zwick, Julie Langford, Michael Decker, David Johnson, Fraser Ottanelli, Barbara Berglund, and Phil Levy—for many stimulating conversations. USF also supplied financial support in the form of a New Researcher Grant as well as grants from the Humanities Institute, the College of Arts and Sciences, and the Research Council. The Copeland Colloquium at Amherst College offered a much-needed year focused on writing among a congenial group of interdisciplinary scholars. Our discussions of catastrophe taught me a great deal and made this a better book.

The Department of Earth and Environment at Franklin & Marshall College gave me the chance to teach in an Environmental Studies Department and at a liberal arts college. Elizabeth De Santo, Dorothy Merritts, and Jim Strick provided particular intellectual and personal support during my two years there, and financial assistance from Franklin & Marshall allowed me to complete the research for this book and obtain the rights to many of the images. The University of Redlands facilitated my return to the West Coast, and I would like to thank Daniel Klooster and the other faculty in environmental studies for the opportunity to put the final touches on the manuscript in such a beautiful setting. Lisa Benvenuti of the Center for Spatial Studies at Redlands created a wonderful map and also served as an excellent fellow instructor on earthquake hazards (my expertise) and GIS (hers). My students at all of these institutions helped deepen my knowledge and gave me hope that the environment will be in good hands in the future.

Like any historian, I relied heavily on capable librarians to identify and track down obscure sources. The staff at the Bancroft Library, the California Historical Society, the Labor Archives and Research Center at San Francisco State University, the National Archives at San Francisco (which has changed its name since my visit), the San Francisco History Center at the San Francisco Public Library, and the California State Archives and California State Library in Sacramento all helped me immensely. The hard-working women and men behind interlibrary loan at Princeton, USF, Franklin & Marshall, and the University of Redlands obtained various essential sources for me, although I am sure they shook their heads at finding yet another request with my name on it.

Over the years, I presented material that became part of this book at many American Society for Environmental History conferences as well as at the Boston Environmental History Seminar and conferences organized by the Association of American Geographers, the Western History Association, the Urban History Association, the German Historical Institute, the Pacific Coast Branch of the American Historical Association, the Shelby Cullom Davis Center at Princeton University, and the Coastal Cities Summit. I would like to thank the commentators, audience members, and my fellow panelists for thought-provoking and insightful conversation. Conevery Bolton Valencius gave me particularly valuable feedback on material from chapters 1 and 2. Earlier versions of portions of this book have appeared in the journal *Management of Environmental Quality* and in *The Nature of Cities: Culture, Landscape, and Urban Space*, edited by Andrew C. Isenberg and published by the University of Rochester Press.

At the University of Washington Press, Bill Cronon and Marianne Keddington-Lang first expressed interest in the manuscript, and after taking over as series editor, Paul Sutter offered excellent editorial guidance and thoughtful comments on the manuscript and Progressive Era environmental history. Regan Huff, Margaret Sullivan, Julie Van Pelt, and many other staff played essential roles in ushering the manuscript into book form. I am grateful to them for their good humor, professionalism, and willingness to tolerate my struggles with deadlines. Amy Smith Bell provided careful copyediting. Craig Colten and an anonymous reader offered invaluable feedback and saved me from several errors and omissions. Any remaining errors are entirely my responsibility.

Finally, I would like to thank family and friends who have provided support and perspective throughout the years. My travels as an itinerant academic (and volleyball player) have resulted in an extensive and diverse network of friends around the country, for which I am grateful. In particular, my parents, Ed and Judy Dyl, have supplied both moral and financial support for all my educational endeavors. My dad did not live to see the completion of this book, but it is dedicated to him.

SEISMIC CITY

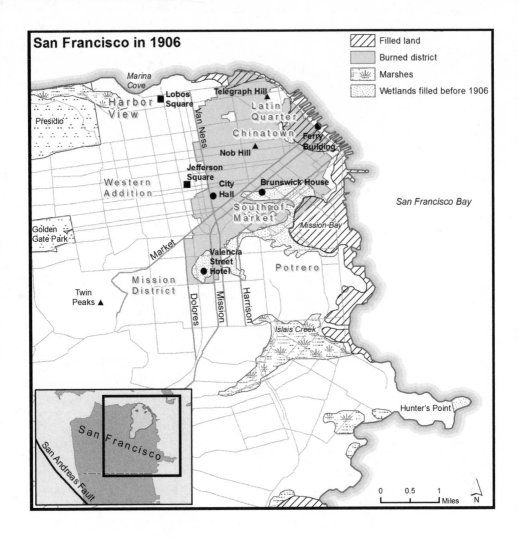

San Francisco in 1906

Filled land
Burned district
Marshes
Wetlands filled before 1906

Marina Cove

Harbor View

Presidio

Lobos Square

Telegraph Hill

Latin Quarter

Chinatown

Ferry Building

Van Ness

Nob Hill

Jefferson Square

City Hall

Brunswick House

Western Addition

Southof Market

San Francisco Bay

Golden Gate Park

Market

Mission Bay

Valencia Street Hotel

Potrero

Twin Peaks

Mission District

Dolores

Mission

Harrison

Islais Creek

Hunter's Point

San Francisco

San Andreas Fault

0   0.5   1
Miles

N

INTRODUCTION

AT 5:12 A.M. ON WEDNESDAY, APRIL 18, 1906, A MASSIVE EARTH-quake struck San Francisco and the surrounding region. The ground shook and twisted for almost a full minute as the earth's crust cracked along a fault line known at the time as the San Andreas Rift. The two sides of the fault shifted as the Pacific tectonic plate crept north and the North American plate rumbled southward. The plates moved as much as twenty-one feet in parts of Marin County, just a few miles north of San Francisco across the bay, and as much as sixteen feet on the penin-sula where the city of San Francisco nestled at the northern end. The Rift, which had been mapped by geologists ten years earlier, lay just to the west of San Francisco, with the picturesque Cliff House on the city's western shore standing only three miles from the fault.[1]

In modern terms of measurement, the quake has been calculated at a magnitude of 7.8, among the largest earthquakes in California history. Alexander G. McAdie, the head of the San Francisco office of the US Weather Bureau in 1906 who had a particular interest in earthquakes, described the temblor as "about as severe an earthquake as can be expe-rienced without total destruction, without great yawning chasms and complete destruction of life and property." The scale of intensity used at the time, the Rossi-Forel scale, rated earthquakes on a scale of one to ten, and scientists classified the 1906 quake as a nine. The destruction extended for at least 350 miles along the north-south line of the fault and for thirty-five miles on either side, covering a total area of 25,000 square miles. The shaking could be felt south as far as Los Angeles, north along the coast more than one hundred miles past the Oregon state line, and east into the Nevada desert as far as the town of Winnemucca—a land area of 175,000 square miles.[2]

Many observers reported, and seismologists confirmed, that the earthquake came in two shocks. The first lasted approximately forty-five seconds, and after a pause of ten to twelve seconds, an even stronger shock hit San Francisco. At least thirty-four aftershocks occurred throughout the day on April 18, with the strongest taking place at 8:14 A.M. and registering a five on the Rossi-Forel scale, meaning it was capable of displacing loose masonry and even wrecking some buildings.[3] At the first shock the combination of motion and sound jarred awake San Franciscans jaded by life in "earthquake country." William Cushing remembered: "My ears were assailed by a chorus of terrifying noises, the creaking and cracking of timber, the crashes of falling plaster and breaking glass."[4] Not all residents felt the full intensity of the shaking. People lucky enough to be ensconced in sturdy buildings on rocky ground did not initially realize the severity of the earthquake, but throughout much of San Francisco, men, women, and children sought safety in the streets.

The earthquake damage was most severe in neighborhoods located near the shores of the bay. There, land that fifty years earlier had been sand dunes, tidal swamps, mudflats, creeks, and even open water housed one-sixth of San Francisco's population and most of its commercial ventures. In those districts cheap lodging houses collapsed, trapping hundreds of the city's working poor. Further inland, City Hall crumbled, a symbol of the chaos that engulfed San Francisco. The shaking also ruptured underground water and gas pipes and cut off electrical power, telephone service, and the telegraph lines that linked San Francisco with the rest of the country. Jack London, who experienced the earthquake from his home in Sonoma Valley, wrote: "All the cunning adjustments of a twentieth-century city had been smashed by the earthquake.... all the shrewd contrivances and safeguards of man had been thrown out of gear by thirty seconds' twitching of the earth-crust." London expressed the contemporary sense that the earthquake challenged the power of technology and the permanence of the urban form.[5]

And the situation would only get worse. Over the next three days, a chain reaction of fires multiplied the devastation of the city and overwrote much of the visible evidence of the earthquake in the process.

Fires, much more than earthquakes, were endemic to the urban environment in the nineteenth- and early twentieth-century United States. Major fires had burned Chicago in 1871, Boston in 1872, and Baltimore in 1904, to name just the most prominent, and San Franciscans had taken precautions after their own "great fires" of the early 1850s.[6] The earthquake, however, had changed the rules when it shattered the underground pipes that conveyed water to the city and funneled it beneath the city's streets and into its buildings. On April 18 more than fifty fires broke out around San Francisco in the first few minutes after the earthquake. As one contemporary observer noted: "The causes of these fires were directly traceable to earthquake effects," including fallen oil lamps, damaged chimneys and flues, overturned boilers and furnaces, shattered gas pipes, and disrupted electrical currents.[7] Initially the main fires moved slowly against the wind, but the blazes soon sped through residential districts filled with wood-frame dwellings. With its water supply cut off, San Francisco found itself at the mercy of changeable winds and roaring flames, and the combination of spreading fires and earthquake damage left 250,000 people homeless by the night of April 21. Over the course of three days, the fire destroyed 514 city blocks—more than half the acreage of the city—and 28,188 buildings. The combined losses of the earthquake and fire amounted to 80 percent of the property value of San Francisco, estimated at between $350 million and $500 million in 1906 dollars.[8]

Such devastation also took a human toll, and the question of the number of deaths caused by the disaster has been a matter of debate since the first attempts to take stock of the catastrophe. In his official report, Major General Adolphus W. Greely, the commander of the army's San Francisco–based Pacific division, listed 304 known dead, 194 unknown dead, and 415 seriously injured. The Sub-Committee of Statistics, appointed by Mayor Eugene Schmitz after the disaster, reported 325 killed by the earthquake or fire, 7 shot, and 352 missing as of April 24. Other accounts described additional deaths by violence and implied much larger numbers of dead among the collapsed rooming houses south of Market, in the Mission, and in the burned ruins of Chinatown and the Latin Quarter. A labor newspaper, the *Coast Seamen's Journal*, succinctly expressed the difficulties of enumerating the victims in its first issue after the disaster. It named six lodging houses that had collapsed, concluding that "none may ever know how many were killed, the majority of the inmates being strangers of limited means, in a strange city." Many of these "strangers" were longtime city residents, but they made up the city's anonymous working poor, white and Chinese, native-born and immigrant alike. Gladys Hansen, the San Francisco city archivist, became suspicious of the low official estimates, particularly since the list of the dead included only twelve Asian names despite the complete destruction of Chinatown. Through extensive research, Hansen identified more than three thousand direct and indirect casualties—a number that she believed was still low.[9] The exact number of dead will never be known, but in both casualties and property damage, the San Francisco earthquake and fire remains one of the worst catastrophes in US history.

"NATURAL" DISASTERS AND HISTORY

The tragic events that took place between April 18 and April 21, 1906, began with forty-five seconds of seismic activity—a thoroughly natural phenomenon for the San Francisco region. Scholars of natural hazards emphasize that disasters are not caused by natural forces but rather take shape through the confluence of a precipitating event and social circumstances that place people at risk. As the environmental historian Ted Steinberg has explained, so-called natural disasters "are produced through a chain of human choices and natural occurrences."[10] The seismic history of San Francisco aptly illustrates this crucial insight. Earthquakes were part of the ordinary framework of life in the city, even in seismically quiet decades, and most represented little more than a thrill or a moment of uncertainty for residents who felt slight movements of the earth. The labeling of California as "earthquake country" has been criticized by scholars for the way it geographically delimits the threat of seismic activity, fostering a false sense of security among residents of other regions of the United States. However, the idea of "earthquake country" and the experience of regular small earthquakes shaped the perceptions of San Francisco residents, creating a locally distinct culture with a distinct historical memory and psychology of risk.[11]

Earthquakes also represent an intersection of two distinct time scales—those of human and natural or geological history. Most people rarely worry about geological forces, which represent an invisible, deep history that has resulted in a planet perceived as primarily stable and unchanging. This is not strictly true, however. Environmental events such as earthquakes, volcanic eruptions, and the tsunamis that sometimes result have shaped the planet's surface since long before humans built their first settlements. These events appear irregular and unpredictable to us, but on a planetary and geologic scale they are also inevitable and thoroughly natural. Thus, it is only a matter of time before cities ranging from San Francisco north to Anchorage, Alaska—destroyed by the second largest earthquake ever recorded in 1964—and east to Charleston, South Carolina, and even New York City face the consequences of an ever-evolving planet.[12] In coastal California, seismic activity occurs frequently enough to serve as a reminder that the earth remains a dynamic place in which humans are not the only agents of change. Geology intersects human history as earthquakes periodically rock cities like San Francisco.

Throughout most of the city's history, however, residents seemed more likely to deny the risks posed by earthquakes than to plan for them. The geographer Kenneth Hewitt has written that the dominant modern view of calamities treats "everyday life and disaster as opposites." Such thinking classifies the relationship between humans and nature as one of two modes: "one normal, secure, *productive* and the other abnormal, insecure and the occasion of losses." In that dominant view disasters exist outside the realm of the normal rather than being integral to and characteristic of the environment of a place.[13] Such a view discourages planning for disaster even when it might be possible to predict the consequences of seismic activity, severe storms, or other events that can precipitate what we call disaster. Paradoxically, the earthquake culture in San Francisco in the nineteenth century and even most of the twentieth proved less than conducive to precautionary planning for earthquake hazards, despite the widespread recognition that seismic activity was normal for the region. Disaster remained something understood as removed from everyday life, and even when major earthquakes struck the city—most notably in 1906 but also in 1865, 1868, and even 1989—residents emphasized restoring the normal over explicit adapation that would have required altering practices of urban development.

The question of why most San Franciscans not only chose to accept the threat of earthquakes—to remain in a hazard zone—but continued practices that increased risk is crucial to developing current and future disaster policies. The sociologist Kai Erikson has suggested that "one of the crucial tasks of culture . . . is to help people camouflage the actual risks of the world around them—to help them edit reality in such a way that it seems manageable, . . . [so] that the dangers pressing in on them from all sides are screened out of their line of vision as they go about their everyday rounds."[14] The historian's task, then, is to identify the specific characteristics of such a culture of risk. In his study of Andean peoples facing hazards from melting glaciers, the historian Mark Carey found that locals chose to rebuild in hazard zones not because of ignorance but because of "complex historically produced social relations." Economic, social, and cultural considerations trumped fear of potential disasters, and local people made active choices rather than being passive victims of disaster.[15] In his work on New Orleans, the geographer Craig Colten notes that attempts to address environmental threats are limited by identification of hazards, available technologies, and "the cost a society is willing to pay."[16] Residents of San Francisco faced similarly complicated circumstances of weighing the risks of life in earthquake country against the environmental, economic, and cultural opportunities offered by the city. Like Carey, I emphasize the choices of San Franciscans of all backgrounds, choices that were made with imperfect knowledge and in the face of constraints such as poverty and discrimination, but that nevertheless represented the active choices of historical agents.

The relative absence of natural disasters from the study of history may contribute to the widespread tendency to ignore or downplay the risks they pose. The San Francisco earthquake, which has been the subject of hundreds of books, initially appears to represent an exception to such historical invisibility. But even the 1906 San Francisco earthquake is unlikely to appear in a history textbook.[17] More tellingly, it is hardly mentioned in many histories of San Francisco. For example, the disaster merits only one sentence in a prominent political history of the city from 1865 to 1932. Gray Brechin's environmental history, *Imperial San Francisco: Urban Power, Earthly Ruin*, spends only a few paragraphs on the earthquake and fire.[18] The relative absence of disasters from historical narratives reflects the ways in which disasters have been understood as departures from history—breaks in the normal order of things—rather than as integral to human history.

Nature itself has seemingly demanded a renewed consideration of the potential impacts of disasters in recent years. Hurricane Katrina's devastation of the Gulf Coast in 2005 and, seven years later, "Superstorm" Sandy's impact on New Jersey and New York dramatically reminded Americans of the power of natural forces even in the twenty-first century. In the immediate aftermaths of these storms, discussions in both popular media and scholarly literature often treated the crises as unprecedented. For example, a 2006 article by an anthropologist and New Orleans resident refers to Katrina uncritically as "a calamity of unprecedented magnitude" in which "with no memory to fall back on, no model to rely on, everyone struggled with even the most basic ways to describe what had happened to the city of New Orleans and its stranded residents."[19]

As this book, and indeed the entire global history of disasters, shows, Katrina was not nearly as unprecedented as this quotation (and many others) suggest. The 2002–11 period saw an average of 394 disasters per year that caused an annual average of over one hundred thousand deaths. In 2004 the massive earthquake and tsunami in the Indian Ocean alone resulted in more than two hundred thousand deaths. Lest we transfer our claims of exceptionalism to that disaster, at least five different earthquakes since 1900 are estimated to have killed over one hundred thousand people. Although death tolls are far lower in the United States, the country consistently ranks among the top five in number of disasters in the early years of the twenty-first century.[20] The ubiquity of disasters demonstrates the importance of understanding them historically, including studying how societies cope with and recover from the multifaceted crises that we label natural disasters.

Disasters also represent particularly powerful examples of the ways in which human societies remain embedded within nature. As the anthropologist Anthony Oliver-Smith has written: "Disasters occur at the intersection of nature and culture and illustrate, often dramatically, the mutuality of each in the constitution of the other."[21] That intersection is, of course, the core subject of environmental history. To take this a step further, scholars have demonstrated how natural disasters of all kinds occur as the unintended consequences of, in the words of the historian Ari Kelman, "everyday decisions made by people who sought to impose social, economic, and spatial order on their environment."[22] Disasters not only remind us of nonhuman nature's ongoing power to affect both the planet and human history, but they also demonstrate how our own actions and decisions—our own efforts to shape nature—in turn often have unforeseen consequences.

CITIES, URBAN ECOLOGY, AND DISASTER HISTORY

If disasters have often been seen as entirely natural, outside the realm of human responsibility, then by contrast cities have often been perceived as outside of nature. Lewis Mumford summed up this prevailing point of view when he wrote: "As the pavement spreads, nature is pushed away."[23] Urban and rural, city and country, culture and nature—these dichotomies have been tropes of American thought since the nation's founding. In the modern United States nature has often been characterized as something out there, in the wilderness, far away from the cities where most people live.[24] Such dichotomies are, of course, false. Nature is all around us, even in the most densely urbanized environment. Our cities and our own bodies are very much part of nature. In San Francisco, seismic activity was not the only manifestation of nature's presence as a force in the city's history. Fire, disease, and capricious weather also played important roles in shaping the experiences of San Franciscans and their construction and reconstruction of their city. Four-legged urban residents such as horses and rats move through these pages alongside two-legged humans (and chickens).

This history is a story of the intersection of natural forces with human choices, nonhuman nature with the built environment. The resulting narrative illustrates the impossibility of separating nature and culture even in the modern city.[25] San Francisco is perhaps a particularly appropriate subject for such a history, as nonhuman nature seems to possess a more visible presence there than in other densely populated metropolitan centers such as New York City. As one guidebook noted in its opening sentence: "It is hard to be unaware of the earth in San Francisco."[26] The spectacular hilltop views of the water and nearby green spaces can conceal the complexity of the city's environmental history, however, including the ways in which nature has shaped that history as far more than an object of contemplation and preservation.

Urban environments possess their own distinct ecologies, whether visible or concealed. They serve as the habitat of not only humans but of many other species as well, and all of those species—humans included—must obtain food and water from their environment. By disrupting the daily functioning of life in San Francisco, the earthquake and fire rendered visible hidden elements of the day-to-day subsistence of the city's residents. A complex network of ecological, economic, and cultural relationships sustained hundreds of thousands of people in a relatively small geographic area. Those relationships included commercial ties with food producers near and far, infrastructures that provided water and electricity and carried away waste, and transportation and communications networks that linked the city with the region and the nation. Ultimately, the very survival of urban residents relied on the flow of subsistence needs into and out of the city. San Francisco in the early twentieth century serves as a case study of an "urban ecosystem" during a period of transition from the Victorian to the modern city.[27] The experiences of the tens of thousands of people left homeless also illustrate the thin layer of technology and civilization that protected even well-off urban residents from the elements and the direct experience of cold and hunger.

The crisis and subsequent rebuilding facilitated changes in San Francisco's urban ecology. In the aftermath of catastrophe residents had to decide whether to widen their city's narrow streets and take better advantage of the scenic potential of its hills and spectacular water views. They had to decide how to address sanitary problems and threats of disease, including a bubonic plague outbreak. Reformers and refugees alike debated what types of housing would be constructed and how neighborhoods would be rebuilt, when and where sewers would be repaired and indoor plumbing installed, and where undesirable industries would be situated.[28] Explicitly or implicitly, such debates represented choices about how people would live in the city and where nonhuman nature fit in the urban environment. The development of

San Francisco in the early twentieth century, and particularly in the months and years after the earthquake and fire, represented a series of conscious decisions about urban ecology that promoted sometimes conflicting visions of the modern, twentieth-century city. The decisions reached had disproportionate impacts on working people and recent immigrants, and they were far from uncontested. Ultimately, however, reactions to the disaster ratified the ideal of the separation of the urban and rural and concealed the importance of nature to the city's history and its future.

Another set of choices facing San Franciscans in the aftermath of the earthquake—choices they were perhaps more consciously aware of than choices about urban ecology—were those of how to rebuild their city, economically and socially. Some economists, urban historians, and geographers have suggested that modern capitalist cities thrive through a process of creative destruction in which reconstruction of urban space fuels economic development and the modernization of infrastructure. In such a view, urban disasters represent an opportunity for rebuilding and improvement through modernization. A variation of this is the idea of disaster capitalism, in which capitalist interests exploit disasters for economic and political gain.[29] These concepts often ignore or downplay the lived experiences of residents of a city stricken by disaster. Despite initial optimism, most ordinary San Franciscans did not experience the process of recovery and rebuilding as one of opportunity. This book asks what disaster capitalism meant for the city's working people in an era of open conflict between labor and capital across the country and in the streets of San Francisco.

In 1906 there was little doubt that the city would rise from the ashes of the fire. The form of the new city that would emerge from the ruins of the old was very much up for debate, however. This history traces different versions of the modern city that surfaced after the earthquake— from refugees who demanded homes to sanitary experts who wanted a city of concrete—and addresses why some succeeded and others failed. These debates occurred within the context of the Progressive Era, a period of reforms that addressed urban ecology through concern with pollution, sanitation, housing, and urban planning. Progressives asserted the perfectability of the city under expert management and through the use of modern science and technology, and reactions to the earthquake, fire, and rebuilding reflected Progressive Era attempts at enhancing urban order—and their opposition. A powerful "politics of place" persisted in San Francisco in the aftermath of the city's destruction as residents of all classes, races, and political persuasions fought for their visions for their city.[30]

The contest over both ideals of the city and the material circumstances of urban life was a story of power and resistance. The concept of vulnerability highlights how some populations face greater risks from hazard events. Differing levels of resilience result from the intersection of existing conditions of inequality with a precipitating event such as an earthquake. As the historian Greg Bankoff has explained: "Vulnerable populations are those at risk, not simply because they are exposed to hazard, but as a result of a marginality that makes of their life a 'permanent emergency.'"[31] In San Francisco the working-class neighborhoods of South of Market, Chinatown, and North Beach were devastated by both the earthquake and the fire. The lives of most residents of these districts were highly precarious even before April 1906. Periods of unemployment were common, and an injury or illness could prove debilitating to individuals and families in an era with few social safety nets. Both the relative normality of risk for working-class San Franciscans and the limited power that they possessed complicate any consideration of choices made by city residents in the wake of the 1906 disaster. However, even individuals facing long-term homelessness and marginalization as refugees mobilized behind their own visions of the possibilities offered by the crisis. For some of the city's disadvantaged residents, the aftermath of the earthquake and fire galvanized them to assert their rights as citizens and their own ideas about the urban environment.[32]

Class was of course not the only factor dividing the city. Even as white San Franciscans prided themselves on their city's relative freedom from the problems of older eastern cities, they worried about the impact of immigration, particularly of new arrivals from Asia and Italy.[33] Those immigrants in turn sought to claim space for themselves in a city that was often anything but welcoming. Chinese residents were confined to the seventeen blocks of Chinatown because of discriminatory rental practices, and they faced constant threats of violence even as trade with China represented an important part of San Francisco's economy. Although the city's large Italian population faced less open discrimination than the Chinese, they too crowded into the poor neighborhoods of North Beach and Telegraph Hill and faced criticism for cultural differences from more Americanized sectors of the city. South of Market, another working-class neighborhood, was home to large populations of Irish Catholics as well as Jewish immigrants from Eastern Europe.[34] The earthquake and fire—and the subsequent refugee camps, rebuilding disputes, labor conflict, and disease outbreaks—demonstrate how both class and race shaped the disaster, the city's recovery, and the broader contours of urban life in early twentieth-century San Francisco. Class, race, and power also remain inseparable from debates about the urban environment. Questions of environmental equity in the wake of the disaster reveal how discussions of urban nature reflected and refracted power relations in the city.

An emphasis on the impact of disaster on disadvantaged populations demonstrates how a disaster is not so much an event as a process—one that is embedded in social relations and in history. Not surprisingly, poor people, people of color, recent immigrants, and women bore the brunt of catastrophe in San Francisco. However, they also organized and fought to enact their own plans for the city, whether by demanding homes and relief funds or resisting efforts to force them out of prime real estate. This story is often one of resistance, including not only resistance by the city's human residents but also forms of resistance by the dynamic natural environment. Nature, ranging from seismic forces to diseased rats, obviously did not intentionally resist urban order, but it nevertheless consistently frustrated efforts at discipline and control. Nature in the city, I suggest, was inherently inimical to elite visions of a tightly controlled, rationalized space, just as urban populations consistently challenged social control efforts.

The earthquake itself is both the starting point of this book (the epicenter, if you will) and a dramatic example of the power of nature in an urban setting, but the environmental, economic, and cultural consequences of the disaster rippled through San Francisco in all directions, and metaphorical aftershocks continued to be felt in the city and the surrounding region for years. Seismic waves had varying effects on the natural and built environments that made up the physical landscape of

San Francisco—from granite hills to low-lying made land, the majestic Palace Hotel to decrepit wood-frame lodging houses. Subsequent metaphorical waves of change also had widely divergent impacts on the city's human population, reverberating along preexisting lines of class, race, and gender. The 1906 earthquake and fire and its aftermath reveal the complexity of San Francisco's existence as part of nature in the early twentieth century. The near-total devastation of the city represented a profound challenge to the prevailing cultural narrative of the modern city's triumph over nature, but in 1906 that seductive narrative of human technological progress prevailed over alternatives that might have led to rethinking patterns of urban development.

The disaster in all its elements—earthquake, fire, and recovery—profoundly disrupted the urban order, both environmental and social. The chaos ranged from tangled wires blocking the streets and iconic structures lying in ruins to tent camps housing refugees, rats feasting among broken sewers, and the reemergence of a dreaded disease. The earthquake challenged the stability of the built environment and the perceived permanence of the city. The presence of rats, disease, untimely rainstorms, and clouds of dust when it was not raining threatened assumptions about the healthfulness of San Francisco's people, neighborhoods, and even climate. And the disruption of spatial divisions of class and race—the presence of thousands of refugees in parks, the devastated infrastructure that forced men and women of all classes to cook in the streets and travel on foot, the destruction of Chinatown that both forced its residents into new parts of the city as refugees and seemed to many whites to offer an opportunity to claim the prime territory as their own, the mobilization of working men and women to affirm the centrality of their labor to both the rebuilding of the city and the functioning of the urban ecosystem—also represented the disruption of social and power relations in the city. The disaster highlighted the contested terrain of urban nature as people struggled to restore, rebuild, and remake their city.

To most San Franciscans, the disorder demanded the reassertion of the control over nature that they saw as characteristic of the modern city. For elites, the crisis also necessitated reasserting control over people, particularly working-class residents who interacted with nature and the urban environment in different ways and who presented their own visions of the city rising from the ruins. In practice, the processes of recovery and rebuilding more often than not reshaped the urban landscape in deeply unequal ways and reinscribed power relations in the city despite the resistance of nonelites.

The earthquake occurred during a transitional period for urban ecology in San Francisco, at a time when new knowledge, developing technologies, and changing ideas promised more control over nature rather than less, and city elites called on local and national experts in reaction to the crisis. Those experts included the social worker Edward T. Devine, the urban planner Daniel H. Burnham, and the public health official Dr. Rupert Blue. Drawing on those experts as well as the visions of ordinary San Franciscans, the recovery and rebuilding represented a recommitment to the city of San Francisco in the face of natural forces capable of its destruction. San Franciscans reasserted their faith in the city and its modern technologies, and many followed Progressive thinking in seeing the disaster as a form of creative destruction offering the opportunity to perfect the urban form.

That ideal modern city would be a place where nature took the form of scenic views and pastoral suburbs rather than the unstable earth, blowing dust, working horses, and hungry chickens and rats that stubbornly persisted in the urban environment. That ideal could not be achieved—the city's seismicity remained, as did its rodents—but belief in the supremacy of technology led San Franciscans to reject a fundamental rethinking of the relationship between the modern city and its natural environment. Ultimately the rebuilding concealed natural hazards rather than eliminating them. The adaptations made by San Franciscans proved incomplete, and allegedly earthquake-proof modern technology provided only imperfect protection against dynamic natural forces. For people to continue to live in San Francisco, now more obviously "earthquake country" than ever, they had to tacitly accept the risk of seismic activity and rebuild their lives. The city's resilience contained a powerful thread of denial, but it also contained an implicit choice to live with dynamic, unpredictable nature in a "seismic city."

ONE

MAKING LAND, MAKING A CITY

WHEN BAYARD TAYLOR'S SHIP SAILED INTO SAN FRANCISCO BAY IN August 1849, he first noticed the ships packing the harbor, one behind the other with their masts reaching to the sky. His ship dropped anchor on the outskirts of that forest of masts, and Taylor boarded a lighter that took him first to another vessel and then finally to a wooden pier extending out into the semicircular cove. Had Taylor arrived a few months earlier, or had a boat not been available to meet his vessel, he might have had to tramp across a quarter mile of mud flats to reach the relatively solid ground of the shore. Once Taylor set foot on the narrow beach, he encountered three sandy hills rising steeply from the water. Colorful tents and small one-story houses constructed from wood, canvas, and adobe dotted the hillsides. Piles of merchandise lay scattered about as merchants offered their wares for purchase. Behind the houses and hills, rocky ridges rose to the sky, and beyond them, out of sight from the harbor, stretched miles of drifting sand dunes. Turning to the south, Taylor saw a wet expanse of tidelands and salt marshes extending far inland with more hills rising in the distance.[1] This unpromising site would quickly develop into the major city of the Pacific Coast, reshaped by an influx of new arrivals who transformed the land and water to serve their needs.

The rapidity and scale of San Francisco's transformation from a motley collection of tents and adobe huts to the metropolis of the Pacific Coast has concealed the contingent and checkered character of the city's growth. San Francisco's success was neither inevitable nor without challenges, and those challenges shaped its development. The hybrid landscape of San Francisco in its early years reflected not only the rapid expansion of human settlement but also the dynamic natural environment. As humans transformed the site, they both encountered and created new hazards. Some, like fires, stemmed largely from changes made to the landscape; others, like earthquakes, were endemic to the site itself. Even something as uncontrollable as seismic activity interacted with the alterations that humans made to the terrain, particularly the fill that soon erased the cove at which Taylor had landed.

The idea of improving, or "finishing," the land dominated the discourse of urban development in the nineteenth-century American West, and few doubted the wisdom of remaking the local environment in San Francisco. J. H. Purkitt summed up this view in 1856 when he wrote: "Nature having given us a safe and commodious harbor, it is for the hand of art to make the port commensurate with the requirements of a great commercial metropolis."[2] Purkitt saw no inherent conflict between nature and artifice; it was the work of settlers in San Francisco to improve upon the site that nature had created for the city. However, dissenting voices soon questioned some of the choices made by the city's developers, asking if they had in fact been improvements in harmony with nature. Even in these early years, urban development had its critics.[3]

The ad hoc character of San Francisco's early development contributed to such questions. San Francisco's growth was largely unplanned, and the city's founders constantly reacted to the environment and natural forces in building the city. Those forces included wind, water, and sand, but they also included hazards, particularly the fires and earthquakes that plagued the city in its first quarter-century. The morphology of cities in hazard-prone locales often reflects adaptations to those threats. Risks also change over time as both technology and the environment evolve.[4] In nineteenth-century San Francisco, choices to protect the city from fire often only increased the hazards posed by seismic activity. Residents weighed cultural and economic imperatives against environmental ones. They imagined San Francisco as an imperial and commercial metropolis dominating the Pacific Coast, and this vision demanded a permanent, stable city—not one buffeted by catastrophe.

Economically, settlers entered a boomtown atmosphere of wild speculation and massive capital investments. Nineteenth-century San Franciscans thus balanced environmental, economic, and cultural factors in
building their city. They experimented with adaptations to the site and
its hazards, but a vision driven by capital speculation, urban growth,
and environmental transformation ultimately dominated the city's first
fifty years. The story of San Francisco's growth is one of repeated crises
and adaptations both to and of the natural environment, but often
adaptations only traded one hazard risk for another.

THE GEOLOGY OF SAN FRANCISCO

In California, frequent geological activity shapes the land. As the
geographer Mike Davis explains, the Mediterranean landscapes of
California are anything but calm, stable ecosystems. Instead, he writes,
"high-intensity, low-frequency events ('disasters') are the ordinary
agents of landscape and ecological change."[5] These agents of change
include seismic activity. The coastal regions of California rest on the
boundary between two tectonic plates and represent the North American edge of the "Pacific ring of fire," a zone of seismic activity and vol-
canoes that circles the Pacific Ocean. The state's mountain ranges rose
out of collisions between the Pacific and the North American plates,
and the plates sliding against each other generates regular seismic activity. The San Francisco Bay Area sits on top of an extensive network
of faults, the most famous of which, the San Andreas Fault, extends 750
miles from the Southern California desert north to the redwoods of
Mendocino, passing only a few miles to the west of San Francisco. The
San Andreas Fault is moving at a rate of one and a half inches per year,
extremely fast for a fault, although that movement is not a consistent,
steady creep. Along most of the fault, including the section near San
Francisco, rocks catch against each other as the plates move, and pressure builds up over time until it overwhelms the locked rocks and they
snap under the strain. Those fractures, earthquakes small and large,
occur on a daily basis along the San Francisco Bay Area's many faults,
although only a few are strong enough to be felt at the surface. When
the pressure becomes great enough, major earthquakes can occur; a
study by the United States Geological Survey (USGS) concluded that

earthquakes of the magnitude of 1906 take place approximately every 250 years.[6]

By geological standards, the strip of land now home to San Francisco is very young. The city's hills, like the coastal region as a whole, are rising rapidly and eroding constantly. The valley that is now filled with water to form the bay is also a manifestation of tectonic activity—"a dropped-down block between the San Andreas and Hayward Faults," in the words of the geologist Doris Sloan. Only twenty thousand years ago, at the peak of the Ice Age, the shoreline lay at least nineteen miles west of present-day San Francisco, beyond the Farallon Islands, and what is now the bay was a wide grassy valley with a mighty river running through it. As the glaciers of the Ice Age gradually melted, sea level rose until finally, about nine thousand years ago, the sea flooded past the Golden Gate to fill the valley and form San Francisco Bay.[7] These events are recent enough that people may have already lived in the region at the time. In fact, the first history of the city described Native American legends that San Francisco Bay formed when an earthquake suddenly opened a gap in the mountains along the coast, and the saltwater rushed in to create the bay out of what had been a freshwater lake.[8] Such stories speak to a long-standing perception of seismic activity as integral to the regional environment.

The bay is an estuary, a place where freshwater and saltwater mix. Every day, the tides carry salty ocean water into the bay and back out again. At the same time, the Sacramento and San Joaquin Rivers convey the freshwater runoff from 40 percent of California's land area into the bay's waters. At a few points along the bay shore, such as at the Golden Gate itself, rocky hillsides rise abruptly out of the waters, but in much of the region vast mud flats and salt marshes form an unstable mixture of land and water along the shores of the bay. Mud flats lie at the border between high and low tide, while salt marshes occur at roughly the average level of high tide. Although they may not sound very appealing, both are highly productive ecosystems. They are also constantly changing, "filling in here, slumping there," as the naturalist Elna S. Bakker writes, particularly when winter brings high tides and heavy runoff from the rainy season.[9]

California's Mediterranean climate features wet winters and dry summers, although annual rainfall varies greatly. Some years, the

Pacific High blocks off the winter rains, while El Niño years can bring unusually wet weather. Both droughts and wet periods can last for years; extremes, more than averages, characterize the region's climate. Rainfall also varies significantly based on local topography as mountains and valleys either block or convey moisture-laden air. San Francisco's distinctive summer fogs occur when the cool air coming off the ocean encounters the warm air over the inland valleys. The hot air rises, and the cold air pushes in underneath, producing the fogs that close in over San Francisco and parts of the East Bay. Early residents of San Francisco complained incessantly about the cold, foggy summer afternoons and evenings, but the fog provides moisture essential to the survival of coastal plant life such as redwoods.[10]

In the wake of the 1906 disaster, geologists described how fault traces had shaped the land in California and how those geological traits in turn had influenced settlement patterns. Streams ran along the depressions caused by the erosion of rocks crushed by tectonic activity. David Starr Jordan, a scientist and president of Stanford University, wrote in 1907 that the "fertile and well watered" valleys formed by old earthquake faults often became the locations of dairies and reservoirs. Harold W. Fairbanks, another contemporary scientist, described how the springs located in rift features attracted settlements while straight fault lines became roads, arguing that "thus for years the rift features have had their influence upon people without the latter recognizing their meaning and importance."[11] The dynamic land beneath San Francisco—hills, valleys, sand dunes, and mud flats alike—continually challenged people building a city there, demanding adaptation, transformation, or both and reasserting itself just when people thought they had succeeded in taming the landscape.

LIFE BEFORE THE CITY

When the Spanish arrived in 1776, the peninsula now known as San Francisco was home to the Yelamu, a small population of about two hundred Ohlone Indians. As the shellmounds around the bay testify, the Yelamu obtained most of their dietary resources from the shoreline, where they collected native species of mussels, oysters, and clams. More than four hundred shellmounds still existed in the early twentieth century, evidence of a long-established human presence in the region. The Yelamu also engaged in hunting and gathering, and like other Native peoples in California and throughout the Americas, they used fire to manage the land to attract grazing animals such as deer and to encourage the growth of useful plants. They did not practice traditional agriculture, probably because the natural environment provided sufficient resources to support a relatively high population density without formal cultivation. The Yelamu also participated in regional trade networks, obtaining valuable foods like acorns via trade with peoples from nearby ecosystems more favorable to the growth of oak trees than their own windswept peninsula.[12]

The members of a 1769 Spanish expedition that got lost searching for Monterey Bay were probably the first Europeans to glimpse San Francisco Bay.[13] Seven years later, the Spanish established Mission Dolores in a fertile valley fed by a creek and built the Presidio several miles away on the cliffs at the peninsula's northern edge. What followed was a familiar and tragic story. The diseases brought by the Spanish almost immediately began killing the region's indigenous peoples, leading to demographic collapse within thirty years. Spanish livestock quickly transformed the local ecology and the long-standing ecological relationships of the Yelamu. By 1830, Mission Dolores had forty-two hundred cattle and two thousand sheep, while thousands of additional imported grazing animals resided to the south at Mission Santa Clara. By that time, not a single Native village remained in the vicinity of San Francisco.[14]

These decades also saw the beginning of the area's establishment as a port. Ships engaged in the fur trade were arriving in Alta California, as the province was known, as early as 1778. The United States steadily increased its commercial interests in the Pacific over the first four decades of the nineteenth century, and American ships transported such commodities as furs, hide and tallow, dried fish and meat, timber, and precious metals from the west coast of North America to as far away as China. Alta California became part of Mexico with that nation's independence from Spain in 1821, and Mexico soon secularized Mission Dolores and abandoned its garrison at the Presidio. In the 1820s and 1830s the Mexican government also made large land grants to encourage settlement of the area, although Mexican law prohibited the granting of land along the coast, maintaining the harbor front as a commons to benefit the community as a whole. Maritime commerce increased significantly in the 1820s (and again in the 1840s) as international traders shipped commodities derived from the region's natural resources across the Pacific Ocean and around the world. Those commodities represented both native species such as sea otters, which were hunted nearly to extinction for their prized fur, and introduced species such as cattle and sheep raised on mission and ranchero land from which indigenous peoples had been dispossessed.[15]

Seeking to claim a piece of this commerce, the English seaman William A. Richardson founded the pueblo of Yerba Buena along the coast of a sheltered cove three miles from the mission in 1835. The name came from a fragrant herb that grew profusely in the area and had been widely used by the Yelamu for teas, medicinal purposes, and decoration. Richardson, who was married to Maria Antonio Martinez, the daughter of the *comandante* at the Presidio, chose the site to expand the hide and tallow trade with the Mexican population scattered around the bay. By the next summer, the town consisted of only three makeshift houses, and even in 1844 it had only fifty inhabitants. The first survey of Yerba Buena had taken place five years earlier, when the Swiss surveyor Jean Vioget had laid out a rectangular street plan. The town was bounded by Pacific Street on the north, Sacramento Street on the south, Dupont Street on the west, and Montgomery Street, which ran along the shore, on the east. Ships landed at Clark's Point, which is now the corner of Broadway and Battery Streets.[16]

At this time, there was little to distinguish Yerba Buena from any other small western outpost whose residents dreamed of great success. The key difference from much of the North American West was the hamlet's location on the cove, a location that meant that future profits would center on maritime commerce rather than overland trade. Richard Henry Dana, who visited the area in 1835, proclaimed with a booster's enthusiasm: "If California ever becomes a prosperous country, this bay will be the center of its prosperity."[17] Dana was notably optimistic, if prophetic. Steve Richardson, who grew up there as the child of William and Maria Antonio, remembered the town as "a dismal thing to look on," with "a wilderness of desolate, forbidding sand dunes" to the west of the little settlement.[18] Wildlife, including such predators as

SAN FRANCISCO UPPER CALIFORNIA
IN 1847.

Yerba Buena in 1847, showing the shallow cove and beach with hills rising just inland. Scattered buildings and ships reflect the trade already taking place. Courtesy of the Bancroft Library, University of California, Berkeley (BANC PIC 1963.002:0538—A).

bears, mountain lions, and coyotes, roamed hills covered with chaparral and lupine. People and animals alike foraged for shellfish along the shoreline, as the Yelamu had done for generations, and men hunted the hills for black-tailed deer and jackrabbits to supplement meat from the region's Mexican livestock.[19]

The United States took control of Yerba Buena with the rest of Alta California in 1846, with no local resistance from supporters of Mexican rule. For the next few years, the town existed in a state of legal limbo and uncertainty, still nominally under Mexican law but ruled by American military governors and a town council of shameless speculators. In March 1847, General Stephen Watts Kearney granted the town property rights to the tidelands along the shores of the cove. Kearney's action not only broke with Mexican precedent but was illegal under US law, which should have preserved the tidal flats as state property. Extralegal or not, the grant laid the groundwork for the town's expansion by facilitating real estate speculation along the shoreline.[20]

The town hired Jasper O'Farrell to survey the newly opened property, and the new lots included 444 beach and water lots, 80 percent of which were entirely covered with water at high tide. With this survey, O'Farrell and city leaders—most of whom were merchants and speculators who directly benefited from land sales—extended the grid of urban space out over the waters of Yerba Buena Cove. At the time, the population of San Francisco was only 459, but the next year, in July 1848, more than four hundred water lots sold for between fifty and one hundred dollars each.[21] Even in San Francisco's infancy, speculators anticipated that the town's growth would depend on its port, and they did not hesitate to commodify both the land of the coast and the water of the bay, delineating and selling lots that consisted of nothing but mud and shallow water. The groundwork had been laid for the building of a city, but in the minds of settlers, the site still needed much improvement.

BUILDING ON WATER

Early arrivals to Yerba Buena inaugurated a long tradition of debating the suitability of the site for urban development. James Ayers remembered that in 1849 the spot had "nothing to recommend it" as the site of a great city save the harbor.[22] Residents and visitors alike were more inclined to complain about the climate, wind, sand, and mud than to praise the location. Eliza W. Farnham's comments were typical. On approaching the city, she wrote: "the San Francisco winds meet you face to face, and search you like an officer of the customs." By the time you reach the town, she continued, "you are thoroughly chilled and dampened" from the winds, and "your eyes, ears, nostrils, and mouth are filled with the sand they have hurled at you."[23] During the dry season the winds and sand made blowing dust a constant bane of residents, but conditions only worsened during the winter rains, which transformed the dusty, unimproved streets into a sea of mud an average of three feet deep. In a January 1850 letter, Robert Smith Lammot described the hazards of crossing Montgomery Street, a major thoroughfare in the business district, during the rainy season. He watched a man, "half-drunk or he would not have attempted it," sink in the mud up to his neck and have to be rescued with a rope. Lammot also wrote of horses trapped "up to their bellies" in mud as their drivers attempted to pry them free.[24]

San Francisco's residents and boosters would continue to debate the suitability of the city's site—whether the forty-three hills represented

MONTGOMERY STREET, SAN FRANCISCO, 1849.

People and animals floundering in the deep mud of Montgomery Street in 1849.
Courtesy of the Bancroft Library, University of California, Berkeley (BANC
PIC 1963.002:0626:02—A).

an impediment to development or a source of civic beauty, whether the
climate was mild or foggy and cold—depending on the interests being
served. Geographers and environmental historians distinguish between
a city's site and its situation. Situation refers to a location's advantages
in comparison to other cities. In San Francisco's case, its harbor provided great opportunities, as almost everyone recognized. However, the
city's site—the actual land it occupied—was less than ideal for urban
development. The geographer James E. Vance Jr. has called San Francisco's history one of "truly phenomenal investment" to render the
land "somewhat less inimical to city-functioning than nature had made
it."[25] Over the course of the city's history, San Franciscans worked

continuously to transform the terrain of their city even as that land-scape helped shape the course of its development, whether through the constant presence of the bay and hills, natural processes such as sub-sidence, or periodic disturbances in the form of major earthquakes.

Even with the advantages of its harbor, San Francisco's eventual dominance of the Pacific Coast in the second half of the nineteenth century was anything but inevitable. Instead, the city's success stemmed from a combination of location, timing, and luck. The most important factor was James Marshall's report of gold in the Sierra Nevada foothills in 1848. That summer, established residents and newcomers alike deserted San Francisco and rushed to the mountains to seek their for-tunes. As word of the precious metal spread, the town became the point of debarkation for men from all over the world suffering from "gold fever." In 1849 forty thousand new arrivals streamed into the little town, two-thirds of them on their way to the mines. They came from all over the world—north from Chile, Mexico, and elsewhere in Latin America, across the ocean from China, Hawaii, and Australia, and of course west from the United States. Some were already there, the native Californios and Native Americans who had survived the first waves of European and American settlement. Most were men—the ratio of men to women in the early days of the gold rush was eleven to one—and they belonged to all social classes, from laborers to lawyers.[26]

Even San Francisco's status as the destination point for gold rush miners resulted from a combination of luck and booster foresight. Early in 1847, the village of Yerba Buena had changed its name to San Francisco to match the better-known bay. The ordinance noted that the name Yerba Buena was "unknown beyond the district," whereas the new name of San Francisco would give the town "the advantage of the name given on the public maps." That recognizable name encouraged California-bound ships to choose San Francisco as their destination. The town's rival at the time was Benicia, which sat at the foot of the Sacramento and San Joaquin Rivers where they empty into the bay. James D. Phelan, the former mayor and leading Progressive politician and businessman, suggested in 1905 that San Francisco became a major urban center rather than a failed booster project because "some cities, predestined to greatness, overcome all impediments and so prove their necessity and fitness," a sort of urban Darwinism.[27] Today we can look back and see San Francisco's rise as anything but predestined—a combination of luck, timing, a promising situation, and massive investment that transformed sand dunes, rocky hills, and marshlands into a metropolis.

In 1848 the town still had a population of less than a thousand people, but prospectors began pouring into the city the next spring. The owners of water lots almost immediately began filling in their property to profit from the new arrivals. They built wharves and structures on piles, then leveled the inland sand hills and used the sand as well as trash and debris to fill in the water around new construction. Bayard Taylor estimated that between fifteen and thirty houses were being finished every day in 1849 to accommodate the influx of people. The result was a makeshift city. Shelters included everything from prefabricated houses shipped halfway around the world to tents, brush houses, and deck cabins removed from vessels.[28] San Francisco's growth in these early years was an ad hoc process in which residents fashioned streets, housing, and commercial buildings from whatever materials were available.

The first pier that could accommodate ocean commerce was completed during the summer of 1849. Its construction required driving more than twelve hundred redwood piles, each as long as three hundred feet, into the mud beneath Yerba Buena Cove.[29] Once completed, ships could dock at the pier, an improvement over transporting their passengers and cargo across the wide mud flat. By this time, the harbor was filled with hundreds of ships. Eight additional wharves stretching out over the shallow cove soon joined the first; the historian Roger W. Lotchin describes "an epic pile-driving battle" as wharf owners competed for lucrative territory in both the cove and the courts. Vessels arrived at the port in 1849 with goods to sell to the men setting off for the mines, only to become stranded when their crews deserted to join the gold rush. With the limited urban infrastructure, more than two hundred of those abandoned vessels were drawn up onto the beach, where they served as warehouses, lodgings, and even a prison. Benjamín Vicuña McKenna, a visitor from Chile, described San Francisco as "a Venice built of pine instead of marble. It is a city of ships, piers, and tides." He added that "the whole central part of the city swayed noticeably because it was built on piles."[30]

In just a few short months, San Francisco's combination of mercantile commerce and gold rush immigration had transformed the site. An 1850 survey incorporated lots that were as much as thirty-five feet underwater into the urban grid. Building on such sites required using wooden piles to anchor buildings, converting ships into buildings, or employing fill to transform tidal lands into solid ground.[31] Another contemporary observer of the city, Théophile de Rutté, declared that already in 1849, "the original crescent of Yerba Buena [Cove] had disappeared," filled in with sand from the hillsides and marked by "a line of giant wharves stretching out into the bay on pilings, each crisscrossed with a series of transversal docks."[32] The combination of trade oriented toward the harbor, the shortage of level land for commercial development, and the suddenness of the city's growth all contributed to this pattern of expansion out over the bay and the improvisation of building a city over water. Other coastal cities, such as New York, Boston, and later Seattle, employed similar development strategies, but San Francisco stands out for both the pace and the scale of its transformation.[33] Residents would face a series of consequences from these choices, however, starting with the threat of fire.

BURNING DOWN THE CITY

San Francisco's early history was not a story of uninterrupted urban growth despite its rapid progress from a few adobe huts to the nation's leading Pacific port. The most dramatic threat to its success was fire; the city experienced six fires between 1849 and 1852, the worst of which claimed the title of the "great fire" until the 1906 conflagration. Early residents and business owners feared the prospect of fire among the tents and frame and canvas houses, not to mention the wooden wharves and planked streets of the commercial district. One company noted in September 1849 that there was "no such thing as fire insurance" in San Francisco and worried that a fire swept by the city's high winds would be unstoppable.[34] Statements like this reflect a widespread awareness of fire as a hazard plaguing nineteenth-century cities. Although we now usually think of fire as a wildland problem—when we think of fire at all—cities possess their own fire regimes. Urban fire regimes are shaped by the natural environment, including vegetation, climate, and topography, as well as by social and political conditions that influence choices of building materials, precautions taken against fire, and the condition of urban infrastructure.[35] By 1849 the new city of San Francisco offered a perfect confluence of fire threats: a windy, hilly environment; a long dry season; flammable construction; a complete lack of protective infrastructure; and relatively open use of fire for cooking, warmth, and light.

On Christmas eve of 1849, the flames came. Bayard Taylor referred to this first fire as "the calamity, predicted and dreaded so long in advance." The fire destroyed over fifty houses, but people began rebuilding within days. Taylor observed: "All over the burnt space sounded one incessant tumult of hammers, axes, and saws."[36] Only five months later, in the early morning hours of May 4, 1850, fire struck again, and three hundred buildings burned over seven hours. In both fires, lack of water for firefighting posed a major problem. In early San Francisco, water came from a few small springs and private wells or was purchased from water carts, which sold water imported from elsewhere on the peninsula or from Marin County. This second fire led the city council to order the digging of additional artesian wells and the construction of cisterns around the town. In the short term, however, San Franciscans rebuilt with buildings even flimsier and more flammable than those that had just been destroyed.[37]

Only six weeks later, the young city burned for a third time. High winds carried the flames through the main commercial section of the city, devastating four of the most valuable city blocks and two major wharves. The few brick buildings in town withstood the flames, and bankers and merchants responded by ordering new "fireproof" brick or iron buildings to protect their investments.[38] Some unlucky residents had lost their property to flames as many as three times in nine months. The city's first granite building, constructed like a fortress to guard against fire, soon marked the northwest corner of Montgomery and California Streets. The first fire ordinance restricted the use of tents and buildings that were nothing more than a wooden frame covered with canvas, but it placed no stricter limits on frame construction even in the center of town.[39]

Reactions to these fires revealed an interesting comparison with another, seemingly less immediate threat: earthquakes. In October 1850 the *Alta California* described how the cry of fire "aroused the sleeping with a suddenness and terror that an earthquake could not have produced." The comparison of earthquake and fire as destructive forces in the urban environment might seem to be a natural one, but the paper and its readers also employed the metaphor for unrelated events. For example, a letter published in November 1850 declared that building a mint in San Francisco would lead to "a new impetus . . . felt, as plainly as an earthquake, by every true Californian."[40] This casual use of earthquakes as the point of comparison for any change that might disturb the city, for better or worse, indicates that residents were aware of the region's propensity for seismic activity. The British traveler William Kelly, who visited the city in 1851, wrote of "the bewildered stranger" with "vague notions of earthquakes and such like vagaries of nature."[41] Even in these early days, such rhetoric distinguished between strangers who feared movements of the earth and more seasoned Californians who had little such concern. The earthquake had already become a touchstone of local culture, even though seismic hazards seemed to pale in comparison to the all-too-immediate hazard of fire.

Late at night on May 3, 1851, fire struck again. A gale force wind drove the flames toward the bay, then changed direction and turned the fire back toward the heart of the city. Within a few hours, the entire business district was burning. The glow of this great fire was visible in Monterey, one hundred miles to the south. The hollow areas beneath San Francisco's planked streets acted as wind tunnels, and as the first history of the city, the *Annals of San Francisco*, described, the fire "ran along the planked streets, and from block to block, almost as if they were but a train of gunpowder," stopping only when it ran out of fuel. Water from the town's small fire hoses only vaporized on contact with the flames, and even the much touted fireproof buildings proved useless. Faith in technology could prove fatal. At Sacramento and Montgomery Streets several people who took refuge in a new, allegedly fireproof iron building suffocated when the heat of the flames warped the doors closed. The men were dead when the building collapsed on them. In ten hours, fire had consumed eighteen blocks, more than three-quarters of the small city.[42]

Once again, San Franciscans were quick to regroup, and only ten days later one-fifth of the burned area had already been rebuilt. As one

GREAT FIRE IN SAN FRANCISCO.

The Great Fire of May 3, 1851, showing the planked streets of the business district that extended out over the water. Courtesy of the Bancroft Library, University of California, Berkeley (BANC PIC 1963.002:0617—A).

resident wrote: "Before a week had passed, the streets were once more marked out; houses were going up everywhere on still smoking ruins." He lamented, however, that "although the inhabitants had learned from sad experience that wooden structures were excellent food for the flames, they were rebuilding in wood."[43] Of course, wood was really the only option if one needed to rebuild as quickly as possible. Mrs. Dolly Bradford Bates noted that the rush to rebuild had very practical motivations. San Francisco was still a city of squatters, and Bates described how property holders had to act quickly "to prevent their lots from being jumped."[44] Property remained unsettled in San Francisco in 1851, and fires were not the only hazard faced by residents.

A sixth fire on June 22, 1851, was notable as much for the violence it engendered as for the damage done by the flames. Three people died in the flames, two more when police targeted them as suspected looters, and another two men were beaten to death by a mob that suspected them of arson. Many citizens blamed the June fire and that of the previous month—which had occurred on the anniversary of the fire of the preceding May—on arson. The fires of 1851 thus contributed to the formation of the Vigilance Committee, the first in a series of controversial vigilante efforts in which the city's "respectable" citizens sought to enforce the law through their own version of frontier justice.[45]

In addition to their political consequences, the fires of the early 1850s inspired San Francisco to look for an outside water source to supplement the city's few wells and the delivery of water in tanks by steamers from across the bay. In June 1851 the town authorized Arzo D. Merrifield to construct a system of pipes to bring water from Mountain Lake, located at the edge of the Presidio, but Merrifield's company soon failed.[46] In the 1860s the Spring Valley Water Company, under the leadership of the engineer Herman Schussler, tapped into the water sources of San Mateo County and built a virtual monopoly in supplying water to San Francisco. By 1871 the city consumed six million gallons of water daily, and several dry years in succession raised doubts about the adequacy of Spring Valley's resources. A city-commissioned investigation recommended eventual municipal control but optimistically concluded that the existing water supplies would be sufficient to supply San Francisco for another fifty years.[47]

Another solution to the threat of fire in the 1850s was the construction of cisterns to store water across the city. Fifteen were built in 1852 alone, with thirty-six dotting San Francisco by 1856 and fifty in use a decade later. The first cisterns were square boxes constructed of tar-soaked planks that were kept filled by periodic deposits from water carts. Most of the cisterns were eventually rebuilt with brick, and their capacities ranged from only 14,700 gallons to over 100,000 gallons. San Franciscans lost interest in the cistern system in the 1860s as the immediacy of fires receded—no major fires occurred in the city during the decade—and people placed their faith in new water mains, reservoirs, and the steam engines of the fire department. Many cisterns, not unlike the region's natural waterways, became clogged with urban wastes like unused building material, and their very existence had receded from local memory by 1906.[48]

The fires of the 1850s also sent San Francisco's wealthier residents on a quest for noncombustible building materials. Large brick buildings became common in the more established residential and business districts, and they proved their worth when heavy brick walls on Washington and Montgomery Streets halted a fire in November 1852. San Franciscans imported bricks from the Atlantic states and from Australia, and they brought in granite from quarries elsewhere in Northern California and even from China.[49] However, wood remained the primary building material in the city, particularly in residential districts. Construction with wood was affordable and quick, and San Francisco was still growing rapidly.

After the string of fires in the early 1850s, San Franciscans adapted by taking the basic precautions of the era to mitigate against the threat of urban fire. They organized a volunteer fire department, imposed basic ordinances governing construction in the city center, and began to develop a water system. Individual property owners, particularly those with greater resources at their disposal, also built more fire-resistant buildings.[50] However, the almost instant rebuilding after each fire reflected the driving force behind the city's growth—capitalism with its ethos of creative destruction. San Francisco's merchants and speculators remained undeterred from their project of building a commercial power. They did, however, seek to protect their investments and reduce the known hazard of urban fire. Flames racing along the piers and planked streets even led San Franciscans to recognize the risks facing a city built on piles. In the early 1850s fill seemed to offer the perfect solution that would allow a new, improved city to rise out of destruction.[51]

FROM A CITY ON PILES TO A CITY ON FILL

Fires were not the only obstacle to development San Franciscans encountered in the early 1850s. The land beneath the city remained a problem as well. Building on the mud flats of the cove had partially addressed the shortage of level ground, but construction on mud flats posed its own difficulties. The sand hills that loomed just inland, impeding both travel and development, represented another obstacle. From the vantage point of 1855, the *Annals* matter-of-factly recounted the solution: "Great quantities of rock and sand were removed from places where they were only nuisances, to other quarters where they became of use in removing the natural irregularities of the ground, and making all smooth and level."[52] For most observers at the time, this transformation of the original site represented nothing but improvement. Nineteenth-century white settlers in the United States employed a rhetoric of "finishing" nature. They believed they could divine nature's intention for a place and complete nature's work through the application of technology.[53] For early arrivals in San Francisco, the presence of the harbor clearly established San Francisco's destiny as the commercial center of the Pacific Coast, and all alterations to the site that facilitated the fulfillment of that destiny represented nothing but improvements. Within the city's formative years, its human residents made major changes, leveling the ground, filling the mud flats and open water of Yerba Buena Cove, and straightening the coastline in the name of destiny and profit.

When the waterfront burned in 1851, boosters saw an opportunity to redevelop that section of the city. The *Alta California* reported that "no part of the city is improving so much, and with such astonishing rapidity as the 'water lot' section." The newspaper added that it was cheaper to fill in the lots with sand than to use piles to anchor buildings and streets. Fill also offered health benefits in comparison with the stagnant, smelly, waste-filled water that had accumulated in the gaps between buildings and streets spanning the mud flats.[54] Technology soon offered assistance with the project of filling the water lots. In 1852 the first steam shovel arrived in San Francisco. The steam paddy, as it was known, worked night and day shoveling sand from a sixty foot sand hill blocking Market Street between Second and Third. It dumped the sand into open boxcars, which horses then pulled along railroad tracks north to the waterfront, where the sand was deposited in Yerba Buena Cove as fill. The machine was said to do the work of twenty Irish laborers with every stroke, and it could move as much as 2,500 tons of sand in a single day. The steam paddy ran steadily between 1852 and 1854 and again from 1859 to 1873, when it excavated sand from the South of Market district to fill Mission Bay.[55]

San Francisco already encompassed thirty blocks of made land by the end of 1853, only four years after the gold rush had put the town on

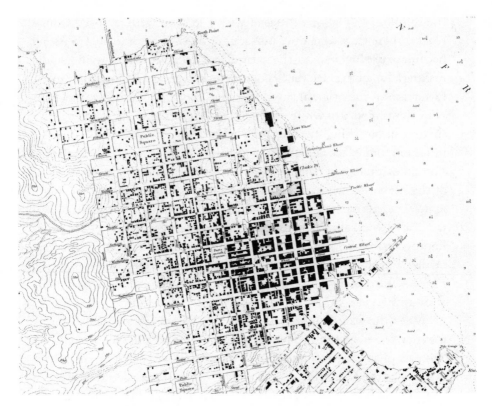

US Coast Survey map of San Francisco from 1853. Dark spots represent buildings, and wharves and fill have replaced much of the original cove. Courtesy of
the David Rumsey Map Collection.

the map. The *Annals* declared that "the old character of the cove has
been completely changed" with "the former semicircle of beach"
replaced by "a straight line of building extending across the middle of
the cove." Gold rush wealth and capitalist speculation made such astonishing feats as leveling hills and filling in the cove possible. After the
initial boom died down, the process of urban construction slowed as
well. Charts from 1857 show that little additional land was added in the
four years after 1853.[56]

The city expanded inland even as it extended its commercial district
out into the bay, and it encountered some of the same obstacles of location in developing to the south and west. The saga of Mission Plank
Road, later to become the major thoroughfare Mission Street, illustrates

the challenges. When it was built in 1851, the road connected the old Mission Dolores and the scattered homesteads around Mission Bay with the growing town of San Francisco, centered three miles away at Yerba Buena Cove. The builders initially planned to drive pilings to anchor the new road across marshland. However, in the vicinity of what is now Seventh Street, they failed to locate solid ground even with eighty-foot pilings. Ultimately, the contractors constructed the road on a wide platform of heavy planks that provided just enough stability for traffic, although the entire structure quickly sank several feet. When the franchise for the road came up for renewal in 1860, the grant was conditional on filling in the swamp between Seventh and Eighth or rebuilding the shaky platform. The new road cut through several large sandy ridges, and these cuts became the sites of toll booths. With the explosive growth of the city, houses soon lined the new road.[57]

Transformations of the land and water had consequences. Even in the short term, evidence indicated that the new land was less than stable. On October 20, 1851, the American Theater opened on Sansome Street between California and Sacramento in a large brick and wooden building. The theater was packed on opening night, and the weight of the crowd caused the walls to sink two inches, inspiring doubts about the safety of the structure.[58] As one contractor testified: "I have noticed . . . a want of stability in the subsoil on the entire water lot property." He complained that even "heavy solid rock and clay" used as fill tended to settle "frequently at the rate of six inches in six months," and the depth of soft mud varied so much that it made the use of piles difficult.[59] The local historian John S. Hittell described how contractors would raise a street to the official grade only to find that "the sand had sunk down six or eight feet" in the single day it took the city engineer to arrive to inspect the fill.[60] In 1854 the city suffered from a recurrent problem with portions of buildings falling. Observers attributed the situation to a combination of inferior building materials and unstable filled ground, and the widespread settling of walls and buildings contributed to the slowing of construction on made ground in the mid-1850s.[61]

Haphazard filling also posed problems for pedestrians negotiating the planked streets of the central city. Dolly Bradford Bates described a harrowing journey across "a hewn timber, which, at least, must have been nearly one hundred feet [long], and at a height of twelve feet . . .

from the green slimy mud." Mrs. Bates started off bravely, but she became dizzy halfway across and clutched at the beam until she regained her courage.[62] Nor was her fear unwarranted. J. H. Purkitt estimated in 1856 that sixty people had died in just four months falling into "man-traps" along the water front, and Henry Edgerton not only warned that "man-traps everywhere abound" but "a general caving in cannot by any means be regarded as an impossibility." In its short history, the city had already seen several wharves collapse, one under the weight of a riot among teamsters in 1853. The wooden piles that supported the buildings and planked streets on the former water lots were also being eaten by shipworms. Several species of mollusks were boring into the wood and threatening to cause the district to collapse.[63] The problems of subsidence, "man-traps," and shipworms indicated the imperfect transformation of the land. Tidal water continued to flow beneath plank-covered streets, and sea animals lived among the piles that supported the city.[64]

These problems and others raised early doubts about the direction the city's founders had chosen. Purkitt, who was generally a supporter of improvement, complained that "the work of piling, capping and filling in has been done in the most reckless and destructive manner" that threatened even the "commercial advantages" of the port.[65] Observers also criticized the initial surveyors and their decision to lay out a grid of streets without consideration for natural topography. In an 1854 report on grading city streets, several engineers called for the preservation of San Francisco's hills. They argued that the hills were "natural advantages" that contributed to the city's unique beauty rather than merely obstacles to travel and sources of material for fill.[66] In a discussion of the absence of provision for parks in gold rush San Francisco, the *Annals* declared that "the eye is wearied, and the imagination quite stupefied, in looking over the numberless square—all *square*—building blocks, and mathematically straight lines of streets" laid out "without the least regard to the natural inequalities of the ground."[67] Comments like these served as the first forays in a debate over whether economic interests should dominate the development of San Francisco to the exclusion of provision for a beautiful and healthy urban environment. They also reveal uncertainty about the course of urban growth even in these early years, as San Franciscans tried to decide how best to develop their city's beautiful but impractical terrain. None of these authors questioned the premise of improving the site, but they did wonder just how much of the transformation constituted improvement.

Meanwhile, as humans debated their plans for the city, the land continued to evolve as it had for millennia. Even without human actions, the distribution of land and water could change at any time. During the night on November 22, 1852, a mild earthquake opened a fissure in a wide sand bank, and the waters of Lake Merced, on the western side of the San Francisco peninsula, burst through to flow to the Pacific. Previously, the lake had no apparent outlet, probably relying on an underground stream, and heavy rains that season may have weakened the lake's sandy banks sufficiently to cause a collapse. Such changes were a natural part of the coastal environment—just as seismic activity was endemic to the region—but they became increasingly problematic as a city grew up along the shores of the bay. The November 22 earthquake was one of just three reported in 1852, a relatively quiet year, but an average of 7.5 quakes were felt in the city each year of the 1850s.[68]

San Franciscans faced a series of challenges in building their city in the fevered atmosphere of gold rush California. Many of those challenges stemmed from the city's site, while others (such as fire) were hazards common to most nineteenth-century American cities. An adaptation to one hazard was not necessarily ideal for another, however, particularly for the vast majority of San Franciscans who could not afford to build a complex and expensive structure such as the Montgomery Block, a brick building that rested on an elaborate raft of redwood logs floating over the bay mud of what had once been the shoreline of Yerba Buena Cove.[69] The city's hilly site encouraged ambitious merchants to build out over the water. When their city on wooden piles burned, they adapted by increasing their use of fill to create what they saw—admittedly with a strong element of denial—as solid land. Fire revealed the limitations of frame buildings, and businessmen sought to adapt by switching to brick in the commercial district. The limitations of both fill and brick would soon become apparent, however, as San Franciscans came face to face with the region's seismicity. The hazards of the urban environment—particularly subsidence, fire, and seismic activity—shaped San Francisco's development in its early years, but most residents saw them primarily as obstacles to be overcome in the construction of the great commercial city of the Pacific Coast.

Small earthquakes were as much a part of life in San Francisco in the nineteenth century as they are today. Amelia Ransom Neville observed that only "alarmists" worried about "slight tremors of the earth." Titus Fay Cronise conceded in *The Natural Wealth of California*, published in 1868 but composed before that year's earthquake, that "earthquakes are, indeed, of frequent occurrence, one or more shocks being felt every year." However, Cronise emphasized that "with two or three exceptions they have been so slight as to cause no alarm—scarcely to attract more than passing attention."[70] In the wake of the 1906 disaster, the scientist John Casper Branner noted that the very frequency of light shocks made them difficult to study since the locals paid them no more mind than a passing mention in conversation. As many as 465 measurable earthquakes shook San Francisco between 1850 and 1906.[71]

Despite the frequency of small quakes, the city did not experience a major earthquake during its formative years. The authors of the *Annals* worried in 1855 that a catastrophic earthquake represented "the greatest, if not the only possible obstacle of consequence to the growing prosperity" of San Francisco.[72] Significant shocks had occurred in the area in 1800, 1808, and 1812, but those had been forgotten by all but a few students of the historical record. In 1836 a substantial quake occurred on the Hayward Fault, which runs under the East Bay city of Oakland and its suburbs. Two years later, a movement of the San Andreas Fault knocked down adobe walls in tiny Yerba Buena. Stronger shocks in 1856 and 1857 affected buildings on filled ground, and a series of quakes in 1863 and 1864 provided another warning. In response to those temblors, the *Alta California* worried: "Earthquakes are becoming a permanent institution in California. Scarcely a week passes without one or more shocks being felt; this season they seem to be more numerous and severe than usual."[73] In fact, the shaking was probably a prelude to a larger quake yet to come, what scientists call foreshocks, but the scientific theories that might have suggested such a pattern remained far in the future. On October 8, 1865, the long-feared earthquake arrived.

Hittell, writing just over a decade later, described the 1865 quake as "more severe than any felt in thirty years." The shaking "cracked the walls and plastering of some weak buildings" and scared more than a hundred people into returning to homes on the generally more stable ground of the eastern states. Cronise, in the same paragraph in which he had called earthquakes "harmless disturbances," noted that quake damage had included "the throwing down of some toppling parapets, and the cracking of certain ill-constructed walls, with slight injury on one or two occasions to a few newly erected brick buildings."[74] Cronise's language minimized the potential hazards by qualifying the damage with such phrases as "slight injury" and "ill-constructed" walls, but even with those qualifiers, it suggested the vulnerability of San Francisco's built environment. The *Alta California* noted a pattern of damage on fill, but the paper also suggested that "tall brick buildings need no longer be considered hazardous" since those that were well made had survived. The avoidance of tall brick buildings was one concession that San Francisco's builders had made to the threat of earthquakes (and perhaps also to the problem of subsidence). Few brick buildings in the city exceeded four stories in height, and none stood taller than five stories.[75] It was a good thing, however, that developers did not immediately follow the *Alta California*'s advice to build taller because the region's string of earthquakes was not over.

On the morning of October 21, 1868, the Hayward Fault moved in a quake estimated at a magnitude of 6.8 to 7.0. The quake killed five people in San Francisco and another twenty-five across the bay in the towns of Hayward and San Leandro, which sat directly on top of the fault. The total property loss was estimated at anywhere from three hundred thousand dollars to five million dollars.[76] The shock shattered some underground water pipes and started several small fires that were quickly extinguished, but the bulk of the damage in San Francisco occurred on about two hundred acres of filled ground in the business district. The *Alta California* reported "something like a slide" along the bay's old water line that damaged California Street and buildings in the area. A house at Folsom and Fourteenth Streets sank four feet.[77] One contemporary observer described "a confused aggregation of cracked walls, demolished firewalls, and wrenched chimneys" in the made land district, adding that "the handwriting of the earthquake may be easily observed by any."[78]

Reactions to the 1868 quake reveal a preexisting knowledge of risk, centered around made land. According to the *San Francisco Bulletin*,

Damage from the 1868 earthquake at Bush and Market Streets. Courtesy of the California History Room, California State Library, Sacramento, California.

"where the muddy deposits of the Bay have been crusted over by filling in sand, and these lands have been built upon, the foundation has always been insecure." J. D. B. Stillman, a physician and writer, took this even further, writing in *The Overland Monthly* that "all past experience tells us that the made lands and estuaries of the bay, that have been filled up with mud . . . may be severely shaken by earthquakes that will pass harmlessly through the firmer ground." Similarly, the mining engineer Thomas Rowlandson declared that it was "well known" to San Francisco residents that earthquake damage "almost wholly took place on alluvial soil, or made ground."[79] Statements like these show that at least some San Franciscans were well aware of the danger of earthquakes in their city and of the specific hazard posed by made land, particularly at those moments when nature reminded them.

The geologist Bruce A. Bolt has written that political action to reduce risk in the aftermath of an earthquake has a half-life of only a year or so, and that was certainly the case in San Francisco in 1868. In the first days after the shock, the *Alta California* praised the survival of every building "constructed as it should be" but noted the presence in the city of too many buildings "dangerous under any circumstances to human life" because of thin walls, slight foundations, and inadequate supports. The *Bulletin* called for "a system of official inspection and a strict revision of the building ordinances."[80] Stillman worried that owners would only patch up damage. He cited an example of a fire-wall on Battery Street that had been replaced after it fell during the 1865 earthquake only to fall again in 1868, "burying two innocent victims beneath its fragments." For Stillman, greed was the problem: "Men, in their eagerness to get to the front in the battle of the money-bags, have encroached upon the dominions of Neptune, until he has called his brother Pluto to his aid."[81] With its colorful reference to Roman deities, this quotation connected the temblor and the expansion of the city out over the water, implying that the quake represented a form of revenge for the alteration of the coastline in pursuit of profit.

Some observers placed the 1868 earthquake in the context of the region's seismic history. Stillman cited the Bay Area earthquakes of the early 1800s, concluding that "few will now be disposed to deny, that *California is an earthquake country*."[82] For Stillman and other cautious observers, the threat of earthquakes demanded that San Franciscans take precautions as their city expanded. Some individuals did react by moving their homes or businesses to locations perceived as more secure. In November the *San Francisco Real Estate Circular* reported a trend of people moving out of high brick hotels and buildings into more modest frame dwellings, which were believed to be safer in earthquakes. Andrea Sbarboro remembered that his family moved from a brick house into a wooden one "until the scare had subsided." Selim Woolworth was one of several businessmen who fled the city. Woolworth sold his Market Street property to William Ralston, who constructed the Palace Hotel (promoted as both earthquake proof and fireproof) on the site.[83] Construction had just begun on the US Mint, located on made land at Fifth and Mission Streets, and the building process was delayed several months to revise the plans to protect the structure against earthquakes. In this case, precautionary measures paid off, as the Mint survived the 1906 disaster. The famed Palace Hotel survived the earthquake with minimal damage but burned in the fire.[84]

In 1868, however, much of the city rushed to rebuild and forget. The *Alta California* declared that all damages would be repaired within two weeks and all traces of the event would be wiped out within two months, following the city's historical pattern of rapid rebuilding after disaster.[85] In his memoirs the printer Edward Bosqui recounted the "mortal terror" and lasting shock felt by some people who experienced the worst of the earthquake. However, Bosqui also praised the newspapers, calling them "very wise and prudent in making little account of the disasters" to prevent more people from leaving California.[86] In fact, the city so desired to wipe the 1868 earthquake from memory that some scholars believe the Chamber of Commerce suppressed a report prepared by a committee studying the quake's effects. It appears more likely that the committee's efforts fizzled out due to internal dissension, lack of funds, and the death of the entrepreneur and civic leader George Gordon, a driving force behind the project. Rowlandson, who was a member of both the local committee and the California Academy of Sciences, did publish *A Treatise on Earthquake Dangers, Causes, and Palliatives* in the aftermath of the earthquake. His cryptic mention of the "present paradoxical position" of the committee with the Chamber of Commerce hints that San Francisco's economic leaders may have been leery of the committee's findings.[87] Ultimately, the reasons for the committee's failure to produce a report seem inconclusive.

In the days and months immediately following the 1868 earthquake, San Francisco's newspapers had called for the city to take precautionary measures to make the urban environment safer during future seismic activity. Citizens voted with their feet, abandoning multistory brick buildings for wooden ones. However, the tension between risk reduction and a return to normal development, driven by economic motives of minimizing cost and promoting growth, quickly led most San Franciscans to choose limited adaptations such as renting a wooden home over a brick one. The hazard of made land was clear to those who read the newspapers closely or looked at the damage, but city leaders proved unwilling to redirect development away from the waterfront.

FILL AND URBAN DEVELOPMENT AFTER 1868

The problem of earthquakes was not entirely forgotten in the years after 1868, but neither did San Franciscans seem overly concerned with the threat of seismic activity. Hittell declared that "the scare [after the 1868 quake] passed off in a few weeks" and optimistically added that "since that time earthquakes have been less frequent and severe than before." The geologist Josiah Whitney wrote in 1869 that the "prevailing tone" in the region was one of "assumed indifference to the dangers of earthquake calamities."[88] Rowlandson complained about "the apathetic conduct of many Californians," but he called leaving the state to escape seismic activity an overreaction. He noted Boston's past history of earthquakes as well as the sequence of quakes that hit New Madrid, Missouri, in 1812 in pointing out that seismic activity was not confined to California. For Rowlandson the solution was scientific research to dissipate the mystery surrounding earthquakes combined with the use of proper building techniques and materials.[89] And research did continue. In the 1890s geologists identified and mapped the San Andreas Rift, as it was known at the time.[90]

Many ordinary San Franciscans also remained aware of the hazards facing their city. Samuel Bowles, who visited the city in the mid-1860s, observed that, because the city was "always exposed" to earthquakes, the citizens were forced "to build strong and low, even for business purposes" and to rely more on wood than other cities of a similar size and prominence. Similarly, in his 1888 *History of California*, Hubert Howe Bancroft wrote that the winter rains, summer fogs, and regular earthquakes characteristic of San Francisco combined with cost considerations to cause most residents to prefer frame buildings.[91]

The architectural historian Stephen Tobriner has demonstrated that many architects and engineers in San Francisco analyzed the damage caused by the earthquakes of the 1860s and attempted to adapt construction practices accordingly. They added "earthquake proof" to "fireproof" as expectations for the city's most prestigious new and retrofitted buildings. They used iron rods to reinforce masonry, built shorter chimneys, and sought out better quality bricks and mortar. New fire codes passed in 1866 required the use of iron anchors and appropriate foundations, and local inventors filed patents for new methods of reinforcing structures, particularly the seawall that was on the minds of the city's residents in 1868.[92] That seawall, as well as other urban development projects, demonstrates the limits of the city's adaptation, however. San Franciscans might keep their buildings low and reinforce them when they could afford to do so, but they were not prepared to rethink their strategies of remaking the terrain of the city despite clear evidence of the hazards of made land.

Instead of fears of earthquakes, the major factor driving urban development, and particularly land speculation, in San Francisco in the late 1860s was the prospect of the completion of the transcontinental railroad. What had looked like a doubtful prospect for a long time was nearing realization, and San Franciscans snapped up new real estate offerings with the expectation of a major boom in demand as soon as the railroad connected California to the east. The settlement of long-disputed land claims left over from the city's chaotic early years—in which Mexican land grants, squatter claims, and sales of questionable legality had made the rightful ownership of large tracts of urban land uncertain— opened up new districts to development in the 1860s.[93]

The demand for a suitable site for a railroad terminus led to another bout of land making in San Francisco, this time along the southern waterfront. Hittell wrote that "the fever of land speculation was so active" that the city had to import a second steam excavator and boasted that "about eight hundred acres that were swamp and bay in 1868" had become "solid land" and "occupied for business purposes" in the subsequent decade. The city filled in much of Mission Bay, completed a bridge across Islais Creek, and began construction on a seawall to protect the harbor from fill that was washing into the bay.[94] The need for a seawall had been debated since at least the mid-1850s as deleterious impacts of filling the water lots came to light. Fill did not always stay where it was placed, particularly under the influence of the tides. Water intruded on land as the tides flowed into the soft fill, and land in turn seemed to be intruding on water as fill washed into the bay and threatened the commercial viability of the harbor. The seawall was built, and then rebuilt to fix a flawed design, in stages starting in 1867. It was still not completed in 1906.[95]

Rock for the seawall and fill for the south waterfront had to come from somewhere. In 1869 developers cut through Rincon Hill to obtain rock to use as fill and to gain easy access to tidelands to the south, including the proposed railroad terminus and potential industrial sites. Rincon Hill had been one of the city's wealthiest residential districts, but the cut left houses hanging precariously over a jagged, unsightly sixty-foot chasm with unstable banks.[96] As Charles Warren Stoddard, who rented one of those houses when its owner fled to safer ground, wrote, the cut "ruined the Hill forever. There is nothing to be done now but to cast it into the midst of the sea."[97] Perhaps because of its impact on a prestigious neighborhood, the destruction of Rincon Hill became one of the few transformations of the land that was widely regretted even in the nineteenth century.

Not all projects to remake the terrain "ruined" the neighborhood, however. One such scheme transformed a thousand acres of the Outside Lands, the lightly inhabited expanse of sand dunes that made up much of the city's western half, to a degree that rivaled the made land of the business district. In the 1860s, San Franciscans began to consider the creation of a local park modeled after New York's great Central Park. The famous landscape architect Frederick Law Olmsted was initially invited to design the park, but he judged the site unsuitable for an eastern-style, tree-filled park. In some sections of the Outside Lands the sand was more than one hundred feet deep and dunes stood sixty feet high. However, in 1871, William Hammond Hall accepted the project of reclaiming this challenging landscape. Through a combination of luck—he discovered the value of barley in anchoring the dunes after a fortuitous spill of horse feed—and experimentation, Hall developed a system of plant succession by which he transformed the sand dunes into a great park of grassy meadows, picturesque lakes, and trees imported from all over the world within six years.[98] Golden Gate Park became one of the gems of the city, almost universally admired for its aesthetic and recreational value.

Even as San Francisco was building an urban retreat to the west, the southern sections of the city were becoming increasingly industrialized. In the late 1860s, Butchertown was relocated to the salt marshes on the city's southeastern side, where the butchers attempted to use the tides as a natural method of removing waste dumped from their slaughterhouses.[99] Other industries demanded more solid ground under their factories and took advantage of the newly filled lands South of Market and farther to the south in the Potrero Hill and Islais Creek districts. The heavy industry in these areas led one visitor in 1869 to compare the city to England's Liverpool and Birmingham for its extensive manufacturing and the "dense cloud of smoke" that hung over the southern neighborhoods. By 1890, San Francisco was home to more than half of the manufacturing businesses in California and produced more than two-thirds of the state's total output.[100]

Rapid growth and new industries demanded a constant influx of new residents. Astonishing rates of population turnover characterized the city's early decades. Between 1850 and 1870 only one in ten members of the laboring classes remained in the city for three decades, and three out of four departed for new opportunities within eight years of arriving. By 1870, San Francisco was the nation's ninth largest city with just under 150,000 people, and that number would double over the next two decades.[101] San Francisco was also one of the most diverse cities in the nation. Throughout these decades the percentage of the urban population born outside the United States remained above 50 percent and sometimes reached 70 percent. Most were white, with large populations of immigrants from Ireland, Germany, Great Britain, Scandinavia, and Italy.[102] The largest group of nonwhites was the Chinese community, which declined in size after the passage of the Chinese Exclusion Act in 1882. However, in 1906 the population of Chinatown remained an estimated twenty-five thousand people, who were confined to the few blocks of wooden buildings and narrow alleys by segregated housing and employment markets.[103]

Chinatown was far from the only distinct neighborhood in San Francisco at the turn of the twentieth century. Social and physical barriers, such as the city's hilly topography, divided San Francisco into neighborhoods separated by class and ethnicity. The South of Market district was crammed with the small homes of Irish working-class families and large boarding houses filled with poor workers of varying backgrounds. They lived and worked among the smoke and smells of the neighborhood's manufacturing plants and foundries. Workers and their families—particularly the more prosperous residents of German and Irish descent—spilled over to the south into the growing Mission and Potrero Hill districts. Much of the low-lying ground in these neighborhoods was made land. To the north, North Beach and Telegraph Hill formed the center of the Italian community, consisting of both long-established and newer immigrants, many of whom lived in crowded and makeshift housing. The city's middle class expanded rapidly into the Western Addition with its block after block of wooden row houses. The newer neighborhoods south of Market and west of Van Ness consisted largely of long rows of continuous wooden buildings subdivided by narrow alleys.[104]

Despite the rapid population increases and turnover, some old-timers remained to recount the city's history of making land. When Rudyard Kipling visited San Francisco in 1889, his reaction echoed that of new arrivals forty years earlier. Unimpressed by the site, he declared that the city "has been pitched down in the sand-bunkers of the Bikanir desert." Kipling added: "About one-fourth of it is ground reclaimed from the sea—any old-timer will tell you all about that."[105] Statements like these show that at least some San Franciscans remembered their city's past, even if most of the city ignored the hazards underfoot. By 1906 one-sixth of the city's population of 410,000 people lived on areas of made ground that were primed for catastrophe.[106]

CONCLUSION

In the aftermath of 1906, the writer John P. Young wondered if "perhaps it was not altogether fortunate" that the test of an earthquake had been deferred. He speculated that San Francisco's citizens might have acted to minimize the risk of severe damage if they had experienced a large quake during the city's early years. However, Young cynically concluded: "There is no evidence that the people of San Francisco, at any time prior to 1906, were impressed by the danger of covering large areas with inflammable wooden structures," despite the obvious risk of fire, so why would they show any greater concern for minimizing the hazard posed by earthquakes?[107] Young did not give early residents of the city enough credit, as they did in fact take precautions against fire. Of course, he had just watched the great conflagration of 1906 tear its way through block after block of wooden buildings, so he should perhaps be forgiven for being unimpressed with the effectiveness of the precautionary measures taken by the city in the preceding decades. It was also a bit simplistic for Young to declare that an earthquake had never tested San Francisco. In fact, the quakes of 1865 and 1868 had been significant tests, and they had revealed many of the hazards that would prove so problematic in 1906, particularly the risks of made land.

But subsequent years lulled San Franciscans into complacency and blurred the memory of those earlier crises. Moderate quakes in the 1880s and 1890s only convinced many residents that they had taken adequate measures to protect their city. At least some observers seemed to forget San Francisco's distinctive challenges. One insurance agent noted that tall buildings had survived these quakes because, he explained: "They are built in the modern fashion, braced as strongly against the elements as are the large business structures of the leading Eastern cities like Chicago and New York, but more strongly."[108] Such statements reflected a faith in modern structures as proof against the forces of nature as well as an assumption that San Francisco's buildings need only match the standards of construction in other American cities. And even where architects took measures to guard against seismic damage, their expensive modern buildings stood alongside cheap frame lodging houses and the small wooden cottages of the city's working classes in neighborhoods like South of Market.

The earthquake and fire that destroyed San Francisco in 1906 came out of nowhere to most residents of the city, but in many ways the disaster could have been anticipated. San Francisco had experienced multiple major fires in its short history, and the prevalence of seismic activity was open knowledge. The city's early years were a saga of crisis and adaptation as natural forces from subsidence to shipworms threatened development. San Franciscans who spoke to old-timers or studied their city's history could even have predicted which areas of the city represented the greatest risk. San Franciscans' apparent tendency to downplay or ignore the danger posed by the combination of filled ground and earthquakes did not stem primarily from ignorance. They knew the region was prone to seismic activity, and certainly after 1868 they knew of the possibility of earthquakes of sufficient force to cause severe damage and threaten lives. They even knew that made land was particularly hazardous, and sometimes—although not always—they took precautions to mitigate those hazards, even as they continued to build in risky areas.

In most cases, however, other considerations trumped a fear of future earthquake hazards. The city's seismic history demonstrates the normality of earthquakes, and it suggests that residents chose to live with periodic shaking. At times they acted to mitigate known hazards, but more often, economic and cultural imperatives took priority. The possibilities of life in the great metropolis of the Pacific Coast seemed to exceed the risks of living there, and faith in modern technology and improvements inspired confidence that the city was protected. San Franciscans knew they lived in "earthquake country" and they knew about the risks posed by made land, but they accepted those risks to continue to develop their city on the unstable ground of the California coastline.

> o economics/culture prioritized over safety / avoidance of earthquakes.

> o risk taking

TWO

CATASTROPHE AND ITS INTERPRETATIONS

IN OCTOBER 1905 THE NATIONAL BOARD OF FIRE UNDERWRITERS bluntly and prophetically declared: "San Francisco has violated all underwriting traditions and precedents by not burning up."[1] Major fires remained a hazard facing late Victorian cities despite improvements in fire departments and municipal water systems since the era of frontier San Francisco. In the most dramatic examples, Chicago burned in 1871, Boston in 1872, and Baltimore in 1904. In the early 1900s fires killed an average of eight thousand people annually in the United States.[2] San Francisco appeared particularly susceptible to fire damage because of the predominance of redwood frame buildings, frequent high winds, and hilly topography that made it difficult for both fire engines and water to reach some parts of the city. More than 90 percent of the buildings in the city were made of wood, some of them four or five stories tall, and brick, stone, and steel structures were concentrated in the business district. Even there, wooden buildings stood alongside the more fireproof buildings, and barely 2 percent of the structures were considered truly fireproof. Almost all buildings lacked modern devices to protect against fire such as sprinkler systems. The city also had many narrow streets and alleys that provided no obstacle to the spread of fire. In the whole city, only Market Street and Van Ness Avenue were wide enough to serve as potential firebreaks.[3]

In contrast to widespread concern about fire, few people in San Francisco worried about earthquakes in the early twentieth century despite the city's seismic history. That mind-set would prove literally disastrous in 1906. Old-timers told stories of the city's history of making land, and some citizens undoubtedly remembered the earthquakes of 1865 and 1868. But explosive growth in the intervening decades meant that the vast majority of residents had never experienced a major earthquake, and the threat of seismic activity seemed sufficiently distant for residents to focus on more immediate concerns of daily life. Such lessons as the hazards of fill had been largely forgotten, and residents placed their faith in modern construction, confident that technology had created a city proof against earthquakes. In the process they ignored the warnings of more knowledgeable experts and evidence that cities remained susceptible to "natural" catastrophes of various kinds.

San Francisco's vulnerability stemmed from both history and geology, a result of the intersection of human choices and natural environmental conditions. On April 18, 1906, as seismic waves reverberated through the land beneath the city in unpredictable ways, they encountered a variegated built environment. Some buildings collapsed because they had been built cheaply and poorly, but the type of land on which they stood played a critical role as well. Other structures survived either because of superior construction or the relative solidity of the ground beneath them—or in some cases because of nothing more than luck. The fires added to the complexity of the disaster, sweeping through vast areas of the city driven by prevailing winds and their own fuel needs with no consideration for the type of ground or the quality of buildings. Neither the earthquake nor the fire, of course, had any concern for the life circumstances of people in its path, but in a city characterized by social and geographic stratification, impacts were far from equal. Understanding the disaster requires consideration of the dynamic interplay of seismic forces, urban fire regimes, social circumstances, and the built environment of San Francisco. The specific characteristics of the city's complex urban environment—most notably unstable made land and densely packed wooden dwellings—transformed a regional seismic event into a disaster of epic proportions.

This chapter begins with a description of the earthquake and the three days of fires that followed. It then focuses on the specific damage caused by the earthquake within San Francisco and relates that damage to the geological and historical features of the urban environment, most of which were identified in the aftermath of the catastrophe. Reactions to the earthquake and fire among both popular observers and the Bay Area's scientific community reflected attempts to come to terms with disaster and its challenge to a narrative of progress that saw modernity as a triumph of human technology over nature. In an attempt to restore order, many explanations linked science and meaning by portraying the destruction as a consequence of construction defects. The disaster became a test that much of the city's built environment had failed, but such a narrative offered a promise of different outcomes in the face of future tests. Rhetoric of scientific analysis of the earthquake's effects also undermined connections that researchers found between seismic damage, fire damage, and historical choices. As a result, contemporary analysis of the catastrophe ultimately contributed to the separation of the earthquake as a seismic event from social and economic factors that shaped the resulting disaster.

THREE DAYS OF CRISIS

Within San Francisco most of the city lay asleep at the predawn hour of the earthquake. At 5:12 A.M. a cacophony of motion and noise abruptly awakened the city's residents—the roar of the rocks of the fault fracturing, followed almost immediately by timber creaking, plaster falling from walls, bric-a-brac and even furniture crashing to the floor, glass shattering, and in some parts of town, buildings shaking, cracking, and collapsing in on themselves. Jesse B. Cook, a police officer on duty downtown, spent the long seconds of the quake dodging falling bricks. Another officer, Michael J. Brady, reported that "the surface of Market Street was rising and falling like the waves on the bay on a stormy day," and some San Franciscans still at home found their own bodies in motion as beds slid across rooms. All lights suddenly went out, and clouds of dust filled the air. James Hopper, a writer for the *San Francisco Call*, declared: "The earth was a rat, shaken in the grinding teeth, shaken, shaken, shaken with periods of slight weariness followed by new bursts of vicious rage."[4]

The earthquake claimed its share of victims, but the death toll would have been much higher if the temblor had occurred later in the day when more people were about in the streets. In the wholesale district a meat market collapsed, killing several market men who were purchasing meat, vegetables, and fruit for their wares for the day. On Mission Street a steel telegraph pole smashed through the driver's seat of a milk wagon, although the driver escaped. Elsewhere on Mission, a herd of beef cattle were being driven up from the waterfront to stockyards at the Potrero. The shock stampeded the cattle, and a falling warehouse struck part of the herd. Patrolman Harry F. Walsh and a bystander from Texas shot a number of the crazed steers, but the stampede claimed at least one human life.[5] The shaking also spooked the city's equine population, and many horses broke from their stables and fled, some escaping only to be killed by falling rubble. Frightened fire horses charged from their stalls in the city's engine houses, and the need to pull the heavy engines using manpower rather than horsepower proved one of many obstacles facing the fire department as it reacted to the disaster.[6]

For residents of many parts of town, particularly neighborhoods north of Market Street and in the Western Addition, the great earthquake initially appeared to be nothing more than an unusually heavy shock. Treating the earthquake as a holiday, men and women left vases, mirrors, and books where they had fallen and ventured out to see the sights. William Douglas Alexander concerned himself primarily with locating a hot cup of coffee—"no easy task ... as there was no water"— and gave no thought to fire as a possible threat to his possessions.[7] Some who remained at their homes approached the day like any other. Josephine Fearon Baxter and her husband decided to do their own washing when their Japanese housekeeper failed to appear for work. Baxter wrote to her parents: "Everyone thought we were crazy to go on washing as though nothing had happened."[8] Mayor Eugene Schmitz, a resident of the Western Addition, was among those who saw little earthquake damage in the immediate vicinity and had no idea of the catastrophe developing downtown and south of Market Street. He finally arrived at the Hall of Justice to oversee the city's handling of the disaster an hour and a half after the first shock, having been fetched from his home by employees of the City Attorney's office.[9]

South of Market Street no one doubted the severity of the crisis facing San Francisco. Market Street was not only the city's main thoroughfare but also the symbolic divide between the working-class residential and mixed-use districts to the south and the upper and middle-class neighborhoods to the north. One out of six San Franciscans lived south of Market, mostly in older, poorly constructed wooden buildings. A mix of small, single-family dwellings, many nestled in alleys or crowded in among other buildings, and large boarding houses where unmarried male laborers rented sleeping space characterized the neighborhood. The earthquake sent many of these ramshackle old buildings collapsing in on themselves, nothing more than "masses of splintered wood," killing many residents and trapping others inside.[10]

On the block of Sixth Street between Howard and Natoma, four large wood-frame rooming houses provided lodging for approximately a thousand low-income workers. The shock of the earthquake caused the Nevada House at 132 Sixth Street to collapse, slamming into the adjacent Lormor, which in turn struck the Ohio House. Ohio House than rammed into Brunswick House, splitting the larger building into three sections and driving part out into the middle of Howard Street. A fire immediately broke out in the wreckage as trapped residents screamed for assistance. James Madison Jacobs, who lived in Room 56 on the third floor, successfully dug his way out of the wreckage and heard "wailings and cries for help in every direction." Eyewitnesses estimated that between 150 and 300 people ultimately died in Brunswick House. A few blocks south, on the 600 block of Howard Street, one wall of the American Hotel fell, severely damaging Fire Engine Station No. 4 next door. Across the street a Chinese laundry collapsed and a fire broke out. Firefighters had to simultaneously try to rescue men trapped in each building, salvage their own equipment, and deal with the flames.[11]

Numerous other residential hotels in the neighborhood also collapsed, and fires engulfed the ruins by midmorning, halting most rescue efforts. The destruction of the large hotels attracted the most attention, but the modest, working-class homes of the district became sites of smaller-scale personal and familial crises as well. Olina Granucci remembered her father rescuing her grandmother through an attic window as her South of Market cottage sank into the fill on which it had been built.[12] As the fires swept through the neighborhood, families like the Granuccis saw their homes and possessions destroyed in minutes.

Other working-class neighborhoods were hit hard by the earthquake as well, particularly the Mission District and Chinatown. Perhaps the best documented of the hotel collapses was that of the Valencia Street Hotel, located at 718 Valencia Street in the Mission District. Police Lieutenant Henry N. Powell described how the street "began to dance and roll in waves," sinking in places and snapping streetcar tracks and underground cables. The hotel itself "lurched forward as if the foundation were dragged backward from under it, and . . . telescoped down on itself like a concertina. This took only a few seconds." In those seconds the four-story hotel sank three stories, leaving only one floor above ground level. Most residents trapped in the lower floors of the Valencia Street Hotel probably drowned within minutes as water flooded into the structure from broken water mains, but rescue efforts continued for two days. The final death toll was approximately two hundred people.[13] The severe earthquake damage in these neighborhoods occurred not only because of the shoddy construction of large wood-frame residential hotels and workers' cottages but also because of the type of ground the structures were built on. A combination of geology and history turned particular blocks into death traps.

Collapsing buildings and stampeding cattle were not the only hazards of the urban environment after the earthquake. During the morning more than thirty explosions occurred along gas lines in severely damaged sections of the city, killing and injuring an unknown number of people fleeing the fires that were engulfing the central city and the South of Market district. Thirteen-year-old James J. O'Brien remembered that "the street blew up" and cobblestones flew into the air as gas mains on Tenth Street exploded. Although the gas was shut off by 7:30 A.M., some remained in the pipes and explosions created craters in the city's streets as large as twelve feet wide and thirty feet long and fed the fires.[14]

The earthquake also destroyed underground telephone and telegraph conduits, cutting off communications both within the city and between San Francisco and the outside world. Most importantly, the earthquake shattered both water mains and service pipes that

The Valencia Street Hotel after its collapse, with a large sink hole in the foreground. Courtesy of the California History Room, California State Library, Sacramento, California.

distributed water throughout the city. Edna Laurel Calhan saw water "shooting in a geyser up in the air" from broken pipes outside her front door. Throughout the city water leaked from hundreds of breaks, leaving the system bereft of water for combating the fires.[15] Lack of water was only one of the obstacles faced by the San Francisco Fire Department. They also dealt with the loss of equipment and horses, the failure of the city's fire alarms and other communications systems, and the death of their chief, Dennis Sullivan. Sullivan suffered fatal injuries when a cupola and section of wall from the California Hotel crashed through the roof of the fire station on Bush Street where he and his wife were sleeping. The impossibility of protecting the city stemmed from the sheer number of localized disasters happening at once; the fallen buildings, people trapped in the wreckage, and fires breaking out all over would have been too much for the Fire Department's resources, even had Sullivan survived.[16]

extreme punishment → relation to Hurricane
Katrina in priorities
of
response

But columns of smoke were rising over San Francisco alongside the
sun on the morning of April 18 as more than fifty separate fires flickered
to life. Overturned stoves and oil lamps, damaged chimney flues, and
broken electrical wires all started fires. Many small flames in private
dwellings were doused before they could spread, but in the dawn quiet,
fires expanded unchecked among the business districts. In his May 1906
report on the conflagration for the National Board of Fire Underwriters, the engineer S. Albert Reed described how almost all of the original
fires started in the areas south of Market Street and east of Sansome
Street "in a quarter characterized by soft ground," where buildings suffered severe structural damage and water, gas, and sewer pipes gave way
with the shifting earth. The rooming houses that collapsed in the earthquake caught fire as fallen lamps and kitchen fires in ground-floor
restaurants ignited the wooden structures. Attempts to rescue trapped
residents had to be abandoned as survivors fled flames approaching
from all sides.[17]

As the fires spread, city leaders attempted to maintain order. Upon
his arrival at the Hall of Justice in Portsmouth Plaza, Mayor Schmitz
issued orders that looters should be shot, applying the rationale that
the city had nowhere to confine prisoners. Schmitz ordered all liquor
sales stopped immediately and instituted a curfew after dark. A local
printer produced five thousand copies of Schmitz's proclamation to
post throughout the city; with the electricity down, the printing press
had to be powered by hand. Brigadier General Frederick W. Funston,
acting commander of the US Army's Pacific Division because Major
General Adolphus W. Greely was out of town, saw the flames spreading
and called for all available troops to report to the Hall of Justice. Troops
began arriving downtown by 8 A.M., and by noon more than fifteen
hundred soldiers were in the city. During the fire San Francisco contained five separate bodies charged with maintaining order: the municipal police, the US Army, the California National Guard, the US Navy,
and ad hoc citizens' committees.[18] Not surprisingly, the presence of
so many law enforcement and military entities created confusion over
whether the civilian government remained in power or whether the city
had been placed under martial law—in fact, the mayor remained in
charge throughout—and several groups, particularly the US Army and

A man moving through the streets during the fire. Note the buckled streetcar rails in the foreground. Courtesy of the California History Room, California State Library, Sacramento, California.

National Guard, came under criticism for their actions. The fire forced the seat of government to migrate first from City Hall to the Hall of Justice, then to the Fairmount Hotel, and finally to Franklin Hall on Fillmore Street, which only enhanced the confusion.[19]

The flames spread so quickly through the South of Market district that by 1 P.M., in the historian Gladys Hansen's words, the neighborhood "had become a single raging fire."[20] Residents fled either east to the Ferry Building, where they hoped to escape across the bay, or north to Union Square and the city's parks as open spaces became places of refuge. As the city's newly homeless dragged whatever possessions they could carry through the rubble-filled streets, they passed sightseers from lightly damaged districts heading downtown to watch the fires. Many people remembered the deafening rumble of trunks being pulled along the sidewalks.

The reporter James Hopper hired a wealthy young man with an automobile to drive him and spent the first day of the fire circling the city and observing the destruction. He wrote of the great buildings on Market Street writhing "like so many live beings" and described the entire wholesale district as a mass of flames. Hopper was only one of many San

San Franciscans watching the fire from Sacramento Street. Photograph by Arnold Genthe. Courtesy of the Library of Congress.

Franciscans who dedicated themselves to observing the spectacle of their city's destruction. Crowds gathered at various points in the city to watch a contest between firefighters and flames. But there was no water, so men and women stood and watched as the city burned.[21] Many San Franciscans believed until the last possible moment that their homes and businesses would be spared. Those in the outer neighborhood of the Western Addition put their faith in the barrier posed by Van Ness Avenue, which they believed to be too wide for the fire to cross. Mary Edith Griswold described how people and furniture lined Van Ness on both sides as refugees encamped with whatever they had saved from the flames, sometimes a rocking chair or bedroom set, in one case a parrot. Vacant lots and parks throughout the city similarly filled with people and their salvaged possessions.[22]

When the fires first broke out, winds in the city were less than ten miles per hour, and the flames moved slowly against a westerly wind. But the conflagration transformed the local atmosphere, creating its own wind tunnel effect. Jack London, who had experienced the earthquake at his ranch in Sonoma County, approached the city on Wednesday afternoon and described the scene: "I watched the vast conflagration from the bay. It was dead calm. Not a flicker of wind stirred. Yet from every side wind was pouring in upon the city. . . . The heated air rising made an enormous suck. Thus did the fire of itself build its own colossal chimney through the atmosphere. Day and night the dead calm continued, and yet, near to the flames, the wind was often half a gale."[23] This phenomenon by which the fire created its own wind system is known as a firestorm. Firestorms have occurred in massive wildland fires such as those that devastated the American West in 1910 and in bombing campaigns during World War II. In peacetime urban settings, firestorms occurred during the Great Fire of London in 1666 and the 1871 Chicago fire. As smaller fires come together into a mass fire, they reshape the atmospheric dynamics and feed on their own energy, creating high winds and intense heat. One observer reported that the San Francisco fire raced up Rincon Hill so quickly that it "outran men and women in flight."[24]

As the winds shifted and built, one fire jumped to the north side of Market and drove northward and westward through Chinatown. It then joined with a second column of flame and sped through the city's older residential portions, consuming wooden structures both great and small as though they were tinder.[25] During the night the combined north fires threatened Van Ness Avenue and the Western Addition, while the south fires headed toward the Mission District. The first night was a harrowing experience for both San Franciscans and their neighbors around the bay. Eric Temple Bell described "the peculiar sound of the flames, like wind blowing through a field of ripe corn" that was audible even eight miles across the water in Oakland. For those in the city, the night of April 18 was lit by the glow of the fire, and the heat of the flames warmed the refugees. Hugh Kwong Liang, who sought safety in the Presidio, remembered periodically spraying water on his canvas tent to prevent it from catching fire from the rain of sparks.[26] Regular detonations of dynamite assaulted the ears of Liang and others throughout the city as the army and the fire department deployed all measures at their disposal to halt the advance of the flames.

The use and misuse of dynamite in a largely futile effort to create firebreaks became one of the great controversies of the fire. With water largely unavailable, a corps of dynamiters formed as early as Wednesday morning, but this group of volunteers had little knowledge or experience. John J. Conlon, a battalion chief with the fire department, blew up the block of Eighth Street between Market and Folsom despite having no previous experience with dynamite. He ultimately questioned the effectiveness of his work. John Bermingham, who was intoxicated at the time, took charge of explosives in Chinatown and the Barbary Coast and later testified that he started sixty fires. An unknown number of Chinese were reported to have died in the explosions in Chinatown.[27] In much of the city, dynamiters employed black powder (gunpowder) that probably started more fires than it put out. Captain Le Vert Coleman, who headed the army's Artillery Corps, complained that the mayor had hamstrung his team's efforts by refusing to allow them to blow up any buildings not adjacent to others already ablaze. This policy, intended to protect private property for as long as possible, prevented the army from creating a sufficient firebreak to halt the spread of the flames.[28]

Thursday, April 19, the second day of the fire, dawned without the sun. The only sign that morning had arrived was a change in the color of the smoke that covered the city and the decreased visibility of the flames. Although the downtown fire was moving slowly, much of the city had already been destroyed. James Hopper walked down Market Street and found himself in "a dead city, not a city recently dead but one overcome by some cataclysm ages past. . . . Fragments of wall rose on all sides, columns twisted but solid in their warp, as if petrified in the midst of their writhing from the fiery ordeal," shrouded in "yellow smoke" amid "a heavy, brooding silence." Cameron King found blocks of former frame houses "only a smoldering ash-strewn plain" with blackened chimneys standing as headstones on each lot. The streets were blocked by "thick tangles of copper wires" lying "dead and lifeless."[29] Early Thursday morning, defenders abandoned the ornate mansions of Nob Hill and the treasures they contained to the flames. The wind had shifted to the east, relieving the waterfront and the railroad depot in the southeastern part of the city, where a group of refugees had gathered, but the fire now threatened the Western Addition, and its defenders dug in at Van Ness Avenue.[30]

That evening the winds shifted again, and the north fire sped back toward Russian Hill and North Beach, which had not been evacuated. A few Italian residents of Telegraph Hill refused to leave and saved their homes with blankets soaked in wine and well water, but hundreds of others died in the streets as they were overcome by the fire and hot gases that made the air unbreathable. The piers and beaches of the northern shore of the city became the site of a makeshift evacuation as all kinds of vessels, from ships to scows and rowboats, were called into service to convey thirty thousand people to safety across the water. Army tugs relieved exhausted firemen and pumped saltwater to fight the blaze all through the night and into Friday morning, when the fire began to run out of fuel as it revisited ground already burned. The defenders had succeeded in preserving the waterfront, which would become critical to the resumption of commerce in the city, and a few buildings along the shore and on Telegraph Hill.[31]

On the south side of the city, another group of men and women faced down the flames in the predominantly Irish working-class residential district of the Mission. Firefighters and residents there had been forced to retreat steadily as the small wooden structures on each block provided abundant fuel for the fire. With all communications systems down, they were isolated from the city's political leadership and the US Army, which may have been a blessing in disguise. The local fire department battalion chiefs developed what Gladys Hansen describes as "a brilliant, ad hoc, sectional defense plan to save the Mission District." They created a firebreak that drove the fire toward a two-block-wide park at Dolores Street between Eighteenth and Twentieth Streets. Thousands of volunteers dismantled small buildings by hand, and Navy and National Guard dynamite squads removed the larger structures. A blacksmith named John Rafferty discovered a functioning fire hydrant at Twentieth and Church Streets, and human volunteers joined with exhausted fire department horses to pull two fire engines up a steep section of Dolores Street to the hydrant; luckily the available hose just barely reached from hydrant to flames. When firebrands jumped the firebreaks, people with mops, blankets, and milk cans full of water beat out the incipient fires. The hot gases of the great fire nearly suffocated the volunteer firefighters who challenged the flames, but for seven hours three thousand residents of the Mission District successfully contained the fire until it finally burned out from lack of fuel.[32]

Saturday morning saw the fire largely stopped at Van Ness Avenue, preserving the Western Addition, and in the Mission. The fire made a brief run along the bay shore before a heavy rain came to the aid of the

Panorama of the city from Nob Hill, looking southwest toward Market Street. The dome of City Hall is visible on the right. The cleared streets indicate that some debris removal has taken place, but gutted structures remain on most lots. Courtesy of the California History Room, California State Library, Sacramento, California.

city's exhausted defenders and doused the last of the flames.[33] Roughly 250,000 people had seen their dwellings destroyed along with San Francisco's wholesale district, financial district, manufacturing district, all large retail stores, and most government buildings. The fire had burned a total of 28,188 buildings, more than 24,000 of them of wood-frame construction, and destroyed 514 city blocks covering 4.7 square miles—or half the acreage of the city. Although wooden buildings burned in great numbers, more than 95 percent of the buildings fronting the burned district were also made of wood. This is not entirely surprising given the predominance of frame construction in the city, but it demonstrates that factors other than building materials determined where the fire came to a halt.[34]

Isolated structures did survive, even in the heart of the burned district. One was the US Mint, located at Fifth and Mission, which was saved by a crew of sixty employees who defended the Mint from the inside, drawing water from an artesian well in the building's court and two large water tanks on the roof. The fire was so hot—reaching temperatures as high as 2700 degrees Fahrenheit—that it melted the glass in the Mint's windows like butter and caused sandstone and granite to flake off the building with, in the words of Mint superintendent Frank A. Leach, "explosive noises like the firing of artillery."[35] Several cisterns left from before the fire department could rely on a municipal water system saved the Montgomery Block in the middle of the burned district. The Italian-Swiss Colony winery located between Battery and Sansome survived when defenders kept the winery saturated for three days and three nights with water from a stream discovered during construction and incorporated into the building in the form of a well.[36] San Francisco's vaunted "fireproof" buildings did not fare as well. The opulent Palace Hotel was widely believed to be the most fire- and earthquake-proof building in the city. The hotel did survive the earthquake with little damage, but it burned after its water supply was drained in a futile effort to fight fires elsewhere on Market Street. Ultimately, forty-two "class A fireproof" buildings were destroyed. Some observers suggested that more buildings might have been saved had their would-be defenders not been forced to evacuate by the police and military authorities, but in buildings left undefended, the fire found its way in through backdoors, windows, and elevator shafts when it could not consume the walls from the outside.[37]

Buildings were obviously not the only structures affected by the shaking. Water pipes, gas pipes, electric light conduits, and city sewers were all badly damaged, especially where they crossed fill. Such technology, often installed within the ground itself, represented a largely invisible infrastructure essential to human survival and comfort in the modern city. Water pipes in particular formed a crucial link between the city and the hinterland that supported a population of four hundred thousand people within an area of only a few square miles. In early twentieth-century San Francisco, the quality of this infrastructure varied widely, but even the most modern systems proved vulnerable to an earthquake of the magnitude of 1906.

Many of San Francisco's sewers were still constructed of brick, but water and gas pipes made of cast iron also broke apart. The forty-four-inch wrought-iron pipe of the Crystal Springs conduit, one of the main pipelines that transported San Francisco's water supply up the peninsula to the city's reservoir system, ruptured in seven places where it crossed three swamps south of San Francisco. Another pipeline, the Pilarcitos conduit, ran for six miles through what engineers had probably considered to be a convenient narrow valley but which in fact marked the San Andreas Fault. When the fault moved, the earthquake shattered the thirty-inch iron pipe, throwing it sixty feet to the side at one point. At least nineteen different ruptures occurred along a single six-mile stretch; in places the pipe had been either pulled apart or telescoped by as much as six feet. The third conduit, the San Andreas pipeline, ran between the other two and suffered relatively slight damage. Although the thirty-seven-inch pipe had ruptured, it was quickly repaired and served as San Francisco's primary source of water for several weeks after the disaster.[38] The water crisis actually could have been much worse. The concrete dam of the Crystal Springs reservoir and the earthen dam at the San Andreas reservoir were both located near the fault. Although they suffered some damage, both dams survived the earthquake intact.[39]

Although the reservoirs' resilience proved crucial to San Francisco's recovery in the short term and the long term, their survival provided no help against the immediate crisis of the fire. On April 18 approximately eighty million gallons of water were stored in the city—a quantity that in theory might have been sufficient to check the flames. However, the earthquake caused three hundred ruptures in the system of pipes distributing water throughout the city, most (although not all) of them where the pipes crossed filled ground. During the crisis water rushed out through the many breaks, leaving the fire department with little water pressure at those few hydrants that were not damaged. The burning and collapse of buildings also left over twenty-three thousand broken service connections that had to be shut off before the system could be repaired and water service restored.[40] Ironies in San Francisco's destruction by fire did not escape contemporary observers. The *Coast Seamen's Journal* caustically noted: "That a city almost wholly surrounded by water in illimitable quantities should have been laid in ashes mainly, if not solely, by lack of water for fire-fighting purposes, is calculated to make one revise the preconceived notion of human intelligence."[41]

The earthquake that struck San Francisco on April 18, 1906, and the three-day conflagration that followed had combined to nearly destroy the seventh largest city in the United States. Nearly all of the city's inhabitants had lost their homes, workplaces, or both. Although it was impossible to predict that an earthquake would hit the city in April 1906 or that it would be followed by a massive fire, attention to history and geology could have alerted San Franciscans that their city was at risk. More important, they could have recognized that specific sites in the city represented particular hazards. That proved small consolation as residents confronted the devastation, however, and they sought various ways to explain how a modern metropolis could fall so quickly and completely.

IN THE WAKE OF CATASTROPHE

The attitudes of many San Franciscans in the aftermath of the 1906 earthquake and fire reflected a new awareness of the power of nature and the fragility of urban structures. By the early twentieth century, most Americans believed that disasters stemmed from natural phenomena rather than punishment from God.[42] According to this way of thinking, technology could mitigate natural hazards, which represented temporary interruptions to progress and civilization. The catastrophe in San Francisco shook that modern faith in technology and human capacity. Mary Edith Griswold, an assistant editor at *Sunset Magazine*, wrote that her fellow San Franciscans believed they had encountered "a power too stupendous to combat . . . the fury of the forces of nature [that] cannot be met by the puny hands of man." Stanford University president David Starr Jordan compared the earthquake to a "devouring dragon, leaving its trail on the hills and destroying the works of man wherever it passes."[43] William Wallace Campbell, an astronomer at the University of California, conceded that the earthquake was "more discouraging" than the fire even though the fire was responsible for most of the damage to the city. An earthquake, Campbell wrote, "brings terror to many souls. When the earth is no longer *terra firma*, but has become *terra mota*, one does, indeed, feel perfectly helpless."[44]

Other reactions drew a more explicit connection between the destruction of human works and a moral or practical judgment on the city. The Irish newspaper *The Leader*, organ of the Irish priest and political figure Father Peter C. Yorke, declared the disaster to be a lesson about "the vanity of brick and mortar," even punishment for "boast[ing] how we had harnessed the powers of nature." The writer Mary Austin also saw a moral lesson in the destruction, blaming the conditions of urban life. She wrote: "The greater part of this disaster—the irreclaimable loss of goods and houses, the violent deaths—was due chiefly to man-contrivances, to the sinking of made ground, to huddled buildings cheapened by greed." Austin concluded that "most man-made things do inherently carry the elements of their own destruction" and asked how much of the damage could have been averted if San Francisco had "wide, clean breathing spaces and room for green growing things to push up between."[45] The moral lessons drawn from the earthquake thus differed—whether San Franciscans should be humble in the face of the power of God or nature or whether they should build better housing and additional parks—but these observers shared a sense of the disaster as an encounter between natural forces and human "contrivances," a confrontation that the city had lost.

Scientists also sought to explain the devastation. The day after the earthquake, Andrew C. Lawson, a geologist at the University of California, urged Governor George C. Pardee to appoint a scientific commission to study the earthquake. The eight-member commission, known as the State Earthquake Investigation Commission (SEIC), undertook a detailed study of damage throughout the region. Their report proved to be a ground-breaking work of both observation and analysis in the young field of seismology. It drew on direct observations by commission scientists and their students as well as canvassing of local residents throughout the affected region, and it ultimately incorporated information from some three hundred individuals. As such, the report reflected the hybrid character of nineteenth-century American seismology, which relied heavily on the observations of untrained citizens. The commission members sought to emphasize the scientific character of their work, but their methods relied on observed intensity far more than on the instrumental measurements that would later characterize the field.[46]

On one level, the studies published by the commission and other professionals, particularly engineers charged with exploring the effects of the earthquake and fire on the built environment, tested the validity of Austin's theory that "man-contrivances" were largely to blame for the scope of the disaster. Scientific and technical reports, like the writings of lay observers such as Austin, reflected a struggle to come to terms with the scope of the catastrophe and particularly with its effects on the urban environment. Many sought to assign meaning or method to the disaster, to craft an explanation that would relieve some of the chagrined helplessness in the face of *terra mota* described by Campbell. They portrayed the earthquake as a referendum on the quality of construction, suggesting that "good" buildings had survived—a premise that restored the prospect that the modern city could triumph over future seismic activity. Such explanations restored order in the face of the manifest disorder of the catastrophe by promising that proper building practices could protect against future damage, but in doing so, they contributed to an atmosphere of earthquake denial driven by political and economic motives and inadvertently provided justification for limited adaptation to seismic hazards.

Within San Francisco, the SEIC documented an unsurprising correlation between degree of earthquake damage and distance from the fault. A more important factor, however, was the type of ground, with made land and marsh land being the worst. The scientists ultimately calculated that the shaking caused by an earthquake was as much as twelve times as great on a marsh as on solid rock, between 4.4 and 11.6 times as great on made land, and between 2.4 and 4.4 times as great on loose sand.[47] For example, Telegraph Hill and the Ferry Building stood only a quarter of a mile apart on the eastern shore of San Francisco, essentially equidistant from the fault. However, the damage on the made ground at the Ferry Building was similar to that along the fault itself—a ten on the Rossi-Forel scale—in contrast to the rating of "scarcely higher than seven" on the rocky summit of Telegraph Hill, where even a number of brick chimneys remained intact. The report concluded: "The degree of intensity which prevailed at any locality in the city depended chiefly on whether the underlying formations are firm rock or incoherent material more or less saturated with water."[48] The commission's report, and other scientific studies from the time, related the damage at particular sites within San Francisco to the history of changes made to the land over a half-century of urban development. Decisions made more than fifty years before by the city's early residents to buy and sell water lots and extend the city out into the bay proved costly in 1906.

Reports of the effects of the earthquake downtown, along the waterfront, and south of Market demonstrate San Franciscans' knowledge of the intersection of made land, modern construction, and seismic hazard even before April 1906. The problem of subsidence, a bane of San Franciscans in these districts since the early 1850s, was well known to local experts such as city engineer C. E. Grunsky. A study by Grunsky's Board of Public Works in 1901–1902 found that, in a single year, part of Harrison Street subsided 2.04 inches between Fifth and Sixth Streets, while Sixth Street sank 1.20 inches between Howard and Channel. The next year the city engineer recorded a maximum subsidence of 2.64 inches on Harrison and 2.04 inches on Sixth.[49] The SEIC also referenced this "constant tendency of the whole district to subside from year to year." Because of this ongoing sinking, cable car tracks on lower Market Street had been constructed on piles to maintain their grade. When the earthquake hit, the tracks remained largely intact while the street on both sides dropped two feet and pavement fissured, leaving the tracks as "a narrow raised path along the center of the street."[50]

The most notable survivor in this section of San Francisco was the Ferry Building, which suffered damage but possessed a sufficiently strong foundation that it remained standing even though it was located seven hundred feet east of the bay's original shoreline. The commission concluded that the earthquake had caused the fill to settle so that the surface sank anywhere from a few inches to as much as three feet. In general, the damage was greatest closest to the waterfront, indicating that "the more recent the filling, the more it would be compacted" by the shaking. Areas that had suffered significant damage in the 1868 earthquake had been compacted during that crisis as well as experiencing gradual settling over time, making them less vulnerable to further compression.[51] The earthquake had accelerated the ongoing, regular

Damage from subsidence at Embarcadero (then East Street) and Lombard.
Courtesy of the California Historical Society (CHS2016_2126).

process by which fill and other loose soil became compacted over time,
with tragic consequences for many structures built on unstable ground.

Climatic variables joined gradual environmental changes shaped
by historical choices, such as subsidence of made land, in contributing
to the impact of the 1906 earthquake. In San Francisco from January
through March, heavy rains exceeding the average seasonal precipi-
tation by two and a half inches had more than made up for a dry fall.
Outside of the city, the first months of 1906 had been even wetter, and
in some areas rainfall exceeded local averages by more than nine inches.
The rains had stopped in April, but ground throughout the region
remained saturated. One investigator explicitly noted how California's
climate (specifically the seasonal concentration of rain followed by long
months of dry weather) made the region susceptible to hazards such
as landslides and earthflows. The waterlogged ground conditions in
the spring of 1906 contributed to landslides, subsidence, and simply

more severe shaking when the earthquake struck.[52] The historical circumstances shaping the events of April 1906 thus included not only long-standing human practices such as the use of coastal fill but also specific environmental factors such as a wet winter that further exacerbated risk. Seismicity intersected with other dynamic environmental variables such as seasonal rainfall.

The earthquake caused other sudden environmental changes that seemed out of place in the modern city and challenged the solidity of landforms. Police officer Jesse B. Cook was only a few blocks from the Ferry Building in today's Embarcadero district when the earthquake hit. He watched as water bubbled up through a sudden crack in the street at the intersection of Davis and Washington. Even when the shaking subsided, Cook remembered: "The sidewalk I was on felt like it was slipping into the bay." He added: "Everyone thought it was, because they knew that this part of the town was all filled in land, filled on mud."[53] Cook's account reflected not only the shared knowledge of San Franciscans about the risks posed by made land but also described a phenomenon not yet named: liquefaction. In a major earthquake, unconsolidated, saturated soil can be shaken so severely that it behaves like a liquid, sinking, flowing downslope, cracking and spreading, and losing the capacity to support larger structures. Water or sand from underground rises to the surface, often leaving lasting traces on the land. In an urban setting like San Francisco, such traces were erased during rebuilding, but liquefaction would recur in some of the same neighborhoods in 1989.

Several of the most dramatic human crises of the earthquake occurred on areas of made land. The location of the Valencia Street Hotel, where an estimated two hundred people perished, had been a lake in 1776 when the Spanish arrived in the region and a swamp until the 1870s. The ground sank six feet in the area, twenty-two-inch and sixteen-inch water pipes shattered, and streetcar rails were twisted into arches as the pavement bucked and crumbled. Less than a third of the frame dwellings in this section of the Mission district remained standing after the earthquake.[54] In the area of Sixth and Howard, where cheap rooming houses collapsed against each other in a deadly chain reaction, the ground had shifted seven feet. This land had been a portion of Mission Swamp where the 1868 earthquake had created a small lake, which had been filled in the intervening decades. Hundreds of people died there in 1906.[55] Each of these catastrophes—and much of the South of Market district as well as parts of the Mission—fell within two areas of particularly high seismic intensity identified by the SEIC. One such area extended from Eighth and Mission to Fourth and Brannan, and traced along the original shore of Mission Bay, encompassing land that had once been tidal marsh or a portion of the bay itself. Another followed the former course of Mission Creek, extending unevenly from Ninth and Brannan to Nineteenth and Dolores and passing near the site of the Valencia Street Hotel.[56] Thus the worst earthquake damage occurred on land that had been waterways and wetlands before being filled in as San Francisco grew.

The SEIC drew connections to both history and geology in its analysis of damage within the city. Most of the northeastern section of San Francisco, for example, suffered relatively limited damage such as chimneys falling and "slight cracking of brick work." The land in these areas consisted of "exposed bedrock on the flanks of the hills." On the lower slopes a thin layer of sand and alluvium covered a rocky base. The East Bay cities of Oakland and Berkeley similarly suffered relatively slight damage because of their rocky ground. On the other end of the spectrum was made land. The scientists explicitly noted the role of "human agency" in creating such risk, and the commission bluntly declared that its findings "unequivocally demonstrated" that made land represented "dangerous building sites."[57]

Working-class people lived in these neighborhoods, but made land also underlay the major commercial and industrial districts of San Francisco. This confluence reflected the reality that in San Francisco in 1906 only the poor had to live near their places of employment. Streetcar lines allowed the middle classes and more prosperous members of the working classes to move away from the congestion and pollution of business districts. Public transit had enabled use of the hills for residential construction, and the wealthy had built their homes atop some of San Francisco's spectacular vistas. The hills offered excellent views, but they also offered relatively solid ground during earthquakes—although the residents of the mansions of Nob Hill had probably not concerned themselves with seismic hazards when they built their showplace homes. The class stratification of San Francisco did not break down strictly along lines of elevation, however. For example, Telegraph

The "Drunken Row" of homes damaged by the earthquake on Howard between Seventeenth and Eighteenth Streets. Courtesy of the San Francisco History Center, San Francisco Public Library.

Hill was dotted with the homes of working-class Italian immigrants. In flood-prone regions such as New Orleans and elsewhere along the Mississippi River, low-income residents and people of color are often forced to live on the lowest, most hazard-prone ground. However, this correlation between class, race, and vulnerability was more ambiguous in San Francisco, perhaps because earthquakes were less common and less well understood than floods.[58] The differential impacts of the earthquake along class and ethnic lines stemmed in large part from the quality of construction and the capacity to recover.

The fire was, if anything, even more indiscriminate than the earthquake in its impact. Few of even the city's most expensive buildings could withstand the firestorm. As one journalist wrote in the aftermath of the flames: "Nob Hill stands almost as bare as when it was primitive, rolling sand."[59] The mansions of the railroad tycoons burned just as did the much-maligned wooden hovels and tenements of Chinatown and

"On the ruins," photograph by Arnold Genthe of a Chinese man surveying the ruin of Chinatown. Courtesy of the Library of Congress.

South of Market. The historian Andrea Rees Davies has suggested that "Chinatown did not burn by natural causes," citing the counterproductive use of dynamite and evidence that firefighters directed resources elsewhere.[60] Firefighters may well have prioritized saving some neighborhoods and structures over others, but it is hard to imagine that they could have saved Chinatown even with maximum effort. The force of the fire exceeded the capacity of the city's resources to counter it, and the fire had no concern for the class or race of its victims. Questions of vulnerability and social justice proved most salient in the months and years after the earthquake and fire as residents of all backgrounds grappled with the challenges of rebuilding their city.

DAMAGE AND DENIAL

The earthquake and fire had laid waste to the city of San Francisco, destroying much of the technological infrastructure that sustained the metropolis. Looking at the ruins of the city, it was hard not to be impressed by nature's power. The writer Charles B. Sedgwick expressed this view when he wrote that the fire had made "our habitations, cities and great lifeworks subject to as easy destruction as are the wonderful creations of ants at the hands of humans."[61] Even as they shared such rhetoric, the region's scientists and engineers set out to study and explain the calamity. In doing so, they implicitly explored the relationship between the urban environment and the specific damage caused by the earthquake. These studies uncovered important knowledge about seismic activity, most famously Harry Fielding Reid's elastic rebound theory. However, despite the best efforts of scientists to remain impartial, they too sought meaning in the disaster and attempted to reconcile a belief in modern progress—manifested in the transformation and control of nature in the city—with the evidence of nature's power.

Expert observers wrote from within the context of political and economic debates about the relative impact of the earthquake and fire and the relationship between the two. In the weeks and months following the earthquake, San Franciscans debated how to characterize the catastrophe that had struck their city. Was the earthquake or the fire principally to blame? Only a week after the earthquake, the San Francisco Real Estate Board passed a resolution that the disaster should be referred to only as "the great fire," never as "the great earthquake." Ernest P. Bicknell, who would play an important role in relief efforts, overheard men traveling to the city similarly resolve "as a fact beyond dispute that the disaster in San Francisco was due solely to fire, to such a calamity, in short, as might occur in any well-ordered city and that the slight tremor which preceded the fire had nothing to do with the tragedy."[62]

Such resolutions echoed efforts in 1868 to downplay the earthquake of that year, and in 1906, San Franciscans similarly feared scaring off investment and potential immigrants to the city. Fire, after all, could strike anywhere, whereas earthquakes seemed to represent a unique and regionally (even locally) specific threat. Such denial stemmed from real economic and psychological motivations for ordinary people as well as for business leaders. It was not, primarily, an exercise in cynicism. This separation of the components of disaster extended beyond the realms of economics and politics to the scientists seeking to understand the catastrophe and its causes. As such, it contributed to the perception of disasters as resulting from natural hazards outside of human control and thus concealed the role of human choices and history in shaping disaster.

Insurance payouts represented one reason why San Franciscans emphasized the effects of the fire over those of the earthquake. Small property holders in particular were concerned about the ability and willingness of insurance companies to meet their obligations. Some people panicked and accepted early but heavily discounted payouts from insurers. Most policies covered fire but not earthquake damage, complicating the situation. The emphasis on the role of the fire over that of the earthquake was often strategic—a means of countering early media reports that the quake had completely destroyed San Francisco and forcing insurance companies to pay. The first insurance adjusters on the scene reportedly believed that the fire had done no more than burn an already ruined city. The results of a secret May 31 meeting of insurance company representatives in New York City were leaked to the San Francisco papers, which stirred up indignation at companies that had voted to pay 75 percent of the dollar value of claims in contrast to "dollar-for-dollar" companies that planned to pay full value. Ultimately the companies acquitted themselves reasonably well, with estimates suggesting that they paid at least 80 percent on the dollar and provided $115 million worth of capital for rebuilding in just the first six months.[63]

Among those who published reports about the structural effects of the earthquake in San Francisco, Frank Soulé, then dean of the College of Civil Engineering at the University of California, was particularly optimistic about the damage. Soulé argued that well-made buildings survived the earthquake with little damage, and he attributed the vast majority of destruction to the fire. Richard L. Humphrey of the USGS agreed that building survival correlated to quality of construction, although he characterized the overall earthquake damage as more severe than did Soulé. John Stephen Sewall of the US Army Corps of Engineers, however, noted that the damage was remarkably localized, writing that he had encountered clusters of buildings "almost totally destroyed" even when adjacent buildings "escaped practically without damage, although I feel quite sure that many of the wrecked buildings were superior in every way." Sewall's findings more closely match those of the SEIC, and his willingness to identify the seeming randomness of destruction may have resulted from his status as a short-term visitor to the city, sent to San Francisco in May 1906 to survey the structural damage. In contrast, Soulé was a longtime Bay Area resident with an interest in promoting the region.[64]

As with many such debates, both sides contained an element of truth. Well-constructed buildings *were* more likely to survive, but other factors (most notably the type of ground) played crucial roles as well. Nevertheless, the correlation between quality of construction and degree of seismic damage became an important element of attempts to explain the catastrophe. The Chamber of Commerce, hardly an impartial observer, declared that "the earthquake damage in San Francisco stands as a monument almost entirely to cheap, dishonest, and insincerely ostentatious construction." The journalist Ray Stannard Baker perceived a "proof of character through fire" in which "good, honest work stood."[65] Several examples offered hope that sufficient "character" of construction could survive in even the most hazardous locations. The Southern Pacific railway tracks, which survived both the earthquake and fire, were located along the old course of Mission Creek. The SEIC concluded that the tracks possessed an "exceptionally strong foundation" and noted that the railroad lands had been filled in with broken rock from nearby hills, particularly Rincon Hill, rather than the more ad hoc and less solid mixtures of sand and urban debris used in many older filled areas.[66]

The US Post Office building at Seventh and Mission was another survivor. The post office had been constructed on twenty-foot piles, and it suffered damage but survived the earthquake even though nearby streets sank four feet. Sewall wrote of the "extraordinarily severe test" that the earthquake had posed for the post office, and this language of the catastrophe as a "test" to be passed or failed by structures was common.[67] The argument that "good" buildings had survived implicitly sought to restore order to the city and reassert the ability of technology to protect against natural forces. However, engineers who explained earthquake damage as affecting only subpar structures provided support—whether intentionally or not—for earthquake denial.

Scientists at the time extended this argument to explain damage to natural features as well as built structures, showing the strength of its appeal. USGS scientist Grove Karl Gilbert, also a member of the SEIC, argued that "natural structures in general are much less sensitive to earthquake violence than artificial structures." In contrast, Charles

Derleth Jr., recently hired as a professor of engineering at the University of California, believed that, just as in the cities where "one can pick out the black from the white sheep in buildings," nature "pointed out her weak and her strong construction" through the earthquake. Humphrey wrote of how "unsound" redwood trees with "defects" such as dry rot suffered greater destruction, although he considered such flawed trees to be unusual among redwoods.[68] Such assessments represented an attempt to assign meaning to the disaster, either through a contrast between the natural and the artificial or by dividing both natural and artificial into "weak" and "strong," with the latter showing resistance to seismic forces.

For many San Francisco readers in 1906, the collapse of City Hall, widely perceived as the epitome of shoddy as well as "insincerely ostentatious" construction (as the Chamber of Commerce had written), represented the prototypical example of the earthquake revealing hidden weaknesses in a building. When the shaking hit, most of the masonry on the building's dome fell, bombarding other parts of the structure in the process. Huge exterior column drums, cornices, and walls crashed to the street. Officer E. J. Plume, who was inside City Hall at the time, heard "reports like cannon" as the building's structure gave way. He watched, fearing for his life, as "huge stones and lumps of masonry came crashing down."[69] In the aftermath of the quake, the city's Sub-Committee on Statistics cited City Hall as a prime example in which "the principal damage by earthquake was due to inferior workmanship, worthless mortar, or faulty design." In contrast, organized labor defended the workmanship and material used, suggesting that the damage was less severe than reported and the building could have been saved. With such debates, contemporary analysis of earthquake damage became intertwined with political disputes between Progressives and labor in which each attempted to portray the other as corrupt.[70]

As they sought to develop scientific explanations for the 1906 earthquake, geologists and other scientists operated within this context of politically and economically driven analyses of the 1906 disaster. In a 1913 article, the new president of the Seismological Society of America, J. C. Branner, complained that "many persons, organizations, and commercial interests" worried that earthquakes would keep business and capital away from California. That concern had led them to engage in "deliberate suppression of news about earthquakes," particularly the 1906 catastrophe. The civil engineer Fred G. Plummer similarly complained that San Franciscans had suffered from a tendency to deny seismic risks prior to April 1906—he recounted his difficulties in finding a copy of a published catalog of historical earthquakes in the city—and had not learned the lessons of 1906. According to Branner, suppression efforts included discouraging geologists from collecting and publishing information on seismic activity. Like many other scientists both before and after him, Branner advocated the accumulation of knowledge about earthquakes—"the terrors that earthquakes have for mankind are largely attributable to our own ignorance," he wrote—and emphasized that most earthquakes were not, in fact, dangerous.[71] The political and economic rationales for earthquake denial thus intersected with, and posed an obstacle to, the scientific quest for knowledge about seismicity.

Other learned observers joined Branner in emphasizing the normality of earthquakes. Derleth noted that "earthquakes are natural phenomena and should not be feared." Scientists and engineers explicitly compared the earthquakes of the Pacific Coast to hazards facing other regions of the country. They suggested, as scholars do today, that few if any locales were free of natural hazards. Yet they too were motivated to defend their state and promote tourism. For example, Plummer tempered his criticism by declaring that "California is the best place on earth to live" as long as its residents adapted to the state's active seismicity. In a 1915 publication reassuring potential visitors to California, Branner wrote that earthquakes offered no more cause for alarm than "wind or rain or snow." He emphasized: "The stories of yawning chasms, and the swallowing up of people and buildings are the veriest fabrications."[72] Branner was not, of course, wrong in these statements, but he wrote with the clear intention of reassuring potential visitors to the city and the state who feared "earthquake country." His essay paralleled the praise that earlier boosters had lavished on the natural advantages of San Francisco. Such statements also ignored connections between the urban environment and seismic hazards, characterizing earthquakes as entirely natural and deemphasizing their ability to affect human cities.

Ironically, the impulse to separate the earthquake and fire, to see them as two distinct events, underlay both earthquake denial efforts and scientific investigations that focused on seismic activity. The Chamber of Commerce and its allies downplayed San Francisco's distinctive environment and the power of nature in favor of the more easily explainable, less terrifying phenomenon of urban fire. But seismologists also, for different reasons, increasingly separated the earthquake from local history and the urban environment as their branch of science expanded after 1906. Even the SEIC ignored the fire except as an obstacle to accurate assessment of localized seismic intensity within San Francisco. The commission saw its work as nonpolitical—Derleth sought funding by emphasizing that their research would be "concerned with the purely scientific phase of our disaster"—yet its decision to attempt to separate earthquake damage from that of the fire helped contribute to the compartmentalization of natural hazards into scientific and social components and the perception of earthquakes as natural disasters unaffected by human history and choices.[73]

San Francisco's susceptibility to earthquake hazards began with the selection of a location subject to regular seismic activity and only intensified as the city's residents filled in waterways to create made land. Urban land, indeed all land, is simultaneously cultural and physical space. In 1906 the South of Market district of San Francisco was a mixed-use neighborhood of industrial workplaces and working-class dwellings, home to Irish and Eastern European immigrant workers and poor transient laborers. Its cheap, wooden buildings were closely packed, densely populated, and built on filled-in marshland vulnerable to extensive seismic damage. Historians have often emphasized the human characteristics of the district but forgotten its physical characteristics. The story of San Francisco's growth is the story of alterations to the city's site—particularly the flattening of sandy hills and filling in of shoreline areas, creeks, and other watercourses. These areas of artificially created land proved to be death traps in April 1906.

If no one could have predicted the earthquake—and scientists still have not discovered a reliable means of predicting seismic activity more than a century later—evidence of the specific dangers posed by a massive temblor was there in the city's history. It was there in the accounts of damage on made land in the 1860s, published in the newspapers and analyzed by leading local scientists. Even without a modern-day understanding of seismology, San Francisco residents had connected the dots to elucidate the risks of made land. A year after the 1906 disaster, one of the subcommittees investigating the catastrophe reported their unanimous opinion that most of the losses "could have been prevented by a clear interpretation and regard for the lessons of 1868 and the fires which have devastated this and other cities."[74] We have seen that a close analysis of the city's seismic history supports the subcommittee's assertion. Ignorance, then, only partially explains the city's lack of preparation in 1906.

In thinking about why San Franciscans chose to take only limited precautions against earthquake damage on made land, we should consider the psychology and potentiality of disasters. From Edward Bosqui in 1868 to William Wallace Campbell in 1906, some San Franciscans applied the term *terror* to describe reactions to earthquakes. Seismic activity, more than most other natural disasters, strikes without warning and literally disrupts the solidity of the ground underfoot.[75] One way to live with the daily threat of earthquakes—the potentiality of catastrophe at any moment—is to set aside risk or resituate it in the realm of ordinary life. Earthquakes become less something to dread than a simultaneously familiar and distant threat against which to take basic precautions, but which must be accepted as part of the surrounding environment. In coastal California earthquakes are part of life, something that has shaped the land and the cities built there, and residents know and accept that risk. Perhaps it is that acceptance of risk, even more than the prevalence of seismic activity, which makes California "earthquake country."

THREE

BREAD LINES AND EARTHQUAKE COTTAGES

AS THE FIRE SWEPT THROUGH THE CITY, HUNDREDS OF THOUSANDS of people fled their homes, many taking with them only a few necessities. They gathered in whatever open spaces they could find in the densely settled city—public parks and squares, vacant lots, and military reservations. Many spent their first nights in the open with neither food nor shelter. On the day of the earthquake, Mary Kelly described how she wandered the streets until evening before arriving at Jefferson Square, not far from where her home had burned to the ground. There she and her family "lay on the hillside all night long without any covering over us, the burning sparks falling all about and around us." The disaster left the Kellys, like hundreds of thousands of San Franciscans, bereft of material possessions, including clothing, bedding, cooking utensils, and other necessities.[1]

Like almost everyone else in the city, Mary, her husband, William, and their children stood in bread lines to collect food rations and improvised ways to survive. Mary lost her job as a cleaning woman after the disaster, and William had not worked since suffering an injury years earlier. Both Mary and William were over fifty and in questionable health, and with no income, the family could not afford the high rents after the fire. With nowhere else to go, they lived in a tent in the refugee camp at Jefferson Square throughout the summer and into the fall before finally moving into a tiny "earthquake cottage" in January 1907. These experiences made Mary Kelly an activist on behalf of displaced refugees. She publicly criticized the actions of camp administrators and the Rehabilitation Committee, and her small, spectacled figure became a fixture in the forefront of marches and on public speaking platforms. She even engaged in direct action by occupying a cottage when officials initially denied her application. Mary Kelly's actions reflected her frustration and anger at the ways in which her life, and those of others among San Francisco's working poor, had become more difficult as a result of the disaster.[2]

In the first days and weeks after the earthquake, everyone experienced the devastation of San Francisco's urban ecosystem—the infrastructure and markets that conveyed food, water, electricity, and even communications. Contemporary hazards researchers appropriately refer to such infrastructure as lifelines, and the severing of these lifelines transformed everyday life in the city. People of all classes were forced into visceral encounters with urban nature as they lived in the parks and cooked in the streets, and they interpreted those encounters based on preexisting assumptions about both nature and their fellow urban residents. Optimists ignored heavy rains and biting winds to argue that life in the refugee camps was pleasant, even healthy, in San Francisco's temperate climate. In fact, they suggested, outdoor living would improve the health and well-being of people left homeless by the disaster. Families like the Kellys, who endured cold, rainy nights in leaky tents or felt the bite of the winds through the walls of rough cottages, disagreed, and they mobilized to assert a right to adequate food and shelter.

Such demands reflected and highlighted the disruption of social relations that resulted from the environmental events of the earthquake and fire. Long-standing spatial divisions of class and ethnicity broke down, and an initial period of class leveling quickly gave way to a resurgence of class and ethnic tensions as disparities in people's ability to recover from disaster became apparent. The devastation of working-class neighborhoods and limited economic opportunities for working-class San Franciscans, particularly women, left tens of thousands reliant on relief and living in tent camps into the fall. Like more recent disasters, San Francisco in 1906 highlighted how preexisting inequality shaped resilience in the face of a devastating event, what hazards scholars call vulnerability. Despite its utility, vulnerability can convey a sense of static inevitability of unequal conditions, and it provides little space for the agency of disempowered populations. The related framework of environmental injustice—the disproportionate exposure to environmental hazards and lack of environmental amenities experienced by people of color and poor people—is rooted more in community activism and resistance.[3] Poor urban residents have a long history of organizing against visible sanitary crises such as vermin in their neighborhoods, concerns that have not always been seen as environmental but that directly reflect unequal access to basic environmental amenities in the form of healthy, livable environments. For the urban poor, the environment represents the places where they live and work, not distant wilderness or pristine nature.[4] For refugees in San Francisco, access to basic amenities of food and housing became the basis for organizing against a relief system geared toward restoring conditions that had existed prior to the earthquake, including their inequities.

Disasters often spark organizing among affected communities, but in San Francisco the mobilization of people like Mary Kelly encountered more conservative forces among the city's middle and upper classes, including the social workers who administered the relief system.[5] Nature in the city became contested terrain as residents disputed the mechanisms for providing food and housing. When San Francisco's parks and public spaces became sites of refugee camps, established neighborhood residents and government officials used the social and aesthetic value of parks to advocate for the further dislocation of refugees. The disaster ultimately sparked a spatial reorganization of housing, forcing many working-class residents out of the central city. Real estate developers promised such amenities as access to idyllic nature to promote relocation of San Franciscans to distant suburbs even as activists like Kelly questioned the costs of living far from employment opportunities. Suburban amenities also often proved more promise than reality as poor suburbanites encountered insanitary conditions and substandard housing. A new landscape of housing emerged in San Francisco after the earthquake and fire, but geographies of class remained central to those new spatial arrangements. Ultimately, the story of San Francisco's bread lines, refugee camps, and earthquake cottages demonstrates how the relief and recovery only exacerbated inequalities along lines of class, race, and gender.

NETWORKS OF RELIEF AND SURVIVAL

Relief efforts relied on San Francisco's place within economic, social, and environmental networks both regional and national. San Franciscans as well as outside observers initially believed that the scale of the disaster represented a challenge to the survival of the city and its people. One contemporary observer wrote that the calamity had shattered "the intensely complicated, interdependent and seemingly ultimate mechanism of a modern city."[6] This "mechanism" of the city, what we might call its urban ecology, represented the processes by which the resources needed to support four hundred thousand human beings flowed into and were distributed within San Francisco. The earthquake and fire disrupted this urban ecology from physical infrastructure to economic markets. The Red Cross director and Columbia professor Edward T. Devine described the cessation of "the flow of capital from mines and farms and factories, through shops and warehouses and markets" that "staggered" San Francisco. He noted that the "ordinary economic life of the city" was not restored for a month.[7] However, even with the severe damage caused by the earthquake and fire, key pieces of the resource networks that sustained San Francisco survived and facilitated both relief efforts and a relatively quick recovery.

When news of the devastating earthquake in San Francisco spread across the country, Americans responded with an overwhelming wave of charity. If anything, initial reports exaggerated the destruction of San Francisco; the city was largely cut off from the telegraph and other forms of communication, which fed fears that it had perished utterly. Responses to calls for aid were generous. Congress appropriated an unprecedented two and a half million dollars, which the US Army rapidly spent in its attempts to maintain order and provide food and shelter. Private donations came in all sizes and from all over the world. Ultimately, the Relief Corporation and American National Red Cross collected more than nine million dollars' worth of donations for relief of the city.[8]

In the initial days and weeks many donations arrived in the form of goods rather than dollars. San Francisco was lucky that both the Southern Pacific railroad tracks and the waterfront were largely unscathed, and these centers of commerce became sites through which donated (and later purchased) relief supplies entered the city. Relief goods began to arrive almost immediately. On April 19, the day after the earthquake, the Los Angeles Relief Committee had already sent seventeen carloads by rail and six by steamer in response to an urgent plea from the governor of California. Donations soon began to arrive from across the country, as railroads reportedly gave relief trains the right of way. At one point, 150 carloads of supplies arrived daily, and Major General Adolphus Greely reported that the first month saw an average of 1,154 tons of relief goods entering the city each day. Not all of the supplies were donations—some were purchases of the relief committee and the army—but these official tallies did not even include massive quantities of goods that never passed through the hands of the army or Red Cross.[9]

San Francisco's people had always relied on commerce to provide the necessities for their survival. Rather than store large quantities of food in the city, both merchants and individuals alike were accustomed to buying small quantities of fresh food every few days, particularly because California's temperate climate meant that fresh produce was available year round. One observer noted that "San Francisco never contained more than three days' supply of food." What food was kept in the city rested in warehouses and large retail stores, almost all of which went up in flames. The army, city officials, and individuals had saved as much as possible, emptying buildings as the fire approached, and these salvaged goods helped feed the city in the first days of the disaster.[10]

Because severe damage was localized in San Francisco and a few other sites around the Bay Area, not all of San Francisco's regular suppliers of food were affected. Vegetable gardens located on the city's outskirts, many farmed by Italian San Franciscans, escaped the fire and continued to provide fresh produce—initially free to the refugees and then available for sale as markets reopened. Italian and Portuguese fishermen used their boats to ferry stranded citizens across the bay to escape the fire, and they quickly resumed their trade of providing fresh fish for urban buyers.[11] Milk was one item for which the perception of need greatly exceeded the actual demand. Huge quantities of condensed milk arrived from around the country, but San Francisco received its milk from dairies located on its outskirts and across the water in Marin County, areas that were relatively unaffected by the earthquake and that had escaped the fire's reach. Not only was the city's supply of fresh milk not significantly diminished, but the Dairymen's Association provided free milk until May 1. Police officer Henry C. Schmitt described how dairymen from the peninsula and wholesale butchers left their wares on the corner for Mission District refugees.[12] Preexisting supply networks thus continued to function outside regular market channels as food producers stepped forward to aid their fellow citizens in the initial days of crisis. Survival trumped profit, as least for a little while.

These local efforts were often more efficient than the efforts of the centralized Relief Committee, which struggled to match donations to needs. An infamous scandal and riot over flour illustrated this problem. When the Relief Committee received sixteen million pounds of flour, far more than it could use, a plan to sell off the excess flour led to a public controversy. Distribution of the flour would have flooded the local economy and undermined the restoration of market conditions, so the committee bartered the flour to milling concerns at below market value or dumped it into the bay. The Minneapolis relief effort, source of 15 percent of the flour, objected that its donation was intended only for use, not for sale. The flour supply also became a point of contention among the refugees, who believed that valuable food had been wasted or exploited for the profit of a few members of the Relief Committee. In July 1906, refugee women, including Mary Kelly, stormed the main relief warehouse and walked out with two thousand pounds of flour. As this example suggests, despite the best intentions of donors, not all of the supplies sent to San Francisco proved useful to the stricken city, and they often exacerbated social tensions.[13]

Getting the relief goods into the city was only the first problem; the next was distributing them to residents. The local transportation infrastructure was so badly disrupted that General Greely identified local transportation as the most difficult problem he faced. With familiar landmarks utterly destroyed, even longtime residents could become lost in the ruins. San Francisco was a relatively compact city, but it had long been dependent on its transit system. The street railway system was completely shut down for over a week, and full transit service was not restored until late in 1906. With horses scarce and automobiles reserved for official business, most San Franciscans walked where they needed to go. Relief officials quickly impressed all available carts and horses, but the harsh conditions and shortages of food for horses that exceeded those for humans—relief efforts should have collected hay and oats rather than milk and flour—posed ongoing problems. Some horse owners allegedly spirited their animals out of the city rather than allow them to be overworked and starved, but the mayor and Relief Committee managed to enlist four hundred teams in distributing food and other relief goods.[14] The logistics of relief remained a problem, with local shortages in camps and long lines at inefficient relief stations hindering the distribution of the donations that flowed generously into San Francisco.

The disaster transformed the city's political leadership just as it did the physical and social landscape. Mayor Schmitz quickly took charge during the crisis, and his decisive leadership received wide praise. However, his decree that looters should be shot on sight, with its protection of property over the lives of San Franciscans, hardly seemed like the action of a representative of the workers' Union Labor Party. As the historian Philip L. Fradkin has emphasized, the decree was selectively enforced, with poor people and ethnic minorities more likely to face dire consequences for looting than the upper-class men and women who raided Chinatown in the days after the fire. Early reactions juxtaposed a fear of looters and other implied working-class lawlessness with concerns about overreactions by guards posted throughout the city. Even General Greely admitted that guards with loose trigger fingers posed a danger to anyone traveling after dark, and Mayor Schmitz condemned vigilance committees formed by residents in various neighborhoods, reserving the authority to threaten violence to the sanctioned extralegal forces of the military and the committees governing the relief. The number of people actually shot for looting remains uncertain.[15] Regardless of the number of violent deaths, the disaster broke down the urban spatial order and its attendant protections to property, wealth, and status, and some anxious residents supported vigilante justice such as the shooting of looters as a way to preserve the sanctity of property and class divisions even as they praised selfless action and social unity.[16]

Mayor Schmitz bypassed the legal structure of government almost entirely during the crisis and recovery. He appointed the Committee of Fifty, charged with managing the immediate aftermath of the earthquake, from among the city's leading businessmen, lawyers, and religious leaders. Not a single member of his own Union Labor Party, even "Boss" Abe Ruef, was an original member of San Francisco's ad hoc leadership in its moment of crisis. Former mayor James D. Phelan—a banker, Progressive reformer, and political enemy of Schmitz—chaired the Finance Committee, which became the de facto leadership of the recovery efforts. The Board of Supervisors put up little fight in the face of its disempowerment, agreeing on April 25 to "confine itself to strictly official duties" and leave all relief and restoration to the mayor and the various committees that had grown out of the Committee of Fifty. Faced with a crisis, Schmitz had handed over the keys to the "labor city" to its economic and social elites.[17]

The organization of refugee camps and the distribution of relief represented a massive bureaucratic undertaking. City officials leaned heavily on the army, first for maintaining law and order during the fire and then for overseeing the initial distribution of relief goods. In early May the American National Red Cross stepped in, mobilizing a staff of rehabilitation workers from among the ranks of professional social workers both locally and nationally. Edward T. Devine arrived to oversee the Red Cross's relief efforts in San Francisco. Devine was general secretary of the New York Charity Organization Society and had extensive experience with social work in general and disaster relief in particular. He worked with local social welfare professionals such as Katherine C. Felton of the Associated Charities of San Francisco, who had trained at Hull House.[18] On July 20, Phelan's Finance Committee joined with the Red Cross to incorporate the San Francisco Relief and Red Cross Funds. Board members of the new corporation included Mayor Schmitz, Governor Pardee, and Devine. Many of San Francisco's leading businessmen and Progressive reformers took positions as heads of committees.[19]

The official relief was not the only source of aid for refugees. As the historian Karen Sawislak has observed of Chicago after the great fire of 1871, many residents and charitable givers "conceived of the urban community in *parts* and in far more personalized terms" and therefore donated their aid to particular social groups to which they maintained ties.[20] In San Francisco the United Irish Societies, with the help of Father Peter C. Yorke, aided the city's Irish community. Italian merchants from New York shipped macaroni, olive oil, and other dietary staples for special distribution to compatriots in San Francisco, and the Italian Consul-General formed an independent relief committee. Chinese San Franciscans received both financial and material assistance from the Qing government in China.[21] Interest groups gathering aid were not based solely on ethnicity. For example, by mid-May the Brewery Workmen's Union had raised over eleven thousand dollars and distributed ten dollars in cash as well as weekly unemployment benefits to all members. Building trades unions provided grants for members to replace lost tools, and the Masons distributed almost $175,000 worth of aid to both members and nonmembers.[22] People thus obtained assistance from their diverse communities, even as city officials marshaled the bulk of the relief donations into a heavily regulated official relief structure. The official relief proved problematic for San Francisco's poor as well as its Chinese and Italian residents, so members of those communities faced greater urgency to provide for themselves and find aid from sympathetic donors.

EARTHQUAKE LOVE IN THE BREAD LINES?

The earthquake and fire destroyed many of the comforts of civilization and transformed daily life for residents of San Francisco. The shattered pipes of the Spring Valley Water Company no longer conveyed water to the city, and the distribution system within the city limits lay in ruins. With no water available for toilets or other modern conveniences, San Franciscans were instructed to "dig earth closets in yards or vacant lots" in the initial days after the earthquake. Drinking water had to be boiled for fear of contamination from the shattered sewage system. *The Refugees' Cook Book* described the "Refugee Filter," a method for filtering water using a tomato can, cotton batting, and pulverized charcoal. By early May drinking water was available, but the supply remained insufficient to accommodate the use of toilets.[23]

With the loss of electric power, the day ended when darkness fell. Only candles were permitted for light indoors, and authorities concerned about fires required those be extinguished by 8 P.M. Fear of fire

Three women and a child gathered around a street kitchen, 1906. Courtesy of the California Historical Society (CHS2016_2123).

required cooking be moved outside; Mayor Schmitz issued strict orders forbidding fires in homes since damaged chimneys had contributed to many of the fires after the earthquake. Stoves literally lined the streets of surviving residential areas for as long as three months as residents waited for their chimneys to be inspected.[24] Employing humor to lighten the hardships, some San Franciscans named their street kitchens after famous restaurants and hotels that had been destroyed. Josephine Fearon Baxter wrote to her parents in Omaha of how she no longer lived a civilized life but struggled to survive; she declared, "we merely exist these days, cook and eat," and she was one of the lucky San Franciscans who lived in the unburned district.[25]

Not only cooking but even obtaining food became difficult with the destruction of markets. On May 1, 128 stations scattered around the city provided food for 313,117 people—nearly everyone remaining in the city. The week between April 26 and May 2 represented the peak in demand, as food distribution became more regularized and those whose homes had survived ran out of supplies purchased before the fire. Most stores remained closed, and even people who had money could find little food available for purchase.[26] Mabel Coxe wrote to her brother: "For the first two weeks, there was nothing, absolutely no place where you could get anything." The city soon began to regain its normal economic functioning, however. By the end of April, even before Coxe's two weeks had passed, the *San Francisco Chronicle* reported that groceries, bakeries, butcher shops, and restaurants were reopening in the unburned districts.[27]

The shared experience of the bread lines initially seemed to undermine long-standing divisions of class and ethnicity. Observers praised the spirit of optimism and brotherhood in the city. Edward Livingston Sr., a merchant, wrote of his pride in how "caste and creed were thrown to the winds. There were no rich, no poor, no capitalists and laborers, no oppressed and oppressors." This rhetoric served to unite diverse groups, suggesting that all were equal in the crisis. The city's longshoremen and other workers joined businessmen and middle-class writers in embracing this ideal of social unity in the immediate wake of catastrophe. On May 2 a labor newspaper argued that the previous two weeks had "demonstrated that in danger and distress class lines are obliterated, class interests forgotten, and the general welfare alone remembered"—a strong sentiment in a city that had experienced regular industrial conflict in preceding years.[28]

However, other commentators singled out the city's elites for praise, frequently expressing open or veiled criticism of the poor in the process. One article declared that "the business men laid aside personal affairs in the hour when personal affairs needed them most, and gave their time and thought to the common good." The *San Francisco Chronicle* complained that socialist orators and their audiences were "lying on their backs in the grassy parks, while the millionaires are working eighteen hours a day to keep the relief stations supplied and to bring order out of chaos." The journalist Ray Stannard Baker recounted an anecdote about a wealthy merchant who provided new clothing to women. When told that a quarter of the women taking advantage of his offer were not deserving, he allegedly responded that "this is the only way I can reach the other 75 percent who are suffering." Baker used this story to illustrate the spirit of service that filled the city in the first weeks after the earthquake and fire, but it also reinforced a prevailing sentiment that some refugees were taking advantage of the charitable impulses of their betters.[29]

As these articles suggest, the sense of unity known as "earthquake love" would not last. On April 29 the army took charge of issuing food rations. Army officials considered food distribution to have been "too lavish in quantity" and "issued without suitable discrimination." To solve this perceived problem of excessive food for refugees, officials established a relief ration equivalent to three-quarters of the ration for an enlisted man. Army and relief officials believed that they needed to wean people off relief rations to avoid creating "dependency" and to restore the system of private enterprise in the city. They sought to reduce the attractiveness of rations by including only meat, bread, and vegetables for all healthy applicants, eliminating luxuries such as coffee, milk, and sugar. They drastically reduced the number of relief stations, and in mid-May they began issuing rations three times a week rather than daily. The Red Cross developed a registration system requiring applicants for food to present a card showing their eligibility when they picked up their rations, with eligibility reconsidered every ten days. In an attempt at shaming, applicants were required to state that they were destitute. Beginning in mid-May at selected camps, tickets for hot meals at camp restaurants began to replace rations of raw food. This change discouraged people not residing in the camps from participating in the ration system, particularly since the quality of food prepared in restaurant kitchens was widely disparaged. These policies—along with the gradual restoration of food markets—proved effective at reducing the number of people receiving rations through May and June. On May 31, 41,236 rations of raw food and 9,159 meal tickets were handed out to refugees. One month later, those numbers had shifted to 9,734 food rations and 16,857 meal tickets. Many San Franciscans remained dependent on aid, but the authorities had succeeded in forcing many others out of the relief system.[30]

These efforts to encourage self-sufficiency may have appealed to social workers, but they proved problematic for many refugees. High prices for food and other consumer goods, along with exorbitant rents, made survival on a laborer's income even more difficult than it had been before the fire. All of the kitchens except one were shut down in mid-September, and even the camp administrator Dr. René Bine objected to that decision and the policy of excluding wage-earners from free meals. He wrote: "Earning $1.00 to $2.00 a day, it is utterly impossible to expect a man with a family to get out of camp, if he must feed 4 or 5 tiny mouths, with butter at $.60 cents a roll, and eggs at $.40 cents a dozen."[31] Bine employed the language of rehabilitation to convey his perception of aid recipients as hard-working people seeking to regain their self-sufficiency, but he was among the minority of relief workers in doing so. As summer rolled into fall, the people remaining in the camps were increasingly perceived as lazy and at risk of becoming dependent. Not surprisingly, refugees themselves contested this characterization, defending themselves as hard workers forced into difficult circumstances by the earthquake and fire and criticizing the policies of the Relief Committee as inequitable and even corrupt.

Disgruntled refugees protested the establishment of camp restaurants to replace the distribution of food for private preparation and consumption. On June 1, 1906, John H. Helms led a rally at Jefferson Square objecting to the soup kitchen there, and in mid-June a much larger protest against the kitchens drew contingents from various camps. The Socialist Party riled up the refugees by distributing five hundred copies of a special issue of *Socialist Voice* on "Relief Kitchen Graft." At a mass meeting of refugees the union leader Walter McArthur and one Mrs. Hosford declared that the soup kitchens "were destroying the individuality . . . and the home life of the refugees," reflecting a middle-class vision of family structures that resonated with many of the refugees while also intended to win sympathy from San Franciscans of other classes.[32]

Protests continued in July, when a group calling itself the Committee of Friends of Refugees called for a demonstration outside a banquet honoring Devine on his departure from San Francisco. A crowd estimated by Mary Kelly at three thousand and by *Socialist Voice* at twenty thousand gathered at Jefferson Square and marched to the St. Francis Hotel, site of the banquet. Posters highlighted the use of relief funds to pay for the luxurious meal, declaring: "Let the whole world know that while we are starving they are feasting." Kelly reported that Devine and other guests fled out the back of the hotel rather than face the crowd. Over the summer of 1906, unsettled conditions in the city led to large crowds at open-air political rallies—*Socialist Voice* lamented a shortage of street speakers—and lectures on the shortcomings of capitalist charity.[33] Organizers circulated among the refugee camps, holding mass meetings, criticizing the Relief Committee, and encouraging refugees to demand shares of donated funds. The march on Devine's farewell banquet inspired the formation of an organization called the United Refugees that conducted protests and advocated a cooperative farming and real estate enterprise.[34] San Francisco was a labor stronghold and home to radical organizations such as the International Workers of the World as well as the socialists, and many residents were receptive to and familiar with working-class organization and political power. Their voices challenged the rose-colored interpretation of life in post-disaster San Francisco, and they contested the conditions of refugee and working-class life in the city, asserting a vision of social and environmental justice in the process.

Women were central actors throughout these refugee mobilizations, engaging in everything from public speaking to direct action as well as quieter advocacy on behalf of their families. In fact, women also played prominent roles within the official relief network both as high-ranking officials, such as Katherine Felton of the Associated Charities, and as rank-and-file employees filling roles as social workers and investigators. Women's public involvement in all aspects of the relief effort reflected a sea change that had taken place in American society over the preceding twenty years as middle-class women had taken on prominent roles in reform movements ranging from the settlement house movement to conservation and working-class women had increasingly entered the paid labor force. The fact that relief efforts related directly to family welfare and domestic life only encouraged women's involvement. Poor and working-class women became advocates within the public sphere, even activists, in response to the crisis and the ways in which the relief system made their domestic lives more public than ever before. The historian Andrea Rees Davies refers to this phenomenon as "politicized domesticity," and to many women it became not only a means to secure crucial disaster relief but also a way to assert citizenship rights.[35]

The demands of refugees in San Francisco prefigured those of later working-class activists concerned with subsistence, housing, sanitation, and transportation in urban neighborhoods, issues central to environmental justice movements. Efforts to secure safe and healthly environments for themselves and their families have also been a consistent focus of women's environmental activism. Movements led by women have ranged from the "municipal housekeeping" campaigns of the Progressive Era to later fights over pesticides and toxics in which women such as Rachel Carson and Lois Gibbs played prominent roles. The circumstances after the 1906 earthquake and fire sparked a similar mobilization among local women as well as men. Although issues such as access to food and water as well as dry, sanitary, and pest-free homes are not always classified as environmental issues, they are very much questions of environmental equity for the urban poor. Even these basic environmental amenities were in question for refugees in San Francisco over the summer and fall of 1906.

LIFE IN THE CAMPS

On May 13, three weeks after the disaster, some fifty thousand people still lived in tents, barracks, and rough shacks in more than one hundred official and unofficial camps throughout the city. Refugees, particularly those who preferred to avoid the official camps and their strict regulations, constructed homes from whatever materials they could scrounge among the ruins. In her travels through the city, the writer Louise Herrick Wall observed shelters "made of fire-warped corrugated iron, of window-shutters, of wooden doors torn from wrecked buildings" and tents created from "coats and bed-comfortables." Such makeshift shelters persisted for months. At the beginning of July, the population in official camps remained 17,499 with another 15,000 people living in irregular camps scattered around the city. Army and relief officials frowned on the unsanctioned camps, finding unacceptable moral and sanitary conditions there. However, enough San Franciscans sympathized with the refugees that police tolerated unofficial camps. For example, squatters were not evicted from railroad land south of the burned district until January 1907, six months after the company first requested their removal. The official camps were very close to capacity, with all of their inhabitants living in tents except for a few thousand in barracks constructed in Golden Gate Park as part of the first (unsuccessful) housing plan. Camp populations remained relatively constant throughout the summer, and on September 1, with winter approaching, approximately thirty thousand San Franciscans remained refugees.[36]

The residents of these camps represented a cross-section of San Francisco's poor and working classes. Irish and Italians made up the largest populations, especially since they had been concentrated before the fire in the South of Market and Latin Quarter neighborhoods that had been destroyed. Italians particularly dominated the Lobos Square and North Beach camps, but many others left the camps and settled in shacks and makeshift shelters on their burned-out property on Telegraph Hill. Others fled the city entirely. Dominic Ghio remembered that many Italian families moved south to join relatives in the fishing industry in Santa Cruz or as far away as San Diego, while Olina Granucci recounted how her entire family relocated to a truck garden south of the city in which her father owned a financial interest. Granucci described how her relatives "were afraid to come back" to San Francisco, where the earthquake and fire seemed like a supernatural punishment.[37] Such relocations could be motivated by fear of seismic activity, the harsh living conditions in the stricken city, the daunting task of rebuilding, or discriminatory attitudes on the part of relief authorities—or, most likely, a combination of these reasons.

The experiences of Chinese San Franciscans in some ways paralleled those of Italians. The anger of first the Earth Dragon and then the Fire Dragon led some Chinese to fear that the end of the world had arrived. Once they got down to the prosaic demands of survival, Chinese San Franciscans were among those who quickly left the army's camps. Relief authorities boasted of the absence of discrimination in their provisions of relief, but the Chinese clearly had a different experience. Chinese refugees were first gathered into a single camp and then relocated multiple times under pressure from white property owners who did not want Chinese near their homes. They were finally isolated in a segregated camp above Fort Point at the eastern edge of the Presidio, exposed to cold winds blowing off the Pacific and far from any possibilities of employment. One survivor remembered that Chinese elders disliked the prospect of "living precariously in canvas tents among hostile Barbarians on the fog-chilled slopes overlooking the Golden Gate." His family left San Francisco for a ranch in Solano County owned by relatives. The Presidio camp quickly dwindled to a mere fifty occupants out of a population of roughly twenty-five thousand Chinese San Franciscans before the fire. Many Chinese crossed the bay to Oakland's relief camps and its small Chinatown, which grew dramatically. Others sought refuge in Chinese fishing and shrimp camps in Potrero Hill and across the bay in Richmond and Marin Country. In general, the Chinese community remained apart from the white-run relief system, because of both outright discrimination and cultural and linguistic differences, and took care of its own.[38]

The discomforts of life in a city suddenly cut off from the conveniences of modern technology were only amplified for those unfortunates living in camps and makeshift shelters. Among the hardships they faced was a heightened vulnerability to the weather. Boosters had long praised San Francisco's climate as ideal (even as some residents complained about the winds and fog), and in 1906 many authorities initially considered the provision of shelter to be a low priority because of the expected "temperate and dry" weather. On April 27 the *Chronicle* waxed eloquent about the "glorious climate of San Francisco, which no earthquake can shatter, and no fire consume," crediting the climate for the supposed good health of the refugees. However, the winter and spring of 1906 had been particularly wet, and that pattern continued in the aftermath of the earthquake. Torrential rains drenched the city on April 22, a day when many people remained without shelter of any kind and which had apparently already been forgotten by the *Chronicle* five days later. Rains returned in late May, and for three days San Franciscans huddled in their shelters, unable to cook outdoors. A retrospective reported that the downpour "all but washed the tent camps away."[39] Mary Kelly complained: "When it rained the water would pour in [to her family's tent] just the same as through a sieve, beating on our faces as we slept and wetting everything that was under it."[40]

The *Chronicle* was not alone in praising the health benefits of outdoor living in the post-earthquake city. William Douglas Alexander wrote to his sister that "the fresh air and out door [sic] roughing it, did me a great deal of good physically," including curing his asthma. The early years of the twentieth century were a time when upper- and middle-class Americans, including President Theodore Roosevelt, embraced back-to-nature movements, outdoor education, and physical exertion

A refugee's makeshift shelter and sign expressing sarcasm about the appeal of outdoor living. Courtesy of the California Historical Society (CHS2015.1917).

to maintain toughness, health, and masculinity. Of course, judgments about the health benefits of refugee life were most often made by those who could retreat to secure shelter in case of inclement weather and who were spared the worst indignities of life in the camps. The poet Amelia Woodward Truesdell wrote of how the thousands of tents scattered over the green hillsides of the city's parks "to the idealist might seem/idyllic as a shepherd's dream." However, the dust, odors, and lack of privacy meant that the simple life "proves both disquieting and crude./ That which in art is picturesque,/ For living proves a coarse burlesque." Kelly reminded her readers that getting soaked by the rain through her tent "was not very pleasant, to say the least, or very healthy for us either, I can assure you."[41] The realities of outdoor living did not match the ideal.

Interpretations of outdoor life in the city, like reactions to the disaster itself, exposed contradictions inherent in early twentieth-century attitudes toward nature. On the one hand, boosters' praise for San

Francisco's site and climate had become canon in residents' mental images of their city. On the other hand, the region's seismic instability—a characteristic of the site that boosters concealed—had just destroyed the city. The common tendency to attribute the destruction almost entirely to the fire represented in part an impulse to deny that San Francisco's location was less than ideal for a great city. Similarly, middle- and upper-class residents who embraced their experience of "roughing it" after the disaster were matching their experience to the expectation that close contact with nature was beneficial. Their rhetoric played down the difficulties of refugee life not only because they experienced those difficulties less acutely than did poorer residents of the city but also because their ideological expectations differed. They filtered their experience through the twin lenses of praise for their city's temperate climate and widespread promotion of the benefits of returning to nature. A letter that Sister Louise McCarron wrote to her mother describing the storms of April 22 reflected these contradictions. McCarron described "a pelting rain and wind" so strong that "it seemed to me [all] would be blown off the earth entirely." She added, "It certainly will purify the city if the people will not be carried off by pneumonia." McCarron's expectations that nature's force would be good for the city conflicted with the immediate concern that the cold rain and wind would lead to residents becoming ill from exposure to those very elements that could cleanse San Francisco.[42]

Assumptions of class and ethnic superiority often colored conclusions about the benefits to be derived from the city's destruction. Charles J. O'Connor, secretary of the Board of Trustees of the Relief and Red Cross Funds, suggested that even during the winter rains "thousands were better off in the refugee shacks than they had previously been in the poorer grade of tenements." Advocates for San Francisco's working classes quickly disputed this notion. The *Coast Seamen's Journal* echoed Truesdell's poem in declaring that "the picnic that lasts over one night in the San Francisco fog and wind loses its charm for the participants." The paper added that the camps were certain to be "decimated either by sickness or exodus." Kelly claimed that she became sick from exposure to the rain and cold in her leaky tent and spent six weeks in St. Joseph's Hospital as a result. Her account described both abuse and theft on the part of the authorities, amounting to a concerted effort to undo her

The Jefferson Square Camp where Mary Kelly lived. The trunks and other salvaged belongings indicate that this picture was taken shortly after the earthquake. Courtesy of the San Francisco History Center, San Francisco Public Library.

family's hard work to survive and a forced return to the primitive circumstances of water pouring into their dwelling. Thus, in the aftermath of the earthquake and fire, San Franciscans debated even their city's climate, and judgments about the weather became part of a debate over the importance of providing high-quality shelter to refugees.[43]

In a densely settled city like San Francisco, the space available for those left homeless by the earthquake and fire was limited. Tents and other housing could be set up on public land, on vacant lots, or on the outskirts of the city, where open land was relatively abundant. Refugees made use of all three options, but each had its disadvantages. San Francisco's only large expanses of public land were Golden Gate Park and the Presidio military reservation, both of which were located far from potential sources of employment. Centrally located parks and squares in San Francisco were both few and small, but by necessity they became the sites of tent camps. Not all San Franciscans supported this use of the city's parks. Park superintendent John McLaren, among others, proposed sending all refugees to the Outside Lands—the neighborhoods to the west of the city that still consisted largely of sand dunes—an option that would have left them distant from jobs and stores.[44] In the absence of other practical alternatives, parks and squares within the city's established neighborhoods became refugee camps.

Both military and civilian officials worried a great deal about sanitation, but this concern seemingly did not prevent them from compromising in the selection of camp sites. A camp in the Mission District was located on land that had previously been a dumping site for garbage from the city's stables. Even piles of manure did not deter more than a thousand people from living there in mid-May. Camp No. 15 at the Presidio and the barracks at the Speedway camp in Golden Gate Park were similiarly located on old dumping grounds where the soil consisted mostly of manure.[45] In the early 1900s, American cities like San Francisco remained home to large numbers of horses, each of which could produce fifteen to thirty pounds of manure per day. Some of this animal waste could be sold to farmers near the city for fertilizer, but much was also dumped at any convenient location—such as a vacant lot.[46] Dumping at the Speedway site continued even with refugee housing under construction, and the kitchen sat only about seventy-five yards from the dump. On May 15, Chief Sanitary Officer George H. Torney declared: "It seems incredible that so little attention should have been paid to the rules of sanitation in the selection of this camp site." Despite his incredulity, work on the Speedway Camp continued, and it opened on May 31 with a soup kitchen for residents. The aged and infirm among the refugees were directed to this camp almost immediately.[47]

Camp inspectors and officials often blamed residents for poor sanitary conditions, and prejudices that they held toward Italians in particular are apparent in their reports. Reports of overflowing garbage pails in the Telegraph Hill area noted that they needed to be emptied more regularly but also complained that "the Mexicans and Italians on the top of the Hill . . . do not follow directions." In reporting on Presidio Camp 4, Captain and Assistant Surgeon W. C. Chidester complained about "the densely ignorant Italians," and reports often juxtaposed references to dirty conditions with mention of residents' ethnicity.

Italian residents of Telegraph Hill after the earthquake and fire. Courtesy of the San Francisco History Center, San Francisco Public Library.

People in these districts had little reason to trust that relief officials would fulfill their promises. Uncollected garbage sat for weeks on street corners and vacant lots. Overflowing latrines were another ongoing problem, and as late as May 21, no Spring Valley water was available in the vicinity of Telegraph Hill, forcing residents to draw their water from a stagnant cistern.[48] Conditions in the Telegraph Hill area reflected both a pattern of neglect of sanitary conditions in working-class and immigrant neighborhoods as well as a population with few options, limited knowledge of sanitary practices, and difficulty communicating with social workers and army officers.

The largest refugee camp was Harbor View, located along the northern shoreline of the city just east of the Presidio with a lagoon on one side and a dump on the other. Conditions at Harbor View further illustrated the contradictions of camp sanitation. Sanitary officials reported that conditions were "very good" while simultaneously describing open sewer mains emptying into standing water.[49] A broken sewer main on Baker Street was first reported on April 26, and camp commander and physician René Bine was still complaining about the sewer and the resulting cesspools in mid-August. The Health Committee responded that the sewer would be repaired when it was determined if it was caused by "defective work of the contractors" or "a disturbance such as occurred on April 18th," an obvious euphemism for the earthquake.[50] Harbor View clearly represented undesirable real estate on the city's outskirts, a place used more as a sink for waste than as a neighborhood of homes. The *Examiner* suggested that relief officials hoped that many refugees would leave the camps rather than live on the "shifting sand dunes" of the Harbor View camp.[51]

Despite its disadvantages, Harbor View housed 1,350 residents in 657 tents in June 1906, and by mid-July, after the closing of several other camps, it became a tent city of 2,800. Many residents spoke only Italian, French, German, or Spanish, making both communication and community difficult. Each night the camp filled with smoke and odors from the burning of garbage at the neighboring dump, and the broken sewer only added to the stink.[52] The camp contained only eight working latrines for its 2,800 residents. Men shared three showers, while women had only one functioning shower. Residents had no access to hot water or laundry facilities. Dr. Bine's requisitions for necessities such as blankets and mattresses were filled only partially or not at all, and his angry letters were largely ignored. The months of July and August finally saw efforts to construct floors for tents in the official camps. Latrines, washhouses, and bathhouses were also built. These represented important steps in making the camps habitable for people who were rapidly becoming long-term residents, but they also highlighted the terrible conditions of preceding months.[53]

On July 27, Bine wrote the following in a report on efforts to promote sanitary practices in the camp: "Sleeping in floorless tents, eaten up by fleas, or pestered by ants and gophers, put into bad humor by having no mattresses, it is difficult to make such as these appreciate that they must keep garbage cans covered, tents swept out (without brooms), and do all they can to help in general sanitation in return for the favors bestowed upon them."[54] Bine was unusually vociferous among camp officials in demanding improvements to his camp's facilities, although as administrator of the largest and roughest camp, he also faced some of the greatest obstacles. His writings reveal him to be ideologically

The Harbor View tent camp. Courtesy of the Bancroft Library, University of California, Berkeley (BANC PIC 1996.006:0565).

more sympathetic to the complaints of refugees that they were treated like animals than to those of some social workers that refugees were undeserving exploiters of relief. Bine's proximity to the hardships of camp life—he lived in the camp, although in better quarters than the refugees—may have helped to overcome any middle-class assumptions about the sanitary standards and morality of the working classes. However, some of his early reports indicate prejudices as well, such as a complaint that Italians "do not seem to be able to keep their tents clean."[55]

Bine was certainly not the only middle-class San Franciscan who found himself as much on the side of refugees as on the side of relief officials, although angry refugees perceived Bine as part of the relief establishment despite his efforts to improve conditions in his camp. Bine's combination of sympathy and prejudice, compassion and sarcasm serves as a reminder that, as with all the figures in this history, he was a complex individual and a man of his time and place. Relief officials generally had good intentions, but their efforts to rehabilitate those in need ecountered the limitations of their own thinking as well as the limitations of available time and resources. The harsh conditions of life in the camps reflected how the earthquake and fire exacerbated inequality in the city. These inequalities manifested in the lack of the most basic environmental amenities such as secure shelter, adequate food, clean water, and basic sanitation. In a precursor to later environmental justice movements and community organizing in response to disasters, residents mobilized to contest those conditions and challenge the narratives that blamed them for living in squalid conditions or praised primitive outdoor living while ignoring the realities of exposure to harsh weather, varmints, and filth as well as the daily humiliations of systems of registration and inspection.

HOUSING AND CLAIMS ON THE RELIEF

In the *San Francisco Relief Survey*, a study of relief programs in San Francisco published in 1913, social workers praised "modern relief measures" that emphasized giving disaster victims "a reasonable lift on the road to a recovery of the standard of living maintained before the disaster." Relief policies designed to restore predisaster standards of living tended, of course, to perpetuate preexisting inequalities.[56] Early twentieth-century San Francisco was sharply divided along class lines, and working-class people lived precarious lives of uncertain employment, with few social safety nets. In 1906, housing rehabilitation plans, contrary to the promise implied in the name, only exacerbated the transience of low-income San Franciscans as fall and winter approached.

The Relief Committee developed a multi-tiered system of grants that reinforced class distinctions based on property ownership, financial resources, and personal contacts—the tangible markers of class status that transcended the comparatively indiscriminate destruction of the earthquake and fire. It is telling that the earthquake cottages have often been referred to as "refugee shacks"; they represented the continued provision of substandard shelter for poor San Franciscans made homeless by the intersection of the earthquake and fire with social and economic conditions in the city. The inequities of the relief process did not go uncontested. Refugees like Mary Kelly challenged the policies of the Relief Committee and, in the process, transformed both the sociopolitical domain of relief policies and the physical landscape of the camps into contested terrain, sites of struggle over both principles and implementation of relief and rehabilitation.

Working-class families could not afford to relocate to other Bay Area cities and commute to San Francisco, as many white-collar workers did.[57] For those remaining in San Francisco, the minimum price for rental housing was six to eight dollars per month for a single room in the aftermath of the fire. Rents in the unburned Western Addition doubled after the fire, and in surviving portions of the Mission District, the increase was 20 to 30 percent. Some rents increased as much as 350 percent. Not only did rents rise, but the overall cost of living shot up by almost 9 percent between 1905 and 1906. Food, clothing, and furniture all became more expensive, and credit was less likely to be available. The poverty line for a family of four or five was approximately six hundred dollars per year in 1906.[58] Low pay and poor working conditions meant that unskilled workers often changed jobs, and they suffered frequent periods of involuntary unemployment. Uncertain incomes made for unstable housing arrangements. Health and nutrition problems were chronic, and an illness or injury to a breadwinner could tip a family over the line from self-sufficiency to dependency. A state of permanent emergency almost universally described the lives of unskilled workers, and skilled workers could all too easily slip into similarly precarious situations.[59]

Even slight increases in the cost of living were a hardship for people who lived paycheck to paycheck—especially since the disaster had also brought a halt to paychecks for many San Franciscans. Only skilled building tradesmen found their services in greater demand during the city's reconstruction than before the disaster. Many households also lost supplementary income from taking in boarders when they lost their homes. The increase in rents actually created new populations of homeless people as tenants were forced out of Western Addition spaces they could no longer afford. Some of these economic refugees joined the disaster refugees in the camps. Landlords were widely blamed for these circumstances. A poem by A. H. Hutchinson even compared landlords to the earthquake and fire, declaring them the new threat to the well-being of the city's population.[60] The post-earthquake housing market increased forced mobility and instability for poor families in San Francisco.

Where they could do so, San Franciscans sought to rebuild their homes and businesses as quickly as possible. They encountered several obstacles, including uncertainty about insurance payments and delays in clearing debris from both streets and private property.[61] Some of the most rapid reconstruction occurred in the Telegraph Hill and North Beach neighborhoods, a fact that should have disproved many of the relief officials' prejudiced attitudes toward the city's Italian population. Telegraph Hill residents were rebuilding by early May, helped by the Bank of Italy, which resumed business only nine days after the earthquake and was one of the few banks in San Francisco prepared to offer loans in the immediate aftermath. Nine months after the earthquake, one observer described the hills of the Latin Quarter as crowded with "big and small houses, one, two, and three stories tall, finished or under construction" with no trace of the "awful ruins."[62]

The hastily erected homes on Telegraph Hill would later be criticized by housing reformers who labeled them tenement houses and objected to crowding in the district, but residents seemed content with their accommodations. When Alice Griffith of the San Francisco Housing Association (SFHA) tried to get neighborhood residents to testify in court against developers in 1911, she found no witnesses willing to testify that their housing was substandard.[63] That same year, an article in the *Overland Monthly* described the new construction in the Latin Quarter as "neat light and airy modern buildings" with "sunny, breezy, spacious" rooftop yards with superb views. There, residents grew flowers and herbs and pet dogs, cats, birds, and even illegal chickens slept among the clotheslines, enjoying the warmth of the sun. This article painted a highly romanticized picture of both life and urban nature in the Latin Quarter, but the contrast between this portrayal and that of Griffith and the SFHA demonstrates how perceptions of life in the crowded immigrant district varied.[64]

For the many refugees who could not obtain loans and rebuild on their own, the substantial funds donated for the city's relief offered hope of assistance. Ultimately the Rehabilitation Committee distributed over three million dollars to a total of 22,916 applicants. Assistance ranged from small cash grants for emergencies and transportation to money to build houses or launch businesses. Katherine C. Felton headed the committee, which included other experienced social workers such as Dr. Herbert Gunn and Lucile Eaves, the former head-worker at the South Park Settlement house in San Francisco who had been in New York working on her doctorate at the time of the disaster.[65] Progressive reformers praised the idea of placing the responsibility for coordinating relief and rehabilitation programs in the hands of "trained experts" who would apply "the deepest lore of modern relief-giving."[66] This faith in professionally trained experts was characteristic of Progressives, but experiences in San Francisco revealed the limitations of the "lore" of relief.

Social workers like Felton, Gunn, and Eaves possessed a dual vision of the purpose of relief grants. Grants were initially intended to aid those in greatest need, but relief workers quickly shifted from relief to "rehabilitation." Funds for rehabilitation would be used to help working- and middle-class San Franciscans restore their former standards of living. As Professor James Motley, who conducted investigations for the *San Francisco Relief Survey*, wrote: "Those who possessed vacant lots, or other property, or who could command means with which to build, gave tangible proof that the foundation of previous thrift and enterprise would serve as a guarantee of wise use of aid."[67] Grants helped recipients build homes, sometimes substantial ones, and start businesses. The committee walked a fine line as it considered both need and capacity to make good use of the funds granted. Thus the class and gender dimensions of relief grants became complicated as the committee weighed conflicting priorities.

The Rehabilitation Committee declared that the moral character of an applicant was less important than the "practical definiteness" of his or her plan to build a home or start a small business, but they failed to realize how class-specific their expectations were. The administrators explicitly divided applicants into four classes of people, each slotted for a different housing plan. The "bonus plan" was intended to aid property owners in the burned district with getting back on their feet. The grant and loan program targeted resourceful men and women who did not own property but who could be stimulated to acquire their own homes. San Franciscans "who had never lived in other than rented quarters and who were not likely to make wise use of a grant" to build a home were provided with "cheap cottages." Finally, "chronic dependents" such as the elderly and infirm would be cared for by the city.[68]

Some displaced people were savvy enough to exploit the Relief Committee's policies. The reformer Lilian Brandt complained that "many who had lived before the fire in two or three-room apartments were found to have developed ambitions for owning their homes" and applied for aid to realize that ambition. This might seem like an admirable goal, but Brandt's words revealed her discomfort with such efforts at class mobility. She criticized a man who bought a lot on the installment plan and applied for a five-hundred-dollar grant to build a house after paying only ten dollars toward his new property.[69] Social welfare advocates like Brandt were generally more comfortable with restoring applicants to their former positions than with using relief funds to provide refugees with an opportunity to improve their position in life. Some did push back against these policies. Helen Swett Artieda, a social worker and member of the Rehabilitation Committee, caustically described the provision of larger business rehabilitation grants to applicants with more resources as "an application, doubtless justifiable, of the scriptural principle, 'unto him that hath shall be given.'"[70]

After-the-fact challenges like Artieda's had little effect at the time, but the Relief Committee's policies were not entirely regressive. They made a surprising number of grants to women, especially given that they emphasized keeping families together, which could have led to a patriarchal preference for grants to male household heads. One simple reason why women received grants was that they applied. In fact, two-thirds of the applicants for the lowest level of aid, the earthquake cottages, were women. The fact that the cottages represented homes—manifestations of the domestic sphere—rather than businesses may have been one factor, but as Motley explicitly noted, the burden of applying for aid "fell more and more on the women" among families lower on "the social and economic scale." Women made up 41 percent of the recipients of bonuses and 18 percent of those receiving grants and loans. A high percentage of these applicants were widows with families, who were perceived to be worthy of aid. Widows were particularly likely to use the money to open boarding houses, one of the few occupations by which a woman could both support herself and maintain her respectability—at least if she rented to the proper class of clients.[71]

The housing offered to San Franciscans with no property, low incomes, and few resources were the earthquake cottages. Cottage recipients had been renters before the earthquake and fire, usually living in less than desirable housing. For example, only 29 percent had access to a private bath before the disaster. Most were married couples, but women who had lost their husbands also made up a significant proportion of cottage residents.[72] Although refugees remaining in the camps in the fall of 1906 were often stereotyped as shiftless, in fact the weekly reports of the camp commanders indicated that 89 percent of men, 39 percent of women, and even one-quarter of children were working.[73] Refugees sought creative ways to improve their economic circumstances in the camps. In Harbor View, Bine reported that two cobblers, one fruit dealer, a barber, and a soda-water stand were doing business in the camp by early August. One woman had opened a "delicatessen store," reportedly with a license from the city, and another planned "to open a 5, 10, & 15 cent store—in a tent, of course." In other cases, Bine discovered an illicit stable at the camp and caught two Italian fishermen relocating their tents to the beach, "a location they thought more favorable for their work."[74] Rather than being shiftless, many refugees possessed an entreneurial spirit, probably trying to fill demand for both goods and services at the isolated camp. Despite their best efforts, however, they could not earn enough money to escape the camps in the economic climate after the earthquake and fire.

Most of the remaining camps were converted from tents to cottages during the fall, with gradual construction of cottages from September through November. Cottages erected on the same public lands that had housed the tent camps drew protests from Superintendent John McLaren and the park commissioners. Relief officials ultimately struck a deal, promising that the cottages would not remain in the parks beyond August 1, 1907 (later renegotiated to October 17 of the same year). With the rapid approach of winter, contractor George L. Leonard remembered the cottages being built at a rate of twenty-five per day.[75] Eventually, at least fifty-six hundred cottages were completed at an average cost of $150.50. The vast majority had three rooms, with a few consisting of only two rooms. For the exterior, McLaren selected a "parkbench green" paint that was intended to make the cottages fade into the landscapes of his beloved parks, although residents generally disliked the color. The cottages had no interior finishes and no insulation. Refugees concerned about the cold could purchase wood and coal burning stoves if they could also afford to install a chimney. Gas stoves and lamps required less maintenance, but capital costs of between $5.25 and $8.00 for gas stoves combined with a fee of fifty cents per month for a single gas jet were beyond the reach of most refugees, forcing them to adopt less expensive methods of heating and lighting. The city attempted to provide sewers and plumbing for the cottage camps, but cottages did not have individual toilets or other modern sanitary provisions.[76] Cottage residents thus had access to only a few of the conveniences that upper- and middle-class San Franciscans were once again taking for granted some eight months after the earthquake had shaken up city living.

As a resident of the Jefferson Square camp, Mary Kelly first applied for one of two hundred cottages being constructed there in October 1906. She was turned down, despite having small children and an invalid husband, because she had joined other refugee activists in objecting to the Relief Committee's decision to charge rents. After months of living in the tent camps for free, refugees struggling to get back on their feet objected to being forced to pay for "cottages built out of Relief money, and built on public ground," in Kelly's words.[77] She and five other women employed direct action to assert their right to housing. They each occupied one of the empty cottages with their families, continuing San Francisco's long tradition of squatting as a response to disputed land claims. Despite harassment from police and contractors, Kelly remained for a month.

Finally, on November 3, with Mary Kelly, an elderly woman, and a fifteen year-old girl still inside, the occupied cottage was physically removed to distant Camp Ingleside as Kelly shouted, "I'll stay with this house if they take it to the end of the earth." Kelly wrote later: "There I remained in that house, like some wild animal which the public was curious to see," for three days, until the cottage was torn down around her. Kelly, hardly a delicate woman, emphasized her respectability by criticizing the language of the "scab teamsters" who hauled her cottage to Ingleside. Traditional gender tropes remained part of her rhetoric even as she undertook direct action against the Relief Committee. In January, Kelly finally received a cottage in Mission Park at 18th and

A refugee demonstration over relief distribution. The woman standing in the door of the cottage may be Mary Kelly. Courtesy of the California History Room, California State Library, Sacramento, California.

Dolores.[78] The physical occupation of disputed cottages by refugee women represented an assertion of their right to both space in the city and the material necessities of urban life in the form of a home, however humble. Kelly's emphasis on the public character of both the donations funding cottage construction and the ground on which they were built reinforced her claim of citizenship as a San Francisco resident who had lost her home to the earthquake and fire.

Refugees like Kelly had different views of the relief funds than did the social workers who administered the money. Publicity about the scale of donations led those who struggled to rebuild their lives to question why those millions of dollars were not helping them. As Bine concluded in his July 10 report, "socialistic organization" was not surprising given that refugees had "no mattresses, tatters for clothes, soleless shoes, no place to wash in and no underwear to wash were the laundry there" and then saw "'6,000,000' [dollars] in the newspapers."[79] Refugees believed that they were entitled to individual shares of the money, and many were insulted by agencies' demands that they fill out applications and prove their worthiness by meeting middle-class standards of domesticity and deference. W. D. Sohier and Jacob Furth, who investigated circumstances in San Francisco for suspicious Massachusetts donors, found an "almost universal feeling among . . . the poorer classes that the relief fund was given for them, belongs to them, and each one is entitled to his or her share, as a matter of right."[80]

In gathering information, Sohier and Furth spoke with individual refugees and met with representatives of the United Refugees, who they described as "well-intentioned" but "visionary and often socialistic."[81] Many of the organizers were indeed socialists and experienced activists. Others were simply working people asserting their interests in a society divided along class lines. Calls for equal sharing of relief funds represented a radical departure from existing charity practices, but much of the refugees' rhetoric called for inclusion in the middle class more than systemic change. The United Refugees asked members to sign a card stating, "I desire to secure a home to be built with the money contributed for relief purposes." This demand was entirely practical in light of the severe housing crisis in San Francisco and the way in which refugee status came to define those who still lived in the camps late in the summer of 1906. However, the demand for an individual home represented less of a transformation of class relations than the achievement of a degree of material stability. The United Refugees dreamed of a home as "permanent relief," a dream that did not come true even for many recipients of funds to rebuild their homes or housing in the form of earthquake cottages.[82] The provision of tiny, poorly built homes, or even a grant that was not quite generous enough, failed to resolve the social problems exacerbated by the disaster, most of which, like rampant poverty and transience, were endemic to the city.

Environmental and spatial circumstances, particularly the dense urban development characteristic of central San Francisco, made further transience seemingly inevitable. Because cottages were constructed on the same public squares and parks that had housed the tent camps, they could remain only if San Francisco was willing to give up its already sparse public spaces for housing the working poor. Conflict between parks and people is a recurrent theme in environmental history; the establishment of both urban and rural parks usually demanded the removal of existing residents, particularly poor people and people of color.[83] The earthquake and fire created a variation of this conflict for the city of San Francisco, with the twist of settling displaced refugees in the parks. As early as May 1906, members of the Committee for Housing the Homeless had been concerned that the use of parks and squares for refugee camps meant that they ceased to be available for the recreation of neighborhood residents, particularly children. Critics of the camps also worried that they were creating an idle and dependent population. This perception of camp residents carried over into politics, as municipal officials denied the right to vote to men living on public property, effectively depriving them of their citizenship. Women, of course, did not yet hold the right to vote in California.[84] As Kelly's rhetoric demonstrates, refugees attempted to reverse this dynamic by asserting a right to live on the city's public lands, in cottages built with money donated for relief of inhabitants of the stricken city. Thus debates over individuals' rights to urban space and the presence of private residences on public open spaces underlay many debates about housing for the thousands left homeless by the disaster.

COTTAGES AND SUBURBAN NATURE

The earthquake, fire, and recovery led to a spatial reorganization of housing in San Francisco. As we saw in chapter 2, the environmental events of the earthquake and fire had differential impacts on the city's neighborhoods, impacts shaped by both geological and historical factors. Social circumstances mattered to some degree—cheap wood-frame structures were more likely to collapse than more substantial structures built of steel and concrete—but it was the recovery that underscored the importance of social differences in shaping the medium- and long-term impacts of the disaster. Both relief policies and economic imperatives forced a migration of working-class families out of central city neighborhoods such as South of Market and parts of the Mission. Such changes had environmental components as well, as propaganda promoting the environmental amenities of suburbs joined economic factors such as the cost of land in encouraging population shifts. Suburban amenities proved more promise than reality, however, and in housing as in other sectors the disaster highlighted and exacerbated class divisions in San Francisco.

In August 1907 the Relief Committee ordered cottage residents to relocate their homes from public to private property, with only Lobos Square Camp remaining open, but poor families found few centrally located, affordable home sites. Kelly succinctly explained the problem: "The cheap lots were so far out that I could not take any of them and pay necessary [street] car fare daily for my family and self, and the owners of the lots which were within the city limits were asking such high rents that I could not touch them." Cottage residents were also expected to pay the cost of relocating their homes, although the Associated Charities assisted many families, relocating 879 cottages at an average cost of seventy-one dollars each and sometimes paying for improvements such as plumbing and repairs. Ultimately, 5,343 shacks were moved, with the remainder burned or torn down for wood.[85]

Most of the relocated cottages remained substandard living spaces. Cottages were selling for as little as thirty-five dollars, so some families purchased more than one and attached them to make larger homes. William and Susan James and their seven children, who were evicted from their Mission District flat after the fire, hauled four cottages from Camp Richmond to a lot on 21st Street in July 1907. Their daughter Florence remembered her parents' stories of the wind whistling through gaps in the walls of the fused cottages and extinguishing the lamps in their new home. Cottages often remained grouped in small communities to share plumbing systems. Only 40 percent were connected to the

A cottage being moved through the streets. Courtesy of the California Historical Society (CHS2016_2124).

city's water mains, and only 15 percent had toilets in the house. In cottage settlements with many houses clustered together, as many as ten families might share an outdoor privy. Very few families could afford to purchase lots, so most ended up paying ground rent—the first time that practice had been widespread in San Francisco. Like the James family, many relocated to the suburbs far out Mission Street, where cottages soon dotted the cheap land, but studies indicated that refugees who had lived in crowded central city camps relocated to suburban settings while those who had lived in camps far from the city center moved closer to employment opportunities. As men and women struggled to regain their economic footing, the prospects generally appeared better in another part of the city.[86] Rather than serving as stable homes for San Francisco's working poor, the camps and cottages reinforced transience among residents. Social workers following up with cottage residents in June 1908 were unable to locate 40 percent, and unskilled workers remained destabilized until 1911, often changing homes every year.[87]

For those like Mary Kelly who could not afford to relocate, circumstances only worsened. Kelly's cottage was torn down and her possessions thrown out into the park on September 28, 1907. She and her family then became truly homeless, "sleeping on the ground with those 'bubonic rats' running all over and about us" in the park, as she complained with (one hopes) a touch of hyperbole. Other residents suffered personal injuries and damaged belongings in the rush to move cottages by the deadline. As they had done on previous controversial issues, refugees mobilized to protect their interests. One group obtained a temporary restraining order delaying the removal, and the United Refugees called for a defense of the cottage camps. Ultimately, however, the refugees and their allies lacked the power to maintain their residence in the city's parks, and all camps except Lobos Square were vacated.[88]

Even when families could afford to move their cottages, they often lost their homes within a few years, this time to demolition. In September 1907 the Board of Health began enforcing new sanitary regulations for the cottages, requiring foundations, fireproof roofs, and plumbing facilities. The board systematically burned cottages without plumbing or where a case of bubonic plague had been found. Residents were given only twenty-four to forty-eight hours notice that their homes would be demolished. In March 1910 the Board of Health launched another campaign to condemn the remaining earthquake cottages, along with other temporary buildings built after the earthquake. Two years later, the board's report again referenced its efforts to eliminate refugee shacks from the city, criticizing the poverty of the occupants as a legacy of the 1906 disaster. San Francisco's working poor, many of whom had not regained their footing after the earthquake and fire, thus suffered from recurring harassment in the name of sanitation and beautification of the city. These constant crises—crises for individuals persisting years after the earthquake and fire had receded as a crisis for the city as a whole—reflected the instability and forced mobility that characterized working-class life.[89]

Negative consequences from the dislocations resulting from the disaster and the relief policies proved lasting. Many missed their old neighborhoods and the communities that had been broken up by the disaster and transformed during the rebuilding. The following ditty reflects ambivalence about both technological progress and the changes in the city after the fire:

> You's can have yer porceline bat' tubs
> An yer 'lectric lighted flats;
> Youse kin live in dese swell 'partments
> What has no mice er rats.
> But for mine de rough an' ready
> Of de life below de slot,
> Before de blaze comes along
> An' scorched us off de lot.[90]

The slot refers to the iron crack running along the center of Market Street that contained the cable housing for the cable car line—and that represented the symbolic division between wealthy San Francisco to the north of Market Street and working-class territory south of Market. The author reminiscenced about the good old days before the fire destroyed his neighborhood and the land-use changes accompanying the rebuilding drove out working families. Changes in housing stock caused by the earthquake and fire included a dramatic shift in older neighborhoods like South of Market toward an emphasis on hotel housing as families moved to more distant suburbs and single male laborers increasingly dominated the housing market. The populations of the Outer Mission, the Sunset, and the Richmond districts increased dramatically after 1906 as rows of houses replaced market gardens and sand dunes. In 1911 three-quarters of San Franciscans resided outside the burned district in contrast to just 45 percent in 1905, representing the movement of more than one hundred thousand people.[91]

Rhetoric emphasizing the idyllic suburban environment that awaited cottage residents helped justify the forced removal of earthquake cottages. Social workers and middle-class observers promoted the idea that even modest cottages could make for comfortable homes with environmental amenities not available in the city. The SFHA emphasized the superiority of refugee shacks over tenement houses, particularly if they were located "in outlying districts of the city, with the advantage of vacant spaces adjoining them, as well as of individual gardens."[92]

Photograph by Charles Weidner portraying a bucolic pastoral scene, captioned "Relief cottage after removal." Note the unpaved roads and concentration of poor dwellings that undermine the suburban ideal. Courtesy of the Bancroft Library, University of California, Berkeley (BANC PIC 1994.022-ALB v.3:23).

Rhetoric of suburban nature and the earthquake cottages emphasizes the ways in which contests over housing in the wake of the earthquake and fire represented environmental disputes—debates over where and how people would live. Racial covenants restricted access to this suburban idyll even as the realities of unequal development re-created insanitary conditions, substandard housing, and environmental risk in suburban settings.

The demand for housing after the earthquake combined with the attractions of suburban settings to spark the establishment and expansion of communities to the south of San Francisco, both along the coast and down the peninsula. In 1907 the local magazine *Western World* ran several articles promoting suburban townsites and their environmental amenities. One author, Mary Edith Griswold, praised "everything which tends to carry people out of the city, and give each family a little patch of Mother Earth to get next to, a big blue sky, and plenty of good clear air." She emphasized the ocean and mountain views of new townsites like Edgemar, Salada Beach, and Valle Mar located along the Pacific Coast south of Mussel Rock, in present-day Pacifica. Before the earthquake and fire, this region was settled largely by dairymen and truck and garden farmers.[93] Located just to the north was Daly City, named after John Daly, who offered space on his dairy farm to refugees from San Francisco after the fire. The inexpensive lots that he laid out there became the site of a settlement of relocated earthquake cottages after 1907.[94]

These new townsites were made accessible by the Ocean Shore Railroad, which promised a commute of only twenty-five minutes from Edgemar to City Hall in San Francisco. Edgemar was to be "a high-class seaside residence community" modeled after the beach suburbs of Los Angeles. Edgemar's promoters described an ideal climate, protected from fogs and harsh winds while blessed with fresh ocean breezes. The location was "the most attractive, healthful and beautiful property on the ocean, near the mountains, close to the city," with lots available for purchase "at moderate price and on the easiest terms." Although the pamphlet promised opportunity for "one and all" on one page, restrictive covenants not only kept out nuisance industries but also prevented "Africans," "Mongolians," and "undesirable classes" from owning property or living in Edgemar, so the promise of a suburban retreat along the coast was available only to white Californians who were at least moderately well-off. Lots in Edgemar could be purchased for 10 percent down and ten dollars per month paid over forty-five months.[95]

An article in *Western World* promoting suburbs on the peninsula revealed even more telling contradictions in the promise of suburban nature. The author emphasized the "scenic beauty" of towns like San Bruno, including their "grand old oaks" and redwoods, and promised an escape from "the fogs and chilling winds" of San Francisco. However, the same article—indeed the same page—also touted the growing town's industrial plants. It described San Bruno as simultaneously a "garden spot" and home to fifteen million dollars' worth of industry. Promotions like this targeted potential working-class suburbanites who might seek employment as well as homes.[96] In another piece, the author noted that "millions of dollars were expended in the improvement [of land] for townsites." The land was "graded and sewered, paved and arbored" in preparation for the construction of "comfortable cottage[s]" and bungalows as well as "more pretentious residence[s]."[97] Thus, even the trees that contributed to suburban neighborhoods' scenic beauty had been planted to replace trees long since cut down to build homes or fuel industry in San Francisco. A constructed nature greeted suburban homebuyers who sought to escape the artifice of the city.

Concerns about crowding and undesirable living conditions in San Francisco persisted and even worsened in the years after the fire, and the earthquake cottages remained symbolic of the problem of housing the city's working poor. A 1909 letter published in a labor newspaper lamented the surviving earthquake shacks and "the squalor contained within them." The writer, J. B. Rueben of the local Masonic relief board, appealed to Ernest P. Bicknell of the Red Cross Relief Fund to spend remaining dollars to relocate the shacks to suburban nature: "Help these, our people—to emerge from their ashes into the pure atmosphere of the undeveloped country. Place them where they may know something of the music of the tides; the birds; the winds; the gush of water beneath stones; the bursting of buds in their own rose-gardens; the rains falling upon sun-shrivelled leaves."[98]

Despite Rueben's romanticized portrayal of nature—remember the James family's intimate experience of the wind whistling through their cottages and putting out the lamps—he revealed a vision of improvement of wild nature elsewhere in his letter. Rueben suggested that the "shack dwellers" could "become the means for reclaiming the arid wastes" of undeveloped land in San Francisco County and south along the peninsula. Suburban growth, even in the form of houses for the urban poor, could thus improve the land as well as the people, although of course those "arid wastes" hardly resembled the land of tides, babbling brooks, and rose gardens Rueben described a few paragraphs later. These contradictions remind us that nature is always an idea as well as a real place of complex ecosystems. In promoting the development of lands outside San Francisco in the aftermath of the earthquake and fire, writers employed whatever tropes seemed to support their arguments, probably without even being aware of their own assumptions and contradictions. Their language reinforced the perception of nature as existing outside the city, in this case in suburbs that promised to offer aesthetic and healthful amenities not available to the urban poor and middle classes.

Historians are familiar with these contradictions of suburban development in the case of the post–World War II suburbs that spread across the American landscape. Suburban residents sought environmental amenities and racial homogeneity in the suburbs, and suburbs south of San Francisco and across the water in the East Bay and Marin County exercised a similar pull in the aftermath of 1906. As in the new suburban developments constructed after World War II, the reality often did not live up to the promises of developers.[99] In the case of San Francisco's early twentieth-century suburbs, the expansion of street railway lines and ferry service made these new suburbs practical for many commuters with jobs in the city. However, other infrastructure such as access to municipal water, paved streets and sidewalks, and sewerage was less likely to be available. The absence of urban infrastructure posed a particular problem for poor people such as cottage residents desperate to relocate their homes to any lot they could find and afford. In a 1908 study, Professor James Motley found that new settlements often had no investment in grading or the construction of sidewalks, and cottage residents who had settled on steep hillsides had to carry water up the hill to their homes. On some lots, transplanted cottages were crowded in as many as sixty to a city block. In general, these families found themselves worse off after the fire than before; among cottage residents 329 had smaller incomes than before the fire, 215 larger, and 92 remained the same. They also traveled an average of 75 percent farther to get to work. Overall, 82 percent of those who had rented rooms before the fire preferred their predisaster quarters to those of two years later.[100] Especially for the poor and racial minorities, new suburban developments were hardly the idyll portrayed in promotional literature.

The various relief plans ranging from substantial cash bonuses to temporary earthquake cottages reinscribed geographic distinctions tied to economic class and racial background in San Francisco. Those residents who owned or could afford to purchase property received assistance in reestablishing themselves on that property while refugees who lacked both land and cash remained temporary tenants of parks with no rights to housing in the city. Refugee activists attempted to assert equity as a principle of disaster relief by demanding equal distribution of donated cash. Mary Kelly and others challenged the value judgments made by social workers as either a deliberate assertion of class interests or a failure to recognize how the destruction of both physical property and economic opportunity by the earthquake and fire had knocked hard-working citizens into poverty. Kelly argued that the refugees she spoke for were "law-abiding citizens, a steady, honest, hard-working class of people who never asked for charity from any one and always paid their own way." The only fault of these men and women was that they were "the poor unfortunates who were shaken and burned out by that terrible earthquake and fire."[101] However, she failed to persuade the social welfare professionals, politicians, and businessmen who spearheaded the relief corporation. Despite the best efforts of activists like Mary Kelly, the earthquake and the relief policies that followed only exacerbated preexisting conditions of poverty and instability.

CONCLUSION

The story has one final twist. Mussel Rock sits on the San Andreas Fault, virtually at the epicenter of the 1906 earthquake. The writer John McPhee has described it as "a good place to sit and watch the [tectonic] plates move."[102] Of course, that also made it a less than ideal place to build homes. New coastal settlements like Edgemar and Daly City proved to be highly susceptible to erosion and landslides as well as at risk from earthquakes. In fact, promoters of the new Pacific coast townsites failed to mention that the Ocean Shore Railroad had suffered significant damage in the earthquake when collapsing cliffs swept over four thousand feet of track into the ocean. The company struggled to keep the tracks open through rain, fog, and landslides before going bankrupt in 1921.[103] As the owners and users of the Ocean Shore Railroad learned the hard way, geological change occurs not only through seismic activity but also through such processes as weathering, erosion, and landslides, and the coastal stretches of the San Francisco Bay Area are even more dynamic landscapes than the region as a whole. The promise of environmental amenities in the new suburbs of San Francisco had severe limitations, and the residents of these growing towns faced continued—and sometimes increased—exposure to environmental risk, both in the short term and in the long term.

Life in San Francisco in the immediate aftermath of the earthquake and fire reflected the intersection of ecology, economy, and culture in shaping urban lives and the urban landscape. The disaster transformed the ecology of life in the city, disrupting lifelines ranging from trade networks to provisions for water, light, heat, waste disposal, and shelter. It also disturbed social relations in the city, initially forcing people of all classes into shared experiences of bread lines and improvisational survival strategies such as cooking in the streets. However, distinctions of class, race, and gender quickly resurfaced in the face of residual economic forces such as land ownership, insurance claims, and business experience as well as a severe housing shortage, tight labor markets, and persistent assumptions about the character of the poor and ethnic minorities. As more resilient community members returned to their homes or arranged new ones, more vulnerable San Franciscans remained in refugee camps. Those camps were situated in the city's parks and in its sinks, areas normally used more for dumping waste than for residences, including vacant lots and outlying underdeveloped neighborhoods such as Harbor View. Even as the city's elites objected to housing displaced people in scarce park spaces, camp residents mobilized to protest the crowded and insanitary conditions of the more marginal camps to which they were increasingly shunted.

Community mobilization is common in the aftermath of a disaster, and activism in San Francisco reflected parallels with later environmental justice movements as refugees demanded basic environmental amenities of secure food, shelter, and sanitary living conditions. Refugees like Mary Kelly also asserted principles of economic and environmental equity through demands for direct distribution of cash grants to the displaced or, failing that, the provision of real opportunities for the stability of home ownership. However, for elites, such claims threatened to extend the disruption of social relations initiated by the earthquake, and refugee claims encountered the class assumptions of social workers and more prosperous residents who instead offered an idealized vision of suburban cottages that ignored practical limitations of transportation and infrastructure as well as the environmental risks of new settlements.

Ultimately the relief and recovery, even more than the environmental events of the earthquake and fire, exacerbated inequalities of class, race, and gender in San Francisco. Rather than reducing transience among the poorer classes, the earthquake launched a cycle of increased instability, undermining opportunities for poorer San Franciscans to achieve the financial, familial, and environmental stability that distinguished the respectable working class from those considered idlers and delinquents—even though disaster had demonstrated just how thin the line between the two groups could be. The disruption of the city's central neighborhoods combined with the dynamics of the rebuilding process to reorganize housing patterns in the city. However, geographies of class still shaped the new spatial arrangements, as poor families were forced out of most central city neighborhoods. Although the nascent environmental justice struggles of the refugees largely failed, they reflected a pattern of urban nature as contested terrain in the disrupted environment of San Francisco, demonstrating how regaining control over urban nature and rebuilding the city meant reasserting control over its people.

FOUR

REBUILDING AND THE POLITICS OF PLACE

DURING THE FIRST WEEK OF MAY 1906, A DELEGATION OF CHINESE officials including the Consul-General of San Francisco, Chung Pao Hsi, held a closed door meeting with Abe Ruef, the chair of a committee charged with identifying a new location for Chinatown after the earthquake and fire. The idea of relocating Chinatown out of the center of San Francisco was not a new one—similar proposals had surfaced periodically throughout the city's short history—but to many white San Franciscans, the devastation of the urban environment appeared to offer the perfect opportunity to seize the valuable land of the Chinese district. In their minds, replacing the crowded buildings and narrow alleys with broad streets lined with white businesses would improve the neighborhood and maximize economic benefits for the city as a whole.

In the meeting, Chinese officials expressed their indignation over the treatment of Chinese refugees before the focus turned to relocation. Ruef and the Chinese dignitaries toured outlying districts of the city that had been proposed as new sites for Chinatown, including Hunter's Point and a plot of land in the Potrero, but the Chinese expressed dissatisfaction with both proposed locations. During the tour Chung floated the possibility of racial integration, "the intermingling of the Chinese among the whites, in the same manner that obtains with other nationalities," in the words of the *San Francisco Examiner*. Ruef rejected such a radical proposal, arguing that racial segregation protected and benefited the Chinese minority.[1] The Chinese did not press for integration, but they did mobilize to contest the proposal to force them out of historic Chinatown—and in the process they faced off against many of the city's leading white political figures.

The proposal to relocate Chinatown was only one among several schemes to remake the urban environment in the aftermath of the earthquake and fire. Another, perhaps better known, drew on the Burnham Plan, a master plan for San Francisco commissioned by City Beautiful advocates led by former mayor James D. Phelan. The document by Daniel H. Burnham, the foremost urban planner in the United States at the time, presented a vision of scenic San Francisco in which new parks and roads facilitated contemplation of the city's water views while improving transportation and commerce.[2] Both Burnham and local political leaders envisioned the ambitious report as a blueprint for future development, a guide for long-term change that would be implemented gradually over the next fifty years. When the earthquake and fire destroyed City Hall—ironically turning to ashes three thousand newly printed copies of Burnham's *Report on a Plan for San Francisco* that had been delivered just the day before—circumstances appeared to have suddenly changed. By wiping out the city's infrastructure, the disaster had seemingly left a blank slate, albeit one covered with debris and rubble, for a reordered city. Burnham, Phelan, and other City Beautiful proponents believed they had a unique opportunity to implement their vision of a new and improved San Francisco.

The first question asked after a massive urban disaster such as the 1906 earthquake and fire is often whether the devastated city *should* be rebuilt. Doubts about the wisdom of rebuilding in the same location arise when people perceive a site to be particularly prone to hazards such as earthquakes or hurricanes. However, modern cities are highly resilient. Their economic functions, capital investments, and cultural and symbolic value to residents and to the nation encourage reconstruction rather than abandonment of the city. As one booster publication explained in 1906, San Francisco "was created by commercial energies and necessities that fire cannot burn nor earthquake destroy, and they exist now as they did before."[3] In the weeks following the catastrophe, the reconstruction of San Francisco was not so thoroughly self-evident as to preclude promotional efforts, but it quickly became clear that San Francisco would again emulate the phoenix that had been its symbol since the fires of the 1850s and rise from the ashes.

After a major hazard event, and once it becomes clear that a city will be rebuilt, many observers have seen the opportunity to improve the urban environment as a silver lining in a time of crisis. This is creative destruction taken to its logical extreme—nature or fate assisting the cycle of destruction and rebuilding that characterizes both capitalism and urban development. Proposed changes can appear either positive or negative, depending on one's point of view. Juxtaposing the proposal to relocate Chinatown and the Burnham Plan highlights the spectrum of possible reformations of the urban environment in the wake of catastrophe. Reading these simultaneous debates together also reveals conflicting visions of the urban environment, both in the realm of ideas and on the ground in San Francisco. This chapter moves from the scenic vistas of the Burnham Plan to the congested alleys of Chinatown. The densely urban district of Chinatown might not normally be seen as part of nature, either now or in the early twentieth century, but it represented a distinct urban ecosystem, one shaped by factors such as racial politics that confined Chinese to a single neighborhood, economic and cultural practices of Chinese residents, and nonhuman species that made the district their home, including those fostered by poverty such as rats and disease organisms. Densely populated neighborhoods such as Chinatown—created by the exclusion of immigrants and people of color from the broader urban environment during these decades—had consequences for the environmental health of residents that represented early manifestations of environmental racism.[4]

Discourses of Chinatown as dark, unsanitary, and exotic relied a great deal on myth, but they also highlighted how Chinatown's urban environment differed—in both perception and material reality—from the various white neighborhoods of San Francisco (which in turn differed from each other, of course). Perceptions of Chinatown's environment lay at the root of the struggle over relocation. To ignore the environmental element in debates over relocating Chinatown risks reproducing the emphasis on pristine, wild nature over urban nature that has too often led both the environmental movement and environmental scholarship to ignore urban issues and environmental justice concerns. To foreground issues of environmental justice demands looking at all types of environments, not just those characterized by bucolic settings and valued for the presence of desirable nature.

The proposed relocation of Chinatown represented an environmental justice issue in another sense as well; it involved the attempted seizure of land by white San Franciscans from residents of color. Racism has spatial as well as social and economic components, and residential segregation is an important contributing factor in environmental inequality. Disasters contribute to what David Harvey has called "accumulation by dispossession," a process through which elites enhance their own wealth and power by depriving more vulnerable residents of their property.[5] In 1906, San Francisco's Chinese population not only challenged racial segregation, albeit obliquely, but also challenged the virulent racism that denied their place in the city and declared their neighborhood to be a blight on the urban environment. In this case the Chinese successfully resisted removal to a less desirable area, but the attempt to relocate their neighborhood reflects a recurrent pattern of relegating people of color to polluted and peripheral environments, a foundation of environmental racism. The victory of the Chinese, the most stigmatized racial group in California at the time, complicates simple assumptions about vulnerability during disaster and demonstrates the contested process of rebuilding. For better or worse, the postdisaster city did not represent a blank slate waiting to be remade. Rather, it remained the home of diverse communities that possessed their own visions for their city, often based on the urban environment that had existed before the earthquake, and that fought to enact their visions rather than those of Abe Ruef, Daniel Burnham, or James D. Phelan.

THE UTILITY OF THE BEAUTIFUL

In calling for urban improvement in San Francisco in 1905, James D. Phelan contrasted the early twentieth-century city with frontier San Francisco. He declared: "A love of the true and the beautiful, a craving for artistic betterments and a sense of public duty have succeeded the hard struggles to tame the wild earth, explore its secrets, raze the forest, build the city, and command the sea."[6] As history, this description was far more rhetoric than reality, ignoring, for example, that the wind-swept San Francisco peninsula never had any forests in need of razing. Elsewhere, in fact, Phelan's writings reflected a mind-set of improving nature very similar to that which prevailed among the early American settlers of the region. "Nature . . . has endowed our city," he wrote, and "provided man but supplements what nature has done, San Francisco may yet become the pride of the American continent."[7] Phelan and his allies in San Francisco's City Beautiful movement followed in the foot-steps of previous critics who questioned the city's unrelenting grid of streets and relative lack of park space.

By the beginning of the twentieth century, a national movement pro-moting the ideal of the City Beautiful promised to reform the nation's troubled cities, proposing aesthetic improvements to the urban environ-ment in the name of both beautification and social uplift. Advocates of the City Beautiful, as the name suggests, believed in beauty's restorative power, and they sought to combine aesthetics and utility. A beautiful urban environment would attract, and even create, a better workforce while enhancing property values. Their vision emphasized conserving and enhancing cities' natural beauty, alongside a fondness for monu-mental classicist architecture, and most saw beautification as one piece in a broader effort at reform of urban problems ranging from corrup-tion to poor sanitation. Beauty was, almost by definition, functional and efficient for City Beautiful supporters who were steeped in Progressive Era faith in efficiency and expertise.[8] In 1898, then-mayor Phelan had engineered passage of a new city charter intended to strengthen and modernize municipal government, laying the groundwork for further reform. And in 1904 he and like-minded Progressives commissioned Daniel H. Burnham to develop a master plan for San Francisco.

Planners like Burnham offered a new blueprint for the chaotic cities of the early twentieth century. They promised that intelligent remaking of the urban environment could control the unruly populations—and unruly natures—that vexed the middle- and upper-class men and women who supported and funded City Beautiful movements. Labor unrest, immigration, civic corruption, inefficiencies in transportation and in capitalism itself, pollution and sanitary challenges—all of these could seemingly be mitigated through what the scholar M. Christine Boyer has called "a perfectly disciplined spatial order."[9] In the early twentieth century, the ideals of Progressives came together with the growth of the municipal engineering profession to offer the possibility of urban planning on an unprecedented scale. In the chaos of the post-disaster city, the promise of transforming that chaos into a redisciplined order—one that would fix the inefficiencies and problems plaguing the city to create an improved, modern metropolis—held a powerful appeal.

Burnham was born in New York State in 1846 but grew up in Chicago after his family moved there when he was a boy. After a failed attempt to make a fortune as a miner in Nevada, he returned to Chicago and began working as an architect in the 1870s. His innovative and profitable firm benefited from high demand after the 1871 fire as well as from the city's rapid growth. However, it was Burnham's work on the 1893 World's Columbian Exposition that brought him national prominence as the leading architect and planner of the City Beautiful movement. He followed up that success with high-profile plans for Washington, DC, and Cleveland before receiving the commission for a plan for San Francisco.

Burnham and his assistants set up shop in a redwood-shingled bungalow on a spur of Twin Peaks. Burnham's so-called "shack" hardly resembled those that would house disaster refugees just a couple of years later. The architect's temporary headquarters was specially constructed and equipped at a cost of more than three thousand dollars. It featured a deck facing the bay and a fireplace to warm the occupants during the city's foggy, chilly nights.[10] Burnham's plan focused on two elements of particular concern to Phelan: parks and streets. The planner proposed a series of major new parks that would increase the green space in the city from 1,400 acres to 9,855 acres, including a massive park running from Twin Peaks southwestward to the ocean. Burnham emphasized that his choices for additions to the park system considered both "natural beauty" and such characteristics as "steepness, inaccessibility or difficulties of drainage" that made an area "ill adapted for private occupancy." This echoed contemporary preservationist proposals to set aside lands that possessed both sublime scenery and few other apparent practical uses, policies that led to the establishment of many of the national parks during these years. In San Francisco, proposed new parks included Twin Peaks as well as scenic coastal locales such as an oceanfront public square in the Sunset District and a park and drive at a reclaimed Islais Creek to the south.[11]

Burnham envisioned these parks as possessing both aesthetic and recreational value, and they were to include gymnasia, libraries, club rooms, and other public buildings. The scenic value of the sites was of utmost importance, however, and Burnham noted that he selected hilltop parks "for their effect from afar, as each hill affords a view of the others." These views had to be pleasing to the civilized eye, and Burnham proposed the construction of terraces where necessary to "modify the hills whose outlines are too ragged or violent."[12] The nature that Burnham sought to highlight was a controlled or tamed nature, a civilized urban nature contrasted with the "wild earth," in Phelan's words, that allegedly had existed before the city.[13]

Burnham did not demonstrate an understanding of the region's native ecosystems, as his mentor Frederick Law Olmsted had several decades earlier with his suggestion that an Eastern-style park was unsuited to the sand dunes of the Outside Lands. Golden Gate Park had demonstrated that the local landscape could be transformed in pursuit of recreational spaces, and Burnham proposed an extension of that transformation. He suggested that "the tops of all high hills should be preserved in a state of nature while their slopes below should be clothed with trees." Elsewhere, he stated that San Francisco lacked trees because residents objected to blocking the sunlight, indicating little awareness that the arid, windswept local ecosystems were home to few uncultivated trees. His experience in the city apparently echoed that of many earlier newcomers to the region. Burnham complained: "The most objectionable features of San Francisco are the wind and the accompanying dust." He suggested that planting trees would mitigate those unfortunate aspects of the environment while also softening "the harshness of the skyline." Burnham's vision for nature in the city emphasized the scenic and the controlled, a constructed nature focused on aesthetic value. He even proposed lighting "by permanent or temporary illuminations" the "chain of forest glades" that would be part of the eastern view from Twin Peaks, thus facilitating visual enjoyment even at night.[14]

The other major point of emphasis in Burnham's plan was San Francisco's circulation network, its streets. Despite his stated goal to "interfere as little as possible with the rectangular street system of the city" in combining "convenience and beauty in the greatest possible degree," Burnham's plan included at least seventy changes to San Francisco's streets, including changes in every section of the city. His ideal design for the streets consisted of a series of concentric rings bisected by boulevards radiating outward from a central Civic Center. San Francisco's hilly topography proved one obstacle to imposing that model on the urban landscape, and its existing street grid represented another. Burnham's solution was to incorporate the hills into his design and to lessen the "embarrassments" that arose from the rectangular grid. Diagonal boulevards would cut through the existing street pattern, and many streets would be widened, extended, and regraded. Contour streets would circle the hills, providing another opportunity to experience the scenic views of the city, the bay, and the Pacific. An Outer Boulevard circling the city along the waterfront would also facilitate enlightening scenic drives. The Association for the Improvement and Adornment of San Francisco (AIASF), the local City Beautiful group that hired Burnham, noted that construction of this boulevard would require filling in large areas along the coast, and they identified it as one of their highest priority projects prior to the earthquake.[15]

Burnham never intended that his plan would be implemented all at once or in its entirety. Instead, he expected it to be "executed by degrees, as the growth of the community demands and as its financial ability allows."[16] This was also the expectation of the Board of Supervisors and Mayor Schmitz when they accepted the completed plan in September 1905. In presenting the plan, the City Beautiful advocate William Greer Harrison related beauty of environment and beauty of character, suggesting that the first would lead to the second. He stated that "San Francisco is not likely to be a great manufacturing center, and therefore we should make it an attractive and beautiful city," a "City of Hills . . . more beautiful than Rome." Supervisor A. A. D'Ancona emphasized San Francisco's natural beauty, declaring that "we should appreciate our beautiful hills, our valleys, our sea and our harbor." Schmitz took issue with the idea that San Francisco would not be a great manufacturing city, but he conceded that it should be made "as beautiful as possible" while waiting for that manufacturing development.[17] This tension between commerce and beauty would become even more pronounced in the postdisaster city, and it would be joined by a greater uncertainty about the desirability and feasibility of urban nature.

Map of San Francisco from Daniel H. Burnham's *Report on a Plan for San Francisco*. Note the proposed diagonal streets, boulevard circling the city, and large Twin Peaks park. Courtesy of the David Rumsey Map Collection.

The initial presentation of the Burnham Plan received little media coverage, but the attention it did receive was generally favorable. Both the *Chronicle* and the *Bulletin* endorsed the plan. The Board of Supervisors authorized the printing of several thousand copies for widespread distribution (which would become the ill-fated copies that burned in the fire). In March 1906 the AIASF proposed that the city undertake three projects from the plan: an extension of the panhandle of Golden Gate Park, construction of the outer boulevard around the city, and raising the grade of lower Market Street. The city also acquired forty-seven acres on Twin Peaks, including the site of Burnham's bungalow, to serve as a park and to contribute to a planned auxiliary water supply. The incremental progress envisioned by Burnham and Phelan seemed to be under way.[18]

A month later, the earthquake and fire did far more than nearly obliterate the written record of Burnham's work. In their aftermath, Phelan, even more than the city's elected officials, took charge of recovery efforts, which he clearly saw as an opportunity to implement the City Beautiful. He praised the aesthetic possibilities revealed by the destruction of the built environment, writing that "now, stripped of buildings, the graceful contour lines [of San Francisco's hills] have excited the admiration of the esthetic and the practical alike and the utility of the Beautiful is preached in the streets and from the hilltops."[19] For Phelan the ruins inspired not regret for the buildings and possessions that had been destroyed but a sense of excitement at the possibilities of the landscape that had been uncovered. Under his watch three subcommittees—the (catchily named) Committee on Extending, Widening, and Grading the Streets and Restoring the Pavement and the Committee on Burnham Plans along with the Committee on Beautification—acted quickly to adapt Burnham's suggestions to new circumstances. One commentator noted that San Francisco was lucky to have a plan for rebuilding in place. "A great fire is always a great opportunity," he declared, but "it usually finds the people unprepared. . . . so the chance passes and the old blunders are perpetuated." San Francisco had had the "foresight" to commission a master plan; would the city now have the "resolution" to implement it?[20]

Burnham himself consulted on an updated plan prepared by his assistant Edward H. Bennett, who had also worked on the original *Report.* The preface to the new document noted that, for practical reasons, the original Burnham Plan had focused on the relatively undeveloped outer districts of the city, but "after the fire the burned district seemed equally inviting as a field of study." This was a straightforward statement of the idea that disaster had created a blank slate for urban redevelopment. Bennett and Burnham declared that the new report was "not a scheme for beautification and adornment" but a "scheme for improvement." They added: "Beauty has been bounteously supplied by Nature and terribly marred by man. . . . Improvement can only be achieved by correcting the errors of the past and planning wisely for the future." Interestingly, the earthquake and fire did not figure in the report as either acts of nature or consequences of human activity. They represented no more than events that had altered the "field of study" for urban planners and Progressive politicians. Aesthetic values remained central to Burnham's proposals despite efforts to emphasize practical questions such as facilitating transportation, and "Nature" appeared as a source of beauty and positive values. The revised plan, like Burnham's original version, proposed the construction of new diagonal avenues cutting through the older sections of the city, now part of the burned district. These proposed avenues would slice through blocks owned by many small property owners, and the report mapped out proposed changes in great detail.[21]

Capitalizing on the 1906 disaster as an opportunity for urban improvement initially had broad support. Just days after the fires were extinguished, the San Francisco Real Estate Board endorsed the "adornment" of San Francisco along the lines of the Burnham Plan. A publication of the Southern Pacific Company suggested that "the fire ha[s] cleared the way" for remodeling the city. Phelan himself suggested that the calamity might be "a blessing in disguise" because it would allow San Francisco to be rebuilt as "one of the wonder cities of the world."[22] Socialists and labor also supported the idea of the City Beautiful in these early weeks. One labor newspaper declared that "by destroying old things," the disaster had "paved the way for new." San Francisco should seize the opportunity to enhance "health, comfort, and safety" and not simply re-create the old city. "Considerations of economy and speedy construction," the paper suggested, should be secondary to "the consideration of permanent value."[23] A wide swathe of San Franciscans seemed to share the vision underlying the City Beautiful movement in general and the Burnham Plan in particular.

Opposition was building, however. Some voices that had endorsed the Burnham Plan the previous year began to question its relevance as the city faced the immediate crisis of restoring economic functions and rebuilding physical infrastructure. At the end of April, the *Chronicle* called for "less talk for the immediate present about magnificent boulevards and more discourse on how we are to resume business." The paper noted that the fire had not wiped out land titles, and thus the "clean slate" promoted by advocates of the City Beautiful did not, in fact, exist. Mayor Schmitz and the *Bulletin* soon joined Michael H. de Young of the *Chronicle* in expressing their doubts about the priority of beautification in the context of disaster. Owners of downtown real estate emphasized the need for rapid reconstruction and opposed changes to the streets as likely to delay rebuilding.[24]

Ordinary citizens and their representatives, including labor leaders, soon joined the wealthy downtown property owners in expressing doubts. Reverend T. P. Mulligan spoke for the city's small property owners when he opposed the extension of the fire limits in part by mocking Burnham: "It is all right for the man from Chicago to camp on Twin Peaks and talk of cutting boulevards here and there, but who is to pay for them? . . . I stand for the people before I stand for the beauty and grandeur of the city." Mulligan noted that frame buildings might appear to be fire hazards, but they were safer in earthquakes than brick. And working people could not afford to build elaborate fireproof structures.[25] Such opposition echoed that following other disasters, such as the 1871 Chicago fire, in which proposals for urban improvement and safety such as extended fire limits ran up against the desires of working people to rebuild quickly and cheaply. Practical economic considerations joined with sentimental attachment to the predisaster city. As one architect noted in 1909, many people felt a "sense of pleasure in seeing old landmarks restored."[26] Whether those landmarks were large or small—the Civic Center or the corner store or tavern—the urban landscape offered touchstones of citizenship and belonging for residents. The dramatic plans of outsiders such as Burnham and elites such as Phelan quickly came to represent the opposite of "improvement" to many San Franciscans, particularly those struggling to get back on their feet in the aftermath of the earthquake.

Political realists like Abe Ruef, the boss behind Mayor Schmitz and the Union Labor Party that controlled the city government, were well aware of the need to expand municipal authority to implement any grandiose schemes for improvement. De Young was right when he noted that the fire had not wiped out land titles along with buildings. (Interestingly, the earthquake had actually moved the ground sufficiently to cause problems for street lines and block boundaries by shifting the "fixed" points that had been used for surveying. Several of the older neighborhoods, including the downtown district, had to be resurveyed and remapped in subsequent years.[27]) Moving forward on the prospect of implementing significant changes, Ruef drafted an amendment to the state constitution that would grant the city increased authority over land use. The amendment was scheduled to go before California's voters in November.[28]

Another prominent plan appeared before the election, however—this one prepared by the engineer Marsden Manson. Manson had received his undergraduate degrees from the Virginia Military Institute before relocating to California in 1878, where he earned a Ph.D. in engineering from the University of California. He had worked as an engineer for the State Harbor Commission, the California Highway Department, and the San Francisco Department of Public Works. In 1908 he would be appointed City Engineer. To Progressives, Manson was just the kind of expert qualified to translate Burnham's ideas into practical plans for urban improvement. Over the summer the political climate had changed, and Manson acknowledged that the ambitious suggestions of the subcommittees could not be implemented. Furthermore, Manson embraced an economic mind-set, declaring that "by virtue of her geographic position, San Francisco is essentially a commercial city." He was an avid outdoorsman and a member of the Sierra Club, but his plan downplayed Burnham's emphasis on scenic beauty and its capacity for social uplift in favor of a more practical focus. As an engineer, a reformer, and a conservationist, Manson believed in the reworking of nature for human use, and he and Phelan were allies both on issues of urban development and in the debates over the proposed Hetch Hetchy water system that would come to a head in the years after 1906. They promoted a utilitarian view emphasizing the greatest good for the greatest number in calling for both a Sierra Nevada water supply for the city and changes to urban infrastructure that they believed offered long-term benefits for San Francisco.[29]

In his report Manson recommended a relatively restrained 7.9 million dollars' worth of improvements to San Francisco's streets, noting their importance as thoroughfares between the waterfront and manufacturing and commercial districts. Wider streets would also serve as fire barriers, reduce congestion, and enhance the value of adjacent property. Branching out from both the subcommittee reports and the original

Burnham Plan, Manson also recommended improvements to the water-front. He argued that the 1906 catastrophe had demonstrated the inadequate condition of San Francisco's waterfront, which he saw as crucial to the prosperity of not only the city but the entire state. He proposed to extend the seawall and to fill in the lots around the newly enclosed coastal areas. The material for filling in this section of San Francisco's coastline would come from the grading of Rincon Hill, where Manson proposed to remove about six million cubic yards of earth covering 120 acres. The removal of Rincon Hill would also open up another 220 acres of previously undeveloped land by providing better street access. This proposal not only echoed the development projects of the 1850s and 1860s, with their emphasis on creating level land along the waterfront, but it even suggested continuing the destruction of Rincon Hill, which had begun in 1869 with the much-lamented Second Street Cut.[30]

Manson's proposal to fill in land along San Francisco's coast failed to take into account one of the major lessons of the earthquake of just six months before—that filled ground was hazardous during seismic activity. It also stood in contrast to Burnham's perspective on altering the urban landscape. Burnham suggested that cutting into hills should be permitted only where it "follows a well-defined plan of terracing and improvements," not "where it is done simply for immediate commercial gain." Burnham did propose to fill in an area around Islais Creek where a widened Mission Boulevard would cross the creek, but he suggested that the area be made into a park.[31] This proposal for a park challenged the overwhelmingly commercial focus of development along the waterfront south of San Francisco, a focus that Manson embraced.

Plans for parks and other scenic and recreational improvements had lost support, however. The San Francisco Real Estate Board abandoned its previous endorsement of Burnham's ideas in favor of Manson's report, which in their words called "only for those improvements which are of strict commercial value and which will immediately aid in the reconstruction of the city from a business standpoint." Opposition to the more grandiose plans continued among middle- and working-class citizens, including both property owners who feared losing pieces of their land to the city and workers who suggested that adequate temporary housing should take precedence over wider streets and more parks. The civil engineer John Galloway noted: "The distant observer may ask why, with virgin ground before it, the city did not cut avenues, widen streets, and build nothing but incombustible buildings." Such improvements did not take priority after the disaster, Galloway explained: "What San Francisco needs is the cheapest building possible in which business may be done, to insure the community enough to eat."[32] The contrast between Burnham's vision of scenic parks and the reality of tent camps of displaced people filling San Francisco's existing open spaces must have been readily apparent to many local observers.

Even Phelan had developed doubts about the expansion of municipal power that would be required to implement his ideas of the City Beautiful. He praised the "town-meeting government" after the fire, in which "the best professional and business men of the city" formed committees to plan for San Francisco's future, largely displacing the elected Union Labor Party government. Phelan correctly perceived the existing San Francisco administration as corrupt, and he hesitated to expand the political power of municipal government as long as it remained in the hands of his Union Labor rivals. He became one of the ring leaders in an attempt to prosecute Mayor Schmitz and other members of the administration for graft, and in the fall, his attention shifted to that effort rather than the amendment that would have enhanced municipal government power with the aim of facilitating changes to the urban plan. In the November election the amendment was decisively defeated both in San Francisco and statewide.[33] The vision of remaking San Francisco had encountered the realities of municipal politics.

Historians have sometimes lamented San Francisco's failure to implement the Burnham Plan after the disaster, implicitly or explicitly portraying it as a missed opportunity to improve the city.[34] Burnham's vision offered a seductive image of a city filled with scenic terraces, efficient parkways, and green spaces. However, it offered few practical benefits for San Francisco's working population, and its vision of nature was an artificially controlled one, in which imported trees smoothed the dramatic hills of San Francisco's dynamic landscape and blocked its chilly ocean winds. Perhaps those trees would even be illuminated by the new electric lights of the modern city. Although such a plan was fully in keeping with California's historical development as a garden spot, it was less a case of living with nature than a proposal for its continued transformation. As such, the mind-set of urban improvement behind the early twentieth-century plans of Burnham and Manson differed less than they realized from the unplanned growth of early San Francisco. The paradigm of "improving" the natural site of the city remained the same, and even the emphasis on commerce above all else resurfaced in Manson's proposals. Although reformers suggested that the devastated urban environment represented a blank slate for changes, they seemed unable to incorporate lessons such as the hazards of coastal fill, and they struggled to consider the social and economic realities facing people who had lost their homes and jobs. A comparison with the simultaneous proposal to relocate Chinatown reminds us of the ways in which the perfected San Francisco envisioned by contemporary elites required excluding at least one population of its residents, revealing the dark side of urban improvement.

CHINATOWN, SANITATION, AND RACIALIZED SPACE

The fate of Chinatown in the rebuilding process raises questions about the relationship between race and vulnerability in cities after hazard events. In the United States, both race and poverty strongly correlate with vulnerability to disaster, and people of color have historically been subject to efforts to force them out of American cities in other contexts (such as gentrification) as well. In New Orleans after Hurricane Katrina, for example, failures of relief and recovery efforts revealed the extent of poverty in the city, particularly among African Americans, and black Americans and progressives rightly worried about the dispossession and displacement of the city's African American population. Marginalized groups possess fewer resources with which to restore their homes and neighborhoods, and this pattern held true in San Francisco in 1906, where most poor San Franciscans found economic recovery to be a difficult and slow process. As detailed in chapter 3, relief policies only reinforced preexisting inequalities along class and ethnic lines. San Francisco's Chinese population experienced particular vulnerability and injustice in the wake of the earthquake and fire, but debates over the proposed relocation of Chinatown demonstrate how the Chinese also found ways to assert power through local and international alliances in defense of their community and its place in the city.

San Francisco's Chinese left the official relief system after discriminatory experiences in the early days of the camps drove them to seek assistance elsewhere. The buildings of Chinatown lay in ruins after the fire, and National Guardsmen and white tourists looted those ruins in the final days of April, before Chinese residents were allowed to return to the neighborhood. Chinese protests against this addition of theft on top of catastrophe had little effect, although the looting was described in the city's newspapers and stolen goods were sold openly in the city and on the ferry. The *Chronicle* described "hundreds of relic hunters" combing through the debris in search of chinaware and other valuables. Such looting flipped the usual script after disasters, in which headlines regularly trumpet elites' fears of looting by marginalized populations. In San Francisco, Mayor Schmitz threatened looters with execution on April 18, but it was the armed would-be executioners and local elites, including "respectably dressed" white women, who took advantage of their relative freedom to move about the city and engaged in looting of Chinese property.[35]

The earthquake and fire proved particularly devastating to San Francisco's Chinese community, not only because of the total destruction of Chinatown but also because much of the community's wealth took the form of merchandise and goods rather than real estate. That wealth thus literally went up in flames, and looting added an element of indignity to material losses. Thousands of Chinese San Franciscans left the city never to return, including several thousand who settled permanently in Oakland and fifteen hundred who returned to China in the first year. Others relocated to smaller Bay Area communities. Most, however, wanted to return to the neighborhood that had been their home.[36]

Chinese had been residents of San Francisco since the days of the gold rush when they, like other immigrants from around the world, were drawn to California by the promise of gold. By 1854 the city contained a distinct Chinese quarter concentrated on upper Sacramento Street and Dupont Street. In settling there, the Chinese were occupying land that had been abandoned in favor of more desirable real estate closer to the wharves; only later, with the growth of the city, did Chinatown become prime real estate. Anti-Chinese sentiment developed in

Shop at Dupont and California Streets selling "souvenirs & relics from Chinatown," reflecting the looting of Chinatown as well as the popularity of disaster tourism. Courtesy of the California History Room, California State Library, Sacramento, California.

those early years and worsened in subsequent decades, particularly as the completion of the transcontinental railroad led to an influx of unemployed Chinese workers and the depression of 1873 threw people of all backgrounds out of work. Throughout the West, struggling white workers blamed Chinese for driving down wages and taking jobs. San Francisco's famous "sandlot uprising" of 1877–78, led by Denis Kearney, targeted Chinatown and Chinese immigration, part of recurrent waves of white violence against Chinese across the West in the 1870s and 1880s.

Western pressure led to passage of the Chinese Exclusion Act in 1882, and the Chinese remained convenient scapegoats for white workers suffering from a combination of real economic difficulties and a sense that they had lost status and opportunities that they perceived to be their birthright as white men. The Exclusion Act prohibited Chinese from becoming naturalized US citizens and largely halted Chinese immigration, allowing only a few merchants and their families to

Captioned "View in Chinatown." Courtesy of the California Historical Society
(PC-PA199_002).

enter the country. Throughout these decades, however, San Francisco's
Chinatown persisted as a dynamic economic center within the city and
home to as many as forty thousand Chinese.[37]

Chinatown's location in the heart of San Francisco was controversial. An 1853 article in the *Alta California* represented probably the first
proposal to relocate the city's Chinese population, and that idea periodically resurfaced over subsequent decades. Calls to relocate Chinatown intersected with a persistent pattern of blaming the Chinese for
epidemics in San Francisco, a pattern that began as early as the "cholera
panic" of the 1850s. In 1876 a physician wrote in the *Pacific Medical and
Surgical Journal* that, in San Francisco, the Chinese "were the focus of
Caucasian animosities" to the extent that "they were made responsible
for mishaps in general. A destructive earthquake would probably be
charged to their account."[38] Although neither the 1868 nor the 1906
earthquake was blamed on the Chinese, white residents considered
them the culprits in disease outbreaks throughout the nineteenth

century and into the twentieth. Health officials and politicians justified such accusations with references to sanitary conditions in Chinatown, reflecting anxiety about the neighborhood's environment, cultural practices of its residents, and inevitable connections between Chinatown and the rest of the city. This phenomenon of racial scapegoating was not unique to San Francisco. Where cities in other parts of the country targeted African American or Jewish populations, in Pacific Coast cities like San Francisco, Chinatowns represented outposts of the racial and cultural "other" within the city. Contemporary theories racialized disease, and fear of contagion became particularly acute when the space associated with the other was located in the center of the city, as with San Francisco's Chinatown.[39]

Concern about disease reflected and highlighted Chinatown as racialized space in San Francisco. Racialized spaces serve to contain and control a minority population, often manifesting conditions of environmental racism in the short term and exacerbating them in the long term. Such spaces and their residents are designated as inferior, and both de jure and de facto practices maintain segregation.[40] The historian Nayan Shah describes how, from 1854 to 1885, recurrent official investigations in San Francisco employed particular spatial metaphors of "dens, density, and the labyrinth" in describing Chinatown, in the process constructing it as a singular, alien urban ecology that posed a sanitary hazard for white San Franciscans. The reports' descriptions emphasized narrow streets, dark alleys, and subterranean passageways, painting a picture of a distinctive urban environment characterized by filth, nuisances, and living conditions often compared to those of animals.[41]

An 1885 pamphlet by San Francisco newspaper editor Curt Abel-Musgrave extended the environmental contrast between Chinatown and the rest of San Francisco. Abel-Musgrave wrote: "Sunbeams that shine on us don't penetrate 50 feet deep into the pestilential dens of the Chinese population, and the fresh breezes which purify the air of our streets and our houses leave the sepulchres untouched in which for 30 years foul and disgusting vapors have been gathering." Abel-Musgrave described how the very air of Dupont Street was "impregnated with bacilli, fungi and stench."[42] Such language emphasized the distinctive environment of Chinatown, characterizing it as different from the rest of the city even to the level of exposure to sun and wind. Abel-Musgrave also assumed a sharp human distinction between "us"—his presumed audience of white San Franciscans—and a racialized other. Sixteen years later, a federal report reinforced the mythology of Chinatown as a place characterized by "marked overcrowding," rooms "entirely devoid of light or means of ventilation," "damp," and possessing "a foul stench."[43] Both official and unofficial discourses thus constructed racialized spaces within the city as environmentally separate and inferior. The assumption that marginalized populations "belonged" in polluted or inferior environments, so baldly expressed in these writings about Chinatown, has continued to shape decision-making on questions of zoning and siting industrial facilities even in the twenty-first century. Such thinking thus represents both a precursor to and a foundational component of environmental racism.[44]

In San Francisco, reactions to epidemics—disorderly nature in the form of disease—emphasize how Chinatown's status as racialized space facilitated containment and social control of its people. For example, in the 1875–76 smallpox epidemic, only sixty out of sixteen hundred victims were Chinese, but immigrants from China were subjected to examination and quarantine, while Chinatown residents had their homes fumigated, their sick isolated, and vaccination imposed on them.[45] In 1880 the Board of Health declared the neighborhood to be a sanitary nuisance and issued a resolution stating, "The Chinese cancer must be cut out of the heart of our city." The mayor and the Workingmen's Party of California backed health officials, but the proposal failed when the municipal administration deadlocked. Ten years later, the city government tried again to force the Chinese to relocate outside the city proper. This time the ordinance passed, but a federal district court declared it unconstitutional.[46]

The quarantines that would have been most immediate in the minds of San Franciscans, Chinese and white alike, in 1906 had occurred just a few years earlier in response to the first confirmed appearance of bubonic plague in the city. On March 6, 1900, a Chinese lumber salesman named Wong Chut King died in the basement of the Globe Hotel in the heart of Chinatown. Wong was forty-one years old and had lived in San Francisco for sixteen years. An autopsy and subsequent bacteriological tests revealed that he had died of the plague.[47] San Francisco quarantine officer Joseph J. Kinyoun imposed an immediate quarantine on Chinatown. Chinese residents noted that the cordons zigzagged around white-owned businesses on the edges of Chinatown, making it clear that the quarantine targeted them racially at least as much as marking off their neighborhood spatially. Police officers escorted white people out and forced Chinese people inside the lines. Trapped residents watched as sanitary officers burned Wong's clothing and bedding in the street and fumigated the Globe Hotel with sulfur. Chinese protests and legal actions succeeded in raising the quarantine after only sixty hours, but Kinyoun reinstated it on May 31. This time the restrictions lasted more than two weeks. Chinese workers lost their jobs, merchants lost income, and food shortages became significant. Health inspectors undertook a house-by-house survey of Chinatown and disinfected sewers and dwellings.[48]

In April 1901, with the number of human plague cases only increasing, state health authorities repeated their initial efforts at disinfection and fumigation of the Chinese district. A "flying squadron" of as many as 150 men cleaned more than a thousand buildings from basement to roof. Floors and walls were scrubbed and sprayed with a solution of bichloride of mercury, and in the words of the State Board of Health, "all the dark rooms, alleyways, and stairways were subjected to a coat of whitewash." Symbolically, and in terms of sanitation, Chinatown was being whitened. Such disinfecting activities were limited to the seventeen blocks of Chinatown, with reports emphasizing that it was never necessary to "invade" the adjacent white neighborhood.[49] Such traditional measures of disinfection were largely ineffective against the plague, and a 1904 campaign of structural change in Chinatown eventually halted the outbreak by rat-proofing the district (see chapter 6 for more details on this campaign). However, the city's reaction to the disease in 1900, particularly the quarantines, reflected Chinatown's status as racialized space, including targeting its population for invasive public health measures justified by a racialized understanding of disease.[50]

The presence of plague led to renewed calls to relocate Chinatown. In May 1900 the *San Francisco Call* actually urged that the neighborhood be burned—a threat that must have seemed very real to Chinese, who were well aware that a conflagration had destroyed Honolulu's Chinatown in the wake of a plague outbreak there.[51] In 1902, Mayor

Schmitz spoke out in favor of extending Chinese exclusion and declared that "their very presence is a pollution and a source of both physical and moral disease."[52] Such language had little downside for a politician in San Francisco and explicitly linked the Chinese presence to environmental hazards such as pollution. A year later, the State Board of Health explicitly called for "the removal of Chinatown from its present site in San Francisco to some outlying and isolated district." Rhetoric demanding relocation in these years emphasized "uncleanliness" and the sanitary hazard allegedly posed by the neighborhood and its residents. One article in the *San Francisco News Letter* cited the "filth and germs of disease" situated in Chinatown, declaring: "The Chinese now have one of the best parts of town, and they have forfeited their right to it by their habits of life." Some white merchants suggested that Hunter's Point, to the southeast of the city near the mouth of Islais Creek, represented the ideal isolated location for the Chinese and hatched a scheme to purchase Chinatown real estate and resettle the existing population.[53] Plans to relocate Chinatown had thus been circulating in the years before 1906, and they emphasized the unsanitary urban ecology of the neighborhood.

The residents of Chinatown did live in unsanitary conditions, but perceptions of Chinatown and the Chinese exaggerated the neighborhood's problems and ignored the role of discrimination in perpetuating crowded and dirty conditions. As the geographer Susan Craddock has observed, dirt was a "class-coded concept" at the turn of the century, and it was often racially coded as well.[54] In Chinatown in the early twentieth century, discriminatory housing practices led to twenty-five thousand people crowded into an area of only seventeen blocks. The Board of Health noted the poor conditions of the streets, sewers, and plumbing in the district—including the prevalence of open sewers and toilets "blocked by accumulation of human excrements"—but these conditions largely resulted from neglect by the city and landowners, the vast majority of whom were white.[55]

Many other working-class neighborhoods were little better, with waterways that resembled cesspools and sewers that were blocked up when they existed at all, but Chinatown represented an easy target for blame because of racial stereotypes and the social and political disempowerment of the Chinese. Sanitation campaigns during the

Progressive Era had a mixed record with regard to social and environmental justice. Sanitary improvements were much needed, and where
they contributed to real improvements in people's health—as the 1904
structural changes in Chinatown arguably did—they offered legitimate
environmental benefits. However, public health measures were imposed
on a disempowered population that was deeply suspicious of Western
medicine, often with good reason given the limitations of medical
knowledge and the unequal application of risky treatments. Health
reforms in these years thus fail any test for community participation
and often exacerbated some health risks in addressing others.[56] The
imposition of restrictive measures such as racially delimited quarantines and the prevalence of myths about the environment of Chinatown
alongside discriminatory measures to segregate the Chinese population reflected Chinatown's status as not only racialized space but also
space under regular threat of dispossession in early twentieth-century
San Francisco.

THE FIGHT OVER RELOCATION IN 1906

The destruction of Chinatown in 1906 provided new impetus for calls
for relocation, with the added twist that, in the eyes of white elites
greedy for real estate, the fire had removed both the structures and the
people that marked the racialized space of Chinatown as inferior terrain, highlighting instead the neighborhood's prime location adjacent
to downtown. The *Overland Monthly* called it "divine wisdom" that "fire
has reclaimed to civilization and cleanliness the Chinese ghetto." The
magazine added: "No Chinatown will be permitted in the borders of
the city." The site of Chinatown was a topic of discussion among the
Committee of Fifty as early as April 24, just three days after the last of
the flames were extinguished.[57]

This, even more than Burnham's proposed changes, seemed like an
issue on which the leading political factions in San Francisco could
agree. Mayor Schmitz, whose political backers in the labor movement
had a long history of anti-Chinese sentiment and organizing, supported
Hunter's Point as the new home for the city's Chinese population.
Phelan, who a few years later would run for the US Senate on a platform
opposing Asian immigration, agreed. One labor newspaper speculated

Ruins along Dupont Street. The sign directs patrons of Sing Fat & Co. to temporary offices in Oakland. Courtesy of the California Historical Society (CHS2016_2125).

that an "overwhelming majority" of San Franciscans would vote to locate Chinatown "on the Farollone [sic] Islands," not only outside of the city but exiled to a small rocky outcrop thirty miles from shore. Such a statement, although probably not meant literally, assigned almost no value to the Chinese quarter and its residents.[58] Mainstream newspapers also expressed support for relocation. In its early articles on the subject, the *Chronicle*'s language disassociated Chinatown from its physical space in the city. The term "Chinatown" referred to the dwindling band of refugees being shifted from one camp to another, suggesting the inevitability of relocation of the neighborhood and its people.[59]

The dispute over rebuilding Chinatown represented a contest over urban space and who would occupy prime real estate in the city. The most frequently mentioned alternate location, Hunter's Point or Bayview, lay at the city's southeastern corner along the shoreline. The area was largely undeveloped at the time, and it offered the scenic views so valued by Burnham. However, it was also home to noxious industries in the form of several tanneries, a small chemical factory, and Butchertown, the slaughterhouse district that had been exiled from more central locations. Proposals to relocate Chinatown thus implicitly equated the Chinese neighborhood with such undesirable elements of the urban environment, echoing the earlier attempts at relocation, including an 1890 ordinance that would have required all Chinese to move to areas of the city zoned for noxious industries. That ordinance passed but was overturned in the courts.[60] Bayview–Hunter's Point later became a predominantly African American community during and after World War II as well as a heavily polluted industrial district—site of a notorious PG&E power plant, a sewage facility, and a naval shipyard that would eventually be designated as a Superfund site—again demonstrating connections between race and exposure to environmental hazards in urban settings.[61]

Sentiments in favor of expelling the Chinese from the city were consistent with overall sentiments among white San Franciscans at the time. The early years of the twentieth century certainly had not seen a decline in racism toward people of Asian descent in California. In fact, discrimination and violence toward Chinese had sparked a boycott of US goods in China and across the Chinese diaspora in 1905. The boycott was in part a reaction to the beating and humiliation of Chinese diplomat Tan Jinyong in September 1903 by San Francisco police, among other incidents of official mistreatment. The historian Yong Chen has suggested that the widespread boycott, which originated in China, strengthened political and psychological ties between Chinese Americans and their country of origin.[62] In the United States, 1902 saw the permanent renewal of the Chinese Exclusion Act, and labor organizations in California pushed for the extension of exclusion to Japanese and Korean immigrants. Four years later the Japanese and Korean Exclusion League, which labor newspapers prominently supported, claimed a membership of more than seventy-eight thousand, mostly residents of San Francisco.[63]

Racial violence persisted as well. A delegation of scientists from Japan—among them the prominent seismologist Fusakichi Omori, who traveled to San Francisco to study the earthquake—had stones thrown at them, and nineteen cases of assaults against Japanese residents were reported in the aftermath of the earthquake and fire. Discrimination remained municipal policy as the San Francisco Board of Education moved to segregate Chinese, Japanese, and Korean schoolchildren; in October 1906 the board sparked a diplomatic incident when it ordered Japanese students to attend a separate Oriental Public School. President Theodore Roosevelt had to step in and negotiate a compromise between the offended Japanese government—which had sent $250,000 in aid to the city after the earthquake—and the Board of Education. According to the Gentlemen's Agreement of 1907, the city would cease its efforts to segregate Japanese schoolchildren and Japan would limit emigration of laborers to the United States.[64]

Thus the political climate in the city seemed to point to the real possibility that Chinatown could be expelled from its central city location. Yet, despite the array of white political support, this grand scheme for urban "improvement" was ultimately even less successful than that based on the Burnham Plan. Chinese ownership of property was not a major obstacle; although Chinese owned thirty-five lots, white landlords controlled at least 80 percent of the property in Chinatown— and they profited handsomely from charging high rents. The Chinese were well aware that these property owners represented crucial allies. An April 29 editorial in the Chinese newspaper *Chung Sai Yat Po* urged Chinese residents to contact their landlords and renew their leases. Both Chinese and white property owners in the district formed the Dupont Street Improvement Club to oppose relocation. They also pledged to construct a more sanitary Chinatown to alleviate some of the fears of white San Franciscans. Many landlords signed new leases with Chinese tenants in May 1906 in an apparent campaign to undermine relocation efforts, and they remained firmly in support of the return of the Chinese despite pressure to consider "the interests of the city at large," in the words of an *Examiner* editorial, above their individual financial interests. They were no doubt motivated primarily by profit, but they also had personal experience dealing with the Chinese as reliable tenants (as well as tenants who were not inclined to complain about property conditions).[65]

The most important group defending Chinatown was, not surprisingly, the Chinese themselves. Chow Tszchi, secretary of the Chinese Legation in Washington, arrived in the city on April 27 and promptly met with Mayor Schmitz and General Greely to represent the interests of Chinese refugees who were being repeatedly moved from one camp to another. Chow must have remained concerned, because two days later he and a delegation of Chinese officials, including Consul-General Chung Pao Hsi and an attorney, met with Governor Pardee. They secured a letter from the governor to San Francisco officials granting the Chinese the right to enter the burned district to return to China-town. Chinese officials publicly announced that the Chinese government owned the lot on Stockton Street where the consulate had stood and planned to rebuild. The statement directly referenced "the report that the authorities intend to remove Chinatown," declaring it counter to "a free country" where "every man has a right to occupy land which he owns." A week later, Chung and another official from the consulate joined Ruef for an unproductive tour of proposed new locations for Chinatown. It was during this tour that Chung raised the possibility of integration of Chinese and white San Franciscans, only to have Ruef reject the idea.[66]

The almost immediate involvement of representatives of the Chinese government in what would seem on the surface to be a local concern represented an unintended consequence of exclusion. Because the Chinese had been prevented from becoming naturalized American citizens, they remained subjects of the Chinese government. Racial tensions, political developments in China, and the 1905 boycott had strengthened those ties, and they gave San Francisco's Chinese population powerful allies that other disadvantaged populations did not possess to the same degree. The long history of discrimination and violence against Chinese in the American West had primed Chinese officials to come to the defense of immigrants in a moment of crisis. Those crises in the past had most often been precipitated by economic circumstances, but the destruction of San Francisco by earthquake and fire represented a new and dramatic crisis that mobilized international support for the city's Chinese residents. San Francisco's Chinatown was also the hub of Chinese America—the entrepôt through which goods, services, information, and even people passed between the mainland and the United States—so losing Chinatown would represent the loss of the capital of the entire Chinese American community.[67]

In addition to diplomatic allies, the Chinese possessed economic leverage. Even in the earliest days after the earthquake, when the proposal to relocate Chinatown first surfaced, the white attorney and politician Gavin McNab expressed concern that San Francisco would lose the property taxes of the Chinese if they were moved south of the border of the city and county. In subsequent meetings, Chinese representatives made it clear that San Francisco's preeminent place in trade with China was in jeopardy if city leaders forced relocation. During the May 4 tour with Chinese officials, Ruef reported being informed that "many of the Chinese merchants had canceled orders for goods, with the expectation of leaving San Francisco permanently."[68] The threat to redirect trade to other Pacific Coast ports such as Los Angeles, Portland, Seattle, or even Oakland reinforced fears among San Francisco's economic and political leadership that their city was losing its preeminent place among western cities—a fear that the earthquake and fire had only enhanced. Chinatown also represented a popular tourist attraction for the city, another source of revenue and status that businessmen were reluctant to lose. Chinese merchants paid one-third of the import duties in the city before the earthquake, and white property owners noted that business in Chinatown had brought thirty million dollars to the city in the preceding year.[69] Thus, despite the poverty and low wages of most individual Chinese people in San Francisco, the district held important places in commerce and tourism, and its defenders were savvy enough to exploit that economic value.

By late May, wealthy Chinese merchants were following the lead of the consulate and publicly stating their intentions to rebuild. Sing Fat explicitly asserted the affinity between the Chinese and other San Francisco residents, using the shared experience of disaster as a source of common ground: "The earthquake and fire treated all alike. We are going back to our own, just as other property owners are." He expressed his commitment to "a new and greater San Francisco" and described his plans to "endeavor to build up a new and greater Chinatown," language that echoed that of supporters of the Burnham Plan and other proposals to improve the city in the wake of the disaster. Although Sing Fat's words conveyed a sense of shared community among all city residents, the same article expressed more combative views as well when it stated that Chinese firms would "fight to the last ditch if any attempt is made by the municipality to move them from the quarter."[70]

During these weeks Telegraph Hill—the center of the city's Italian community and, as such, the home of another racially stigmatized group in early twentieth-century San Francisco—surfaced as another possible location for Chinatown. When this news became public, residents formed the Telegraph Hill Protective Association and resolved to oppose any move to locate Chinatown in their neighborhood. Defenders compared the effort to previous fights against the quarrying of the hill. "I fought years ago for the preservation of Telegraph Hill against the greed of contractors who would have leveled it with dynamite and steam shovels. I'll fight again to preserve it against possession by the Chinese," declared Rev. Father Carraher, a leader of the campaign. The comparison between the threat of the literal physical destruction of the hill and the settlement of the Chinese in the neighborhood demonstrated the close connection in the minds of San Franciscans between physical and social space in the city. Telegraph Hill was a physical space under threat of demolition by quarrying, but it was also a neighborhood with a particular social and cultural character that could be similarly threatened by a change in the ethnicity of residents.

This reaction of course also revealed the limitations of possible alliances across ethnic lines. Carraher asserted his support for the City Beautiful vision as part of his argument against the Chinese, calling on prevailing racial stereotypes in the process. "What do the Chinese care about broad streets?" he asked. "What do they care about boulevards and parks?" He suggested that Chinese preferred "a dark street, a narrow street or alley or a subterranean passage, a hole below ground."[71] In calling up mythic images of Chinatown as a dark place filled with subterranean passages—even after the fire had thoroughly disproven rumors of the existence of such passages—Carraher sought to form political alliances by juxtaposing the City Beautiful vision of a new San Francisco of wide streets and open park space with the congested, sunless environment of the Chinese quarter, which he implied to be the natural environment of Chinese people.

Ultimately, the alliance of Chinese political leaders, Chinatown merchants, and white landlords proved more powerful than racial fears and stereotypes. As with the defeat of the Burnham Plan, the status quo held and Chinatown maintained its long-standing location in central San Francisco. Ruef's committee on the Permanent Location of Chinatown disbanded in early July, a concession that the Chinese and their allies had won. Some changes did take place during the rebuilding, however. Streets were widened and connected to other main streets in the downtown district, removing some of the idiosyncrasies of the street layout, and new construction generally followed the city's sanitary regulations regarding provision for air and light. Contrary to a May 12 letter to the *Examiner* declaring that "the Chinese will not live where there are wide streets," such changes in the urban environment did not drive out Chinatown's residents.[72]

Both Chinese merchants and white landowners rebuilt not only with sanitation in mind but also with attracting tourists as a major consideration. The San Francisco Real Estate Board suggested that all buildings in the district should be constructed in "imitation oriental" style, and architects generally followed a version of that decree, employing ornamentation such as tiered pagoda towers, fringe-tile roofs, dragon decorations, and bright color schemes over multistory, steel-framed structures. As a whole, the new Chinatown had a more "oriental" appearance than the pre-fire neighborhood, although that character consisted largely of ornamental façades. Look Tin Eli, the manager of the Sing Chong Bazaar, enthusiastically declared it "so much more beautiful, artistic, and so much more emphatically Oriental" than pre-fire Chinatown. Yet this new Chinatown had its modern elements as well. Eli contrasted the view of the district on "any bright, sunny day" with night and "the wonderful transformation when the hundreds of thousands of electric lights bathe the streets and façades of the wildly fantastic buildings in a blaze of glory."[73] The splendors of the reconstructed Chinatown included both a sanitized traditional appeal and modern features like electric lights.

Tourism only increased, although nostalgia for the seemingly more authentic predisaster Chinatown developed as well. An advertisement in a 1909 pamphlet for tourists promoted "Chinatown—Dug From the Ruins," featuring an "original refugee house . . . filled with relics of the most scientific nature, the fruit of the earthquake and fire." This language echoed both disaster tourism and the well-to-do looters digging

Postcard of "New Chinatown" showing California Street after the rebuilding. Note the elaborate "Oriental" pagoda towers and wide street. Courtesy of the California Historical Society (CHS2016_2131).

through the actual ruins of Chinatown three years earlier in search of what they saw as exotic relics—and ignoring the property rights of the Chinese in the process.[74] Tourism around both Chinese "exoticism" and disaster reflected a quest for authentic experience as a counterpoint to the attractions and promises of modernity. This quest for authenticity through Chinatown tourism traced back to the 1880s and only increased after the earthquake, even as the district's residents more consciously exploited the desires and pocketbooks of tourists.

Arnold Genthe published his famous photographs of old Chinatown in 1908 and 1913. The timing was partly instrumental; most of Genthe's collection of negatives burned in the fire, and the old Chinatown images were the only ones to survive, thanks to a prophetic warning by his friend Will Irwin that the city "could burn down at any time." But the perception by Genthe and his publishers that a market existed for publication of images of old Chinatown reflected nostalgia for the predisaster city, including an enclave seen as the repository of an exotic culture. In preparing his photos for publication, Genthe excised signs of the integration of the Chinese and white communities in San Francisco, cropping or scratching out non-Chinese figures and English-language signs. The result portrayed an artificial distance between Chinatown and the rest of the city, a distance that seemed to be closing with the modernization of the Chinese quarter after the earthquake but that also remained integral to its appeal to tourists.[75]

Paradoxically, as tourism capitalizing on a stereotypical orientalism increased after the earthquake and fire, San Francisco's Chinese community downplayed traditional practices such as gambling, opium smoking, queues, and foot-binding in pursuit of greater cultural integration and racial equality. The San Francisco journalist and photographer Louis Stellman declared the 1906 fire "perhaps the most powerful westernizing agency [sic] ever applied to the Chinese." To Stellman, writing in 1913 or 1914, the fire had destroyed a "wall" separating the Chinese and white populations of the city.[76] The Chinese accepted the profit potential of tourism emphasizing exotic differences even as they pursued a vision for the city more in tune with Chung Pao Hsi's call for racial integration that Abe Ruef had summarily rejected. Shops in Chinatown shifted from serving primarily the local Chinese community to offering goods intended to appeal to tourists.[77] More famously, many Chinese men took advantage of the destruction of records in the fire to claim US birth and additional "paper sons" and "paper daughters" when they applied for new documents. These efforts to get around the restrictions of the Chinese Exclusion Act and to eliminate some of the distinct practices that had helped keep Chinese outside the American mainstream reflected Chinese residents' desire to claim membership in the broader community. Just as they had fought to retain their neighborhood in the heart of San Francisco, they sought to remain the integral part of the city that they had been for decades.

CONCLUSION

Contrary to the widespread belief that San Francisco after the earthquake and fire represented a blank slate for "improvements," the disaster-stricken city proved to be a difficult place in which to implement reforms. Not even the presence of a blueprint such as the Burnham Plan or an apparent consensus among the city's political classes as with the relocation of Chinatown proved sufficient to impose dramatic changes on the broader populace. The politics of place proved more complicated than the proponents of a tabula rasa had anticipated—whether they took the form of an alliance between the Chinese and their white landlords or the protests of small property owners who wanted to rebuild as quickly as possible even if it meant rejecting wide boulevards and re-creating a wooden city. The ambitions of planners, engineers, and politicians like Burnham, Phelan, Manson, and Ruef encountered messy urban politics and people's attachment to the old city. Reshaping the urban environment—whether through the scenic parks of the Burnham Plan or by expelling Chinatown—proved no easier when the city lay in ruins. Creative destruction might make room for new skyscrapers, but small merchants and homeowners clung tenaciously to their more modest plans for reconstruction.

The Chinese victory over relocation reflected the successful defense of urban space transformed from inferior to valuable by the devastation of the earthquake and fire. The attempt to relocate the racialized space of Chinatown to more marginal real estate such as Hunter's Point represented an attempted dispossession, one that the Chinese resisted through both international and local alliances, an unexpected assertion of power under conditions of vulnerability. In 1906, San Francisco's Chinese escaped relegation to an environment dominated by noxious industries, an example of avoiding the worst conditions of environmental inequality. The language of the debate, however, reveals the prevalence of environmental racism among white San Franciscans, who perceived the city's Chinese population as belonging in a polluted and isolated landscape. The Chinese avoidance of such a fate stemmed from their own initiative and their ability to leverage economic and diplomatic alliances. However, the failure of their tentative challenge to racial segregation reflected the limits of that power and the sometimes mixed role of racialized space, which could be a means of containment and social control but also a base of economic and cultural power for a marginalized community.

For the Chinese the politics of place meant a rejection of the bayside views and noxious industries of Hunter's Point in favor of the crowded, central district that was their home. The failed attempt to relocate Chinatown, like the failure to implement Daniel H. Burnham's expansive vision, showed the difficulty of transforming urban space in the context of disaster. Rather than being a blank slate, the devastated city remained a complex matrix of property and power relations in which people often mobilized around the need to restore the city rather than transform it. Visions of the city as it had been remained powerful in the minds of San Franciscans of diverse backgrounds even as buildings lay in ruins.

politics of place
racialization/segregation

FIVE

DISASTER CAPITALISM IN THE STREETS

ON MAY 5, 1907, SAN FRANCISCO'S STREET CARMEN WALKED OUT ON the job, shutting down the majority of the city's street railways. It might seem an odd time for a strike, with the city still struggling to rebuild barely a year after the earthquake and fire, but the strike represented the latest chapter in years of conflict between the Carmen's Union and the United Railroads, the largest of San Francisco's street railway companies. Patrick C. Calhoun, president of the United Railroads, had teams of armed strikebreakers ready to operate the cars, and violence broke out almost immediately. A gun battle on May 7—thereafter known as Bloody Tuesday—claimed two victims and left at least twenty wounded. San Franciscans feared that tragic day would set the tone for an unprecedently bitter struggle between labor and capital. As detailed in chapter 3, the aftermath of the earthquake and fire had stoked the anger of many members of San Francisco's working classes, who faced an increased cost of living and limited employment opportunities and who questioned the distribution of relief money. For his part, Calhoun was determined to break the Carmen's Union, and he believed that political and economic circumstances in 1907 would allow him to do just that.

The so-called natural disaster of the earthquake and fire might at first appear to have little in common with the strike that shut down San

Francisco's street railways the following spring. However, in a 1913 study of the city's transit system, the electrical engineer and mass transit expert Bion J. Arnold linked them as "the two great catastrophes" that had befallen transportation in San Francisco. Of the two, he considered the strike to have had the greater impact, citing declines in both ridership and earnings, proxies for the normal functioning of the city's capitalist economy and spatial order.[1] For many San Franciscans the economic crisis known as the Panic of 1907 represented a third catastrophe in these two years, one that threatened personal well-being and the city's recovery from the earthquake and fire. Rather than being three distinct and unrelated catastrophes, these three crises were interwined, and each possessed environmental, economic, and cultural components. The connections between these crises from seemingly disparate areas of urban life illustrate the impossibility of separating environmental events such as the 1906 earthquake from their broad social and economic contexts.

Most of this story takes place in an oft-neglected part of the urban environment—San Francisco's dusty, broken, chaotic streets. If Daniel H. Burnham's grand, scenic "view from atop the hill" represents one perspective on San Francisco's urban environment and one vision for the city, another perspective stays on the ground amid the rubble through which San Franciscans labored at rebuilding their lives and their city. This, too, is the ground of environmental history.[2] This chapter focuses on embodied experiences of work and mobility in the modern city. The carmen produced transportation for other San Franciscans through their labor, and in doing so, they reshaped others' experiences of both the built environment and nonhuman nature. Their labor allowed passengers to ride the streetcars rather than walk the city's steep hills, avoiding much of its wind, dust, and rain in the process. Their labor also transformed distances, effectively shrinking the city and making suburban living possible.[3] As such, transit infrastructure and the labor that made it work were central to the urban ecology of the modern city and mediated San Franciscans' experiences of the environment in which they lived.

As with so many other aspects of urban life, the earthquake and fire disrupted this system by shutting down the trains and damaging all components of the city's transportation infrastructure—from the streets themselves to the streetcar tracks and the power plants that provided electricity. The carmen navigated challenging new working conditions in a city filled with debris, and they also lived the disaster's disruption of social and economic relations, particularly its exacerbation of inequality. The carmen's demands for higher pay and shorter hours reflected both the specific circumstances in San Francisco after the earthquake and fire and a broader context of class conflict. The streetcar strike took place in an era of ongoing conflict between labor and capital from the 1870s to World War I, a time of near "class warfare," to borrow a phrase used more than once by San Franciscans in these years. These labor conflicts reflected the unsettled state of the American economy under relatively unregulated industrial capitalism. Most Americans faced uncertain working conditions, and recurrent economic crises buffeted the country. Although we will hear from Calhoun and other members of San Francisco's elites, this chapter focuses on the perspective of the strikers and other ordinary San Franciscans as they negotiated the complications of life in the postdisaster city—a place marked by both environmental and economic disruption and chaos.

In this context of industrial conflict, San Franciscans openly debated ideas now labeled disaster capitalism. Disaster capitalism suggests that the reshaping of urban space benefits a capitalist economy, and natural disasters that annihilate the built environment thus represent more opportunity than crisis. Scholars and public intellectuals have analyzed disaster capitalism as a phenomenon of the late twentieth century and twenty-first century in which disasters have sparked privatization efforts and uneven redevelopment, but in San Francisco in 1906, residents debated questions of disaster capitalism in a very different political, cultural, and even environmental context.[4] Private control was more broadly contested, and corporations like the United Railroads faced a number of voices calling for public ownership of essential infrastructure such as street railroads. Infrastructure systems—from roads and railways to water pipes and sewers—shape how urban residents interact with the natural world, and the disruption of infrastructure by the earthquake and fire opened space for both retrenchment and rethinking of urban ecology, including debates over who should control such systems.[5]

For organized labor as a whole, the city in ruins initially promised a chance to reassert the centrality of labor to urban life. The city, they suggested, could not be rebuilt without the calloused hands, strong bodies, and practical skills of working men. Such a narrative challenged the dominance of capital and the widespread focus on the financial side of rebuilding. It asserted the agency of workers, and it emphasized a down-to-earth vision of the city as a place of labor and the home of working people. Similarly, the carmen sought to leverage their essential role as the operators of transit in the city, facilitators of its daily economic functioning and the spatial integration of its diverse neighborhoods, with their strike. Such arguments—and the streetcar strike itself—challenged the preeminence and power of capital in building, rebuilding, and maintaining the city. However, the striking workers encountered political as well as environmental and economic turmoil in San Francisco in 1907 and 1908.

Resource flows facilitated rebuilding by bringing lumber, labor, and capital to the city in the wake of the earthquake, but those environmental and economic connections also contributed to the economic downturn that interrupted the city's recovery in 1907. The San Francisco earthquake and fire triggered that recession, which affected not only San Francisco but the entire nation. In the twenty-first century, one of the fears associated with major disasters, particularly those that threaten large cities, is that they could trigger global financial collapse by disrupting investment markets and bankrupting the international insurance system. Such a fear is, unfortunately, supported by events in 1906 when, even with a less connected world, the financial effects of the earthquake and fire in San Francisco reverberated to London and back, undermining the carmen's strike in the process.[6]

THE ENVIRONMENT OF THE STREETS

In the days, weeks, and months after the earthquake, residents of San Francisco complained about the condition of its streets and transportation infrastructure. In the words of one observer, the earthquake and fire had left the city's streetcar system "with miles of twisted road warped by fire," other sections "sunken and out of line" from the shaking, and "miles of overhead wires and poles in ruins."[7] The fire burned

Damaged streetcar rails and pavement, Howard Street at Fourteenth. Courtesy of the California Historical Society (CHS2016_2122).

pavements of all kinds so badly that they proved unsalvageable, and the force of the earthquake threw basalt blocks and cobblestones out of alignment. In the areas most strongly affected by shaking, streets buckled and sank, and buried pipes for water, gas, and sewer systems were torn apart. Fallen bricks, tangled wire, and twisted iron pipes blocked the streets for months.

Constant construction and teaming activity perpetuated a disorderly urban environment even with rebuilding fully under way. In August 1906, Sister Eugenia Garvey of St. Vincent's School in the South of Market district described the "clouds of lime dust" that "almost blind us everyday as we stand on the corner of the streets awaiting the [street] cars which run most irregularly." The next July, more than fourteen months after the last of the fires was extinguished, merchant Paul Verdier complained that his "clientele would not come shopping in the dusty district" because their gowns would be ruined.[8] Verdier described a city in which economic conditions may have been returning to

Street scene during reconstruction, showing debris being cleared at the site of the Hearst Building at Third, Kearny, and Market Streets, 1906. Courtesy of the California Historical Society (CHS2017_2264).

normal, but the environment remained disrupted. Reported "clouds of dirt in the down town streets" stemmed from both destruction and rebuilding as well as more routine sources such as manure from urban horses and, in some areas, the sand that had been a scourge of the city since its founding. Specific environmental conditions in San Francisco worsened the dust problem, particularly the lack of rainfall in the summers and the near-constant winds. In late September 1907, the editor of *Western World* complained about the "disgracefully dangerous" streets and "hideous public ruins, that spell 'earthquake' to every stranger."[9] Clearly, the reconstruction of San Francisco still had a long way to go, and the reality of the rebuilding process must have seemed far removed from rhetoric of the City Beautiful.

Streets are a part of the urban environment often ignored by historians, but they were a crucial space of daily life in early twentieth-century cities. In the spread-out cities and suburbs of the twenty-first-century United States, most streets serve only as transportation arteries, but in

San Francisco in 1906 streets were spaces of business and commerce in which male and female pedestrians crossed paths with street railroad cars, horse-drawn conveyances, men on horseback, and even a few automobiles and bicycles. Working-class domestic and social life spilled out into the streets by a mixture of choice and necessity. The streets were a place to hang laundry and gossip with neighbors and, often, a place that had to be traversed for such daily tasks as obtaining water or using a privy.[10] The disaster broadened these uses of the streets. Street kitchens became widespread during the months when residents were forbidden to use chimneys because of the risk of fire. People forced to live in confined spaces in refugee camps relied on common areas as extensions of their homes, and even families who could afford houses often lived in crowded conditions that more closely resembled the pre-earthquake residence patterns of the poor than those of the Victorian middle class. And, as Verdier's concerns about the "dusty district" remind us, moving through the city's streets inevitably required at least some degree of exposure to the elements, whether wind, rain, or dust, even if upper- and middle-class people expected the modern city to minimize that exposure in the name of comfort and civilization.

Residents were forcibly reminded of their city's inconvenient hills when the earthquake and fire disrupted transit service, and ordinary San Franciscans found themselves with few alternatives to walking the city. The destruction of central neighborhoods in the fire also forced people to relocate to more distant locations. One labor newspaper went so far as to declare that: "Since the fire, the city has become more hilly than ever. That is to say, the people have been scattered over the hills in search of homes."[11] Statistics supported this claim. A 1913 study found that sixty-six thousand people had relocated from the central city—referred to as the "walking district"—to more distant neighborhoods after the 1906 disaster. In the process they had become "dependent on [street]car service." Settlement of those outlying districts had been delayed because of the hills separating them from central San Francisco and the limited availability of transit.[12] The earthquake and fire forced San Franciscans into more direct encounters with nonhuman nature as they experienced the city as "more hilly" when its topography had not, of course, changed. Even simple things like being forced to seek housing in distant neighborhoods rather than in the flatter areas of the central district could dramatically affect peoples' experiences of daily life.

Different residents encountered the streets in different ways. For most people, of course, the streets were transit corridors of one kind or another. Many San Franciscans navigated the city's streets on a daily basis, whether they were trudging the hills on foot, trotting on horseback, clinging to crowded streetcars, or speeding around in the pricey new automobiles that were all the rage in San Francisco after the earthquake. For many, local streets and alleys also served as extensions of domestic space. But for some San Franciscans, the streets represented a different kind of space—their workplace. For teamsters, draymen, and the carmen who operated the street railways, among others, the chaotic environment of the streets was where they worked long hours, often ten- or eleven-hour days of negotiating not only the built environment of pavements and train tracks but also the natural environment of wind, dust, rain, and hills.

The historian Thomas Andrews defines a workscape as a dynamic environment "shaped by the interplay of human labor and natural processes." Workscapes involve land, air, water, and bodies of all kinds (human and otherwise), but they involve a cultural element as well, as people use language and other available symbols and ideologies to make sense of the world around them.[13] The streets of a bustling city like San Francisco were not exactly like the workscapes that Andrews describes in the Colorado mines—for one thing, few people spent time in the mines unless they were employed there—but the concept helps illuminate the complexity of relationships in the streetscape. The streets were a place where human labor encountered nonhuman nature on a daily basis, and debates about control of and access to the streets invoked cultural contexts, both local and national. San Francisco's streets were also, like Colorado's mines, a place where workers organized repeatedly in the early twentieth century to improve the conditions of their labor. Understanding the demands and motivations of the striking carmen, as well as understanding the various responses of other San Franciscans, requires that we consider the streets as both work environment and transportation environment, as a place where people encountered nature and each other within a complex matrix of environmental, economic, and cultural factors. The disruption of the earthquake, fire, and rebuilding highlighted those intersections and helped make the streets into contested terrain in which people fought for control of the urban environment in 1907 and 1908.

TRANSIT IN THE LABOR CITY

San Franciscans in 1906 were highly dependent on public transit for getting around their "city of hills." By that time, electric streetcars had largely supplanted San Francisco's famous cable cars. Streetcars facilitated the geographic expansion of the city as workers relied on the system for travel between homes in outlying neighborhoods and jobs in the city center, and the carmen's labor—with the aid of the United Railroads' electrical plants—produced the transportation relied on by many San Franciscans. The expertise and physical labor of the carmen navigated streetcars up and down the hills and managed the experiences of riders of diverse classes and genders. San Francisco had almost three hundred miles of transit tracks in 1906, and passenger trips totaled approximately eighteen million per month in a city of four hundred thousand people.[14]

Public transit arrived early to San Francisco. Regular ferry service across the bay to Oakland began in the early 1850s, and horse-drawn omnibuses began operating in 1852. Horse-drawn streetcars were introduced eleven years later, and by 1870 a network of streetcar lines linked most parts of the city.[15] Most of the city's streets were laid out in a grid pattern that ignored topography in favor of regularity on a map, and this lack of concern with the natural contours of the hills—seen by Burnham as a failure to exploit scenic potential—created streets with impractically steep grades. In fact, the challenges peculiar to San Francisco's site motivated the invention of a city icon, the cable car. Horses struggled to pull cars up the steepest hills, particularly with the unreliable braking systems of the mid-nineteenth century, and a horse that lost its footing could be dragged back down the hill by a car loaded with passengers. Cable cars used technology from California's mines to open up the hills to settlement beginning in 1873.[16] Labor disputes went hand-in-hand with the expansion of transit in the city, with the first streetcar strike taking place in January 1874. Four years later, the legislature fixed fares at five cents, which remained the universal fare almost thirty years later in 1906.[17] The first electric trolley in San Francisco began running in 1891, and despite resistance from cable car companies, electric lines quickly began to replace both horse and cable cars. By 1906 only twenty horse cars remained, and cable cars had declined from more than a thousand to approximately two hundred.[18]

In 1901 and 1902 an Eastern-owned corporation headed by Patrick Calhoun (grandson of John C. Calhoun of South Carolina) purchased the Market Street Railway and three smaller lines and renamed them the United Railroads. The company immediately became the dominant presence in San Francisco's transportation sector. It also found itself embroiled in labor disputes. Employees had organized the Carmen's Union in 1901, and the next year they struck with broad public support and won the ten-hour day—down from eleven-and-a-half hours—while retaining a daily wage of $2.50.[19] The carmen's success reflected the broader context of relations between labor and capital in San Francisco in the first years of the new century when a booming economy encouraged a surge of union activity. The number of unions in San Francisco increased from ninety in 1900 to 162 by 1902, with a total membership of roughly forty thousand men and women.[20]

Sharp class conflict engulfed San Francisco in 1901, with fifteen thousand workers out on strike or locked out, and industrial conditions contributed to the success of the new Union Labor Party in local elections that year. Although then-mayor James D. Phelan had been elected as a friend of labor, his support of employers proved a bitter disappointment for workers. The city's polarization demonstrated the need for a stronger voice for labor in municipal politics. Andrew Furuseth of the Sailors' Union, abandoning long-standing nonpartisanship, declared, "I found that we had a class government already and inasmuch as we are going to have a class government, I most emphatically prefer a working-class government." The new party's first candidate for mayor, Eugene L. Schmitz, won election by a plurality in November of that year, further cementing San Francisco's reputation as the "labor city."[21] By 1904, not only did labor interests control the municipal government but one-third of San Francisco's workforce belonged to unions—three times the national average.[22]

The young Carmen's Union thus formed at a moment when organized labor's power was peaking in San Francisco, both in the workplace and in the realm of politics. In 1903 the carmen again sought higher wages, arguing that the cost of living had increased and their wages were substandard. The United Railroads countered by pointing out that carmen in the city were already being paid more than anywhere else in the country except the mining town of Butte, Montana. The dispute went to arbitration, and in the hearing Tirey L. Ford, general counsel for the United Railroads, attempted to portray the carmen as well paid by citing their desire to consume fresh produce. According to Ford, by complaining that they could not afford tomatoes and green peppers, the carmen "unwittingly disclosed extravagant habits of living" since these vegetables were "a dish for millionaires" in the spring. The company and its witnesses also argued that thousands of idle men in San Francisco would be happy to be employed by the railway at existing wages, and they declared that the working conditions of the carmen were generally pleasant and comfortable. Climatic conditions in San Francisco, they claimed, were favorable year-round, and carmen did not face the seasonal unemployment endemic to many trades.[23] These arguments show how environmental factors—ranging from food choices to weather—were integral to perceptions of urban labor.

These arguments also reflected both economic realities and ideological debates in which workers demanded wages that would allow them to maintain the "American standard of living" and support their families in reasonable comfort. The line between "skilled" laborers such as the carmen and "unskilled" laborers was fluid, and slight changes in economic, environmental, or personal circumstances—such as a recession, a bad winter, or a health problem—could drive working-class people from stability into transience. In the case of the carmen, at the time of the 1907 strike, 65 percent of the platform men had been with the company for two years or less, a statistic that suggests the instability of their lives.[24] Debates about wages and working conditions therefore played out in this context of uncertainty and anxiety as workers sought to improve their situations while companies attempted to maximize profits. The new owners of the United Railroads had paid an inflated price for the company and promptly watered down the stock, so they almost certainly felt pressure to keep costs down in order to maintain the company's earnings.[25]

In 1904, Mayor Schmitz brokered a deal between the Carmen's Union and the United Railroads that narrowly averted another strike, and a contract signed the next year further increased wages, creating a graduated scale from 25 cents per hour to 27.5 cents per hour. This contract took effect May 1, 1905, and was to remain in place for two years.[26] Of course, in the meantime, the earthquake and fire shocked everyone in the city and dramatically altered the urban environment and with it the conditions of labor for the carmen. The 1907 dispute between the carmen and the United Railroads called on many of the same arguments as labor conflicts earlier in the decade, and it integrated the effects of the catastrophe into existing debates. Politics came into play as well. The Union Labor administration was undeniably corrupt, but between 1902 and 1906, Schmitz and Abe Ruef, the party's behind the scenes "boss," had managed to mediate between labor and capital in San Francisco, restraining both sides and preventing the city from being torn apart.[27]

When the earthquake brought streetcar service to an abrupt halt, it only intensified and highlighted the issues facing San Francisco's transit system. Even before the earthquake, articles appeared in the *San Francisco Examiner* almost daily discussing the condition of the streets, the need for expansion of the street railway system, the (poor) quality of service, and the advantages of municipal ownership. Then the earthquake and fire damaged not only the United Railroads' network of tracks but also its power plants. The company acted quickly to get some lines up and running, spending as much as twelve thousand dollars a day. In the heart of the burned district, cars were running on Market Street within ten days after the earthquake, and twenty-seven lines were back in operation by July 21.[28]

The United Railroads exploited the crisis to gain municipal approval for the installation of overhead trolley lines. Overhead lines represented the quickest and cheapest way to restore service, but many San Franciscans opposed them on aesthetic grounds, calling them a blight on the city's streets. The potential dangers of overhead electrical wires had also been a concern since the introduction of the electric trolley in the early 1890s, and cable car companies had fueled those fears to undermine a competing technology. For two years the United Railroads had been locked in a dispute with property owners and proponents of beautification, such as James D. Phelan and Rudolph Spreckels. Opponents of overhead lines wanted the company to install underground conduits for its electrical wires, which were much more expensive but would leave the streets free of unsightly and potentially hazardous overhead wires.[29] In the aftermath of the fire the United Railroads took advantage of pressure to restore service as quickly as possible and executed an end run around the opponents of overhead lines, bribing the mayor and Board of Supervisors to obtain a permit to rebuild with overhead trolley lines.[30] This strategy was reminiscent of later disaster capitalism described by Naomi Klein, among others, in which private companies use crisis conditions to implement controversial policies.[31] In 1906 the political controversy around this incident would come to a head with the graft investigations of Mayor Schmitz and the supervisors beginning in October.

The destruction of preexisting infrastructure allowed the United Railroads to convert much of the mishmash of transit systems that it had inherited into uniform electric trolley lines. This could represent a positive example of disaster capitalism, with its exploitation of damage to update infrastructure, but local residents perceived few benefits. Calhoun boasted that 91 percent of the company's mileage was back in operation eight months after the disaster, but in the fall of 1906, San Francisco residents were still complaining about the slow process of restoration. In December, Annie Haskell wrote in her diary: "Oh, I have no language to express myself about the cars. I waited in a pouring rain for a half hour for the Castro, and not one came. Then I took the Valencia, stood up and walked up the hill in the mud."[32] Haskell's words reinforce the experience of unruly nature—the pouring rain, mud, and hills—in urban San Francisco as well as the ways in which streetcar travel could mitigate that experience, or fail to fulfill its promise to do so, particularly for working-class people like Haskell. A year later, even supporters of the United Railroads asked, "What, pray, could be worse than the service of the electric cars these days?" One described San Francisco's transportation facilities after the earthquake as "the worst in America," with "rattle-trap cars" that were "dangerous and uncomfortable."[33] Overcrowding and delays were rampant, and not until 1910 did the company manage to fully restore its track mileage to pre-earthquake levels.[34]

Carmen gathered around a streetcar for the first ride after the earthquake and fire. Mayor Eugene Schmitz is driving. Courtesy of the San Francisco History Center, San Francisco Public Library.

Before returning to the seemingly political topics of strikes and bribes, it is important to think further about the cultural associations that San Franciscans had with street railways in the early twentieth century. What made the transit system such a central issue in local politics? In addition to daily encounters with the urban environment while waiting for and riding streetcars, people had daily and personal interactions with one of the city's most prominent and controversial corporations through the street railway system. In his 1913 report Arnold described how "there exists in the street railway business an exceedingly intimate point of contact between the corporation and the patron—the street car." As representatives of the company and producers of transportation, trainmen brought an "additional human element" that became part of the perceived "personality" of the corporation. Patrons also directly encountered the company's physical property in the form of cars and tracks, fixtures of the urban environment and essential infrastructure for mobility.[35]

A 1909 article in *Organized Labor* conveyed the frustration of working people like Annie Haskell who relied on an overcrowded street railway system. It described men and women alike waiting on the street corner "seeing car after car, packed and jammed, pass by, before there is one with even standing room."[36] Although *Organized Labor* appealed to union members as its readers, such frustrations were hardly class-specific—although the most crowded lines were generally those leading to the rapidly expanding working-class residential districts. Arnold contrasted the street railway business with other utilities, but in an age when business was not yet as impersonal and global as it is in the twenty-first century, such visible, direct corporate contact was less common than we might think.

The railroad as the symbol of corporate reach and corruption was also a staple of Gilded Age political rhetoric, which portrayed the railroad as an octopus with its tendrils reaching into all parts of American life. In a study of the Great Railroad Strike of 1877, the historian David Stowell argues that many people saw the railroad as a symbolic and physical manifestation of the encroachment of capitalist industrialization. Railroads brought disorder and danger to American cities in the form of noise, smoke, and the very real hazard of accidents, threatening other uses of the streets ranging from walking to play. Stowell emphasizes the street as a contested space and refers to the Great Strike as a "spontaneous rebellion against that invasion of the people's streets" as well as a reaction to specific workplace grievances.[37]

By the early twentieth century, Americans were far more used to the railroad than in 1877, and the electric street railway system represented less of a nuisance to urban residents. However, frustrations similar to those from thirty years earlier persisted. Accidents still happened, particularly in the chaos of narrow city streets. *Organized Labor* was undoubtedly overdramatic when it referred to "the carnival of death, for which the United Railroads has become famous" and "the victims ground under the blood-thirsty wheels of the traction company, from the little boy to the aged father," but such language reveals, at a minimum, a concern for the safety of San Francisco's streets. One article reported that eighty-three people had been killed by streetcars in San Francisco in 1908 alone.[38] Reports on the conditions of the streets and transit system reveal other safety and traffic flow concerns. Horse-drawn vehicles would "ride the rails" of the street railways, and a broken axle or fallen horse could thus block an entire transit line. South of Market resident Thomas A. Maloney remembered teamsters deliberately stopping on the tracks at one steep grade to get a push over the hump from the streetcar. Street sweepers worried about being run down by teamsters and other drivers who failed to see them. On some of the steepest hills in the city, insufficient brakes and poorly designed switches left passengers' lives "continually in danger."[39] And the railways could still represent a nuisance as well as a hazard, as the controversy concerning overhead trolley lines indicates. Finally, as the labor history of San Francisco—and indeed the entire nation—attests, the first decade of the twentieth century remained a period when many Americans contested the premises of industrial capitalism and organized to mitigate its inequalities or even promote alternative economic systems.

In an essay on streetcar strikes written in 1888 and republished in San Francisco in 1907, the lawyer and writer Leigh H. Irvine compared street railway tracks to highways and argued that neither should be privately owned. He declared that "the steel rails of a modern trolley system" were no different from "the path of a nomad." Both were "modifications of the surface of the earth" to facilitate transportation, be it by horse or by streetcar. Irvine was no fan of street railway corporations, but he did not care for strikes either. He argued for public ownership of the infrastructure of streets, tracks, and power plants, with private companies granted nonexclusive franchises to own and operate the cars that ran over the tracks. Like many Americans living through the dramatic class conflict of the late nineteenth and early twentieth centuries, Irvine sought a middle ground that would prevent future strikes while preserving the rights of all parties from union men to railway companies. Irvine's emphasis on the inherent character of streets and the tracks constructed on them, along with his focus on streets as public property, provides insight into debates about access to and control of the streets and public transit at a time when Patrick Calhoun himself boasted that the United Railroads was the largest property owner in the city.[40] An additional factor in San Francisco was the Eastern ownership of the company. Calhoun was an outsider, and civic pride came into play as opponents of overhead trolley lines described their beautiful city being despoiled in the service of profit for financiers living thousands of miles away.[41]

Thus, although San Franciscans may have been dependent on their street railways, those railways could still represent a few people getting rich while the majority struggled to make ends meet. The frequency of residents' interactions with the street railways fostered their resentment of Calhoun and the United Railroads. A crowded or late train or even a rude trainman could feed hostility toward the corporation that appeared to be prospering in hard times. San Franciscans' very reliance on the street railway system contributed to a desire to take back control

of the means of moving around the city, and in fact, demands for municipal ownership employed a language of reclaiming public control over
private profit. The question of ownership of San Francisco's streets
became an issue during the 1907 strike—the strike committee asked
bluntly, "Who owns the streets of this city?"—and the new city charter
passed in 1898 had called for eventual muncipal ownership of utilities,
including street railways.[42]

Components of urban infrastructure from the streets to the water
system were essential pieces of the city's urban ecology, as the destruction of streets, streetcar tracks, and water pipes by the earthquake and
fire had underlined. The disaster capitalists of 1907 faced a coalition
of political actors promoting public control over that infrastructure,
in sharp contrast to the late twentieth and twenty-first centuries when
disasters became opportunities for widespread privatization. The striking carmen believed that they could leverage their role as the labor
power behind the transit system and take advantage of frustration with
Calhoun's corporation and its claim on the public space of their city's
streets. But in 1907 they would find that the political and economic
ground for organized labor in San Francisco had shifted even as the
physical ground beneath the city had moved a year earlier.

FROM UNITY TO DIVISION

In 1906 many members of the middle and upper classes articulated ideas
now associated with disaster capitalism, seeking to frame the city's
destruction as an opportunity for urban redevelopment. For example,
William D. Wood declared confidently: "San Francisco will actually
benefit by this great calamity." He suggested that trade and commerce
would barely be interrupted while "the activity of business and construction" would receive a boost from the rebuilding. In just a short
time San Francisco would be reconstructed as "the most modern city
in the world."[43] Wood, who was a former lawyer, land speculator, and
mayor of Seattle, was expressing the common view at the time that San
Francisco could—and would—turn the disaster into a blessing. For
these optimists, not only would the city be revitalized, but the earthquake and fire represented the chance to replace the old and dated with
the new and modern. Such thinking had facilitated rebuilding in the

wake of earlier, smaller crises, including the fires of the 1850s and the earthquakes of the 1860s. In fact, businessmen and politicians were not the only observers in 1906 to note the potential opportunity for financial interests in the wake of the earthquake and fire. In the *Socialist Voice*, W. V. Holloway described the disaster as "a Godsend to the greater capitalists." He emphasized that "the misfortune of the many is the opportunity of the few."[44] For regular people, Holloway proved to be more prophetic than Wood.

San Francisco's union members initially shared the optimistic vision that the city's destruction presented an opportunity. Perhaps, they reasoned, disaster capitalism could benefit workers as well as capitalists, laborers as well as financiers. They saw labor, not financial capital, as most essential to rebuilding and thus as the core of urban prosperity. Such ideas challenged those who discounted the importance of workers' physical labor in favor of an emphasis on wealthy capitalists in their skyscrapers and funds from around the world to finance rebuilding. Initially, in fact, not only money but also workers—specifically male laborers and tradesmen—flowed to San Francisco, drawn by the opportunities of rebuilding. Materials such as lumber also arrived in the city in vast quantities as San Franciscans mobilized regional, national, and international economic ties.

Labor did appear to possess leverage in a city buried under the rubble of fallen buildings. In its second issue after the earthquake, the *Coast Seamen's Journal* declared that "one power can with certainty be invoked in the great task [of rebuilding] and that is the power of labor. The new city of San Francisco will be the product of the workers' hands and brains, not of the financiers' credit." Six months later, the same paper suggested, perhaps less confidently, that the disaster had revealed that property value resided less in land than in buildings and improvements, which could be rebuilt only with the sweat equity of workers. The paper hoped that this "fundamental lesson" would "equalize" relations between labor and capital that had already failed to live up to earlier optimism.[45] Father Peter C. Yorke, spokesman for the city's Irish workers, declared that San Francisco would arise "more glorious" through "good honest decent work from the first course of the foundation to the very capstone of the corner." For Yorke the disaster explicitly represented not only a chance to rebuild a great city but also an employment opportunity for workers who would perform the labor of rebuilding. He warned, however, that "San Francisco shall not be built by scabs."[46]

Labor leaders initially expected to work in partnership with business and municipal government, still in the nominal control of the Union Labor Party. Only days after the fires were put out, the San Francisco Labor Council (SFLC) and Building Trades Council (BTC), the two major labor coalitions in San Francisco, announced that union wage scales would remain the same as before the catastrophe. They believed they were acting in accordance with a citywide desire to resume business-as-usual, and they therefore expected employers to join them in maintaining existing wage scales and conditions of employment. Member unions suspended plans to demand higher wages or shorter hours in the spirit of working together to restore the city.[47]

Labor leaders such as Father Yorke did worry about the possibility of a flood of men drawn to the city by the promise of reconstruction jobs, and they emphasized that all workers hired need not be union members but insisted that work conditions be consistent for all employees. They sought to counter advertising campaigns by the California Promotion Committee and the Southern Pacific Railroad to attract workers to the city. In a laudatory book on the rebuilding of San Francisco, Rufus Steele observed that half of the building tradesmen working in the city were newcomers, and historians have estimated that as many as forty thousand men came to the city in the wake of the earthquake and fire. This represented an unusual influx of workers, but it was not surprising in an era characterized by widespread "tramping" in search of work. The jobs in San Francisco proved both short-lived and risky, however. Steele praised the urgent reconstruction—"there is no more lurid or splendid sight than a skyscraper going up at night"—yet even he felt it necessary to note the dangers faced by workers. "The misleading half light ... made every step a positive risk of limb and life," he wrote. He downplayed that risk, though, when he suggested that men did such work out of "zest" rather than desperate necessity.[48] Working conditions would, in turn, become one point of contention in labor disputes that followed the earthquake and fire.

Like other forms of "earthquake love," industrial cooperation under disaster capitalism was short-lived. In its meeting of May 25, 1906, the

SFLC condemned increasing rents and the imposition of "onerous conditions" upon labor.[49] By June the first signs of labor conflict had returned to San Francisco as the Sailors' Union, Marine Cooks and Stewards, and Marine Firemen reiterated a request for a modest wage increase of five dollars per month that they had first presented in January. Steam schooner owners refused to grant the increase, and the United Shipping and Transportation Association locked out the workers, briefly including the longshoremen. Violence ensued when employers attempted to hire nonunion crews, and private armed guards shot and killed a union sailor named Andrew Kellner. Radicals in the city tried to stir up resentment; the *Socialist Voice* declared, "Nowhere in the United States today is there a greater degree of capitalistic exploitation than right here in San Francisco." The paper gleefully announced in August that "the class war is raging in San Francisco." The socialists blamed unions for agreeing to fix wages after the fire as well as capitalists for *not* agreeing to fix the cost of living.[50]

The strike lasted until October, when the union won its wage increase. The strong market for building materials—which entered the city through the port—aided the strikers, and labor leaders believed that public support was on their side because of post-earthquake living conditions: "Three months ago the public could see nothing but a 'scarcity of lumber' in the seamen's attempt to raise wages. To-day [*sic*] the public feels the necessity of raising its own wages." As rents doubled and tripled in some parts of the city, people blamed "real estate men and landlords," and organized labor anticipated widespread sympathy for their campaigns.[51] Unlike the socialists, more moderate labor leaders worried about a return to a state of conflict, however. The *Coast Seamen's Journal* caustically declared in late September that "the progress made has been mainly toward bringing about an industrial war. This, considering the past history of the city, is quite consistent with the idea of 'resuming the normal.'" A year after the earthquake and fire, the *Labor Clarion* drew on military metaphors in urging labor to prepare for battle.[52] Just a few days later, on May 5, 1907, the Carmen's Union voted to strike, and the entire city faced the prospect of a protracted struggle that would undermine its still recovering transit system. The hopes of cooperation between labor and capital had been crushed under the weight of the realities of the rubble-filled city. Instead of diverse classes coming together to rebuild, San Francisco descended into a bloody contest over control of the streets and a recession that struck yet another blow against its working people.

THE STREETCAR STRIKE

The streetcar strike of 1907 is usually considered as just one incident in the longer history of industrial relations in San Francisco in the early twentieth century, but placing it in a broader context provides additional insights not always factored into traditional labor history with its focus on politics and organizing.[53] The economic, social, and environmental circumstances after the earthquake and fire affected everything from the carmen's decision to strike to the eventual outcome. Economically, the disaster had inflated the cost of living, particularly rents, and provided a boost to some workers, such as those in the building trades, while hurting others. Socially, the crisis had created a frustrated population of displaced refugees, brought an influx of laborers to the city, and shifted residence patterns, forcing many people to relocate to outlying neighborhoods. And environmentally, the earthquake and fire had devastated the city's streets, making the daily grind of the carmen more difficult, creating new obstacles to travel, and forcing a new awareness of the persistent power of natural forces even in a modern city. When the ground itself could shift underfoot so dramatically, people worried about security in all facets of their lives. Like building tradesmen and laborers who hoped that the rebuilding process would reinforce their centrality to the community, the carmen sought to leverage their critical role as producers of the mobility of urban residents and the spatial integration of the city. All of these factors came together with the political to influence the course of the streetcar strike that took place just as San Franciscans were trying to put their city back together.

In the fall of 1906, San Francisco's street carmen had briefly struck against the United Railroads, seeking three dollars per day for eight hours of work, but Mayor Schmitz brokered a settlement. Arbitrators granted a wage increase to between thirty-one and thirty-three cents per hour, depending on seniority, but to the frustration of the carmen,

Resumption of streetcar service on lower Market Street. Note the piles of debris. Courtesy of the California History Room, California State Library, Sacramento, California.

the settlement preserved the ten-hour day. Thus, the next spring, the carmen walked out again. Union president Richard Cornelius explained that "the earthquake and fire radically altered our employment" by greatly increasing "the volume of work per man" as well as the cost of living. The carmen were also reacting to recent increases in the wages of their counterparts across the bay. They sought a wage scale of thirty-one to forty cents per hour, matching that in Oakland, or an eight-hour day at three dollars per day.[54]

The carmen were not the only group in San Francisco to use the strike as a tactic to navigate the difficult conditions for working people in the recovering city. Laundry workers and telephone operators, most of them women, were also on strike, as were the metal trades unions. In all, 17,500 San Francisco workers were idle in labor disputes in May 1907.[55] The *Labor Clarion* declared the situation to be as grave as those created by the forces of nature thirteen months before and, again drawing on the recurrent theme of unity in crisis, appealed to citizens to once again lay aside "class distinctions, class prejudices," this time in support of organized labor. The paper claimed that Patrick Calhoun of the United Railroads and Henry T. Scott of the local telephone company "regard their employees as mere machines—machines that require neither care nor consideration." It was the duty of all good San Franciscans to support the men and women who were striking for fair treatment.[56]

Violence on both sides marked the streetcar strike, with a total of six people killed and 250 injured over the next five months. The first volley took place on "Bloody Tuesday" when a gun battle outside the United Railroads carbarns along Turk Street left two dead and at least twenty others wounded. News outlets reported a crowd of as many as five hundred—"composed of ordinary hoodlums," in the words of the *San Francisco Chronicle*—indicating widespread community involvement with the strike. The *Bulletin* noted the presence of a "certain lawless, turbulent element" that used strikes as an opportunity to provoke further conflict.[57] This riot drew a proclamation from Mayor Schmitz requesting that "all persons not having any business upon the streets" remain at home, a plea that echoed his attempts to maintain order after the earthquake and fire. With class tension higher than at any point since 1901, SFLC leaders acted to head off a general strike, even as socialists urged workers to "Tie Up the Town."[58] As the strike wore on, localized violence continued, but the threat of a general strike soon dissipated. Calhoun's strikebreakers, armed with revolvers, kept the streetcars running while the strikers called on fellow union members and San Francisco's historically sympathetic populace to show solidarity.

Accounts of the degree of public support for the strike varied widely, and both sides claimed to have the majority of the city behind them. The strikers initially received strong support from other unions, including those in the building trades. Unions affiliated with the BTC contributed more than $170,000 to strike funds while those with the less wealthy SFLC, of which the Carmen's Union was a member, contributed $46,000. The Carmen's International Association contributed over $86,000 and other unions outside San Francisco added almost $30,000 more.[59] Support took nonmonetary forms as well, including sabotage such as felling trees across tracks in outlying areas of the city. On May 13 refugee residents of the Richmond Camp threw objects at the cars and blocked the tracks with bonfires and debris. Newspapers that

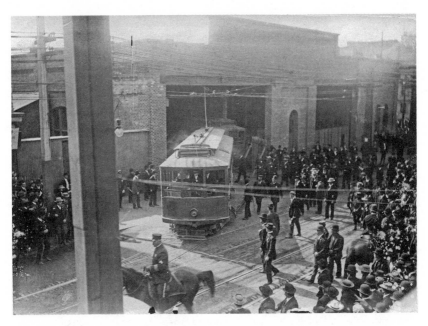

A streetcar under police protection leaving the United Railroads carbarn during the 1907 streetcar strike. Courtesy of the California History Room, California State Library, Sacramento, California.

opposed the strike contrasted the genteel women riding the cars with the coarse strikers down on the streets, but working-class women also asserted themselves as visible supporters of the strike by occupying sections of track "with babies in their arms."[60]

Since Calhoun employed strikebreakers to run the cars, the union's call for a boycott was essential to the strike's success. Many residents of the "labor city" joined the boycott, and according to one historian, ridership of the streetcars dropped by 75 percent as San Franciscans walked to work. Arnold found that the strike had almost twice the impact on ridership of the earthquake and fire, causing a decline of fifteen million rides in one month. However, the *Examiner* reported forty thousand riders on May 14 and the *Chronicle* fifty thousand the next day, indicating the limits of the public's willingness to walk.[61] The union offered an alternative means of transportation for their supporters in the form of horse-drawn "strike wagons" or "Union Buses." Critics of this alternative transportation called it extortion, and it did provide a

Strike wagons and other alternate means of transportation on Market Street during the 1907 strike. Courtesy of the San Francisco History Center, San Francisco Public Library.

source of revenue for the carmen, to the tune of more than $40,000 in fares over six months of operation. One critic claimed that the fares varied widely based on the perceived social status of riders and their degree of support for the strike.[62] The union also tried to enforce the boycott by publishing lists of people "seen on the [street]cars" along with their businesses and addresses, and it identified and praised businesses that had contributed financial support to the strike, thus incorporating a call for supporters to patronize pro-labor businesses.[63]

Labor suggested that the earthquake's destruction of the city had prepared people to support the strike by disrupting streetcar service and reaccustoming people to walking San Francisco's hills.[64] This logic could of course be turned around. The loss of streetcar service during the strike could make its value more obvious to residents who had taken the citywide transit system for granted. Another motivation to support the striking carmen might have been the specter of accidents caused by inexperienced replacement drivers; during the 1907 strike twenty-five San Franciscans died and another nine hundred were injured in streetcar accidents.[65] The increase in accidents emphasized how public transportation remained a bodily experience and a source of risk for riders of the streetcars as well as operators and pedestrians.

Both the strikers and their opponents employed a rhetoric of a right to the streets. The weekly magazine *Western World*, a consistent opponent of the strike, declared the union's demand for a boycott to be "a prohibition against the individual's right to use the streets, for conditions in large cities are such that a man cannot make the best use, or even ordinary use, of the streets unless he rides street cars." The same article added that, to the public, "cessation of street-car travel is a blockade of the streets against use."[66] Similarly, the carmen and their supporters declared repeatedly that "the people own the streets" even though "the companies may own the cars, the rails, the wires." Their rhetoric emphasized that the people had granted Calhoun and the United Railroads a franchise to operate in San Francisco, and they therefore retained a base level of control over the street railways and possessed a right to a safe and efficient transit system. The prominence of the question of ownership and control of the streets during—as well as before and after—the 1907 streetcar strike reflected how the urban environment was both the ground and the object of struggle between labor and capital. Strikers mentioned living wages and increasing rents, but they also referred to public ownership of the miles of property and essential travel corridors that were the streets.[67] Calls for public ownership of the streets represented part of a campaign to restrain private capital, represented here by the United Railroads, and harness essential infrastructure in the name of the greater good of San Francisco and its people rather than in the pursuit of private profit. As a primary form of transportation around the city, the streetcars meant different things to different people, and the physical and rhetorical ground on which the strike unfolded reflected the practical and ideological importance of the city's streets as part of the urban environment.

POLITICS, SCANDAL, AND THE FAILURE OF THE STRIKE

Initially in the spring of 1907, the SFLC and the BTC joined together in support of the strike, but scandal and factionalism consumed San Francisco's political scene over the summer and fall, shattering organized labor's unity and undermining the carmen's chance of victory. The Union Labor Party technically controlled both the mayor's office and the Board of Supervisors when the strike began, having swept to victory in 1905 in a demonstration of political power by organized labor. However, the administration was corrupt, as many other city governments had been, and a three-year-old graft investigation against Mayor Schmitz, his ally and adviser Abe Ruef, and members of the Board of Supervisors picked up steam in the fall of 1906. The financial backing for the campaign came from some of the city's richest men and its leading Progressives, including Phelan and Spreckels. In November 1906, Ruef was indicted for receiving a bribe, and the scandal quickly spread.[68] Sixteen members of the Board of Supervisors confessed to taking bribes, and in May 1907, Mayor Schmitz was indicted as well. Ironically, the specific corruption case at issue centered around the controversial decision the previous spring to allow the United Railroads to rebuild using overhead trolley lines, and indictments also came down against Calhoun and several other United Railroads officials for paying the bribes. In June, Schmitz was convicted of extortion and removed from office, and the sixteen supervisors resigned the next month.[69] Thus, even while the carmen were out on strike, organized labor was losing its political hold on the city.

This political crisis deeply affected the labor movement. The SFLC passed a resolution that disavowed any "connection, direct or implied, with the 'Union Labor' party or any other political party or organization." The use of quotations around the name "Union Labor" attempted to disassociate the labor movement as a whole from its corrupt electoral representatives. In fact, many labor leaders had been ambivalent about the Union Labor Party even when rank-and-file support was enthusiastic. According to the historian Judd Kahn, the formation and electoral success of the Union Labor Party was a direct response to the sharp divisions between capital and labor in San Francisco—"a political solution to the social problem," in his words—and the graft trials shattered this fragile balance. Although the existence of corruption was undeniable, the city fractured over whether the prosecution should focus on bribe-takers (Union Labor Party officials) or bribe-givers (corporations and wealthy business people, particularly Calhoun and other representatives of the United Railroads). The SFLC resolution called for the prosecution of "every corruptionist—briber and bribed," but labor in the city became divided and preoccupied with electoral politics in the middle of the industrial struggles of 1907.[70]

In particular, the labor movement split over the mayoral candidacy of BTC leader Patrick H. McCarthy on the Union Labor Party ticket in 1907. Despite the BTC's support for the carmen's strike, many labor leaders backed McCarthy's opponent, Dr. Edward Taylor. Taylor was a reformer who ran on a good government ticket and promised to prosecute the corporations accused of bribery in the scandal.[71] The precarious alliance between the SFLC and the BTC in support of the carmen and other strikers did not survive the additional stresses of political chaos, fracturing by August 1907, and one historian has suggested that "the rank-and-file union members became little more than pawns in a struggle for control of San Francisco politics."[72] To consider tension between the different factions of organized labor in the city as strictly political oversimplifies the situation, however. Disaster and its economic effects had exacerbated long-standing tensions between the SFLC and the BTC, which represented different classes of workers and which saw their members affected differently by the earthquake and fire. The members of the building trades, of course, were among the few who could seemingly prosper economically from the destruction of the city. In November 1906 one estimate counted fifty-five thousand men employed in the rebuilding of San Francisco, forty thousand of them skilled workers in the building trades and fifteen thousand of them unskilled laborers.[73]

The membership of the building trades unions increased steadily from 14,500 in January of 1906 to 20,000 in August and peaked at almost 30,000 early in 1907. With the high demand for skilled tradesmen, wages increased about 20 percent, or roughly one dollar per day—a substantial increase, although at best barely enough to keep pace with the rising cost of living. Wages for bricklayers peaked at eight dollars per day in January 1907, when plumbers were earning six dollars per day and electricians five dollars. Laborers, who earned an average of only thirteen dollars a week, saw only a minimal increase in their wages in 1906 and 1907. The carmen, with their demand for three dollars for an eight-hour day, were still far behind most workers in the building trades in earnings, although they earned more than unskilled laborers. In general, the earthquake and fire increased the differential in wages between skilled and unskilled workers, who experienced a decline in real wages.[74] Thus the prosperity of the BTC unions after the earthquake exacerbated existing inequities among San Francisco wage earners, and it seems likely that the carmen's insistence on striking stemmed at least in part from their desire to keep pace with rivals in the building trades.[75] Their emphasis on altered economic conditions in the city as a motive for the strike supports this theory. Of course, strike supporters also blamed landlords for rising rents and corporations like the United Railroads for alleged increased profits, but one would not expect them to openly critique potential allies within the labor movement.

Business interests, particularly the Merchants' Association and the city's banking industry, seized the opportunity of the graft trials to redirect the prevailing discourse in San Francisco away from class conflict and corruption toward economic development and progress.[76] The scandal ultimately petered out as 383 total indictments resulted in the punishment of only one man: Ruef. Although Schmitz was forced out of the mayor's office, he went on to be elected to a series of terms on the Board of Supervisors. Many business leaders who supported the prosecution of the union men objected when the prosecution also went after Calhoun, whom they admired in particular for his handling of the strike.[77] The strike saw a last burst of violence on Labor Day of 1907. A riot broke out when union supporters attacked a streetcar, resulting in the death of an iron worker named John A. Petersen and more than a dozen other injuries. That tragedy proved to be the last gasp of the strikers, and the Carmen's Union lifted the boycott in mid-September. The end of the boycott amounted to an admission of defeat, although the strike technically continued until the November election of Taylor as mayor made it clear that labor would receive no assistance from the municipal government. The broken Carmen's Union had dissolved by the end of 1908.[78]

THE ECONOMIC CRISIS OF 1907 AND 1908

We need to consider one final context for the streetcar strike and its aftermath. The graft trials may have deflected attention from the economic problems facing San Francisco in 1907, but they did nothing to alleviate the difficulties faced by the city's working people as they tried to rebuild their lives after the earthquake and fire. Many had lost all of their material possessions, including their homes, household treasures, and the tools of their trades, and men and women struggled to regain their footing in the face of skyrocketing rents, limited housing options, and a job market transformed by the crisis. A May 1907 headline in the *Socialist Voice* referred to "a conspiracy to reduce the standard of living in San Francisco."[79] Although aid had poured into San Francisco initially, national economic conditions soon combined with local circumstances—including the strikes by the carmen and other workers—to undermine the city's recovery. By the spring of 1907, the country had fallen into a recession known as the Panic of 1907.

A June article in the *Coast Seamen's Journal* explicitly blamed "the industrial troubles of the present or recent past" on the "general upheaval caused by the great fire," specifically the combination of the increased cost of living and expectations of higher wages.[80] This analysis was more accurate than the paper probably realized. The earthquake of April 18, 1906, was both a direct and an indirect cause of the economic difficulties facing working-class San Franciscans in 1907 and 1908. Of course, the earthquake and fire directly transformed the urban environment, and with it the conditions of life and work faced by residents. In addition, economic aftershocks of the earthquake affected global gold flows, thereby helping to cause the Panic of 1907 and the subsequent national recession. This recession was in turn felt on the ground by men and women in San Francisco.

The San Francisco earthquake and fire had both immediate and delayed effects on national and international financial markets. In the week following April 18, 1906, the New York Stock Exchange suffered a 12.5 percent decline with stocks perceived as directly affected, such as railroad and insurance companies, taking deeper hits. The United Railroads' stock suffered one of the deepest declines.[81] Over subsequent months, insurance payments to San Francisco policy holders were so large that they created highly unusual gold flows between England— British companies had issued half of the fire insurance policies in San Francisco—and the United States. By October 1906, San Francisco companies and individuals had received an estimated one hundred million dollars in insurance payments, forty-eight million dollars of which had come from British firms. Ultimately, as the economists Kerry Odell and Marc D. Weidenmier explain, "quake-related payments to the United States represented 40 percent of seasonally adjusted British gold exports for all of 1906."[82] The Bank of England responded to these unprecedented circumstances—a 14 percent reduction in the country's gold money stock and the largest two-month net outflow of gold in the years from 1900 to 1913—by "rais[ing] interest rates and discriminat[ing] against American finance bills." These actions pushed the United States into a recession, beginning with a short panic in March of 1907 and culminating with a much larger crisis in October. Nationally, industrial production crashed by 30 percent in the second half of 1907 and GNP declined by 6.7 percent, sparking bank runs in New York in the fall and eventually spreading back across the Atlantic.[83] These unexpected and largely unrecognized economic impacts of the earthquake and fire remind us of the complexity of the global economic system even in the early twentieth century and, perhaps more important, emphasize how natural forces like seismic activity could reverberate through even something as seemingly removed from nature as global finances.

The recession was first felt in San Francisco in the spring of 1907, and it worsened in the fall as the regular seasonal cycle of unemployment drew itinerant laborers to the city. These seasonal arrivals only increased competition for scarce jobs among men and women already out of work because of the recession and the lingering effects of the earthquake and fire. In January 1908 the *Labor Clarion* declared that "the army of unemployed is increasingly daily" in San Francisco and called for public works projects to provide jobs. *Organized Labor* called the depression the worst the city had seen since 1894. The Associated Charities provided work for some unemployed men by hiring them for construction and road repair. A report described the recipients as "chiefly men newly arrived in San Francisco who expected to profit by the demand for labor created by the rebuilding" and found that 15 percent of the aid recipients were union members. Nationwide, unemployment reportedly reached 35 percent in all trades in 1908.[84]

The recession not only led to privation for working men and women in San Francisco but also affected the progress of the rebuilding. In September 1908, *Organized Labor* declared that "the final blow intended to lay low the strong labor organizations of San Francisco was nothing more or less than *starvation*." The paper accused financiers of a conspiracy to "starve the building mechanics and laborers out of their homes and their unions" by refusing to lend money to finance rebuilding efforts. The next spring, the same paper complained that San Francisco's streets and municipal buildings were in "worse condition" than in the first year after the fire and "yet there is an army of idle men looking for work every day." Not only had rebuilding stalled, but the condition of the urban environment had worsened—and yet there seemed to be no money or desire on the part of the city's leaders to address those two problems. A few months later, the Irish community paper *The Leader* blamed insurance companies, "real estate sharks," and landlords for the "thousands still suffering as a result of the great disaster of 1906."[85] The claims of conspiracies on the part of financiers, landlords, and even insurance companies were probably groundless, but such accusations reflected ongoing class antagonisms in the city as well as the perceived shortage of available work for both skilled and unskilled laborers. Organized labor's hopeful vision of disaster capitalism, the promise of prosperity for workers as their labor rebuilt the city, had already fallen apart by 1907 and 1908, replaced by recession and widespread unemployment.

Although much of California experienced prosperity between 1908 and 1913, the problems of seasonal unemployment and low wages persisted in San Francisco. In April 1909, *Organized Labor* complained that "the old California and San Francisco standard of living . . . is no longer for those who produce in mine or factory, on the streets or buildings."[86] This rhetoric adapted the "American standard of living" that was a staple of labor's demand for a living wage in this era to the more specific "California and San Francisco standard of living," a reference to San Francisco's history as a relatively high wage city as a result of its strong unions and isolated labor market. The emphasis on workers as producers was a staple of labor rhetoric, and the list of work environments linked sites of natural resource extraction and manufacturing with the buildings where craftsmen plied their trades and the streets where the carmen, teamsters, draymen, and other less skilled laborers toiled. There was no quick fix for problems of high unemployment and low wages in the city. In 1912 the State Labor Commissioner estimated the presence of thirty-two thousand unemployed men in San Francisco, and the *Coast Seamen's Journal* described the city as a "land of idleness, hunger, and misery."[87] Economic and environmental conditions in both the city and the expansive hinterland with which it shared a labor market fostered cyclical unemployment even as skyscrapers signaled the resurgency and modernity of San Francisco's central business district.

CONCLUSION

The carmen might have lost their strike and their union by the beginning of 1908, but debates over control of the city's streets and its transit system were far from over. Organized labor and Progressive reformers found common ground on the issue of public ownership of municipal utilities, including the street railroads. Reformers believed that municipal ownership would remove one of the major sources of corruption in city government by eliminating negotiations over franchises and rates, and they argued that government could run utilities more efficiently than private business since its focus would be on the public good rather than profit. Both the graft scandals and the 1907 strike only increased the determination of many San Franciscans to find alternatives to the United Railroads.[88] *Municipal Railway of San Francisco*, a 1915 publication by the lawyer Martin S. Vilas, emphasized that a municipal railway could facilitate development of outlying neighborhoods, provide efficient service, pay its workers well, and raise money for the city.[89] Rather than fearing a loss of competition from the entrance of government into the street railway business, supporters expected competition from city-run railways to force private companies to improve their service and their treatment of workers.

Like Vilas, organized labor embraced a utopian vision of higher wages, shorter hours, and labor peace on municipally owned lines.[90] Unions proved to be strong supporters of an expanded role for government in providing for the needs of urban residents. Their rhetoric continued to emphasize that "the streets of the city belong to the people" and a vote in support of municipal acquisition of the Geary Street Railroad was "a vote for the people and against private monopoly." A bond issue financing the city's purchase of the Geary Street line finally passed with the required two-thirds of the vote in December 1909.[91] This vote began San Francisco's gradual acquisition of privately owned lines, and the renamed Municipal Railway opened at the end of 1912 to a cheering crowd of fifty thousand, although the city did not acquire complete control over its street railway system until 1944.[92] The Carmen's Union might have lost their battle with the United Railroads, but their vision of public control of transit in the city eventually triumphed.

However, in 1907 and 1908, disaster capitalism and creative destruction provided limited opportunity at best for working people in San Francisco. The streetcar strike stemmed from environmental, economic, and cultural circumstances that left the carmen feeling underpaid and overworked, and the earthquake and fire exacerbated those conditions. To make matters worse, the disaster reverberated through international financial markets, causing the Panic of 1907 and subsequent recession. Thus financial cycles—like the lives of urban residents of all classes but particularly the poor—proved subject to environmental forces even in the twentieth century. The uncertainty associated with an unstable economy in turn motivated men and women to engage in industrial struggles in pursuit of higher wages and more secure employment that could counter the constant threat of relegation to transience.

Although ordinary San Franciscans had successsfully defended their city and neighborhoods against the dramatic physical changes proposed in the Burnham Plan and Chinatown relocation, circumstances after the earthquake and fire precluded reform of urban conditions to benefit labor. The streetcar strike sought to leverage economic and environmental disruption to improve the status of the carmen, but urban politics and economic crisis—both intertwined with the earthquake and fire—limited the possibilities of working-class mobilization. Rather than offering an opportunity to reassert the centrality of labor in rebuilding and running the city, the earthquake undermined working San Franciscans by contributing to economic volatility on local, national, and even international levels as well as fostering an underlying fear that nothing, not even the ground beneath the city, was stable. In the city, as everywhere in nature, everything proved to be connected to everything else.

SIX

PLAGUE, RATS, AND UNDESIRABLE NATURE

AS MARGUERITE BRINDLEY TRIED TO SLEEP HER FIRST NIGHT BACK in her home on Taylor Street, which had miraculously survived both the earthquake and the fire, she "was wakened about three by hearing the rats, which have come in swarms, nibbling at the woodwork."[1] Brindley and other humans were not the only residents of San Francisco forced to flee from the flames that engulfed the city in April 1906. The movements of rats went largely unmarked in the crisis, but the fire drove them from their burrows. Afterwards, some rats, like the city's people, found new homes in new parts of the city while others returned to live among the ruins. But where many humans struggled in the chaos of the postdisaster city, San Francisco's rodent population thrived. Rats grew fat on garbage dumped in messy vacant lots or left uncollected in overflowing garbage bins. They congregated around the makeshift kitchens of the refugee camps and burrowed into the walls and basements of broken buildings. They took full advantage of access to dark, subterranean spaces provided by broken sewers and water pipes. San Francisco's rats, like its people, had come from all over the world through the city's bustling port, one of the unintended consequences of global trade. And just as the rats had been stowaways traveling against the will of ships' captains, if not necessarily without their knowledge, fleas in turn had hitched rides hidden in the rats' fur and the humans' cargo. By the turn of the twentieth century, some of the rats and fleas that came to San Francisco from Asian ports carried a legendary scourge of civilization in their bodies: the bubonic plague.

The dramatic death tolls of epidemics like the plague in fourteenth-century Europe and smallpox in the Americas from the sixteenth through the nineteenth centuries can overshadow the ongoing significance of disease in history, but epidemic disease remained a very real danger facing residents of early twentieth-century cities. In the United States just a few decades earlier, waves of cholera and yellow fever had threatened the lives of urban residents, particularly poor people who lacked the resources to flee to healthier environs when an epidemic broke out. In urban environments, dense human populations combined with poor sanitation to provide ideal conditions for diseases to flourish. Cities had grown too big, too fast, and scientific knowledge, sanitary practices, and technological developments took decades to catch up. Humans acted as hosts and carriers for disease organisms, as did animals such as rats, fleas, flies, and mosquitoes, each of which thrived in urban environments. Epidemics, like earthquakes, were far from natural crises despite the central roles played by nonhuman agents. The ways in which humans structured and produced both urban spaces and social relations contributed to outbreaks of disease just as much as the presence of germs did. Epidemics in turn have political and social repercussions. Tiny viruses and bacteria have decided wars and brought down governments, reminding us of nature's power to shape history.[2]

The impacts of the bubonic plague in San Francisco were more subtle, just as the 172 confirmed deaths hardly rank with history's great epidemics. However, coming as it did at a time of upheaval in the urban environment, the plague provides another angle through which to understand how San Franciscans perceived nature in their city. It also reminds us of the diverse residents of the city, human and otherwise. The characters in this story include not only Dr. Rupert Blue of the US Marine Hospital Service, Wong Chung of the Chinese Six Companies, and ordinary San Franciscans such as Marguerite Brindley. The bacteria *Yersinia pestis*, two species of flea (*Nosopsyllus fasciatus* and *Xenopsylla cheopis*), and of course San Francisco's rats (*Rattus norvegicus*) also played central roles, influencing the course of the outbreak and the city's history. Ultimately, both the causes and the consequences of the bubonic plague outbreak reflected the inescapable connections between ecological, economic, and cultural factors.

Although San Francisco's human residents saw their urban environment as distinctly modern as the twentieth century began, their San Francisco was very different from the twenty-first-century American city. Perhaps most prominently, in 1900 a variety of nonhuman animals ranging from working horses to chickens raised for eggs and meat shared the urban environment with humans. The decades from the mid-nineteenth century to the early twentieth century represented a transitional period as an ethos of modernity increasingly called for the exclusion of these elements of nature from American cities, a process that the historian Ted Steinberg has called the "death of the organic city." In the organic city, horses represented the primary means of transportation, and the manure they left on city streets fertilized farms and gardens that produced food for urban dwellers.[3] In San Francisco the earthquake and fire accelerated changes such as the replacement of horses with automobiles and the removal of chickens from people's yards to industrial farms outside the urban center. The 1907–1908 plague scare provided sanitary reformers with funds and public support to clean up the city and hasten this transition from the organic city to the modern, sanitary city.

In 1908, Dr. Rupert Blue, head of the campaign, declared: "The disease must be built out of existence. This is the hope of San Francisco and in time that city will be one block of concrete throughout, and the gateway to the Orient closed against plague."[4] Blue's words reflected both the belief that modern technologies such as concrete could prevent disease and the older tradition of blaming the Chinese for infectious diseases in San Francisco. The war on rats likewise combined scientific understandings of disease with assumptions about proper urban citizenship coded by ethnicity and class. It targeted undesirable urban nature—a category that encompassed not only pests and disease organisms but also working and food animals and even the practices of immigrant populations—for removal from the city, replaced with sanitary technologies of concrete and industrial food production. Such a vision might seem to have little in common with the City Beautiful, but it shared a faith in modern technologies and municipal engineering with Daniel H. Burnham's vision. Blue ignored any concern with beauty, however, focusing solely on the perceived utility of a concrete city insulated from the risks characteristic of urban environments. Although these changes in urban ecology did result in improved sanitation that benefited all of San Francisco's residents, the city's poor and recent immigrants suffered under the burden of these programs, frequently losing their homes and subsistence strategies such as raising chickens in the backyard.

THE THIRD GREAT PANDEMIC

In the early twentieth century, the plague was both a legendary scourge and a very real threat. The outbreaks in San Francisco were part of the third great pandemic of bubonic plague, following the sixth-century Justinian plague and the famous medieval "Black Death" that hit Europe in 1347 and killed an estimated twenty-five million people. Scientists have concluded that each wave of the disease was caused by a slightly different strain, but the discovery of DNA of the plague bacillus in the bodies of victims of the Black Death provides conclusive evidence that *Yersinia pestis* was to blame. The disease lay quiescent for centuries, surviving and evolving among wild rodents in the Himalayan borderlands. In the 1860s it broke out among humans in the southern Chinese province of Yunnan. It spread to Canton and Hong Kong by 1894, then surfaced in India, where it killed twelve million people between 1898 and 1928. In 1907 alone, as plague recurred in San Francisco, 1.3 million people died in India. Traveling by sea in the bodies of rats and their fleas, the disease spread around the globe, striking fifty-one countries between 1894 and 1910. Despite being relatively unknown, the third bubonic plague pandemic killed at least fifteen million people worldwide, mostly in Asia, before petering out in the 1950s.[5]

In San Francisco, as discussed in chapter 4, the first appearance of the plague was concentrated in Chinatown, and both health officers and most white San Franciscans racialized the disease and confined their attempts to address it to the Chinese neighborhood. Reactions to the outbreak in 1900 reflected complicated municipal and state politics along with uncertain scientific understanding of the disease. Local, state, and federal authorities disputed both the existence of plague and the appropriate means of containing it, if in fact it did exist. Throughout 1900, after the San Francisco Board of Health and the Marine Hospital Service confirmed their diagnosis of plague in the death of Wong Chut King, those health authorities encountered opposition from San Francisco business interests and even Governor Henry T. Gage. The governor publicly accused city officials and San Francisco quarantine officer Joseph Kinyoun—who had attempted to extend his quarantine of Chinatown to the entire state after the Chinese successfully challenged the legality of targeting their community—of fabricating plague cases. Gage went so far as to attempt (unsuccessfully) to make it illegal to perform bacteriological tests for plague in the state of California. When Eugene Schmitz took office as mayor, he tried to dismiss four members of the Board of Health because they persisted in stating that plague had reached San Francisco.[6] Even the city's two leading medical journals disagreed on whether the plague in San Francisco was real. Not until February 1903 did all parties involved officially concede that plague existed in the city.[7]

The San Francisco Board of Health argued that the attempted coverup of the plague had done more harm than good. They suggested in 1903 that "suppression of the truth" had only aroused fears disproportionate to the real scope of the disease while ignoring the success of the "splendid defense against its attack."[8] This statement downplayed the severity of the outbreak and, somewhat ironically given the haphazard efforts to contain and treat the disease, emphasized the effectiveness of the medical community's response. Both health officials and municipal leaders concluded that denying the presence of an epidemic was counterproductive to health, morale, and the city's reputation, however. When the disease resurfaced, San Francisco's leaders quickly acknowledged the new outbreak and called in medical authorities to coordinate the response.

In 1900 neither the role of rats nor that of fleas had been confirmed, and health officials in San Francisco treated the plague like any other infectious disease. The bacteriologist Wilfred H. Kellogg later reminisced that in 1900 "we knew the rat was important, but we did not proceed as if we did."[9] Nineteenth-century theories on the transmission of plague focused on dirt, tainted food, and the "miasma" theory in which noxious odors were believed to transmit disease. These theories continued to influence public health practices even after the development of the germ theory and bacteriology. The deaths of millions in Asia had spurred research, and by 1897 scientists were beginning to identify connections between the bubonic plague, rats, and fleas. Experiments by Paul-Louis Simond had even proved that fleas transmitted the plague between rats, but his findings would not be widely accepted for several years. New scientific knowledge traveled more slowly than the disease itself, and in 1900 health authorities in the United States worked from a mixture of false assumptions—such as the idea that plague had a preference for people of Asian descent—and half-guessed truths. Surgeon-General Walter Wyman even published a 1900 monograph on plague that downplayed the role of "the bites of insects" and endorsed the racial theory of plague.[10]

The response to the later outbreak benefited from a new certainty about the mechanism by which the disease spread. Between 1903 and 1905, experiments by the Indian Plague Commission confirmed Simond's discovery that fleas transmitted the bubonic plague between rodents. The plague was in fact a rodent disease first and foremost. When rats died of the plague, their fleas would seek out another host, and humans contracted the plague when bitten by infected fleas.[11] Thus unsanitary conditions contributed to the spread of the plague only, in the words of a Citizens' Health Committee report, "in so far as they favor infestation by rats." In his 1909 official history of San Francisco's campaign against the plague, Frank Morton Todd wrote: "Bubonic plague is not a filth disease—it is a rat disease."[12] Of course, the particular circumstances of the 1907 outbreak in which Chinatown was largely spared forced white San Franciscans to find an alternative to earlier racialized explanations for the disease, making scientific explanations more convincing.

In fact, the reason for the plague's relatively light death toll in San Francisco in comparison to Asia probably had little to do with either sanitary conditions in the city or measures taken to combat the disease. When a flea bites an infected animal (or human), it ingests the plague bacilli along with blood. Inside the flea, enzymes from the plague organism form clots that block the flea's stomach. These clots allow plague germs to grow but also prevent new meals from nourishing the flea, causing it to bite more aggressively in a futile attempt to assuage its hunger. Each bite injects plague into the skin of the flea's victim. If the flea cannot dislodge the clot of blood, it will starve, becoming another victim of the plague. Some species of flea are more susceptible to these plague-induced clots than others, and the Asian rat flea, *Xenopsylla cheopis*, is particularly vulnerable. *X. cheopis* lived in San Francisco in the first decade of the twentieth century, but the dominant species of rat flea in the city was *Nosopsyllus fasciatus*, the northern European rat flea. This flea transmits the plague only about one-third as efficiently as *X. cheopis*. This quirk of ecological luck is the most likely explanation for why San Francisco's bubonic plague epidemic claimed only hundreds rather than thousands of victims.[13]

San Francisco's defense against the plague also benefited when Wyman replaced the prickly Kinyoun with Dr. Rupert Blue, a thirty-three-year-old officer with the US Marine Hospital Service who had previously encountered the plague while stationed in Italy. Blue's diplomatic skills were better suited to the volatile political debates about plague in San Francisco than Kinyoun's, and he proved to be an innovative thinker capable of devising new ways to fight the epidemic.[14] Even without certain knowledge of how the plague spread, by 1903 Blue arrived at a strategy of targeting Chinatown's rats. On February 6, 1904, the city and state boards of health, the San Francisco Board of Supervisors, and the Marine Hospital Service jointly passed a resolution that essentially launched the rat-proofing of the district. The resolution called for the destruction or paving of "all cellars, basements, and underground places."[15] A total of 625 parcels of real estate in Chinatown underwent improvement (only sixteen of which had Chinese ownership). Looking back from the vantage point of 1909, Todd concluded that these efforts had successfully "built out" the plague from San Francisco, and only the special circumstances following the earthquake and fire allowed the disease to return.[16] Todd's knowledge of the successful campaign against the 1907 outbreak colored his perspective on efforts to eliminate the plague from 1900 to 1904, but the earlier campaign nevertheless made drastic changes in the physical structure of Chinatown that eliminated much of the neighborhood's rat habitat. Contrary to long-standing discourses about Chinatown's unsanitary conditions, it was one of the more sanitary sections of San Francisco after 1904, and the campaign in Chinatown would serve as a model when the disease resurfaced in the city.

"A RAT PARADISE"

Despite San Francisco's previous experience with plague, the disease's return caught the city unprepared. In 1907 the city lacked laboratory facilities and a supply of Yersin's antiserum with which to protect people against infection. Hospital facilities were also inadequate. Worse, the earthquake and fire had suddenly transformed the city into prime habitat for rats. Broken water and gas mains and sewer pipes allowed rats full access to migratory routes and hiding places. Building scraps and piles of brick littered vacant lots in the burned district and provided ideal homes for rodents. The flimsy shelters, makeshift cooking arrangements, and limited sanitary facilities used by refugees served as both dwelling places and food sources. When Blue returned to the city in September 1907, he worriedly reported to Surgeon General Wyman that "rats abound in large numbers in the whole city, where conditions for their maintenance are ideal." Frank Morton Todd described the burned district as "a rat paradise."[17]

Todd's assumption that circumstances after the earthquake allowed the plague to return was only partially correct. Even though plague had apparently disappeared from San Francisco's human population after rat-proofing measures in Chinatown, the disease almost certainly remained in the bodies of the city's rats and their fleas. The omnivorous brown or Norway rat (the dominant species of rat in San Francisco in the early twentieth century) thrives around humans, who provide an abundant supply of its favorite food: grain. Rats also consume food scraps and undigested food particles found in human waste. Sewers thus represent excellent rat habitat, offering plenty of cover as well as a steady supply of food.[18] Studies have found that rat populations spike during wars because of "disrupted supply networks, individuals' makeshift food hoarding, and degraded housing stock"—all conditions that existed in San Francisco after the 1906 disaster. In an even more direct comparison, rodent populations exploded after a 1993 earthquake in India, and a plague outbreak struck the area the next year.[19]

The earthquake and fire also disturbed and scattered rat populations. In the 1900–1904 outbreak, the disease was largely confined to
Chinatown and adjacent areas not because of sanitary conditions but
because of the habits of Norway rats. When left undisturbed, the vast
majority of rats live out their entire lives within territories smaller
than a city block and often no bigger than a single building. Rats prefer
to remain on familiar territory with reliable food sources and nesting
sites, and they hesitate to cross even an alley or street unless pressed.
Norway rats will, however, migrate if their home territory is disturbed
by such activities as sanitary improvements or by a crisis like the fire.[20]
Thus, both the rat-proofing activities in Chinatown in 1903–1904 and
the devastation caused by the 1906 disaster may well have scattered
rats around the city, carrying the plague with them to new sectors of
the urban environment.

On May 27, 1907, a seaman named Oscar Tomei died of the plague
in Marine Hospital Service custody in San Francisco. He had lived on
board a tug in the bay for the previous five or six weeks, coming ashore
to eat at a lodging house near the waterfront. At first, Tomei's seemed
like an isolated case, but another man fell ill on August 12, and by the
end of the month, health authorities had identified fourteen cases. The
epidemic would only worsen over the next few months, ultimately
killing 77 people of 160 total cases.[21] The plague outbreak peaked in
September, October, and November 1907, before cold, rainy weather
sent rats deep into hiding, where they had little contact with humans,
and reduced the number of fleas to spread the disease. Plague proved
to be a seasonal disease in San Francisco, albeit one with a fairly long
season. Flea numbers began to increase again at the end of the winter
rains, sometime between February and April, and peaked in June.[22] As
fleas carrying the disease multiplied, they infected additional rats, who
in turn carried fleas and plague throughout the city. The human residents of San Francisco found themselves at the mercy of the ecology of
a disease that scientists had just begun to understand.

The first attempts to make sense of the return of the dreaded disease
relied on the old racialized associations of disease with Chinatown.
These assumptions quickly encountered the reality that it was white
people, not Chinese, who were dying in 1907. Even though Chinatown
had burned in the fire, the recently constructed cement foundations

survived. The Chinese and their landlords appeared to have learned their lesson about links between disease and the built environment. Health officer Richard H. Creel described Chinatown as "by far the most sanitary district in the city of San Francisco from a structural point of view" after the fire. Rupert Blue similarly observed that "no human cases were found in that portion of the city where all of the buildings were provided with concrete basements."[23] Chinatown's near immunity from the new outbreak thus provided direct evidence of the efficiency of fighting the disease by altering the built environment.

Ultimately, the 1907 outbreak of bubonic plague affected every district in the city except the outlying Sunset and Richmond districts, where the population density was relatively low. However, working-class neighborhoods and immigrant communities—including the Latin Quarter, Lobos Square, and areas along the waterfront—became the primary foci of the disease. The crowded Latin Quarter, home to mostly working-class Italian immigrants, was the site of as many as half of the total plague cases. One couple who became infected shared a house on Telegraph Hill with thirty-five people. William C. Hobdy of the Marine Hospital Service described the building, which had survived the fire, as "swarming with vermin, especially fleas." After the fire many of San Francisco's Italian residents outside the refugee camps lived in similar houses or hastily thrown together shacks that Creel described as "ideal rat harbors." Life in the camps was hardly safer. Starting in September, eighteen cases struck the Lobos Square refugee camp, which housed two thousand people in newly constructed wooden earthquake cottages. These cottages had no foundations to prevent rats from gaining access. The camp's communal kitchen had recently been closed, leaving private individuals responsible for food preparation and disposal of kitchen waste that could attract rodents. In general, the shortage of housing and exorbitant rents after the earthquake and fire forced poor people to scramble for shelter, making it more likely that they would find themselves living in close proximity to rats.[24]

Poverty was only one risk factor related to infection. Among the working classes, recent immigrants—with Italians being the largest group—were most susceptible to both the disease and efforts to reconstruct the urban environment to counter it. The Board of Health Report for

Backyard of a dwelling in San Francisco, including a pile of wood and other rat harbors. Courtesy of the National Library of Medicine.

1907–1908 described the nativity of seventy-two of the plague victims: 61 percent were foreign-born, almost twice the percentage in the city's population as a whole, and 90 percent were classified as white.[25] Despite new theories disassociating the disease from dirt, the Board of Health continued to emphasize poor sanitation as a major factor in suscepti-bility to plague, referring to "the amount of filth that had been allowed to accumulate," the "disgustingly unsanitary conditions of buildings," and the residents' "criminal neglect in matters sanitary."[26] Such phrases can be read as coded critiques of poor people and immigrants, but most rhetoric around the 1907 outbreak deemphasized questions of social class and sanitary practices in favor of the solution of structural change—"building out" the plague.

Universalizing the danger rather than blaming specific social groups became particularly important in the context of mobilizing San

Franciscans behind the war on rats. In the official rhetoric of the campaign, stories of plague cases emphasized contact with rats rather than ethnicity or class. For example, deaths among the Bowers family of the Mission district were traced to a funeral the family's two young sons had held for a dead rat found in a cellar. Similarly, a doctor and his family reportedly became infected after opening a wall to investigate a "foul odor" and discovering rat cadavers, presumably the source of the odor as well as the fleas that infected the family.[27] Todd's account declared that most of the victims were respectable white people, "subsisting on a generous diet and dwelling in houses that would commonly be called 'sanitary,'" and referred to the plague as a "danger that was common to all parts of the City." The San Francisco lawyer and Progressive Augustin C. Keane explicitly attributed the infection of the Lobos Square refugee camp to its proximity to a stable rather than to unsanitary living conditions among the refugees.[28] Blaming rats and the urban environment, rather than any group of people, served to engage more San Franciscans in the campaign against the plague. The crisis of the plague outbreak became an opportunity for sanitary reformers to educate immigrants, working-class families, and the city as a whole about public health.[29]

This seemingly scientific perspective inspired a citywide war on rats that demanded the participation of and sacrifices from all citizens. Observers like Creel and William Colby Rucker of the Marine Hospital Service recognized that totally eradicating the rat from San Francisco would prove impossible because survivors would only reproduce at a faster rate.[30] The key to victory for humans was to eliminate sources of food and rat habitat—what we might refer to as changing the ecology of the city. Rats had thrived for thousands of years in urban environments, but new strategies of sanitation and new technologies of concrete offered hope that rodents could be "built out of existence" in early twentieth-century San Francisco. In practice, poor people, particularly those of marginalized ethnicities, bore the brunt of the combat between San Francisco's people and its rats. Surveillance by health inspectors, criticism of such practices as the keeping of chickens, and the expenses of meeting new structural requirements all fell most heavily on San Francisco's working-class residents.

In 1907, unlike in the earlier outbreak, neither city nor state officials made any attempt to deny the existence of plague in San Francisco. Nevertheless, city leaders worried about the potential economic impact of the disease's recurrence, particularly as the city struggled to rebuild in the wake of the earthquake and fire. The municipal treasury was already strained, but in September, when it became clear that the city was facing a full-fledged epidemic, the Board of Supervisors appropriated twenty-five thousand dollars for antiplague measures. New mayor Edward R. Taylor, a physician, requested federal assistance, and the Marine Hospital Service sent Dr. Rupert Blue, architect of the earlier cleanup of Chinatown, to oversee the fight against the disease. Colby Rucker, who had worked with Blue in fighting a 1905 yellow fever epidemic in New Orleans, joined him in San Francisco.[31] The cooperation in 1907 contrasted sharply with the rivalry and obstructionism among the various city, state, and federal officials seven years earlier.

Even before Blue arrived in the city, men who had worked under him during the previous outbreak began organizing to systematically combat this new appearance of the disease. They divided the city into thirteen sanitary districts, with each field office headed by a surgeon who commanded a corps of inspectors, assistant inspectors, foremen, and laborers. By November the campaign employed 284 men—a number that peaked at 919—and had trapped thirteen thousand rats in a single week. These men also inspected houses and buildings for susceptibility to the plague, a process that was nothing if not thorough. According to the official history, "all the premises in thirty square miles of territory were entered and examined, not once but many times."[32]

These health inspectors were at the core of San Francisco's antiplague campaign. Their sanitary census of every building in the city identified how many people lived or worked there, whether anyone had recently been sick, and of course whether any known cases of plague— human or rat—had occurred in the vicinity. They inspected the physical structure of each building and the sanitary practices of the inhabitants. Aided by guinea pigs who were sent in ahead of human inspectors to attract any hungry fleas in the building, the health inspectors checked if the ground floor was permeable to rats, searching for

Dr. Rupert Blue and his staff during the war on rats. Blue is seated in the middle of the front row, third from left. Richard H. Creel is on the left in the second row, and William Colby Rucker is standing on the right in the front row. Courtesy of the National Library of Medicine.

evidence of the animals or structural problems such as wooden basements. They observed garbage receptacles, analyzed waste collection and disposal practices, and inspected plumbing and sewer connections. The inspectors reported nuisances and violations of sanitary ordinances, and violators were served with notices and fined if they failed to abate a nuisance.[33] Through surveillance and enforcement of new sanitary regulations, health inspectors sought to transform the city into a clean, plague-free, and rat-free environment.

Citywide, inspections resulted in 82,554 abatement-of-nuisances notices. Yellow placards marked premises that failed to meet the new standards, and newspapers published convictions for sanitary offenses. These methods of shaming persuaded most people to improve their property—only 370 arrests took place—but some San Franciscans resisted the unexpected and often prohibitive expenses. In Butchertown the owners of hog pens initially refused access to rat catchers, while members of the Builders' Exchange fatalistically noted that rats "follow civilization and cannot be driven away."[34] The sanitary crews sometimes dealt with resistance to cleanup efforts by simply barging into the premises and beginning the work. Perhaps most important, the courts initially supported the Board of Health's claim of broad powers to abate rat harbors as sanitary nuisances.[35]

Of course, the campaign against the plague faced several obstacles. It was difficult to quarantine refugees without homes, and finding a place to house the sick quickly reached a state of crisis. During August, cases were brought to the City and County Hospital at Potrero Avenue and Twenty-second Street, described by the Board of Health as "an old, dilapidated, most unsanitary wooden structure, erected as a temporary hospital thirty-five years ago and used ever since in spite of repeated condemnation by successive Boards of Health." Although this characterization of the condition of San Francisco's public hospital reflected a degree of bitterness on the part of the board, which had repeatedly and unsuccessfully campaigned for a new hospital, it was probably also an accurate description. On August 12 and 13 the hospital treated four plague patients, and an elderly Irish-born orderly named Jeremiah O'Leary contracted the disease from one of them. In late August two more hospital employees took sick, and on August 27 a patient named John Casey, who had no signs of plague upon admittance, developed the disease. Fleas and the plague bacilli had infested the hospital, and on August 27 it was placed in quarantine and closed to all nonplague patients.[36]

The infestation of the hospital exacerbated fears among the community. One health care worker refused to treat O'Leary and resigned. The Board of Health reported that doctors themselves constructed a "rat-proof galvanized iron fence sunk in concrete" around the infectious disease pavilion when laborers "threw down their tools and refused to come near the building."[37] The city attempted to fumigate the hospital with sulfur, but rats simply burrowed deep into the foundation or retreated to the sewers and waited until the fumes had cleared. Ultimately, the hospital had to be condemned, and it was demolished and burned in an ironic echo of the great fire. Over the winter, patients were housed in abandoned stables at the Ingleside racetrack or at the Plague Hospital, which for two months consisted of tents without flooring before the completion of "simple cottages" in a new rat-proof compound. Early rains made conditions miserable for patients and health care workers alike throughout the fall, and the racetrack buildings leaked both that winter and the next.[38] The fate of San Francisco's public hospital serves as a reminder that the city's practice of modern sanitation and provision of medical care remained very much a work in progress. The 1907 outbreak of bubonic plague galvanized changes, but those changes—like the construction of a new hospital—were forced by the challenges of epidemic disease rather than occurring spontaneously in the course of urban development.

City leaders mobilizing the community to constructive action against the disease did not have an easy task. The chief surgeon of the Isolation Hospital, Arthur O'Neill, observed in his report that "the very name 'plague' seems to strike terror into the hearts of the community," and the panic shown at the hospital's infestation was undoubtedly not an isolated incident.[39] At the same time, throughout the fall, health officials encountered what William Hobdy of the Marine Hospital Service described as "the apathy of the public and the studied indifference of the press" when asked to take specific measures against the disease. For the medical experts heading the plague campaign, panic seemed a more appropriate reaction than apathy. In December 1907, 1.4 percent of rats inspected for plague were infected, a percentage as high as in the worst epidemics in modern times.[40] Faced with a brief winter in which to address the problem of infected rats or face an even greater outbreak in the spring, Blue and the Board of Health called a meeting of leading citizens in early January. Perhaps preoccupied with their plans for rebuilding, San Francisco's elites did not perceive the same crisis that the medical community did. Blue sent out six hundred invitations to the meeting, but only sixty men attended. However, those who did adopted a resolution calling on Mayor Taylor to appoint a Citizens' Health Committee to mobilize the populace.[41]

San Francisco's long history of citizens' committees traced back to the infamous Vigilance Committees of the 1850s. In a crisis the leaders of San Francisco often formed, and joined, committees to take over aspects of governance. Although the activities of the citizens' committees were not as dramatic in the first decade of the twentieth century, they remained a kind of extralegal branch of government, supplementing both elected and legally appointed city officials. Most recently, of course, citizens' committees had been a central part of San Francisco's response to the earthquake and fire. The new Citizens' Health Committee consisted of twenty-five members, twelve of them with medical degrees. Their stated purpose was "to bring about a general co-operation of the people of the city with the sanitary authorities" and, more closely approaching the bloody history of the vigilance committees, "to organize the community for the starving and destroying of rats."[42] Whereas San Francisco's leading citizens had once mobilized to respond with quasi-official violence to crime and arson by members of the city's underclass, they now proposed to unite the city's human community in a war against its rat denizens.

As in the earlier plague outbreak, the primary concern of San Francisco's merchants and businessmen was the potential economic impact of plague and, in particular, the threat of a quarantine of the city. Members of the Citizens' Health Committee met with nineteen consuls of foreign governments to emphasize the city's progress in combating the disease and to avert embargoes.[43] Observers in San Francisco and elsewhere in the Bay Area believed they had learned a lesson from the earlier epidemic—the existence of plague in a city need not "of itself seriously threaten" commerce as long as the community took "prompt and vigorous action" against the disease.[44] The Citizens' Health Committee organized ten committees and forty-two subcommittees representing various industries and social and fraternal organizations. One of the first projects was to raise money for the campaign. The committees collected more than $177,000 by assessing both corporations and individuals appropriate amounts. The largest assessment demanded $30,000 from the Southern Pacific Railway, but some individuals gave as little as fifty cents. This money allowed the committee to employ hundreds of inspectors and laborers as well as purchase rat traps and poisons, pay bounties, and print seven hundred thousand pieces of literature.[45]

Each subcommittee was charged with communicating the urgency of antiplague efforts to its constituency, and most adopted aggressive scare tactics centered around the threat of quarantine. The health risks posed by the plague took a backseat to the economic threat, when they were mentioned at all. A card posted in drugstores throughout the city threatened that "though you may have business to attend to now, you certainly will have none to bother you should the City be quarantined."

Circulars printed in three languages declared that a quarantine "would be a death blow to the industrial life of the city."[46] Organized labor as well as business interests adopted the rhetoric of plague as economic threat. The San Francisco Labor Council's resolution to assist the campaign called for cooperation to "avoid the calamity of a quarantine."[47]

The San Francisco lodge of the Elks sent their members an elaborate circular of several pages that incorporated both economic and health-related scare tactics. The letter evoked memories of hardships in the days immediately following the fire, declaring that in the event of a quarantine all stores would be closed, everyone would stand in line for food, and each person would receive only the regular army ration. The first part of the document ended with the dramatic statement, capitalized for emphasis, that "the awful days of April, 1906, will be as heaven compared to hell, should our city be quarantined." This letter underscored certain health risks from the plague; a "short history of the plague and plague conditions" mentioned the danger of "painful and horrible death" while emphasizing that the disease could "be controlled by PROPER sanitation." The document headed off objections to the killing of animals, presumably in reference to the antirat campaign, with the statement that "in India, where there is a religious feeling against the destruction or killing of any animal or insect, the plague takes from 250,000 to 1,000,000 people a year." The Citizens' Health Committee considered the Elks' letter to be an exemplary piece of propaganda and reprinted it.[48]

Distribution of literature was not the only way that the committee worked to mobilize people. In Todd's words, "for several months San Francisco was a city of meetings," a total of 162 over six weeks. A well-attended mass meeting on January 28 passed a resolution urging both strict enforcement of health regulations and popular cooperation with the cleanup. This resolution emphasized that the sanitary collection of garbage and the extermination of rats demanded the participation of all men, women, and children of San Francisco. One syllabus for presenting the topic to schoolchildren declared: "To protect life one must watch one's neighbors and report them if they are uncleanly," thereby attempting to establish a network of citizen informers watching for sanitary violations. A questionnaire given to ten thousand employees of large businesses included the question, "Have you succeeded in convincing your neighbors that San Francisco is facing a real danger, not only of a sanitary nature, but more particularly of a vital commercial and financial nature?" This question reveals not only the attempt to enlist the entire citizenry in a campaign of education and surveillance, but also the judgment that the financial threat from the plague exceeded the health risks.[49]

The Citizens' Health Committee was clearly aware of the importance of reaching San Francisco's immigrant population, many of whom lived in relatively insular, non-English-speaking communities and in neighborhoods identified as plague foci. They published their circulars not only in English but also in Italian and Greek, and they translated literature into Japanese for publication in Japanese-language newspapers. Ministers preached rat destruction and cleanliness in their churches. Children took home "kitchen cards" listing rules for eliminating rats. To reach working-class people, rent collectors distributed circulars to tenants, and saloon keepers posted notices in their establishments. San Francisco's various labor organizations fully backed the campaign, with the San Francisco Labor Council, the Building Trades Council, and the City Front Federation all forming subcommittees.[50] At least one observer considered Blue's efforts to involve the entire community to be crucial to the campaign's success; Augustin Keane praised Blue for bringing "the citizens of San Francisco into the ranks of his workers."[51]

The antirat and cleanliness measures intruded on the domestic sphere, so mobilizing women to support the campaign became an important strategy. The men who ran the Citizens' Health Committee initially sought to enlist women through their husbands, but women quickly became an independent force in the war on rats. They formed their own subcommittee, called the Women's Sanitation Committee, which later became a permanent organization known as the Women's Public Health Association of California. The subcommittee mobilized women from sixty organizations and forty-five churches, demonstrating that women could be reached through their own organizations, not just through male family members. Women not only hosted and attended meetings but also scrubbed and cleaned the city's schools, a task probably seen as an extension of their domestic roles. Once mobilized, women also acted as inspectors of hotels, restaurants, lodging houses, streetcars, and even factories.[52]

In an ironic reversal of the committee's original plan, the enthusiasm of women for the campaign became a way to motivate men to participate. Women's roles as household consumers made their patronage crucial to the success of many businesses, and Todd reported warnings to butchers and produce dealers that "housewives were reaching a general understanding that no butcher shop, vegetable stall or fruit stand that was not clean and wholesome" should be patronized.[53] Many women thus embraced the campaign against the plague as an extension of their traditional roles governing cleanliness and consumption within the home. They became important players in the 1908 campaign and maintained their public authority on matters of sanitation and health by creating a permanent organization after the committee's men had returned to other concerns. These developments paralleled the national trend of Progressive middle-class and upper-class women's involvement in reform efforts known as the municipal housekeeping movement.

The effect of the massive campaign to mobilize the citizenry of San Francisco in the war on rats was to transform the plague into a new problem for the city's working-class residents. Initially, the disease represented another in a long list of threats to their health that endangered individuals, their families, and friends and neighbors on a daily basis. Although the plague's reputation and high fatality rates augmented fear, it was hardly unique as a threat. Fewer San Franciscans died of the plague in 1907–1908 than of tuberculosis, typhoid fever, or diphtheria. Tuberculosis caused an average of seven hundred deaths per year in San Francisco between 1906 and 1915.[54] However, the war on rats expanded public health demands placed on San Franciscans in the name of combating plague. Inspectors invaded their homes and businesses, insisting that they change daily practices and pave their property. The sanitary city had no space for the chickens, gardens, and stables of the poor, calling instead for costly concrete backyards and in the process contributing to the perceived separation of the city from nature.

These demands most dramatically affected recent immigrants, particularly Italians, many of whom came from rural backgrounds and gravitated to employment in familiar and accessible trades such as fishing, farming, selling produce at the market, and driving horse-drawn scavenger wagons. The vast majority of Italians emigrating to San Francisco came directly from the city or village where they were born rather than from other cities in the United States. In 1911 the Progressive reformer Lawrence Veiller noted the need for "sanitary control of diverse foreign peoples seeking to adjust themselves to urban conditions of living." According to Veiller, reformers encountering these immigrants faced "the problem of regulating their habits of life, of protecting them from themselves and of protecting the community from the results of their ignorance and carelessness." In San Francisco, too, residues of rural life—industries seen as insufficiently urban and modern—and the immigrants who dominated them became targets of the campaign to sanitize San Francisco into a modern city.[55] At times, individuals benefited when landlords and the city installed plumbing and sewers for their use. In other cases, they watched as their homes were torn down in the name of sanitation and their employment saddled with new restrictions.

PAVING THE CITY

By changing people's daily living habits and altering the physical landscape of the city, Dr. Rupert Blue and his allies sought to transform San Francisco from an ideal rat habitat to an inhospitable environment for rodents. Frank Morton Todd identified the "rat harbor formed by board walks in gardens and backyards, planked back areas, and floors close to the ground, in basements and cottages" as "the danger that was common to all parts of the City."[56] Ordinances and health inspectors targeted as sanitary threats both these elements of the built environment and practices such as garbage collection and the use of manure for fertilizer. The campaign against the plague became an opportunity for health officials to promote changes in urban living habits that they had long advocated.

Blue's war against San Francisco's rats consisted of five components: trapping, poisoning, exposing rats to natural enemies, cutting off their food supply, and eliminating their habitat. Bounties of five cents per rat, later increased to ten cents, encouraged trapping. The Citizens' Health Committee spent over twelve thousand dollars on rat bounties

Rat catchers with their morning catch. Note the debris-filled vacant lot behind them. Courtesy of the National Library of Medicine.

in the opening months of the campaign. Bounties also helped monitor the spread of disease among the rodent population since the bodies were brought to the campaign's headquarters, where they were tested for plague. Rat catching was not left to civilians—men were employed as professional rat catchers, earning wages of $2.50 per day as well as bounties per rat. Over 350,000 rats died in traps, and hundreds of thousands more were poisoned. In total, an estimated two million rats died. Many of these animals "died in the sewers and were washed into the bay, where they could be seen floating in rafts near the outfalls."[57] Thousands of rat corpses floating in San Francisco Bay hardly seems characteristic of a successful sanitary campaign, but reducing the existing rat population was only part of Blue's strategy. Even more important was enforcing sanitary practices and rebuilding the urban environment to make it inhospitable to rats—creating the modern, sanitary city, paved with concrete.

The new campaign did not entirely abandon the long-standing practice of disinfection of premises. In an echo of 1900–1901 in Chinatown, buildings where cases of human or rat plague were found received the full treatment of fumigation with sulfur dioxide gas and washing with bichloride of mercury solution. Cleanup crews burned bedding and clothing. Rat holes were flooded with toxic solutions and poisons, particularly the Danysz rat virus, a poison that targeted the animals. Men stuffed cracks in walls and floors with chlorinated lime to kill fleas and their eggs. At first, cleanup efforts radiated out from the initial foci of infection, but eventually the campaign encompassed the whole city.[58] Experts ultimately concluded that all these efforts at disinfection were less potent than the new, plague-specific strategy of rat-proofing. Richard H. Creel even characterized disinfection and poisoning and trapping of rats as "ineffective." As an example, he described "a large two-story frame dwelling located in the center of the city and in a good neighborhood" that had been the site of a human plague case and a cleanup effort. Trappers caught plague-infected rats within two months after the disinfection of the property. However, removing the wooden planked yard and replacing the plank floor of the basement with a concrete one eliminated the infestation. Writing in 1910, Creel used the San Francisco experience as his primary case study of the effectiveness of rat-proofing in combating bubonic plague.[59] Copies of Todd's *Eradicating Plague from San Francisco* were sent to physicians around the world, and Blue became internationally recognized as an expert on plague outbreaks. He would ultimately use the success of San Francisco's war on rats to launch a distinguished career that included a stint as surgeon general from 1912 to 1920.[60]

To support the San Francisco campaign, the Board of Supervisors passed a series of ordinances addressing unsanitary practices and structures. Floors in basements had to be concrete, and foundations had to be built of concrete, brick, or stone and extend at least one foot above the ground. Obviously, both older frame houses and new wooden dwellings constructed in a hurry after the fire rarely met these requirements—and these were most often the homes of the city's poorer residents. To rat-proof a building, all wooden floors had to be removed from yards and replaced with concrete, gravel, or packed earth, materials that did not provide hiding places for rats. In total, 6,433,100 square feet of the city of San Francisco (including sidewalks, basements, stables, and chicken yards) were rebuilt with concrete in just two years.[61]

Even the most ardent supporters of rat-proofing recognized that all of these changes were costly. Health officials considered the "immense outlay of both money and labor" essential, however, if plague was to be permanently eradicated from the city.[62] Private citizens paid for many of the improvements after health inspectors discovered nuisances on their property. According to the Board of Health, the Citizens' Health Committee served as a "mediator between the authorities and the citizens who were required to spend considerable sums of money" to make their homes and businesses conform to new sanitary regulations.[63] Not surprisingly, many property owners resisted these unexpected and often prohibitive expenses. Todd described "hundreds" of cases in which "it was extremely difficult to convince the owner that his innocent plank wall or bit of flooring was a danger." San Franciscans spent an estimated one million dollars to rat-proof their property, and some reverted to claims that the plague did not in fact exist in the city when their property failed an inspection. This denial was not surprising given the history of San Francisco newspapers and officials denying the existence of plague. Presumably many residents, particularly those for whom these changes represented major expenses, genuinely believed that the disease was merely an excuse for authorities to impose additional hardships during difficult economic times.[64] The vast mobilization campaign certainly played a role in pressuring San Francisco residents to cooperate with the sanitation campaign, as did the evidence that the Board of Health possessed the political authority to condemn their property if they failed to act. In total, health officials destroyed 1,713 houses and disinfected 11,342.[65] The houses condemned and torn down were almost exclusively the homes of the poor, many of whom had lost their previous residences in the fire and now lost those they had scrambled to reconstruct in the wake of the disaster.

Small wooden buildings could be made rat-proof by elevating them off the ground, preventing rats from easily entering through the floor. Similarly, small sheds and wood piles could be balanced on elevated platforms. In the city's outlying districts, where the plague outbreak was less severe, ordinances allowed houses of less than eight hundred square feet to be elevated eighteen inches off the ground in lieu of constructing concrete foundations.[66] This technique of elevating houses proved its effectiveness in the Lobos Square refugee camp, where eighteen people were stricken with the plague starting in September 1907. As in other infected areas of the city, the disinfection and fumigation of the camp failed to prevent the disease's recurrence. However, when the cottages were raised off the ground, the plague disappeared. The success of "rat-proofing by elevation" demonstrated another aspect of changing the ecology of the city to make it inhospitable to rats.[67]

SANITIZING THE CITY

The transformation of San Francisco into a more sanitary city consisted of several components. Paving the city with concrete was one. Another involved choices about the place of animals in the urban environment. Rats obviously were to be excluded from the modern city. Cats and dogs were generally accepted as useful and loved companions. Horses, which were central to transportation and portage, also remained, but the new antiplague ordinances established a distance between horses and humans that had not previously existed. In 1906 it remained normal for many working-class people to live in close proximity to animals of all kinds. For example, before the fire the upper stories of a building near Telegraph Hill were home to sixteen families while the basement housed twelve horses and an assortment of rabbits, chickens, dogs, cats, and rats. The same basement provided storage for the wares of vegetable venders, one of the professions common among the neighborhood's Italian residents. However, such living habits were increasingly seen as unsanitary vestiges of rural habits. In October 1906, Henry A. Fisk of the Commonwealth Club declared these living quarters shared by humans and nonhuman animals to be "absolutely unsanitary" and unacceptable in modern San Francisco.[68]

During the campaign against the plague, Todd described "the ordinary stable" as a "complete rats' boarding house," and he and Keane blamed several plague cases on close proximity between stables and human dwellings. They particularly condemned wooden houses constructed over ground floor stables. One stable reportedly contained more than two hundred rats. In another case, a lodging house where two people contracted the plague and trappers caught twenty-six infected rats was located near five stables. In May 1908, when San Francisco instituted formal regulations governing rat-proofing in stables, the city had 5,292 stables. The Stable and Carriage Owners' Association formed an active subcommittee of the Citizens' Health Committee and persuaded the owners of those stables to install 3,967 concrete floors.

Health inspectors threatening the destruction of a woman's backyard stable.
Courtesy of the National Library of Medicine.

Another 903 stables were temporarily rat-proofed on the condition that
they be torn down within two years. Over four hundred stables were
eliminated entirely from the city.[69] The earthquake and fire represented
a turning point in the replacement of horses with automobiles in San
Francisco, and the rat-proofing of stables and paving of the city contributed to that process.

While horses remained as work animals, animals used for food
production were almost entirely exiled from the city in the wake of
the plague. The Board of Health considered "chicken coops and other
places where live animals were kept" to be "dangerous harboring and
breeding places for rats," and chicken coops became the target of a special ordinance.[70] San Francisco contained some sixteen thousand
domestic chicken yards, most located in thinly settled suburbs and in
the densely populated poorer quarters of the city, where Todd referred
to them as "thick among the houses." Chickens were an important element of the subsistence strategies of poor families. In 1904, a dozen eggs

cost an average of twenty-three cents, ranging from nineteen to forty-five cents depending on the season, and eggs were a staple ingredient in most meals. Chickens could also provide a source of meat, and a successful backyard chicken farmer could earn extra income by selling eggs and young chickens to neighbors. Chickens kept in backyards were fed grain and table scraps, which sanitary officials suspected supported as many rats as fowl. The 1908 rat-proofing ordinance required that chicken yards have concrete floors and be surrounded by brick or concrete walls at least a foot high topped by a six-foot wire net. Such elaborate chicken coops were prohibitively expensive for most practitioners of the domestic chicken industry, and the new regulations forced eleven thousand people to dispose of their birds. Those with the financial resources to remain in the business covered their chicken yards with 676,000 square feet of concrete and gravel.[71]

San Francisco's working poor resisted the loss of their chickens. Frank Morton Todd observed sarcastically that "sacred among the palladia of American liberty is [the] right to keep chickens." As a proponent of the sanitary measures, Todd mocked the vehemence with which people defended their right to raise chickens on their property and expressed his frustration with their resistance to the war on rats. He went on to list the factors that made chicken yards "one of the most troublesome problems" facing the rat-proofing campaign. Specifically, Todd referred to "the number, the varying intelligence, and the temperamental diversities of the people that keep chickens—their passive resistance, and infinite stratagems, and degrees of 'pull' when threatened with prosecution." His defamation of the character of people with chickens in the yard demonstrated the class and ethnic tensions that underlay an antiplague campaign in which sanitation officers inspected and judged the homes of working-class people, many of them immigrants. Todd's "passive resistance" and "infinite stratagems" reflected the weapons of the weak deployed by the poor, and his reference to degrees of pull implied that some chicken owners successfully lobbied to retain their birds. Perhaps because of this resistance, the Board of Health's efforts to rid San Francisco of chickens did not end with the plague campaign. Four years later, in 1911–12, the board reported that 275 chicken yards containing 3,213 chickens had been shut down after a round of inspections while another 69 had been remodeled. Not a single chicken yard passed inspection, indicating that sanitary officials were looking to shut down the city's remaining chicken keepers.[72]

The elimination of San Francisco's domestic chicken trade went hand in hand with the rise of industrialized chicken factories in the greater Bay Area, particularly in the city of Petaluma. As early as 1894, Petaluma's exhibit at the Midwinter Fair in San Francisco featured the new technology of incubators. The Petaluma Incubator Company—"'progression' is our motto"—sold incubators, brooders, and other chicken farm equipment nationwide. Petaluma boosters dreamed that the chicken industry would make their town "the leading manufacturing city of the Pacific Coast," surpassing even San Francisco, and half a million hens already lived there in 1895. In 1912 the California Chicken Company opened in Mayfield, thirty-two miles south of San Francisco, with ambitions to put "the chicken raising business on a business basis." They emphasized the "remarkable cleanliness" of their operation, which resulted from "the underlying principles of sanitation rightly applied."[73] Exiling chicken raising from San Francisco thus opened up urban markets to these large companies located in nearby more rural areas. It was also part of a broader and ongoing process in which food production became disconnected from the city.

Chickens were not the only food animals targeted for exile from the urban environment, and the war on rats was likewise not the only motivation behind the process. The same ordinance that discussed chickens also made it illegal to "keep or feed" rabbits, guinea pigs, turkeys, geese, ducks, doves, and pigeons, except in coops meeting strict regulations. The dairy industry was also gradually forced from the city. In 1902, San Francisco's chief sanitary inspector had worried that "the gradual extension of the city" meant that dairies and cattle raising were being driven outside the borders of the city and county, where they were no longer subject to inspection. Most dairies were owned by Italian and Swiss immigrants who had only short-term leases on their land, and the demand for land on the city's outskirts in the aftermath of the fire led to a 50 percent reduction in the number of dairies in San Francisco between June 1907 and June 1909. Officials no longer worried about dairies leaving; in fact, a 1910 ordinance regulated the keeping of cattle "with a view to clearing out all of the dairies within the city limits." Because of the Bay Area's moderate climate, milk was not iced in transit, and dairies supplying the city did not move far. Approximately 130 dairies remained within one hundred miles of the city, most located in Marin County, but San Francisco had taken another step in gradually distancing itself from its food supply.[74] In this case, change occurred less because of fear of the plague than because of the geographical expansion of the urban area in the wake of the earthquake and fire, although strict antiplague ordinances targeting stables may have played a role as well.

San Francisco's stables not only housed horses and dairy cows but also contributed to a cycle in which the city's excess manure fertilized rural gardens in southern San Francisco County and adjacent San Mateo County that grew vegetables and fruit for the urban center. As in many of the industries targeted in the war on rats, Italian immigrants made up a high percentage of both these farmers and the men who transported vegetables and manure to and from the city, the newer immigrants having gradually displaced the Chinese in the industry.[75] The plague brought scrutiny to this practice of "truck and garden farming," which appeared to be unsanitary. Dead rats could be discarded with stable manure, then in Todd's words, "the vegetable grower's wagon stops at the barn on its way back from market, [and] loads up on manure and bubonic rats" before returning to the gardens that fed the city. In response to the possible transport of plague, the State Board of Health prohibited "the hauling of manure from San Francisco to any other county." In response, truck farmers faced with losing a valuable source of cheap fertilizer "threatened to shut off . . . the City's supply of green vegetables." Stable owners left with no easy means of disposing of manure also objected to the new law. A compromise allowed manure to be sent out only in metal-lined wagons "from stables certified to be sanitary and equipped with rat-proof manure bins." The cost of inspection would be born by the San Francisco Gardeners' and Ranchers' Association.[76] In this case, the sanitary regulations, rather than protecting the city, focused on preventing the spread of plague from the city to the vulnerable countryside. The effect of these restrictions on the cycle of urban manure fertilizing rural gardens was to further separate the urban and the rural, the city and the farms that provided sustenance to its population.

Postdisaster San Francisco faced a challenge in disposing of refuse produced by its human residents as well as its animal ones. In San

Francisco in the early twentieth century, Italians from the northern province of Genoa dominated the waste trades. The stigma attached to waste-related trades meant that they offered opportunities for immigrants from marginalized ethnic groups to establish businesses. In San Francisco an Italian man who wanted to enter the scavenging business need only save enough money to purchase a wagon and a horse.[77] Under the city's privatized system of garbage collection, licensed private scavenger wagons made individual arrangements with householders along their routes. The high rates charged by scavengers provided an incentive for residents to find illicit means of disposing of their waste. Scavengers in turn had to pay to have their collections incinerated at the Sanitary Reduction Works, the company with an exclusive franchise to dispose of the city's refuse, so they too engaged in illegal practices such as burning scrap paper in furnaces in the manufacturing districts, contributing to pollution and posing a risk of fire. In 1903 the Department of Public Health described the city's system of garbage collection as "neither scientific nor sanitary" and suggested municipal garbage collection as the solution. Things became even worse after the fire when scavengers often surreptitiously dumped garbage on the suddenly abundant empty lots.[78]

When human garbage collectors did not complete their jobs, rats stepped in as natural scavengers. Thus the first step in eliminating garbage as a food source for the city's rats was to reform human residents' methods of disposal. Women led the campaign to educate San Franciscans about the importance of using metal garbage cans with lids that sealed tightly. City officials passed yet another ordinance regulating garbage receptacles, pickup schedules, and even defining garbage to include virtually all organic matter. As part of the war on rats, the city distributed fifty thousand new garbage cans.[79] The people most affected by the new regulations and strict enforcement of garbage collection were those for whom scavenging represented a subsistence strategy. Licensed professional scavengers were one such group, but another was the poorest of the poor, who use the waste prevalent in any urban environment. San Francisco's rag industry—in which poor people scavenged rags that they sold to dealers for eventual reuse or recycling into products such as paper and shoddy cloth—was an example of such an economic niche that was shut down by the increased attention to sanitation.[80] Thus the crackdown on garbage, like that on chicken coops, targeted strategies employed by the city's poor in their struggle to eke out a living.

Although in San Francisco the plague outbreak provoked the city to strictly regulate garbage disposal, the change was part of a nationwide trend in which professional sanitary engineers began to take over municipal refuse programs in the early twentieth century. Engineers persuaded public health officials that technology could solve garbage disposal problems.[81] In San Francisco the technological panacea was the construction of new municipal incinerators. The city purchased the existing Sanitary Reduction Works plant as well as lots on which to construct two new incinerators, but in an example of not-in-my-backyard syndrome, none of the city's residents wanted them in their neighborhood despite promises that the new incinerators would not spew noxious odors. Fears of nuisances and reduced property values certainly were justified. The pollution from the existing plant spread over a half-mile radius around its site south of Market, and the earthquake and fire had forced more people to move into the vicinity, leading to a noticeable increase in the number of complaints. Two new sites were eventually selected, one in North Beach and the other south of Army Street in the Islais Creek district.[82] By June 1913 the Islais Creek incinerator was finally nearing completion, but it failed to meet guarantees that it would not emit odors, gases, or smoke. The plant operated only intermittently as the city sought reimbursement from the contractor for breach of contract, and the structure eventually became a warehouse. The second planned incinerator was never built.[83] The technological solution to the problem of solid waste disposal had fallen short.

Damage to San Francisco's sewer system represented another sanitary crisis in the wake of the 1906 disaster. In 1900 the Board of Public Works had noted that the city's sewer system was in urgent need of repairs and improvements. It developed a systematic plan for sewers and drainage in the city, and a bond issue to provide funding passed in 1903.[84] Construction had barely begun, however, when the earthquake struck. The temblor shattered several of the main sewage pipes and dislodged the line and grade of other pipes. Brick sewers collapsed completely. The authorities in the war on rats targeted the sewers as the "great highway" of rats as well as a source of "protection, food, and drink" for the rodents. Broken sewers provided rats with easy access to an underground network running throughout the city and connecting wealthy areas with poor ones.[85]

In fact, the city's sewer system had been in crisis for nearly its entire existence. Perhaps the worst site was Channel Creek, formerly Mission Creek but widely known as "shit creek," which ran through the lumber yards, warehouses, and factories south of Market. Captain Fred Klebingat described the creek as "an open sewer . . . as thick as soup." The rumor among the longshoremen was that "if you fell overboard you'd not last more than two minutes" because "if you took two gulps of that stuff it would be the end of you." The Citizens' Health Committee found that sewage accumulated at the mouth of the creek and nearby lumberyards and warehouses swarmed with rats.[86] Even after the sanitary reforms associated with the plague, in 1910 an area of two square blocks in the Potrero district became known as "'The Red Sea' nuisance" when the haphazard filling in of railroad properties created a pond cut off from the bay. Plumbing from nearby dwellings and factories emptied into the pond, creating a serious health hazard. To mitigate the problem, the Board of Health forced the factories to construct a private sewer and connect it to a main city sewer. In the long term the board suggested that the city address this body of water as it had so many others in its history—by filling it in. This would not only "abate an insanitary condition that has long existed" but also "open up to use a valuable tract of land."[87] Of course, this solution ignored the earthquake's recent demonstration of the risks of building on filled land.

Early underground sewer systems, including San Francisco's, were constructed before the era of germ theory, when the prevailing belief that running water purified itself meant that discharging sewage into waterways was seen as an appropriate means of waste disposal. In the late nineteenth and early twentieth centuries, sanitary authorities became concerned about bacteria, although an awareness of the dangers posed by industrial wastes and toxic materials did not develop until after World War I. The technology of sewer systems also lagged behind that of water supplies. The increased flow of water from new innovations like indoor plumbing flooded city sewer systems. San Francisco's sewers had expanded steadily from 128 miles of mains in 1880 to 307 in 1900 and 332 in 1905, incorporating growing suburbs as well as improving coverage of the central city.[88] The city's rapid outward expansion in the wake of the fire strained the capacity of the damaged sewer system, however. The region around Islais Creek, which drained the outer Mission, Glen Park, and Sunnyside districts, had no sewer facilities at all as late as 1910. Many of the city's vegetable gardens as well as Butchertown and other noxious industries were located there. Robert Langley Porter, a physician with the University of California, remembered "millions" of "great, big, fat rats coming down at low tide to feed" along Islais Creek. The threat of contaminated food from inadequate sewers thus paralleled the concern with bubonic plague spreading from urban stables to agriculture on the suburban periphery.[89] On the other side of the city, sewage from the rapidly developing Sunset district accumulated in a cesspool in Golden Gate Park, where it contaminated first the sandy soil of the park and then its water supply.[90] Uncontained urban waste posed a sanitary threat to food sources and open spaces—rural elements that remained within and adjacent to the metropolis.

Even sewage outlets that did not directly contaminate gardens and parks were less than sanitary. In 1908 more than 125 sewer outlets discharged their contents along the bay shore. The historian Matthew Morse Booker has suggested that San Francisco Bay was probably at it most polluted in the early twentieth century because of flows of sewage and industrial wastes. Most of the sewer outfalls were nothing but wooden boxes, and they lacked screens to prevent rats from entering. Waste accumulated behind bulkheads and backed up in blocked outlets. At Polk and North Point Streets near Fort Mason on the city's north shore, 250 feet of sewage flowed out over the ground. The Citizens' Health Committee concluded that the existing sewer system was "a terrible menace to public health" and endorsed a proposed bond issue to raise funds for a new system.[91] The measure allocated another four million dollars for improvements to supplement the bond passed five years earlier. The new system reduced the number of outlets discharging along the shoreline to four and located those remaining points where powerful tidal currents would sweep the waste out to sea. The stated goal was "no perceptible pollution of the waters of the bay."[92] In the aftermath of the earthquake and fire, San Francisco's campaign against plague and rats joined with the growing concern over water sanitation to provide the impetus for improvements to the city's sewer system.

Removal of sewage outfalls was not the only improvement the waterfront needed if it was to meet San Francisco's new standards. The San Francisco Gas & Electric Company dumped waste from their gas works into the bay, killing fish that then washed onto the beach to provide a feast for rats. Garbage from ships also washed ashore and attracted hungry rodents.[93] As one of the few areas not destroyed in the fire, the waterfront remained in its original makeshift state as the rebuilding of the city commenced. Most wharves were constructed of wood and offered no protection against rats. Because plague spread via ships, the waterfront represented a particularly important site in the war on rats. The committee feared that unless conditions at the waterfront improved, "the money expended and the work done in the attempt to eradicate plague from this city will be wasted," as the disease would just reenter the city from ships in the harbor. They proposed "the installation of a concrete seawall, bulkheads, and properly constructed modern piers" along with the planned improvements to the sewer system.[94] These structural improvements accompanied practices intended to prevent rats from traveling between ships and shore, including funnel-shaped metal rat guards on the lines anchoring ships to docks, regular disinfection and fumigation of ships to kill rats on board, and careful inspection of cargo.[95]

The efforts to rat-proof the waterfront and vessels passing through San Francisco's port not only protected the city from diseases associated with commerce but also sought to avoid infecting the countryside with plague from the city. William Hobdy described his work overseeing the fumigation of all kinds of vessels, from transpacific liners to lumber trawlers, passenger ferries, and steamboats, as a constant effort to "prevent the spread of the Plague from San Francisco to the various Bay and river ports that are now so intimately connected." San Francisco's place at the center of regional trade networks meant that rat-borne disease threatened the entire Pacific Coast. Ship owners and captains were as sporadically cooperative as other groups affected by the campaign. Hobdy frequently reported ships escaping from the harbor without undergoing disinfection, particularly when their destination port was

Debris and wood scraps being burned during the sanitary campaign. Courtesy of the National Library of Medicine.

too small to have harbor authorities to check if vessels had been certified rat-free. He also complained of insufficient staff to patrol the waterfront and enforce measures to prevent rats from moving between ships and solid ground.[96] In retrospect, these policies were imperfect at best as measures for rat control. Fumigation and disinfection that killed rats but not their fleas could simply incite fleas to bite the only remaining warm-blooded food source: humans. And both rats and fleas crossed to and from shore in grain sacks and other containers.

The paving of San Francisco during the war on rats laid a total of nearly 6.5 million square feet of concrete to replace sidewalks, basements, floors, stables, and chicken yards.[97] Such changes, along with updates to the sewer system and new practices of waste disposal, represented improvements to long-standing sanitary hazards in the city. The crisis of the plague inspired efforts to modernize the city's infrastructure by raising public awareness and building support for new policies and for bonds to finance new construction. Building a modern, sanitary city was a long-term process, however. In 1911–12 the Board of

Health reported that 1,308 houses and 406 stables were destroyed as antirat measures, the same year that an additional 275 chicken yards were shut down. The San Francisco Housing Association continued to complain that immigrants, specifically Italians and Mexicans, kept "chickens, goats, cows and horses" in their living rooms and cellars, as well as dogs under their beds, and called for "regular inspection" to counter these practices. Even between 1918 and 1920, "animals removed from premises" remained a significant sanitary violation, with more than a hundred cases each year.[98] San Francisco's poor continued to be subjected to the loss of their homes and livelihoods in the name of sanitation even as they simultaneously benefited from a more healthful urban environment.

THE PERSISTENCE OF PLAGUE

San Francisco was not the only Bay Area city stricken with plague in 1907–1908. Across the bay, Oakland experienced twenty cases in two years, with another in 1911. In Oakland the percentage of infected rats was as high as in San Francisco, although the disease affected fewer people. Cases also developed in Berkeley, Point Richmond, and further inland in Contra Costa County. In fact, while the plague lay dormant in San Francisco between 1904 and 1907, the only human cases in the region were three in Contra Costa County and one in East Oakland.[99] In rural areas of the East Bay, plague spread via contact with ground squirrels, which had presumably been infected by fleas from rats escaping from ships. Sanitarians in the Bay Area guessed at this connection as early as 1903, and more recent research has confirmed that rats and wild rodents such as ground squirrels and meadow mice can live in close association and exchange fleas. In 1908 researchers established that ground squirrels in Contra Costa were dying en masse from the plague, the first confirmed epizootic among wild animals in North America.[100]

The widespread infection among ground squirrels—seventeen hundred infected squirrels were discovered in the years after 1908—threatened any hopes of containing and eradicating the plague. San Francisco responded to the news of ground squirrel deaths by banning the importation and sale of ground squirrels in the city. (Squirrel legs were often used instead of frog legs as a delicacy in Chinatown.) With the disease seemingly under control in San Francisco, Blue and his associates launched an ambitious campaign to create a "10-mile squirrel free zone" around population centers and to eradicate the disease among ground squirrels across the bay.[101] Not surprisingly, this campaign proved unsuccessful. Plague raced ahead of its pursuers, spreading from county to county even as the squirrel body count exceeded seven hundred thousand. In 1912 infected squirrels were found in nine California counties, and despite poisoning and hunting programs, plague-positive squirrels continued to turn up in counties believed to be free of the disease.[102]

The plague did not return to San Francisco after 1908, but it periodically resurfaced in other California cities. One case developed in Los Angeles in that year, and thirteen cases were scattered among six northern California counties between 1910 and 1914. Oakland suffered an outbreak of pneumonic plague—the more virulent form that could spread via sputum from person to person—in 1919 that killed thirteen of fourteen people infected. The first victim had been squirrel hunting in the foothills of Alameda County just before coming down with the disease.[103] In 1924 and 1925 pneumonic plague broke out among Los Angeles's Mexican community. In an echo of San Francisco's treatment of Chinatown in 1900–1904, four poor Mexican neighborhoods were quarantined and twenty-five hundred homes damaged or destroyed in an effort to contain the disease. More than forty people died. A rat epizootic occurred in the area prior to the first human infection, and the infection was traced to both rats and squirrels, particularly those living near hog farms that received garbage from the city of Los Angeles. City authorities followed the example of their northern neighbor and spent several million dollars on their own antiplague campaign. Overall, including the San Francisco outbreaks, California suffered a total of 372 plague cases and 257 deaths from 1900 to 1925.[104]

Although individual cities could be made less susceptible to plague, the disease established a permanent foothold in western North America. Plague-infected squirrels have been found in fifteen western states. Wild rodents, particularly ground squirrels, became a reservoir from which the disease has occasionally flared up among animals and infected humans. Such reservoirs, which also exist in Asia and Africa, are believed to be the source of the pandemics that have earned plague its reputation as a global killer. In 1953–54 scientists trapping rodents on San Bruno Mountain just south of San Francisco found the plague bacilli in their fleas, and sure enough, an epizootic struck the region's rat population in 1954. The scientists concluded that undetected plague outbreaks could easily occur among suburban and rural rodent populations, and the study confirmed that plague persisted among Bay Area rodent populations despite the best efforts of Blue and other sanitarians earlier in the century.[105] About a dozen people contract the plague in the United States every year, and a 1983 outbreak consisted of forty cases. Most of the victims lived in rural New Mexico, and many of them were Navajo. In 2015 cases at Yosemite National Park forced a brief closure of several campgrounds and temporarily brought the disease back into the national news.[106] Despite the best efforts of health authorities to contain the disease, plague escaped their control and became endemic to the United States. Ironically, through their efforts to clean up and protect cities like San Francisco, urban authorities and resources transformed the disease from an urban to a rural problem.

CONCLUSION

When the earthquake and fire disrupted the urban environment in San Francisco, the flames drove rats from their burrows. Broken sewer pipes, makeshift human housing arrangements, and rubble-filled vacant lots provided the city's rodents with abundant food and shelter. As displaced rats settled into new territories, they carried with them fleas and the bubonic plague, leading to a resurfacing of the dreaded disease. Targeting those rats, health officials emphasized their ability to control and eliminate the plague through sanitation reforms and paving basements, stables, and backyards. The aftermath of the earthquake and fire provided no shortage of discourses of catastrophe, but in contrast to the fire's sweeping destruction, the more manageable crisis of the plague provided an opportunity for authorities to implement plans for improvements.

In 1908, Augustin C. Keane declared optimistically that the war on rats had made San Francisco "virtually invulnerable to epidemics" and "probably the world's most sanitary city." In combination with the rebuilding after the fire, San Francisco had become "the first twentieth-century city."[107] Keane overstated his case, but the war on rats did transform the urban ecology of San Francisco, not only for rodents but for humans as well. The campaign accelerated the modernization of San Francisco in the form of an updated sewer system, municipal garbage collection (even though the new incinerator failed), and the replacement of wooden structures with rat-proof concrete ones. The changes certainly made the city healthier; overall rates of infectious disease declined by an impressive 75 percent in the aftermath of the cleanup efforts.[108]

When Dr. Rupert Blue called for San Francisco to be "one block of concrete throughout," he envisioned a city protected against the disorderly nature of not only disease, rats, and squirrels but also of vegetable gardens and chicken coops. Such outposts of the rural in the city, managed more often than not by recent immigrants and members of the working classes, became sanitary threats to the city and its residents. The historian Adam Rome has observed that, during the Progressive Era, native-born Americans worried that new immigrants "made no effort to distance themselves from the messiness of nature."[109] When that messiness seemed to spread disease, particularly the bubonic plague, it became an easy target for reformers. The war on rats largely shut down the domestic chicken industry and interrupted the use of manure from San Francisco to fertilize the suburban farms that produced food for the city. Thus the city became increasingly isolated from food production in the name of sanitation, changes that contributed to the perception of cities as existing outside of nature. Although environmentalists may look back with nostalgia on a city more integrated with its hinterland, those changes made the urban environment healthier for its human residents. All San Franciscans did not experience the burdens of change equally, however. In the long run, working-class residents and members of marginalized ethnic groups certainly benefited from improved sanitation, but in the immediate context of the war on rats, thousands lost their homes as well as elements of their subsistence strategies, such as the chickens in the backyard.

SEVEN

SYMBOLIC RECOVERY AND THE LEGACIES OF DISASTER

IN 1911, HARBOR VIEW REMAINED A RELATIVELY UNDEVELOPED stretch of land on the northern shore of San Francisco. An unfinished seawall—begun in 1893 by the silver baron James G. Fair but abandoned a year later—partially enclosed shallow Marina Cove. The neighborhood possessed an open waterfront and lovely views, but steep hills impeded travel to the central city, keeping it as less than prime real estate. During the 1906 earthquake, several parts of the district, including an area of fill that had once been a spring-fed lake called Washerwoman's Lagoon, suffered from shaking as severe as anywhere in San Francisco, rated as a nine or ten on the Rossi-Forel scale. At the United Central Gas Company plant, which had been built on made land, brick walls cracked and fell along with the plant's chimney. The earthquake also wrecked a large gas container and killed one worker. The temblor broke the Baker Street sewer, a bane of camp commander René Bine and residents of Harbor View refugee camp, and wrenched frame buildings off their foundations throughout the neighborhood. In its characteristic linking of ground type and earthquake damage, the State Earthquake Investigation Commission (SEIC) noted that this site combined made land and the point of a sandpit that had been extensively graded. On a filled section of nearby Union Street, the shaking moved a sidewalk ten feet to the north and caused it to sink ten feet s original grade. Street paving and the cable conduit there ⟨⟩red more severe damage than at any other point in the city." The ⟨⟩C report concluded that such damage "unequivocally demon-strated" that "such places are dangerous building sites, especially in regions subject to seismic disturbances."[1]

As detailed in chapter 3, the underused land owned by the Fair Estate became the site of the Harbor View refugee camp. Although many residents disliked the location, a few sought to remain after the official camp closed. For example, Mrs. Shorter, a widow with several children whom Bine described in the language of the time as "a very nice colored lady," wanted to construct a shack and maintain her laun-dry business from the camp.[2] Both her race and her status as a single mother situated Mrs. Shorter on the margins of the community, and she presumably saw the Harbor View neighborhood as an affordable place to live with sufficient demand and the necessary resources to sup-port her laundry, a callback to the old days of laundries surrounding the now-filled lake. The makeshift homes and small businesses of working-class people like Mrs. Shorter dotted the landscape of Harbor View over the next five years.

As Mrs. Shorter and many other San Franciscans struggled to make a living in the postdisaster city, the more prosperous planned a trium-phant celebration of the city's rebuilding. Even before the earthquake, some city leaders had proposed a world's fair to commemorate the opening of the Panama Canal projected for 1914. Ironically, the disaster may have boosted San Francisco's bid for the fair, and the city beat out New Orleans for the right to host the Panama Pacific International Exposition.[3] The event promised to simultaneously celebrate "the benign beauty of nature at its best" and human control over nature, manifested in the canal, the reconstructed city of San Francisco, and the fair itself.[4] Symbolic, commemorative projects such as the exposi-tion can play a key role in urban resilience after disasters, providing both psychological and tangible signs of progress toward recovery.[5] The exposition ultimately served as both a symbolic demonstration of the city's recovery from the earthquake and fire and a practical tool of urban development.

As with previous plans for urban space, such as the Burnham Plan, the Panama Pacific International Exposition balanced praise for the natural beauty of San Francisco and Harbor View with proposals to dramatically transform the site to facilitate appreciation of that beauty and advance development goals. As one promotional brochure declared: "A topography of great natural beauty and variety permits and demands unprecedented architectural, landscape, color and lighting effects." The setting "spurs artists and architects to supreme efforts, inspires them to avail of nature for the perfection of art."[6] In the minds of San Franciscans, nature and artifice would come together to create an exposition, and a city, of unprecedented splendor.

The exposition also served as a model city in a more literal sense. For proponents of the Burnham Plan and city planning in general, the carefully planned, centrally controlled "cities" of world's fairs—epitomized by the famed White City at Chicago's 1893 Columbian Exposition—offered exemplary models of urban development. Some observers at the time emphasized the Panama Pacific International Exposition as instant city. Frank Morton Todd, the official historian of the fair just as he had been for the war on rats, wrote that the exposition as city was "not a mere figure of speech, but a gritty reality." He added: "What had to be done on the Exposition grounds amounted to the creation of a city with every known convenience."[7]

The history of the construction process—the "gritty realities" of the acquisition of land and the transformation of the site—reveals much about the mind-set of leading San Franciscans only a few years after the earthquake and fire. In building this temporary city as a paean to their own city's resilience, they reenacted familiar processes of urban development. The instant city of the Panama Pacific International Exposition echoed San Francisco's rapid early growth, and the choice of a waterfront site meant that construction required filling of 184 acres—a process undertaken with almost no recognition of seismic risks.[8] Despite the widespread acknowledgment of the risks of made ground in 1906—specifically reinforced for Harbor View in the findings of the SEIC—the city's planners and architects failed to implement any lasting recognition of made land as hazard zone. Ongoing patterns of waterfront development reveal the degree to which San Franciscans ignored the lessons of 1906. Narratives of urban growth and technological progress, along with the lure of profit, continued to trump evidence that supported a new, more cautious approach to urban development.

Initial visions of the rebuilt city had often assumed that San Franciscans would take every precaution to prevent a recurrence of disaster. In May 1906, for example, one labor newspaper declared it "certainly a settled question" that "the new building laws will provide for thoroughly earthquake and fire proof structures within the burned district." Such changes in regulations proved to be anything but settled. As in Chicago after the 1871 fire, proposals to extend the fire limits in San Francisco into the South of Market district drew opposition from small homeowners. At a rally of concerned property owners, the Rev. T. P. Mulligan declared: "Better a city of shacks owned by the people than a city of skyscrapers owned by Eastern capitalists." Mulligan called frame buildings the "safeguard" of the poor, and worried that "the extension of the fire limits will mean our ruin." The proposal went down to defeat when Mayor Schmitz threw his support behind the opposition to extended fire limits.[9] This decision set the tone for a rebuilding process that would downplay risks in the service of restoring what city leaders saw as the "natural" place and form of the city and promoting its future growth.

By many measures, San Francisco bounced back rapidly from the earthquake. The city's population recovered to 1906 levels in only three years, and the 1910 census counted 416,900 residents of the city—an increase of almost 75,000 people since the last official count in 1900. Most of the central business district was rebuilt quickly, with little serious consideration of moving the economic center of the city away from the hazard zone of made land. As the contemporary writer John P. Young put it: "Nature had marked out the burned district as the proper place for the conduct of important commercial operations." He explained: "The bay was still in its old place, and the wharves and their facilities for handling commerce, had escaped destruction." These words reflected not only how San Francisco's site (most notably the bay and its suitability as a harbor) remained central to its economy but also how the survival of important infrastructure influenced choices made in rebuilding. Writing only a few years after 1906, Young insisted: "Time and experience have not impaired the ... desirability of locating as near to what was the old cove of Yerba Buena as possible."[10]

For Young, these words were a statement of fact, not an attempt to persuade his readers of the safety of the made land district. The burned district remained "the proper place" for San Francisco's economic center because of a combination of nature and artifice. But that choice to rebuild in the same location meant ignoring clear evidence that filled ground along the waterfront represented a hazard zone in the seismically active Bay Area.

In keeping with that mind-set, waterfront development continued in the aftermath of the earthquake and fire. In 1907, San Francisco's seawall—begun back in 1867—extended 9,803 feet, with an additional 11,000 feet planned. From 1908 to 1915, work on the seawall extended it from Harrison Street south to King Street. Some of the streets behind the new seawall still consisted of planks on pilings as late as 1912, and people used whatever materials they had on hand as fill. Captain Fred Klebingat remembered, "The fill behind the seawall was just like any dump," a place where "city rubbish" of all kinds could be discarded.[11] Some of the rubble from the city's destruction in 1906 was used as fill along the coastline, including in Mission Bay, in the Islais Creek tidal marshlands, and perhaps in Marina Cove, although some scholars have suggested that the disposal of debris in Harbor View has been the subject of more rumor than fact.[12] This followed long-standing practices of getting rid of waste by dumping it into the water, a habit that traced all the way back to the precarious structures perched on piles and surrounded by tidal waters in the gold rush era. Despite the widely known impacts of seismic activity on made land, San Franciscans did not seem inclined to rethink their historical pattern of urban expansion through coastal fill.

As the rebuilding progressed, concern about the consequences of decisions such as not extending the fire limits and making new land began to surface. Richard L. Humphrey of the US Geological Survey worried that the rebuilt city would be "a duplicate of the former city in terms of defects of construction."[13] The low cost and easy availability of wood led to its widespread use for both temporary and permanent construction. Schmitz approved the construction of one-story "temporary" structures without a permit, and many of them remained in use for years. One observer, F. W. Fitzpatrick, lamented the lumber pouring into the city for reconstruction, calling it "forty million dollars' worth of kindling with which to make another $300 million fire."[14] More than 90 percent of the new construction after the disaster was either wood, with its vulnerability to fire, or brick, widely known to be hazardous in earthquakes. The promises of modern technologies and building materials also increasingly supplanted another long-standing seismic precaution, strict height restrictions for buildings. By 1908 twenty-five new steel frame skyscrapers built by the city's wealthy corporations soared above pre-fire height limits. Although local architects and engineers showed interest in methods of earthquake-resistant construction, the city did little to enforce existing building codes during the rebuilding period, and it actually reduced building code standards over the next few years.[15]

San Franciscans did worry about another conflagration as a result of vulnerabilities in the city's water system, and in 1908 voters approved a five-million-dollar bond issue for construction of an auxiliary water supply for fire protection. That system, long advocated by the fire chief, combined fire mains drawing from freshwater reservoirs and duplicate high-pressure pumping stations utilizing the saltwater of the bay in emergencies. The pipe system would incorporate cutoff valves allowing any block to be isolated in case of breaks. The city also proposed to purchase two fireboats and rebuild the network of cisterns around the city.[16] The system was completed in 1913, a quick timeline by municipal standards. The Board of Public Works noted that the two saltwater pumping stations were built of reinforced concrete "specially designed to withstand earthquake shock" and the system featured special pipe joints that allowed for extra lateral motion in "the filled-in lower portions of the city."[17] This open provision for earthquake risk shows that the lessons of the 1906 disaster had not been entirely forgotten, but these precautions occurred within the context of fire prevention, the aspect of the disaster that was both more visible and more acceptable for an American city—and that required less dramatic rethinking of San Francisco's patterns of development. It was easier to attempt to protect the "filled-in lower portions of the city" from conflagration than to think seriously about a shift away from waterfront development.

Despite the steady progress on the high-profile auxiliary water supply system, other improvements in San Francisco's protection from fire occurred slowly. More than two years after the earthquake, fire engine companies no. 1 and 2 remained out of service. Five years later, in 1913–14, the fire chief noted that many companies were still housed in temporary frame structures hastily erected after the 1906 disaster, buildings that he considered "totally unfit for habitation." Recommendations for the construction of new cisterns and improved fire protection for the outlying residential districts recurred in the fire chief's reports year after year from 1908 to 1915—an indication that his recommendations were being ignored. The fire department also pushed for modernization, particularly conversion from horse- to motor-driven equipment. In 1912–13 the fire department still used 373 horses against just seventeen motor-driven apparatuses, even though it noted that the more modern equipment had "passed the experimental stage."[18] Thus San Francisco's preparations for fire, although improved, remained imperfect and in some cases—as with closed companies and decrepit temporary buildings—showed the lasting effects of the 1906 disaster years later.

To the casual observer, an obvious problem facing a city that had burned to the ground was a lack of water. Although San Francisco's elites were well aware that the cause of the city's destruction had not been an absolute water shortage but rather earthquake damage to distribution pipes, they had long been concerned about the city's water supply. In 1900, San Francisco still relied on the Spring Valley Water Company and its peninsula supplies, the adequacy of which had been questioned for three decades. Many San Franciscans also perceived Spring Valley as a corrupt corporation holding the city hostage with its monopoly on water, and some were happy to place the blame for the city's destruction on the company. The city's new charter provided for the acquisition or construction of a municipally owned water system, part of the same push for public control by Progressives that would lead to the municipal railroad and a change that seemed overdue at a time when most large American cities no longer depended on private water companies.[19]

Although San Francisco's acquisition of Hetch Hetchy Valley as a water source is often directly attributed to the earthquake and fire, the city had begun pursuing water from the Sierra Nevada mountains six years earlier, when the Board of Supervisors launched an exhaustive study of possible options. In July 1901 the city filed a claim on water from the Tuolumne River, with proposed reservoirs at Hetch Hetchy and

Lake Eleanor. Hetch Hetchy was a U-shaped glacial valley, an isolated place where waterfalls crashed over soaring granite cliffs to feed small lakes and the river itself, a place spectacular enough that it had been designated part of Yosemite National Park a decade earlier. The preference for water from the Sierras, some 150 miles from San Francisco, reflected not only the limited options for a closer source but also, in the words of the Board of Public Works, a preference for a "pure and wholesome" supply "remote from the centers of population" and therefore unlikely to be contaminated before reaching the city.[20]

Even before the fire, the debate over San Francisco's claim on distant mountain water took shape along lines that have become famous in the annals of conservation. The fight over Hetch Hetchy is best known as the paradigmatic clash between proponents of utilitarian conservation, who believed in the use of natural resources for human needs, and John Muir's preservationists, who saw national park lands as inviolate and valued sublime wild areas for recreational and spiritual benefits. Supporters of the plan described water for San Francisco as "the highest possible beneficial use to which water can be put," as city engineer C. E. Grunsky wrote. In the early twentieth century, the residents of San Francisco consumed as much as forty-four million gallons of water in a month. In early 1903, however, the secretary of the interior denied San Francisco's application. He argued that, as "scenic features of Yosemite National Park," it was his duty to preserve Hetch Hetchy Valley and Lake Eleanor in their "natural condition." Undaunted, San Francisco appealed the decision, only to be denied again in December. Even after that second denial, the Board of Public Works continued to insist that it could "be assumed with a reasonable degree of confidence" that San Francisco would eventually get access to the waters of the Tuolumne.[21]

In the immediate aftermath of the earthquake and fire, a few observers suggested that the disaster had demonstrated the risks of relying on a single, distant water source, as proposed in the plan to tap the Tuolumne. Herman Schussler of the Spring Valley Water Company, with an obvious incentive to maintain his company's monopoly, argued that multiple conduit lines from different sources provided a safer and more secure water supply than "a long, single pipe line, bringing water from a source from 150 to 200 miles distant." Schussler quoted Professor

Charles Derleth Jr., who asked, "In light of our present catastrophe how much more danger must there be of earthquake destruction upon a line of so extended a length?"[22] These voices calling for caution would be drowned out by the demand for water from the Sierras.

The 1906 disaster provided a new impetus and a persuasive new justification for the city's claim on the Tuolumne River. In May 1908 a new secretary of the interior changed the earlier ruling and granted San Francisco reservoir rights. The 1910 elections demonstrated broad local support for the plan, despite its high price tag, when San Francisco voters favored, by twenty to one, forty-five million dollars' worth of bonds to finance the project.[23] On the national level the fight was far from over, but Congress finally passed the Raker Act in 1913, clearing the way for construction to begin. The first water from Hetch Hetchy did not arrive in the city until 1934, and the entire process ultimately cost eighty-nine lives and $102 million in bond measures as well as $41 million for the purchase of the Spring Valley Water Company.[24] The catastrophe did not initiate the city's quest for Sierra Nevada water, and it did not reshape the dispute, instead serving as one more point of argument. The fire has usually been considered a trump card for supporters of the dam, but some opponents such as Schussler sought to use the disaster as an argument against the plan as well. Here, as in other issues circulating in San Francisco in 1906 and subsequent years, the earthquake and fire became integrated into the discourse, a shared experience subject to interpretation and appropriation in environmental and political debates.

In that vision of using and transforming nature in service of the city, Hetch Hetchy encapsulated the mind-set of many urbanites in both the nineteenth century and the early decades of the twentieth. The technological sublime of a spectacular dam providing water and power to Bay Area cities triumphed over the natural sublime of the unaltered valley. In the 1910s, as construction of Hetch Hetchy was in its early stages, that vision also took shape closer to home along the shoreline of San Francisco, where the city's elites planned and built a spectacular fair that would both celebrate and represent progress with its fusion of nature and artifice. That vision and the Panama Pacific International Exposition's scenic waterfront location echoed elements of Daniel H.

Burnham's ideas for San Francisco as the City Beautiful, but the exposition further ratified decisions to downplay the hazards revealed in 1906, particularly the choice to continue making new land along the shoreline.

REMAKING THE LAND AND SEA

In his official history of the Panama Pacific International Exposition, Frank Morton Todd discussed the transformation of the site as emblematic of the fair itself:

> It was a common enough operation, in an engineering way; and yet . . . there is something of almost epic quality about this man-handling of the old Earth, and re-making of the land and sea even on so limited a scale—and something peculiarly appropriate to the end in view: an exposition of Man's ways with his environment. One of the best of the exhibits at San Francisco was one that few visitors took into account as such, and that was, 70 acres of the solid ground under their feet, and some of the largest of the palaces, where there had lately been 12 to 20 feet of water.[25]

With these words, Todd acknowledged both the general invisibility of the "re-making of the land and sea" as well as the ways in which it too represented an exhibit of the modern city and its place in nature. The choice of the Harbor View location reflected awareness of the site's potential to link the city and its natural surroundings through its dramatic scenery, but it was also motivated by practical concerns of urban development and integrating peripheral neighborhoods. The acquisition of the site and the use of fill to create solid ground echoed many of the ongoing themes in San Francisco's development during this period. In obtaining the necessary land, the Exposition Company ran roughshod over poorer tenants and immigrants. While landowners received compensation and concessions, renters received no assistance when their lives were uprooted, even though they contested the process in both formal and informal ways. Complications in the acquisition of land and its transformation demonstrate how the elite San Franciscans behind the Exposition Company remained determined to have their way with the city's environment and its people, even as nature and marginalized people pushed back.

As with so many of the developments in San Francisco in the wake of the 1906 disaster, the genesis for the idea of an exposition to celebrate the opening of the Panama Canal dated from before the earthquake. Reuben Brooks Hale first suggested the possibility in 1904. Hale was a prominent businessman, active in the Merchants' Association as well as the Association for the Improvement and Adornment of San Francisco (AIASF) and the California Promotion Committee, and an exposition promised to bring both publicity and tourist dollars to the city. San Franciscans had long believed a canal cutting through the isthmus of Panama would provide a huge economic boost to their city, not unlike the expectations they had for the transcontinental railroad several decades earlier. Hale doggedly pursued his idea even with the city in ruins; he and his allies filed articles of incorporation in December 1906 despite being forced to hold meetings in temporary wooden buildings.[26] If anything, the earthquake and fire added to the impetus of the project, which even then seemed to offer a means of both fostering and commemorating the city's recovery. The specter of urban revival combined with impressive fundraising efforts to allow San Francisco to triumph over New Orleans in 1910 and win the right to host the official exposition.

Next came the practical challenges of choosing a site within the city and building the planned extravaganza. The Exposition Company considered three potential locations for the fair: Golden Gate Park, the Lake Merced area in the southwest corner of the city, and Harbor View. Advocates of Harbor View based their arguments on its beauty, its practicality, and its potential to foster long-term development, including continued recovery from the 1906 disaster. They praised the location on the water with views of the Marin hills, Mount Tamalpais, and the islands in the bay. "If nature had been building an exposition site to order it could have added nothing to the attractiveness of the surroundings of Harbor View," gushed one publication.[27] Many of the arguments cited the potential for urban development offered by the Harbor View site. The project would "do more than anything else to rehabilitate all of the burned section," a statement that reflected both the reality of uneven recovery efforts and anxiety about the city's ongoing rebuilding in 1911. Other rhetoric emphasized the long-term utility of developing the neighborhood. Supporters complained that people were leaving San Francisco for residences across the water in Marin and the East Bay. In their minds, Harbor View, like other outlying districts, represented "miles of splendid homesites" that were "now but dreary wastes." The fair would leave behind permanent improvements including a seawall, docks, sewers, water pipes, and electrical connections as well as additional transit lines to facilitate settlement. At least some proponents of the site saw the opportunity to benefit directly; James McNab, who originally proposed the location, owned a residence overlooking the district.[28]

Some San Franciscans vehemently opposed the plan. A telling letter reproduced in the official history of the exposition objected to "misappropriating the public funds to fill in mudholes and a part of the bay to make land valuable for a few Millionaires who spend their money in New York City." The Harbor View site would be constructed largely on private land, and it thus drew particular criticism as benefiting wealthy landowners over the city as a whole. Although this letter writer objected primarily to the profiteering of "a few Millionaires," the references to fill also indicate a widespread awareness of the prevalence of making land as a development strategy in San Francisco.[29]

Once the Harbor View site had been selected, the Exposition Company faced the task of obtaining the land. The company ultimately acquired seventy-six city blocks consisting of nearly two hundred separate parcels of land. This process was predictably complex. Some owners were difficult to locate; in six cases, titles had been destroyed in the 1906 fire, and in another case of defective title, the owner had recently been killed in a streetcar accident. Todd reported that some of the "cheerful Latin denizens of the neighborhood" were happy to mislead the company, intentionally or otherwise, "by giving options on property they didn't own." Where possible, the company preferred to negotiate leases with the existing landowners, but it purchased seventeen parcels outright when unable to agree on lease terms. For smaller owners hesitant to accommodate the exposition, the company had few qualms about engaging in condemnation proceedings.[30]

When dealing with reluctant larger landowners, the company employed a more conciliatory approach. Fifty-five acres, including many water lots, belonged to Virginia Vanderbilt, the daughter of James G.

Photograph by Willard Worden of Harbor View in 1911. Marina Cove is visible in the background. Courtesy of the Bancroft Library, University of California, Berkeley (BANC PIC 1999.025—D).

Fair, wife of W. K. Vanderbilt, and an absentee landowner as a resident of New York City. Another sixteen acres were the property of her sister, Theresa Oelrichs, and both women were initially reluctant to lease their lands. In mid-January, Vanderbilt finally agreed to a lease, and Oelrichs followed suit two weeks later. The Exposition Company promised to fill in water lots on Vanderbilt's property and bring them up to official grade, along with repairing and strengthening an existing retaining wall and installing sewers in streets adjacent to the property. The terms of the lease also allowed Vanderbilt to hire an engineer to ensure that the work was done to her satisfaction. At issue was the "character of the fill," which had to be "of such weight and consistency as to afford a proper and adequate foundation" for future buidings.[31] Vanderbilt's (or her lawyer's) evident doubts about the quality of improvements to her property indicated some concern about filled ground in practice, if not in theory, and would prove to be a thorn in the side of the Exposition Company as it began to transform the site.

While the company granted concessions to Virginia Vanderbilt, it proved less accommodating when dealing with poorer residents of Harbor View. Kate F. Austin, who owned the block bounded by Bay, Octavia, Francisco, and Laguna Streets, received the substantial sum of $23,333 in a court settlement after the Exposition Company initiated condemnation proceedings, but residents of 119 refugee shacks on her property received no compensation for the loss of their homes, which were torn down as soon as Austin and landlord Horace Woolley could oust the occupants following the sale of the property.[32] Renters, many of whom were non-English speakers, generally received no consideration from the Exposition Company. Mrs. Mary Suters wrote that "the Earthquake and Fire broke me up in Business and left me without a dollar." She had made ends meet for herself and her two boys by running a boarding house in Harbor View. "I am now compelled to move to other quarters at double the rent for the same amount of room and will loose [sic] half of my boarders," she wrote, adding in case there was any doubt "your taking over this property works a hardship and an expense on me." Mrs. Suters asked the Exposition Company to provide compensation equivalent to one month's rent. Her request was refused.[33] The rejection of claims like Mary Suters's, couched in respectful terms of hardship and requesting a relative pittance in compensation, highlighted the company's lack of concern for poorer residents of San Francisco.

Some of those working-class residents, particularly the "Italian[s] and other foreigners," resisted the appropriation of their homes. Four residents of a block on Van Ness refused to pay the rent demanded by the company as their new landlord, "in view of the fact that they have been served with a notice to quit" the premises. One saloon operator withheld his rent of $54.50 per month from August 1912 to February 1913, when he was apparently the last remaining tenant on the site. He was finally forced out when his lease expired in April 1913, and his saloon was torn down a few days later.[34] More formal methods of resistance included the use of the court system. Residents of refugee shacks adjacent to Austin's property had obtained an injunction in January 1912 against the Department of Public Health's planned demolition of their homes, which was apparently still in effect in late September when health officer R. G. Brodrick suggested that Harris Connick of the

A Harbor View home purchased by the Panama Pacific International Exposition Company, probably destined for demolition if not removed by a buyer. Courtesy of the San Francisco History Center, San Francisco Public Library.

Division of Works could "hasten the removal" of the shacks since they were now on Exposition Company land. The company and the Board of Health joined forces in the project of "modernizing" and cleaning up San Francisco, removing the makeshift, unsanitary homes of the poor in the name of progress. The land acquired by the Exposition Company included about four hundred dwellings and other structures, of which the company moved roughly forty to other sites and destroyed the remainder.[35] This destruction of homes, like the demolitions overseen by the Board of Health over the years, echoed the destruction of the earthquake and fire and reinforced the transience of the city's poor.

Ultimately, the exposition site covered 635 acres, of which 184 had to be reclaimed from tidal marshes and Marina Cove itself. The process began with great ceremony on April 13, 1912, as exposition president Charles C. Moore sailed out to the dredge and "pulled the lever that started the long stream of sand and mud flowing shoreward to make the ground," in Todd's words.[36] Despite the confidence of engineers, the process of making land proved more challenging than expected.

The San Francisco Bridge Company was hired to fill in the cove, parts of which were twelve feet deep at high tide. The agreements with Vanderbilt and Oelrichs stipulated the quality of fill that would be used to transform their water lot properties, and a law firm representing their interests hired the engineer Charles L. Reynolds to oversee the process. Reynolds found a number of problems with the operations of the Exposition Company and the contractor as well as the environmental conditions of the site itself, the biggest being an "underlying deposit of ooze, silt, slime and sewage" that had accumulated at the bottom of the basin. Those deposits reflected both the natural conditions of a shallow lagoon and the legacy of decades of settlement in the region, particularly the discharge of sewage and the partial seawall that limited tidal action. The cove's slimy, sewage-ridden floor did not meet the contract stipulations, and as Reynolds emphasized, the "character of the fill" would affect the property's value after the exposition. Under Reynolds's careful eye— he spent four-and-a-half months taking daily samples and exercising what he described as "constant vigilance" and "aggressive diplomacy"— more than 327,000 cubic yards of "sewage, ooze, and generally undesirable material" were discharged through a floodgate and replaced with "substantial sands." Borings found that the final fill reached as deep as 23.8 feet on parts of the property, indicating that almost nine feet of material had been displaced. The need for so much additional fill created supply problems and forced the dredges to dig sixty-five feet down in search of suitable sand. The project also suffered from contract disputes, broken dredges, and cost overruns; it ultimately cost the Exposition Company almost 50 percent more than the original budget.[37] The total project of filling in the Harbor View and Presidio blocks took six months and required 1.7 million cubic yards of material.[38]

The broader goal of urban development meant that transformation was not limited to the future site of the exposition. The fair offered an opportunity to implement plans that had existed for a long time in the minds of San Francisco's development-minded leaders, such as tunneling through the city's inconvenient hills. "The most distinctive and significant feature of modern city building may be expressed in one word—TUNNELS," the Civic League of Improvement Clubs declared dramatically. Other cities across the United States and around the world had been building tunnels, including Pacific Coast rivals Los Angeles and Seattle. The Civic League called on the competitive instincts of San Franciscans in declaring that Seattle had "found it profitable to wash into Puget Sound a hill one-third the size of Twin Peaks." They asked, "Have we less enterprise?" Tunnels would connect the city's isolated neighborhoods to its downtown and facilitate commercial development. Peripheral neighborhoods like Harbor View, "once a dreary waste of swamp . . . will within a few short years be the scene of swarming commercial activity."[39]

Opponents of the proposed Fillmore Street tunnel quoted those words about Harbor View as they argued that the tunnel would benefit only a few wealthy landowners and merchants. They noted that assessments would be much lower on the newly filled tidelands than on the established solid ground of the hills, so wealthy owners of water lots would disproportionately benefit from the project. Mrs. W. Smith laid out this class-based argument in a letter objecting to the proposed tunnel assessment. She complained about wealthy landowners who "have ever since the fire got big rents." Smith declared: "It is time for justice to be done and not make the poor always pay the bigest [sic] part and let the rich go free." In her handwritten letter, Smith referenced the long-standing complaints about landlords profiting from the 1906 disaster by raising rents, and she identified herself as a taxpayer in asserting her right to object. The Civic League vision of a bustling industrial neighborhood did not appeal to many San Franciscans with homes on the hills around Harbor View, who juxtaposed "the pure breezes from the bay and the marine hills" with "the fumes from the steel plant and the dust from the coal bunkers."[40] At issue in the tunnel debate were conflicting visions of the future of Harbor View, whether it would be a residential district taking advantage of scenic views and coastal character or whether it would become a commercial port and industrial district, as well as class resentment in a city that remained divided along socioeconomic lines.

Mrs. Smith and other opponents of the Fillmore Street tunnel won in 1913, in part because delays made it clear that the project could not be finished in time for the exposition, which removed the sense of urgency as well as the motivation of providing access to the fair.[41] The

Fillmore Street tunnel was never built, but the exposition did inspire construction of other tunnels connecting San Francisco's established districts to the site. The Stockton Street tunnel linking downtown to Chinatown, North Beach, and the exposition opened in December 1914. The Twin Peaks tunnel, part of Bion J. Arnold's plan for San Francisco's transportation system, became the world's longest streetcar tunnel when it opened in December 1918 after more than two and a half years of construction.[42] Such projects represented the ongoing transformation of San Francisco's site in the name of urban development, the remaking of both land and sea that Todd saw as characteristic of the modern city and that had been central to San Francisco's history for more than half a century.

THE TEMPORARY CITY

The engineers and architects planning and constructing the Panama Pacific International Exposition were well aware of its temporary character. It was truly an instant city, built in three years and intended to stand for less than one. As one engineering pamphlet explained, "The ideal of Exposition engineering is to produce a construction which combines with a short life, low cost, speedy completion, sufficient strength and capacity, low wrecking cost and high salvage value." The massive undertaking called for "practically the complete design, construction and administrative organization for a living city," with all its challenges and opportunities. The exposition might be intended to look permanent—indeed, both the buildings and the grounds at the Panama Pacific International Exposition sought to convey a sense of age—but its construction balanced questions of safety with concerns about controlling costs.[43]

The art historian Sarah J. Moore has written that the "impermanence" of the exposition "permitted an embrace of grandeur and contained order possible only in the realm of dreams."[44] Yet, as we have seen in the process of filling in exposition land and the debates over the Fillmore Street tunnel, this façade of order concealed a messy process of urban development in which the relatively smooth operation of the final project elided environmental and social complications. In building the Panama Pacific International Exposition, engineers and architects had to reckon with the challenges of building on the unstable ground of fill, and they had to at least consider the environmental hazards that had afflicted San Francisco in the preceding decade, including earthquakes, fires, and even rats.

The papers of the Panama Pacific International Exposition reveal remarkably little concern about seismic activity. A letter from the San Francisco meteorologist Alexander G. McAdie to the architectural board mentioned the subject of earthquakes in a postscript, calling it "not especially pressing" but suggesting that the architects could consult the Seismological Society about nearby faults. Most of McAdie's letter concerned the problem of climate.[45] The engineer Arthur H. Markwart, assistant director of works, noted in several writings that all buildings constructed on sand or fill should be built on piles, in part for "greater safety in case of earthquake," and leases contained standard clauses releasing the Exposition Company from its obligations "in case of war, epidemic, fire, earthquake or other casualty of nature." However, these were the only written discussions of earthquakes despite the fact that organizers could hardly have forgotten the events of 1906. One other precaution, that building strength should be increased 25 percent for wind, also addressed the stability of exposition structures. The concern with wind on San Francisco's exposed northern shoreline was probably real, but such structural reinforcement might also be expected to pay dividends in case of seismic activity.[46] The exposition engineers may also have kept quiet while incorporating seismic safety measures in their designs. The historian Stephen Tobriner notes that several of those engineers published on earthquake-resistant construction in other contexts.[47]

In contrast to quiescent faults, the problems of building on new fill could not be ignored, particularly in a city with long experience with filled ground's tendency to settle. One memo candidly noted, "Ordinarily considerable difficulty is experienced in the case of new fills." Engineers carefully measured and tracked settlement, finding a uniform rate of roughly one inch per month from March 1913 into 1914. Markwart suggested that settlement was not a major concern "since it has been decided to support all structures and heavy exhibits by means of piles," although he characterized the "supporting power of the soil" as "very low." Test piles sank into the fill, however, and engineers reluctantly accepted that the piles would have to be much longer, and therefore more expensive, than they had originally planned. Water also geysered up out of seemingly solid ground, leading to watery pockets in the fill, and piles floated up after being driven into the surface. Eight hundred thousand feet worth of piles were ultimately used, and the Transportation Building required piles over one hundred feet long. The design of the Palace of Machinery accommodated heavy exhibits with a floor that "could be opened almost anywhere" for the addition of new piles, and forty-five thousand feet of piling supported the massive structure (reported to be the largest frame building ever constructed at the time).[48]

Another accommodation to settlement—and one that, like pile foundations, might have provided some protection from seismic activity as well—was the use of wood stave sewer pipes to provide "some flexibility . . . on account of the probable settlement of the fills." This precaution had a downside as, in Todd's words, "a section of it in marshy ground floated to the surface and had to be anchored down with a wooden platform and sand ballast."[49] During the fair the Exposition's wells filled with sand, and the attempted remedy of pumping out the sand caused the ground around the wells to settle, in turn destabilizing buildings in the vicinity.[50] These were the early twentieth-century manifestations of problems that had plagued construction on fill since San Francisco's early days, and they indicated a construction process far less smooth than the image of order projected by the final product.

If engineers considered earthquake hazards obliquely at best, they openly addressed the threat of fire. The Panama Pacific International Exposition was, after all, primarily a wooden city. During construction Douglas fir from the Pacific Northwest filled the Harbor View docks. Exposition engineers noted that wood was low cost and "suitable for the short life required," but San Franciscans were well aware of the risks of fire in a city built of wood.[51] The exposition became the first world's fair to install automatic sprinklers in major buildings, and it also maintained its own fire department and incorporated a high-pressure water system for fire protection. That fire protection system, like the exposition itself, was intended to be temporary, and San Francisco's fire chief noted it would be "terminated" at the close of the event.[52]

Fire appeared to be the greatest hazard facing a wooden fair, but San Franciscans remained cognizant of the problems posed by poor sanitation and its companion: rats. The underdeveloped state of Harbor View and the exposition site extended to its sanitary condition. The site incorporated Lobos Square, where the refugee camp had been a locus of the plague outbreak, as well as broken and inadequate sewers on both city and Presidio land. During the construction phase, the sanitary condition of the Presidio stables generated a year's worth of complaints from the exposition's director of works, and the Exposition Company itself stabled three hundred horses on the grounds.[53] The filled ground suffered from the familiar problem of stagnant water under and around buildings, and as one inspector complained, workmen used that water "for toilet purposes," adding to the sanitary hazard. By September 1914, perhaps unsurprisingly, some of the exposition buildings harbored rats. After initial complaints about difficulty getting access to the grounds, sanitary inspectors began placing traps and poison as well as tracking evidence of the rodent population. The problem apparently persisted through the fair, as Chief Sanitary Officer C. C. Pierce described plans for an antirat campaign "immediately following the close of the Exposition."[54] The sanitary problems of the temporary city bore a strong resemblance to those of urban nature more broadly.

Nature at the Panama Pacific International Exposition was intended to be more beautiful and more spectacular than that of the regular city, however. Plant life played a crucial role in the spectacle and illusion of the exposition. John McLaren, the longtime San Francisco landscape gardener best known for his stewardship of Golden Gate Park, headed the Department of Landscape Engineering. His son Donald noted the challenge facing their team when he wrote: "All the areas to be planted were originally composed of drifting sands, or sands which had been pumped in from the bay." Plants were transported from all over the region and the world, including one thousand redwood trees shipped from the Santa Cruz Mountains. California native species like redwood and manzanita were interspersed with non-natives such as palm trees and eucalyptus, which proved particularly popular because of their rapid growth. McLaren addressed the poor soil by bringing in massive amounts of loam and fertilizer, including street sweepings from the city as well as manure from elsewhere for a total of thirty thousand cubic yards of fertilizer.[55] Sand shipped in from Santa Cruz and other beaches to the south lined the walkways to produce the desired tints of gold or

The Palace of Fine Arts at the Panama Pacific International Exposition. The architecture and landscaping convey a feeling of age and permanence at odds with the temporary character of the fair. Courtesy of the California History Room, California State Library, Sacramento, California.

pink.[56] The natural sands of the Harbor View district were thus replaced with fill topped with imported soil and sand, and the construction of the fair drew natural resources from the city's hinterland of redwood forests and scenic coastlines.

The landscaping created a powerful illusion of age and permanence in the temporary city. As Todd wrote: "Visitors found all these palaces [on fill] surrounded by tall trees looking as though they had stood there for years, and all these courts brilliant with palms and flowering shrubs." Many observers emphasized the feeling of age conveyed by the plantings. Rose Berry declared: "No visitor walking about could dream that hundreds of tons of earth and fertilizer had been placed so recently upon salt sand beds." She further emphasized that the effect—and the Panama Pacific International Exposition as a whole—was thoroughly planned, "no accident brought it about."[57] The artful use of trees, shrubs, and flowers ratified and concealed the erasure of the cove and the transformation of water and marshes into solid ground to create the sense that the exposition had stood for years. Nature thus assisted in the illusion of permanence.

A bird's-eye view of the Panama Pacific International Exposition that illustrates its grand, orderly layout and its setting on San Francisco's northern shore. Courtesy of the San Francisco History Center, San Francisco Public Library.

The rhetoric of the exposition praised the natural setting, as organizers hoped to exploit California's reputation for stunning beauty to attract and entertain visitors. That rhetoric, like so many ideas about nature, proved deeply contradictory. It celebrated both the natural beauty of the site—in the process usually ignoring how much it had been transformed during construction—and the triumphs of humans over nonhuman nature represented by both the Panama Canal and the city of San Francisco. On the one hand, the architects sought "to make the landscape an integral part of the Exposition picture, by fitting the Exposition to the landscape," including adopting a palette based on "the coloring of earth, sky, and sea." Nighttime illumination used "even the tones of the fog."[58] Todd described how visitors "drank in the liquid vision of sea and mountain and ships and forts and islands, . . . the benign beauty of nature at its best."[59] Nature thus provided a backdrop in harmony with the artifice of the fair, even the source of inspiration for its designers. The bay, the mountains visible across the water, the California sky—usually blue but sometimes foggy—all became part of the exposition itself and received praise as among the most beautiful of its exhibits.

In other rhetoric, however, and even sometimes in the same publications, promoters spoke of the Panama Pacific International Exposition as commemorating a contest between "man" and nature. Such a view matched characterizations of the exposition as celebrating modernity and progress. The Palace of Machinery, for example, "spelled a new chapter in man's growing control of the forces of nature," according to Todd. The massive palace was, of course, built on fill that had been open water in 1912, but Todd here referenced not the construction of the building but its exhibits of technology such as electricity and the internal combustion engine. Another official publication boasted of San Francisco as a city "which has risen in less than a lifetime from a lonely spot on a deserted ocean to a cosmopolitan metropolis of world influence . . . a city which has battled with Nature's sternest forces and conquered." The completion of the Panama Canal represented a similar triumph of human ingenuity, "the final victory in man's most gigantic battle with Nature."[60] The temporary city, again like the permanent city of which it was both representative and a part, enacted the improvement of nature in the service of human needs. To many observers, the fair represented the perfection of a section of San Francisco's northern shoreline that had not reached its true potential in the city's first half century.

Nature did not entirely favor the exposition, however. In advising the architects, McAdie noted a potential conflict of "beauty vs. comfort." Designs could either maximize the spectacular views of Harbor View or protect visitors from the worst of its winds.[61] His warnings about the climate proved prescient. The winter and spring of 1915 were among the wettest in memory as contractors raced to complete the Panama Pacific International Exposition in time for its grand opening on February 20. In December, rain poured through holes in the roofs of new exhibit buildings as "rain squads" scurried to mark wet spots on the floors for repairs. The men shot straight up from the puddles to use bullet holes to mark the locations of leaks. Conditions worsened in January and February as it rained twenty-seven of the thirty days leading up to opening day. The weather largely cleared on February 20 before the rains returned. The wet weather depressed attendance during the first months of the exposition.[62]

Nature remained part of the display, despite the winter and spring rains. Artifice and technology could enhance California's natural attractions. Beauty reflected the combined effort of artists, "skilled gardeners and the California climate," and "all that modern science can do in lighting effects." The most spectacular of those lighting effects was a battery of forty-eight multicolored searchlights called the Scintillator that took advantage of foggy nights to create a spectacular display over the Marina. On clear nights, the Panama Pacific International Exposition simulated fog with "artificial clouds of steam and smoke" to create the same effect.[63] The design of the Palace of Fine Arts also utilized existing natural features, remade in the service of the goals of the architects and artists behind the exposition. The local writer Ben Macomber described the lake at the Palace of Fine Arts as "a real sheet of water" revealed when mud was "scooped out" of the "old Harbor View bog." This popular exhibit thus incorporated not only the palace but also the transformed lake bordered by trees both newly planted and retained from a resort in the area that predated the exposition.[64]

Other exhibits went beyond this mix of preexisting nature and artifice to fabricate distant natural attractions. In the "Joy Zone," the popular Grand Canyon and Yellowstone displays showcased replicas of those two great tourist attractions of the West and examples of spectacular American nature. The six-acre Grand Canyon attraction, built by the Atchison, Topeka & Santa Fe Railway, featured a virtual train ride along the simulated canyon complete with imported desert scents as well as a gift shop selling Navajo blankets. The Yellowstone concession included an enormous relief map of the park and reproductions of Old Faithful and Yellowstone Falls.[65]

Several exhibits included references to natural disasters, perhaps surprisingly given the city's general desire to downplay its own recent catastrophe. An attraction reenacting the Dayton Flood of 1913 attracted slim patronage and closed after a few months. Other exhibits were more successful, even when they directly addressed local crises. If open discussion of earthquakes seemed constrained during the process of planning and building the Panama Pacific International Exposition, it proved less forbidden during the fair itself. One exhibit displayed seismological recorders designed by Japanese scientists, although Todd's brief mention in his official history included no commentary on their potential special interest for San Franciscans. At the American Red Cross exhibit, "a reproduction of Refugee Camp No. 5, in Golden Gate

Night illumination at the Panama Pacific International Exposition, with the Scintillator light show in the background. Courtesy of the San Francisco History Center, San Francisco Public Library.

Park" stood alongside dioramas on disaster relief in Dayton, China, and Italy. Todd called this "a most impressive exhibit of what a little money and a good organization will do to mitigate the severities of fate." The US Public Health Service—apparently taking an educational approach to its exhibit—displayed a model of "bubonic rats at work burrowing through a dwelling and feasting in its neglected, open garbage can."[66] The presence of such exhibits referencing, intentionally or otherwise, San Francisco's recent history of environmental crises indicated that such incidents had not fully receded from residents' memories, but the displays' focus on institutional and educational solutions emphasized the Progressive project of perfecting the city and urban life through controlling and managing urban nature.

Insurance also drew praise. Fair organizers held an "Insurance Day" and a "Fire Underwriters' Day" to celebrate the profession. Todd declared the interest in insurance "natural to the locality" after San Francisco's experience in 1906 and praised "the providential power of insurance" for aiding in the city's restoration. In good Progressive fashion he emphasized the "expert and scientific character" of insurance in spreading risk across the community.[67] Working-class San Franciscans might have been struck by the juxtaposition of praise for insurance alongside the reconstruction of refugee camps in which those who lacked the financial advantages of insurance money had remained for months. The narrative of disaster implicit in such displays was one in which institutions like the Red Cross and the insurance industry insulated the city against the consequences of natural forces such as earthquakes. As we have seen, in practice, those institutions worked less than smoothly to cushion the social and economic impacts of natural hazards for all urban residents.

In its function as a symbol of the city's recovery, the Panama Pacific International Exposition also included a six-day-long "Nine Years After" celebration around the anniversary of the earthquake. People gathered to watch parades featuring "floats representing ruin and rebuilding," and they gasped at the burning of imitation refugee shacks on Marina Green, lighting effects that simulated flames engulfing the Tower of Jewels (known as "The Burning of the Tower"), and the real burning of an old barge in the bay. The event portrayed the disaster as a drama and morality play in which "a people's light-hearted and conquering courage" had drawn universal praise and led to "the miracle of restoration" that was the city in 1915 and the exposition itself.[68] With this event the fair commemorated the disaster and formalized the story of regeneration and progress. The exposition capped the narrative of the city's rebirth as an even greater city than before, a place where the creative destruction of disaster had made room for a more modern and more beautiful city—a fitting host for an event that claimed to be the culmination of progress. Both exhibits and promotional rhetoric also revealed the contradictory relationship between nature and the modern city as they praised a natural site that had to be transformed at great effort and expense to create the illusion of nature under control and in harmony with the palaces and statuary of the Panama Pacific International Exposition.

The exposition's status as a temporary city meant that it had to be dismantled. After the closing, Todd wrote, "The men that built the wondrous city were eager to tear it down. . . . They showed the same ardor for destruction that they had shown in creation." Not all San Franciscans shared this "ardor for destruction," however. The deconstruction of the fair called up memories of San Francisco's burning just a few years earlier. As buildings came down, Todd noted evocatively, "The dust rose like smoke from the wreckage." He added, "Thousands came to see it—and couldn't look."[69] The construction and dismantling of the temporary city can be seen as "a ritual reenactment-in-reverse" of the 1906 disaster. In building up and tearing down the temporary city, San Franciscans reasserted the primacy of human agency over nature's destructive power.[70] The end of the temporary city also meant a resurgence of the practical challenges concealed by the exposition's spectacle, including a renewed reckoning with the challenges of fill and other obstacles to the grand promises of urban development that had helped justify the Panama Pacific International Exposition. The idealized vision of the temporary, model city again gave way to the complicated, contested reality.

Not everyone wanted to see the exposition come to a close. Some people had been so moved by the fair that they organized to preserve it, forming the Exposition Preservation League. Supporters of preservation contrasted the exposition's "architectural beauty unparalleled" and "verdant lawns" with the condition of Harbor View before the fair, "muddy stretches covered with the putrefying washes of a salt lagoon," dotted with "buildings constructed from the flotsam and jetsam of the sea" and beautified only by "sickly geraniums on tin cans."[71] Such rhetoric juxtaposed the planned, orderly palaces and gardens with the haphazard homes of the area's poor residents in 1912. However, dreams of preservation encountered the reality of the temporary character of the buildings, which had not been designed to last beyond the fair's ten months. The advocates of preservation convinced the Park Commission to accept the popular Japanese Pavilion for installation in Lobos Square, only to watch it collapse in a high wind while it was being moved.[72] The Palace of Fine Arts building did survive, and it remains as a San Francisco icon following a reconstruction in the 1960s and a seismic retrofit in recent years.

Leased lands had to be restored and returned to owners, and the water lot properties that had posed such challenges in constructing the exposition remained obstacles to the process of restoring the site quickly and cheaply. The fill often did not meet lease requirements stating that the property should be filled to within two feet of the official grade of adjacent streets. Faced with the legal obligation of further improvement, the Exposition Company first suggested using the debris from the fair as additional fill and then offered cash settlements to Vanderbilt, Oelrichs, and other landowners in lieu of fulfilling its obligation. Both proposals were rejected, although the owners did agree to allow the company to leave the piles that it had installed underground.[73]

The contradictions of fill came to the forefront in the debate over how best to prepare the water lot properties of the exposition site for future development. The leases signed with Vanderbilt, Oelrichs, and Hartland Law stipulated that fill must "afford a proper and adequate foundation for the erection of structures or buildings thereon." In an apparent attempt to avoid the financial obligations inherent in fulfilling that clause, the Division of Works suggested its impossibility. It questioned if filling was "desirable and advantageous" without first knowing the future use of the property. The exposition engineers declared that "filled areas will not support buildings without the use of piles," and settlement precluded heavy structures such as factories and warehouses for many years. San Francisco's history had of course revealed such problems of building on made land, but plans for the exposition had downplayed them. Now engineers emphasized the difficulties posed by fill, at a moment when admitting its limitations served the company's interests. Ultimately, the Exposition Company had to again contract the San Francisco Bridge Company and its dredge to add additional fill to the properties. The earlier heavy dredging of the bay floor in the vicinity meant that the dredge had to venture farther out to sea to find suitable fill, and the process dragged on for more than a year.[74]

The question of the future uses of the land underlay disputes over fill. A letter from the assistant director of works suggested that the objections of one of the large landowners, Hartland Law, to proposals to use debris for fill stemmed from the possibility that he would lease his land for market gardening after the exposition. Such a use would obviously require adequate soil, but it also contradicted the grand promises of neighborhood development. Although Law might have been hedging his bets in his communication with the Exposition Company, in other situations he advocated for development. In January 1916, Law called to order a meeting of roughly fifty property owners in the district, who convened to prevent the neighborhood from "reverting back to the state it was in before the Exposition took it over." Law reportedly envisioned a "restricted residence district." Concern for the future of Harbor View extended beyond local landowners with financial interests. The *Examiner* also worried about "the lurking bugbear of possible wharves, factories and unsightly tenements."[75] The newspaper feared not only regression to an unsightly working-class district but also industrial and commercial development on a site that San Franciscans had come to value as orderly and beautiful recreational space.

Preservation advocates proposed the acquisition of the Marina as "a memorial of the Exposition, for a public park, and as a part of the Scenic Boulevard of San Francisco." This resolution invoked Burnham's vision for the city and emphasized the Marina's picturesque character and commemorative value.[76] Todd praised the company for acquiring a "tier of blocks under water, which, in case it ever got into the wrong hands, might have been filled, and used in such a manner as to spoil the whole Marina scheme." Although he had celebrated the process of making land elsewhere in his history, ironically the prospect of additional fill now became a fate to be avoided to protect the scenic character of the former exposition site.[77] This land would eventually be developed as recreational and green space. Marina Green, Chrissy Field, and the Palace of Fine Arts remain to this day as popular leisure spaces that help fulfill the City Beautiful vision of scenic recreational spaces along San Francisco's waterfront.

It took a few years, but the neighborhood eventually developed into a residential district, although not quite the one envisioned by Hartland Law. Instead of widely spaced houses on large lots, construction of contiguous houses on narrow lots began in 1924. Four-story apartment buildings with ground-floor garages soon marked the street corners.[78] The Panama Pacific International Exposition also succeeded in its goal of symbolizing San Francisco's recovery from the 1906 disaster. Millions of visitors stayed in the city's eighty-one new hotels, took in its sights, and experienced the fair with its promotion of controlled nature, progress, and modernity. Ultimately, nineteen million people passed through the gates.[79] The "temporary city" had been a rousing success, so popular that many San Franciscans wanted it to remain a permanent fixture of the urban environment. But that very success concealed the limitations of the model of development that it promoted. Like the permanent city, the temporary city demanded the transformation of nature with little concern for risk, particularly seismic hazards.

SEISMIC RISK AND DEVELOPMENT

The Panama Pacific International Exposition was an exceptional event in the city's history, but the dismissal and downplaying of environmental hazards characteristic of the Exposition Company continued in subsequent decades. Despite an increasing attachment to green space, overall attitudes toward urban development and urban nature changed very little in the decades from 1915 to the explosion of environmental consciousness in the 1960s. Commerce and development continued to trump both safety and preservationist impulses within the city and around the Bay Area.

Even scientists and engineeers who had become very aware of seismic hazards after 1906 downplayed the risks faced by the city and its residents in subsequent years. In 1921 the Commonwealth Club of California held a discussion on earthquakes featuring some of the region's most prominent scientists. The discussion began from the premise that earthquakes "are less destructive to life and property than more common phenomena such as thunderstorms, tornadoes, and conflagrations" even though "their mystery and power have a stronger appeal to the human imagination." The threat posed by earthquakes, the Club suggested, stemmed more from their effect on the human psyche than from their potential to threaten cities like San Francisco. And that psychic effect derived from their mysterious and exotic qualities, not from material hazards. In this view, scientific research would eventually uncover the "natural laws" governing earthquakes, and this knowledge would in turn dispel the mystery and eliminate the fear of earthquakes among common people.[80] The Club's reasoning echoed that of almost two generations earlier in the wake of the 1868 earthquake, when scientists had likewise emphasized the normality of earthquakes alongside the need for additional research.

The featured speakers at the meeting worked to fit their presentations to this premise as much as possible. The eminent geologist and professor Andrew Lawson noted that earthquakes were not peculiar to California but afflicted other regions as well. Bailey Willis, a professor of geology at Stanford, emphasized that seismic activity had created the distinctive topography of the Bay Area. Without earthquakes, Willis declared, "there would be no San Francisco bay, there would be no Coast range." He added, more ominously: "There will be a next earthquake." Both Lawson and Willis encouraged more research into earthquakes. Willis explicitly denounced those who urged that discussion of the 1906 earthquake be silenced. He appealed to the pride of San Franciscans when he declared: "The city that rose upon the ruins of 1906 . . . will look out for itself, will investigate earthquakes, and will see that future earthquakes do not do the damage which that one did." Willis's frustration with the status quo in 1921 came through when he noted that better records of seismic activity existed for the period between 1850 and 1895 than for subsequent years, including those after 1906.[81] His insistence that San Francisco would be better prepared for future earthquakes thus represented more rhetoric than belief. He sought to motivate the city's financial and political elites, but he was clearly dissatisfied with the status quo in the early 1920s regarding support for seismological research and preparation for future seismic activity.

Charles Derleth Jr. represented the engineering profession at the gathering. He too tried to strike a balance between acknowledging seismic hazards and recognizing the realities facing engineers and architects. He noted that many building designers and owners in San Francisco had incorporated lessons from 1906, but he emphasized that many others had not done so, "either from incompetence or indifference, or motives still worse." Derleth listed practical precautions for building in earthquake country, including anchoring foundations on firm ground or on piles; not coupling together sections of a building that would vibrate differently in a quake; avoiding top-heavy buildings; and eliminating high risk features such as masonry arches. For Derleth these strategies for building with relative safety supplanted restrictions on building in hazard zones. He emphasized that engineers were well aware of how types of ground affected the intensity of shaking but noted that fixed sites and limited funds constrained the measures they could employ to avoid risk. "We may admit that frame dwellings in closely built districts are a fire hazard or that brick structures with wood frames and wood roof are inadquate to withstand earthquake shocks safely," Derleth declared. "Yet industrial and financial conditions will always require their reasonable use."[82]

Derleth's attempt to promote earthquake-resistant practices even as he conceded their limitations in the face of the realities of San Francisco real estate represented the best one could hope for in the early 1920s. The historian Stephen Tobriner, an ardent defender of the seismic safety efforts of San Francisco's architects and engineers, concedes that Derleth's calls for attention to soil conditions and avoiding situating important buildings on known hazardous ground "never entered the [building] codes" in these years. Even when architects considered earthquake safety in terms of precautions taken aboveground with bracing and other architectural components, they were usually unable or unwilling to make any major changes in practices that emphasized the hidden risks belowground.[83] Overall, seismic risk continued to be minimized in construction in San Francisco in the early 1920s as local narratives downplayed the effects of the earthquake in 1906—emphasizing the fire as the primary destructive agent instead—and the risks of future seismic activity.[84]

CONCLUSION

The Panama Pacific International Exposition was certainly a success as a symbol of San Francisco's recovery from the 1906 earthquake and fire. Yet that symbol of resilience also ratified choices about urban land use, and particularly land making along the shoreline, that had created hazardous ground in the decades leading up to 1906. The temporary city reenacted a version of San Francisco's rapid early growth, including its propensity for waterfront development and its dream of improving nature to perfect the urban environment. The Panama Pacific International Exposition promised orderly, controlled nature that offered scenery and inspiration without any challenge to human progress and control. For the ten months of the fair, that illusion largely held—at least after the drenching rains of the winter and spring of 1915 ended—but a closer look at the site's construction reveals how urban nature remained unruly beneath the monumental palaces of faux travertine, the constantly flowering gardens, and the spectacular nightly light shows of the exposition.

Ten months was not long, however. The temporary character of the exposition concealed many of the site's hazards—hazards that were often only exacerbated by preparations for the fair. When the Marina District saw new residential construction in the form of wood-frame apartment buildings in the 1920s—the fulfillment of the Exposition Company's plan for the development of a marginal neighborhood of the city—the risks of the made land beneath the neighborhood's apartment buildings had already been forgotten. In the 1920s and later decades, development around the region proceeded with little concern for seismic hazards.

CONCLUSION

ON OCTOBER 17, 1989, SAN FRANCISCO AND THE SURROUNDING region faced another strong earthquake, the largest since 1906. A magnitude 6.9 quake shook the region at 5:04 P.M., just as people across the country were tuning in to the World Series game at Candlestick Park, and a riveted nation watched the crisis unfold on television. The epicenter was sixty miles southwest of the city, in the Coast Range mountains not far from Santa Cruz. The quake killed sixty-three people, led to almost four thousand injuries, and caused as much as $10 billion worth of damage throughout the region, including $2.5 billion in San Francisco.[1] In the city itself, the intensity of the shaking caused by the Loma Prieta earthquake did not approach that of 1906—Loma Prieta was far from the "Big One"—yet it still caused severe damage, evidence that the modern city and its structures were only marginally more secure than they had been in 1906.

Major structures around the region failed dramatically. Although the Golden Gate Bridge suffered no discernable effects, a section of the upper deck of the Bay Bridge crashed onto the lower deck, and horrified television viewers saw a car plunge over the edge. Freeways on fill proved unexpectedly vulnerable. In Oakland the Cypress Street viaduct—a mile and a half section of Interstate 880—collapsed, killing forty-one people. Bill Harp, who was driving on the Cypress at the time but survived, remembered: "The freeway was literally falling apart." The damaged section corresponded exactly to a section constructed on fill,

271

between sections anchored on natural sediments.[2] In San Francisco the Embarcadero Freeway nearly suffered the same fate, and most of the area's major freeways, including I-280 and Highway 101 on the peninsula and I-980 and the MacArthur Maze in Oakland, incurred damage.[3]

Damaged freeways in Southern California in the 1971 San Fernando earthquake had revealed a significant design flaw in many freeway structures, but politics and budgeting challenges in California in the intervening decades had limited funding for seismic retrofits and testing of retrofit programs. The Cypress Freeway had in fact undergone a retrofit in the early 1980s, and CalTrans engineers assured Californians that such retrofitted structures were "earthquake safe." Subsequent research showed that the retrofit cables themselves were fundamentally flawed—two out of three failed in a UCLA study—but the state made no effort to replace inadequate retrofits.[4] Even a structure like the Golden Gate Bridge that had escaped unscathed remained at risk. Later studies by the US Geological Survey showed that an earthquake with an epicenter closer to the bridge could have grave consequences. They projected that a quake on the scale of 1906 would bring down the approach viaducts and cause "catastrophic damage" to the suspension structure itself.[5] The freeway failures in 1989 and subsequent studies showed that too many of the major engineering projects since 1906 failed to live up to optimists' assurances of seismic safety.

The familiar risks of the urban environment also persisted. In San Francisco the worst damage occurred on the relatively new fill of the Marina district, former site of the Panama Pacific International Exposition. Scientists labeled that stretch of made land a "ground-failure zone" where lateral-spreading cracks, liquefaction, settlement, and buckling of the ground occurred. The former Marina Cove, where the new fill proved even less stable than older filled areas, saw the most severe crises. Ground sank as much as twelve inches, and liquefaction sand boils—where a combination of water, fine-grained sand, and bits of urban debris were ejected from liquified ground—dotted the made land where the palaces of the exposition had been erected seventy-five years earlier. A three-hundred-meter-long crack split the middle of the Marina district along the southeast side of the liquified area. It ignited a major fire and caused the collapse of three four-story, wood-frame corner apartment buildings. In total, seven buildings, all but one of them constructed in the 1920s, collapsed entirely, and another sixty-three had to be condemned.[6]

Gas and water pipes shattered throughout the Marina district and the city as a whole. The smell of gas permeated the Marina, and flames rose from broken gas mains. An hour and a half after the quake, Assistant Chief Harry Brophy reported: "There's gas all over the place." Ultimately 13.6 kilometers of gas mains had to be replaced. The water system similarly required 123 repairs in the Marina district alone. Twenty-seven fires broke out within minutes, and the worst burned for more than four hours. Just as in 1906, damage to the water system hampered the efforts of firefighters. Not only did the municipal water system suffer a total loss of flow to both customers and fire hydrants in the Marina, but the Auxiliary Water Supply System (AWSS) sustained six breaks in the South of Market district that rendered it ineffective as well. The city's lone fireboat, the *Phoenix*, did not regularly carry a firefighting crew, and that was the case on October 17 as well, but when it finally arrived around 7:00 P.M., it proved instrumental in allowing firefighters to finally get the last fire under control. An unusually calm October evening also aided the neighorhood.[7] The fires and building collapses in the Marina revealed how badly San Franciscans had underestimated the hazards posed by the new land they had created there, and they highlighted the inadequacies of precautions taken after 1906.

Unlike most residents, seismologists were not surprised by the effects of the quake. As one scientific article bluntly put it: "There were few surprises as to the locations of liquefaction."[8] Various studies by earthquake experts had essentially predicted the consequences of a major earthquake for the Marina district, but the Loma Prieta quake revealed a substantial knowledge gap between those professionals and politicians and the public. Residents certainly knew about earthquake risks in San Francisco, but just as many Americans were shocked to learn of the predictability of the damage from Hurricane Katrina in New Orleans, specific risks had not always been communicated to the populace. As one assessment in the wake of the disaster noted of the Marina: "The area's seismic vulnerability was not well known by residents in 1989, nor was it reflected in the city's emergency planning for earthquakes."[9] The recurrence of this failure to translate scientific knowledge regarding hazards into specific policies and local awareness undermines simplistic assumptions that knowledge of risks will lead to precautions. San Franciscans were only marginally more prepared for seismic hazards in 1989 than they had been in 1906 or even 1868.

The Loma Prieta earthquake also revealed the limitations of technical solutions to the seismic hazards facing the urban environment. Some bridges and buildings that had been retrofitted to resist earthquakes suffered structural damage while others that had not been retrofitted escaped unscathed. Places where fills had been compacted to make them less susceptible to liquefaction performed well on that measure but proved no more resistant to shaking than noncompacted fills, leaving structures at significant risk. Geologists noted that existing federal policy was "biased toward returning to pre-earthquake conditions, even when those conditions represent high earthquake risk." The practical impact of such policy had been to "inhibit upgrading of hazardous structures."[10] It was sobering for both San Francisco residents and outside observers to see how promises of protection had fallen short in practice. Scientists in the aftermath groped for evidence of the success of technical solutions, sometimes ignoring contradictory evidence in the process. For example, an analysis of responses to the earthquake criticized the performance of the AWSS on one page—noting that breaks elsewhere had left it with no water pressure in the Marina—while later praising it as an example of a "lesson learned" and declaring that it had "served San Francisco well."[11] Ultimately even fully implemented disaster prevention programs such as the AWSS had mixed results in the crisis of 1989. Although technical solutions appeal to scientists and engineers and offer hope to many in a society that maintains a great degree of faith in progress, earthquakes continue to challenge promises of environmental control. The Loma Prieta earthquake of 1989, like the devastating Northridge quake that followed only five years later, reminded Californians that earthquakes remained a threat to their modern cities.[12]

In the aftermath of those two earthquakes, as well as the earlier 1971 San Fernando earthquake, California officials began to take the threats posed by seismic activity more seriously. Statewide legislation addressed such hazards as construction on active fault traces, unreinforced masonry buildings, and inadequate building codes. Other legislation required municipal hazard mitigation plans, mapping of seismic hazards, and disclosure of hazards to buyers (but not renters). Such measures helped to reduce damage in earthquakes, including in 1994, but they had little to no effect on land use practices.[13] In fact, the 1972 Alquist-Priolo Act restricting construction on the surface trace of active faults had unintended consequences. With building restricted, urban areas in the Los Angeles region developed the fault zones as green spaces—and they became amenities that added value to adjacent real estate. Hazard zones along fault lines like the San Andreas thus attracted residents willing to pay a premium to live on some of the riskiest land in California.[14]

Many cash-strapped local governments continue to put hazard preparedness on the backburner despite state and national requirements, particularly in regions that have not recently experienced significant earthquakes. For example, the 2011 hazard mitigation plan of Colton, California—a small, working-class city in San Bernardino County bisected by the San Jacinto Fault and only a few miles from the San Andreas—caustically noted the consequences of funding limitations. It recommended relocating a fire station and emergency operations center located in a floodplain and liquefaction zone, noting that the alternative was to leave the building in its current location and "hope it survives to help coordinate the response" to an earthquake. The plea for a full time emergency services coordinator referred to the alternative of "continu[ing] to under fund and under staff Disaster Preparedness planning in our City." The only one of its proposed hazard migation projects that Colton could afford to undertake was an inexpensive weed abatement program to address fire threats.[15] San Francisco is better prepared than Colton, but even there the 2014 hazard mitigation plan gives an expected completion date of 2042 for a Soft Story Seismic Retrofit program to protect buildings like those that collapsed in the Marina district in 1989. Yet the plan also references the 2008 forecast by the Working Group on California Earthquake Probabilities of a 63 percent chance of an earthquake with a magnitude 6.7 or greater striking the Bay Area within thirty years.[16] Although seismic forecasts are notoriously unreliable, they suggest an urgency for both retrofit efforts and real changes in land use practices that is not reflected in the existing allocation of resources.

Even new construction remains at risk from the same foreseeable, yet somehow unforeseen, problems that have plagued San Francisco almost since the city's founding. In the fall of 2016, the fifty-eight-story

Millennium Tower, a luxury residential building located in South of Market and completed in 2009, made the news for having sunk more than sixteen inches since its completion. The culprits included a deficient foundation and a concrete-heavy design that left the building weighing three times what similar-sized steel structures weigh. The tower is now also leaning six inches off center, and sewer connections and elevators could fail as a result. The city's department of building inspection admits that it had no procedures in place to inspect the building's structural integrity and lacked the technology to evaluate the computer models used by developers. Other reports suggest that the department knew the building was sinking excessively before the first residences were sold and covered it up. One engineer consulted by owners of the building's luxury condominiums suggested "lopping off the top 20 floors" to reduce the weight of the building and prevent further sinking.[17]

In 1989 the Loma Prieta earthquake revealed the folly of decades of urban development choices when it devastated not only the Marina district but the Bay Area's transportation infrastructure as well. One of the recurrent patterns—dating back all the way to 1868—has been a refusal by policy makers and city leaders to heed scientists who warned about seismic hazards, whether those scientists were the geologists of the State Earthquake Investigation Commission after 1906 or their counterparts in the 1970s and 1980s who found existing retrofit procedures insufficient and predicted liquefaction of fill. Scandals like the Millenium Tower show how developers and city officials continue to ignore the city's seismic history. These repeated failures undermine assumptions that either greater knowledge or new technical solutions can eliminate the risks of living in earthquake country. For all that cities remain the ultimate reflection of the human capacity to transform our environments, they also remain subject to natural forces that transcend our sense of control.

This book argues that disasters are part of the urban environment, endemic to many cities including San Francisco. The percentage of Americans living in cities continues to increase. In 2010 more than four of every five Americans lived in an urban area with a core population of over fifty thousand people—in other words, a city. Globally, the percentage of urban dwellers continues to rise as well, with more than half of the world's population now living in cities and that percentage only expected to grow over the next few decades. Many of those cities, like San Francisco, are threatened by some form of natural disaster. Those disasters, too, are projected to increase in both frequency and intensity in the coming decades, particularly as climate change leads to more extreme weather conditions and larger storms.

The types of disasters faced by cities can vary over time. For example, San Francisco, like other nineteenth-century American cities, suffered a series of major fires, the last one being the conflagration that followed the 1906 earthquake. Since then, fires have remained under control in the city, but seismic hazards persist, as the 1989 Loma Prieta earthquake dramatically demonstrated. Environmental hazards like earthquakes—and for other cities, floods, hurricanes, tornadoes, and wild fires—represent recurrent threats to urban areas. They are part of urban ecosystems even though most people see them as anomalous and react with minimal concern for reducing the future vulnerability of the urban environment and its residents. Disasters occur in part because cities are often built in risky locations in the path of natural forces such as seismic activity but also because alterations to the environment, such as those that occur in the construction of a city, increase susceptibility to hazards and create new consequences accompanying an earthquake or weather event. Thus, altering the land to create prime real estate in San Francisco also created unstable ground that was subject to severe shaking each time an earthquake struck the city, leading to catastrophe in 1906. Periodic natural occurrences become disasters when they encounter an unprepared urban environment teeming with people. Disasters are thus one piece of evidence for understanding cities and their human residents as part of the natural environment.

City leaders and developers implicitly assume the natural landscape to be unchanging even as the built environment undergoes periodic reconstruction, even creative destruction, as part of urban history. In this paradigm the only evolution that takes place results from human activity; nature itself is expected to be immutable—or nature is not part of the city at all. However, in geologically active places like San Francisco—or in coastal areas like not only San Francisco but other American metropolises threatened by disaster such as Los Angeles,

New Orleans, Miami, and even New York City—the landscape is naturally dynamic. Under normal circumstances human residents can manage these changes—for example, by rerouting or filling in river courses and building seawalls and waterfront piers. Humans and their cities are less prepared for sudden, catastrophic events such as earthquakes and hurricanes. In fact, attempts to build for permanence can often make urban environments less adaptable to crises. Instead of change occurring only through human initiative, the relationship between the natural environment and the city is a reciprocal one in which humans alter the environment—often with unforeseen consequences—but nonhuman nature in its various manifestations shapes the city as well.

Disasters and the processes of relief and recovery highlight the unequal distribution of power within cities like San Francisco. In 1906 the provision of relief funds for reconstructing homes and businesses followed preexisting class lines. In particular, the temporary tent camps and earthquake cottages that served as housing for the poorest refugees reinforced the transience that defined poverty in early twentieth-century San Francisco—in contrast to the immobility that Hurricane Katrina highlighted as a characteristic of poverty in early twenty-first-century New Orleans. Refugees in San Francisco organized to protest the distribution of relief, but they lacked the power to influence official decision makers who governed a centralized rehabilitation process.

To many residents, the crisis of the earthquake and fire represented an opportunity to shape the new city according to their particular visions for urban development, and diverse San Franciscans contested both the physical and social landscapes of the city during the processes of recovery and rebuilding. Some, like the Chinese who fought the relocation of Chinatown, succeeded in defending their visions of the city, showing that the postdisaster city was far from the blank slate desired by many reformers. Organized labor, which nominally controlled the municipal government in 1906, also sought to assert itself as a political force in the aftermath of the earthquake, only to be undercut by city elites and economic circumstances. Skyrocketing rents and a recession—triggered in turn by the global financial reverberations of the earthquake and fire—combined with uncooperative business interests and local political scandal to undermine labor's efforts to reassert its centrality to the construction and functioning of San Francisco.

Nature in the modern city was a source of contradictions and disputes both within and independent of those visions of urban development. Nonhuman nature could be a source of peace and prosperity, as envisioned by promoters of idyllic suburbs and by Daniel H. Burnham with his emphasis on San Francisco's scenic vistas. It could also be a source of disorder, even a hazard in its own right, as with the rain and winds buffeting refugees and the rats that brought the bubonic plague to the city. Plans for the modern city thus ran the gamut from Burnham's promotion of controlled, scenic nature to Rupert Blue's call for a city of concrete, sanitized of nonhuman animals ranging from rats to chickens. The disaster itself and the debates about urban nature that it sparked demonstrated the complexity of power relations in the city and the ways in which environmental, economic, and cultural forces interacted in shaping its history.

The story of San Francisco's recovery is a story of change in many ways. As San Franciscans made the transition from a Victorian city to a modern one, a process that the earthquake first interrupted and then accelerated, they expelled most animal species from the urban environment (or, at least, they attempted to do so). They implemented new sanitary regulations and built new infrastructure, including improved sewers as well as high-profile projects with local and regional impacts, like the Hetch Hetchy water system. Working-class residents and Progressive reformers came together to attempt to assert control over city streets and utilities, first through strikes and protests and later through muncipal ownership of the street railways and the new water system. Yet many things did not change. Foremost among those was a development mind-set that ignored potential hazards and the dynamism of urban nature. The process of making land in the name of "improvement" continued to characterize coastal development despite the 1906 earthquake and clear evidence that such fill represented hazardous ground.

The recurrence of disasters in San Francisco's history highlights the limitations of both a mind-set of ignoring nature and a focus on technical solutions to the hazards facing the city. Fireproof construction fell far short of its promise of safety in 1906, and both modern structures in general and earthquake retrofits in particular too often failed in 1989. Twenty-first-century disasters in other parts of the nation and the world—from Hurricane Katrina in New Orleans in 2005 to the earthquake and tsunami that hit Japan in 2011 to "Superstorm" Sandy and its devastation of New York and New Jersey a year later—serve as repeated reminders that even our most modern cities remain susceptible to nature's force. The promise of insulation from the vagaries of nature is one of the core promises of modernity, but it remains imperfectly—not to mention unequally—realized. Just as neither Rupert Blue's dream of San Francisco as "one block of concrete" free of rats and associated sanitary hazards nor Daniel Burnham's vision of a city of scenic drives and artificially lighted forests could be fully realized in the early twentieth century despite the "opportunity" offered by the devastation of existing urban infrastructure, so the common twenty-first-century belief that we can protect our cities from earthquakes, extreme weather, and sea level rise seems likely to be proven false.

Assertions that we now live in the Anthropocene suggest that we as humans shape nonhuman nature through our actions, and in many ways we do. However, such an emphasis on human agency reifies the separation of nature and culture, placing our species outside of and beyond nature once and for all. Our history of attempts to reshape and control nature have gone wrong as often as they have gone right, and they have often had unintended consequences—like those of made land in San Francisco. Disaster history suggests a broader, more complicated interaction between human history and the natural world, one in which both nature and humanity possess agency. If we can never fully control nature, we must learn to live with and embrace nature's dynamism.

NOTES

INTRODUCTION

Map: Produced with Esri ArcMap™ 10.3 by Lisa Benvenuti, Center for Spatial
Studies, University of Redlands. Sources: streets—Esri Data and Maps,
StreetMap NA, 2013; marshes and land fill digitized from San Francisco Historical Creek Map, Oakland Museum of California Creek and Watershed
Information, http://explore.museumca.org/creeks/SFTopoCreeks.html;
shoreline digitized from U. Graff, "San Francisco and Environs," Map G
04362 S22 1906 G7 Case XB, Bancroft; burned area and Presidio digitized
from "Map of San Francisco, California: Showing the limits of the burned
area destroyed by the fire of April 18th–21st, 1906, following the earthquake
of April 18th, 1906" (US Army Corps of Engineers, 1906), Historic Maps of
the Bay Area digital resource, Earth Sciences and Map Library, University
of California, Berkeley.

1   State Earthquake Investigation Commission, *The California Earthquake of
    April 18, 1906: Report of the State Earthquake Investigation Commission*, vol. 1
    (Washington, DC: Carnegie Institute of Washington, 1908), 25, 148–49;
    Gladys Hansen and Emmet Condon, *Denial of Disaster* (San Francisco: Cam-
    eron and Company, 1989), 13.

2   Calculations conducted in 1958 initially estimated the 1906 earthquake at 8.3
    on the Richter scale, but those numbers have been adjusted using data on
    more recent earthquakes in California. Estimates of the area affected by the
    quake differ in various analyses. I have used the numbers from the report of
    the State Earthquake Investigation Commission, *California Earthquake of
    April 18, 1906*, vol. 1, 2–3. McAdie is quoted in Hansen and Condon, *Denial
    of Disaster*, 14.

3   Hansen and Condon, *Denial of Disaster*, 13–14; State Earthquake Investigation
    Commission, *California Earthquake of April 18, 1906*, vol. 1, 410–16.

4   Cushing is quoted in Malcolm E. Barker, ed., *Three Fearful Days: San Francisco
    Memoirs of the 1906 Earthquake and Fire* (San Francisco: Londonborn, 1998),
    77.

5   Jack London, "The Story of an Eyewitness," *Collier's*, May 5, 1906.

6   For histories of urban fire, see Mark Tebeau, *Eating Smoke: Fire in Urban America, 1800–1950* (Baltimore, MD: Johns Hopkins University Press, 2003); Christine Meisner Rosen, *The Limits of Power: Great Fires and the Process of City Growth in America* (New York: Cambridge University Press, 1986); and Karen Sawislak, *Smoldering City: Chicagoans and the Great Fire, 1871–1874* (Chicago: University of Chicago, 1995), among others.

7   Barker, *Three Fearful Days*, 34; Frank Soulé, "The Earthquake and Fire and Their Effects on Structural Steel and Steel-Frame Buildings," in *The San Francisco Earthquake and Fire of April 18, 1906 and Their Effects on Structures and Structural Materials*, 131–58 (Washington, DC: Government Printing Office, 1907), 136.

8   John Bernard McGloin, *San Francisco: The Story of a City* (San Rafael, CA: Presidio Press, 1978), 137–41; Kerry Odell and Marc D. Weidenmier, "Real Shock, Monetary Aftershock: The San Francisco Earthquake and the Panic of 1907," *Journal of Economic History* 64, no. 4 (2004): 1003 (1002–27). These losses amounted to between 1.3 percent and 1.8 percent of US gross national product in 1906. Philip L. Fradkin has suggested that numbers such as these actually understate the economic impact of the 1906 San Francisco disaster; see Fradkin, *The Great Earthquake and Firestorms of 1906: How San Francisco Nearly Destroyed Itself* (Berkeley: University of California Press, 2005), 346.

9   "San Francisco in Ruins," *Coast Seamen's Journal*, April 25, 1906, 4; Gladys Hansen, "Who Perished: A List of Persons Who Died As a Result of the Great Earthquake and Fire in San Francisco on April 18, 1906," (San Francisco: San Francisco Archives, 1980), 3; Hansen and Condon, *Denial of Disaster*, 153; Ted Steinberg, *Acts of God: The Unnatural History of Natural Disaster in America* (New York: Oxford University Press, 2000), 44.

10   Steinberg, *Acts of God*, xxi.

11   Ibid. As the historian Greg Bankoff has noted: "Disasters do not occur out of context but are embedded in the political structures, economic systems and social orders of the societies in which they take place." He suggests that repeated disasters may well shape the evolution of such societies as "societies and destructive agents are mutually constituted and embedded in the natural and social systems as unfolding processes over time." Bankoff, *Cultures of Disaster: Society and Natural Hazard in the Philippines* (New York: Routledge Curzon, 2002), 152, 158.

12   For one expression of these ideas, see Simon Winchester, *A Crack in the Edge of the World: America and the Great California Earthquake of 1906* (New York: HarperCollins, 2005). For a discussion of the intersection of geological and cultural time, see Anthony Oliver-Smith, "Peru's Five Hundred Year Earthquake: Vulnerability in Historical Context," in *Disasters, Development, and Environment*, ed. Ann Varley, 31–48 (New York: John Wiley & Sons, 1994).

13   Kenneth Hewitt, "The Idea of Calamity in a Technocratic Age," *Interpretations of Calamity from the Viewpoint of Human Ecology*, ed. Kenneth Hewitt,

3–32 (Boston: Allen & Unwin, 1983), 22–25, emphasis in the original. Stephen J. Pyne makes a similar argument about urban fires in Pyne, "Afterword: Fire on the Fringe," in *Flammable Cities: Urban Conflagration and the Making of the Modern World*, ed. Greg Bankoff, Uwe Lübken, and Jordan Sand, 390–96 (Madison: University of Wisconsin Press, 2012), 391.

14 Kai Erikson, "Notes on Trauma and Community," in *Trauma: Explorations in Meaning*, ed. Cathy Caruth, 183–99 (Baltimore, MD: Johns Hopkins University Press, 1995), 194–95.

15 Mark Carey, *In the Shadow of Melting Glaciers: Climate Change and Andean Society* (New York: Oxford University Press, 2010), 191–92. See also Review of Mark Carey's *In the Shadow of Melting Glaciers: Climate Change and Andean Society*, ed. Jacob Darwin Hamblin, H-Environment Roundtable Review, vol. 1, no. 4 (2011).

16 Craig E. Colten, *An Unnatural Metropolis: Wresting New Orleans from Nature* (Baton Rouge: Louisiana State University Press, 2005), 11–12.

17 For example, although Ted Steinberg has written a history of natural disasters, including a chapter about San Francisco, the earthquake only rates a single clause in a discussion of Hetch Hetchy in Steinberg's excellent US environmental history textbook, *Down to Earth: Nature's Role in American History*, 3rd ed. (New York: Oxford University Press, 2013).

18 Labor histories and public health histories of San Francisco constitute a partial exception to this trend. William Issel and Robert W. Cherney, *San Francisco, 1865–1932: Politics, Power, and Urban Development* (Berkeley: University of California Press, 1986); Gray Brechin, *Imperial San Francisco: Urban Power, Earthly Ruin* (Berkeley: University of California, 1999), 107–8, 153–54.

19 Adeline Masquelier, "Why Katrina's Victims Aren't *Refugees*: Musings on a 'Dirty' Word," *American Anthropologist* 108, no. 4 (2006): 736 (735–43). Subsequent research on Katrina often did a better job of considering historical precedents and parallels.

20 Debarati Guha-Sapir, Philippe Hoyois, and Regina Below, *Annual Disaster Statistical Review 2012: The Numbers and Trends* (Brussels: Centre for Research on the Epidemiology of Disasters, 2013), 1; Bruce A. Bolt, *Earthquakes*, 5th ed. (New York: W. H. Freeman, 2006), 319–23. US Geological Survey, "Earthquakes with 50,000 or More Deaths," 2013, online at http://earthquake.usgs.gov/earthquakes/world/most_destructive.php, accessed January 20, 2014.

21 Anthony Oliver-Smith, "Theorizing Disasters: Nature, Power, and Culture," in *Catastrophe and Culture: The Anthropology of Disaster*, ed. Susanna M. Hoffman and Anthony Oliver-Smith, 23–47 (Santa Fe, NM: School of American Research Press, 2002), 24–25.

22 Ari Kelman, *A River and Its City: The Nature of Landscape in New Orleans* (Berkeley: University of California Press, 2003), 89.

23 Mumford quoted in ibid., 10.

24 For the most well-known articulation of the problems with these dichotomies,

see William Cronon, "The Trouble with Wilderness; or, Getting Back to the Wrong Nature," in *Uncommon Ground: Rethinking the Human Place in Nature*, ed. William Cronon, 69–90 (New York: W. W. Norton & Co., 1995). Philip J. Dreyfus argues for the prevalence of this thinking in late nineteenth-century San Francisco. Dreyfus, *Our Better Nature: Environment and the Making of San Francisco* (Norman: University of Oklahoma Press, 2008), 67–100.

25 Notable works of urban environmental history that have raised similar questions include William Cronon, *Nature's Metropolis: Chicago and the Great West* (New York: W. W. Norton & Co., 1991); Andrew Hurley, *Environmental Inequalities: Class, Race, and Industrial Pollution in Gary, Indiana, 1945–1980* (Chapel Hill: University of North Carolina Press, 1995); Joel A. Tarr, *The Search for the Ultimate Sink* (Akron, OH: University of Akron Press, 1996); Martin V. Melosi, *Effluent America: Cities, Industry, Energy, and the Environment* (Pittsburgh: University of Pittsburgh Press, 2001); Matthew Gandy, *Concrete and Clay: Reworking Nature in New York City* (Cambridge, MA: MIT Press, 2002); Kelman, *A River and Its City*; Colten, *Unnatural Metropolis*; Matthew Klingle, *Emerald City: An Environmental History of Seattle* (New Haven, CT: Yale University Press, 2007); and Michael Rawson, *Eden on the Charles: The Making of Boston* (Cambridge, MA: Harvard University Press, 2010). Environmental histories of San Francisco include: Brechin, *Imperial San Francisco*; Dreyfus, *Our Better Nature*; Richard A. Walker, *The Country in the City: The Greening of the San Francisco Bay Area* (Seattle: University of Washington Press, 2007); and Matthew Morse Booker, *Down by the Bay: San Francisco's History Between the Tides* (Berkeley: University of California Press, 2013).

26 Clyde Wahrhaftig, *A Streetcar to Subduction and Other Plate Tectonic Trips by Public Transit in San Francisco*, rev. ed. (Washington, DC: American Geophysical Union, 1984), 1.

27 Other environmental histories that address similar ideas about urban ecosystems and the flow of resources into cities include Cronon, *Nature's Metropolis*; Brechin, *Imperial San Francisco*; Jared Orsi, *Hazardous Metropolis: Flooding and Urban Ecology in Los Angeles* (Berkeley: University of California Press, 2004); Melosi, *Effluent America*; and Tarr, *Search for the Ultimate Sink*.

28 Use of the term *refugees* to describe displaced people has become controversial in some circles. In the aftermath of Hurricane Katrina, many disaster survivors and observers, particularly in the African American community, objected to the term. They associated it with foreigners who were nationless or stateless, and as such, they saw the label of *refugees* as an attempt to exclude them from the community of US citizens and deprive them of rights and resources associated with citizenship. Such fears echoed the long history of discrimination in the nation and in the South in particular, but the debate largely ignored the historical context of natural disasters. The term *refugees* was widely used in 1906 to refer to San Franciscans who were displaced from their homes, and I have followed the people of the time in using it here. For

a discussion of the debate over the term *refugees* after Katrina, see Masquelier, "Why Katrina's Victims Aren't *Refugees*."

29 The term *creative destruction* comes from the economist Joseph Schumpeter. For urban development as driven by episodes of destruction and rebuilding, see Max Page, *The Creative Destruction of Manhattan, 1900–1940* (Chicago: University of Chicago Press, 1999). The concept of *disaster capitalism* has been presented most prominently by Naomi Klein, although her formulation is historically specific to the period since the mid-1960s that has seen the global rise of neoliberalism. Klein, *The Shock Doctrine: The Rise of Disaster Capitalism* (New York: Henry Holt and Company, 2007). Kevin Rozario has explored the historical roots of this thinking and applied the concept to San Francisco. Rozario, *The Culture of Calamity: Disaster and the Making of Modern America* (Chicago: University of Chicago Press, 2007).

30 Page uses the phrase "politics of place" to refer to attachment to places in the city; see Page, *Creative Destruction of Manhattan*, 252–53.

31 Bankoff, *Cultures of Disaster*, 12. The literature on *vulnerability* is voluminous. An example of the use of the concept in analyzing a more recent earthquake is Robert Bolin and Lois Stanford, "Constructing Vulnerability in the First World: The Northridge Earthquake in Southern California, 1994," in *The Angry Earth: Disaster in Anthropological Perspective*, ed. Anthony Oliver-Smith and Susanna M. Hoffman, 89–112 (New York: Routledge, 1999).

32 Andrea Rees Davies similarly argues that the disaster led to the mobilization and political activation of some San Franciscans, particularly women of various classes. Davies, *Saving San Francisco: Relief and Recovery after the 1906 Disaster* (Philadelphia: Temple University Press, 2012).

33 San Francisco's African American population was only 1,654 in 1900, of a total population of 400,000 people. Anna Naruta and Jamille Teer, "Pre-Quake Demographics," in *The Unshakable: Rebirth of S.F. Chinatown in 1906* (Brisbane, CA: Sing Tao Daily, 2006), 5. For a detailed history of racial formations in nineteenth-century San Francisco, see Barbara Berglund, *Making San Francisco American: Cultural Frontiers in the Urban West, 1846–1906* (Lawrence: University Press of Kansas, 2007).

34 Fred Rosenbaum, *Cosmopolitans: A Social and Cultural History of the Jews of the San Francisco Bay Area* (Berkeley: University of California Press, 2009), 170–71.

CHAPTER ONE: MAKING LAND, MAKING A CITY

1 Taylor's account of his arrival is excerpted in Malcolm E. Barker, *San Francisco Memoirs, 1835–1851: Eyewitness Accounts of the Birth of a City* (San Francisco: Londonborn, 1994), 178–87. This description combines material from Taylor's account with similar accounts from the period.

2 J. H. Purkitt, *Letter on the Water Front Improvement Addressed to the Hon. James*

Van Ness, Mayor of San Francisco (San Francisco: Whitton, Towne & Co, 1856), 4.

3   Linda Nash explores ideas about "finishing" nature in California in the nineteenth century, focusing on the Central Valley and medical discourse. She explores the implications of these ideas for irrigation in the rural areas of California's Central Valley, but they apply to urban settlers as well. My argument here is inspired in part by her questions. Nash, "Finishing Nature: Harmonizing Bodies and Environments in Late-Nineteenth-Century California," *Environmental History* 8 (January 2003): 25–52. Richard White also discusses this mind-set of improving nature in *The Organic Machine: The Remaking of the Columbia River* (New York: Hill and Wang, 1995), 57–58.

4   Greg Bankoff, "A Tale of Two Cities: The Pyro-Seismic Morphology of Nineteenth-Century Manilla," in *Flammable Cities: Urban Conflagration and the Making of the Modern World*, ed. Greg Bankoff, Uwe Lübken, and Jordan Sand, 170–89 (Madison: University of Wisconsin Press, 2012).

5   Mike Davis, *Ecology of Fear: Los Angeles and the Imagination of Disaster* (New York: Vintage Books, 1998), 17–18.

6   John McPhee, *Assembling California* (New York: Farrar, Straus and Giroux, 1993), 247–49; Simon Winchester, *A Crack in the Edge of the World: America and the Great California Earthquake of 1906* (New York: HarperCollins, 2005), 167–71, 180.

7   Doris Sloan, *Geology of the San Francisco Bay Region* (Berkeley: University of California Press, 2006), 134, 144–45.

8   Frank Soulé, John H. Gihon, and James Nisbet, *The Annals of San Francisco* (1855; reprint, Berkeley, CA: Berkeley Hills Books, 1998), 154–55.

9   Sloan, *Geology of the San Francisco Bay Region*, 135; Elna S. Bakker, *An Island Called California* (Berkeley: University of California Press, 1971), 39–44.

10   Bakker, *An Island Called California*, 64–69; James E. Vance Jr., *Geography and Urban Evolution in the San Francisco Bay Area* (Berkeley, CA: Institute of Governmental Studies, 1964), 28.

11   David Starr Jordan, "The Earthquake Rift of 1906," in *The California Earthquake of 1906*, ed. David Starr Jordan, 1–62 (San Francisco: A. M. Robertson, 1907), 2; Harold W. Fairbanks, "The Great Earthquake Rift of California," in Jordan, *California Earthquake of 1906*, 326 (319–38).

12   Philip J. Dreyfus, *Our Better Nature: Environment and the Making of San Francisco* (Norman: University of Oklahoma Press, 2008), 12–19; Alan Leventhal, Les Field, Hank Alvarez, and Rosemary Cambra, "The Ohlone: Back from Extinction," in *The Ohlone: Past and Present*, ed. Lowell John Bean, 297–336 (Menlo Park, CA: Ballena Press, 1994); Matthew Morse Booker, *Down by the Bay: San Francisco's History Between the Tides* (Berkeley: University of California Press, 2013), 117–18.

13   McPhee, *Assembling California*, 238–39.

14   Dreyfus, *Our Better Nature*, 22–28.

15   David Igler, "Diseased Goods: Global Exchanges in the Eastern Pacific Basin, 1770–1850," *American Historical Review* 109, no. 3 (2004): 705–7, 713–15 (693–719); James P. Delgado, *Gold Rush Port: The Maritime Ecology of San Francisco's Waterfront* (Berkeley: University of California Press, 2009), 38–40; John P. Young, *San Francisco: A History of the Pacific Coast Metropolis* (San Francisco: S. J. Clarke Publishing Company, 1912), 83–89.

16   Dreyfus, *Our Better Nature*, 34–36; Roger W. Lotchin, *San Francisco, 1846–1856: From Hamlet to City* (New York: Oxford University Press, 1974), 7; Soulé, Gihon, and Nisbet, *Annals of San Francisco*, 172; John S. Hittell, *A History of the City of San Francisco and Incidentally of the State of California* (San Francisco: A. L. Bancroft & Company, 1878), 77–85.

17   Quoted in Barker, *San Francisco Memoirs*, 62.

18   Quoted in ibid., 67.

19   For mentions of wildlife in early San Francisco, see ibid., 38, 41, and 65. For plant communities, see Bakker, *An Island Called California*, 55–60. For wildlife native to the Bay Area, see Galen Rowell and Michael Sewell, *Bay Area Wild: A Celebration of the Natural Heritage of the San Francisco Bay Area* (San Francisco: Sierra Club Books 1997), 90–93.

20   Booker, *Down by the Bay*, 37–38, 42–47.

21   Soulé, Gihon, and Nisbet, *Annals of San Francisco*, 180–83; Young, *San Francisco: A History of the Pacific Coast Metropolis*, 119, 147.

22   Ayers is quoted in Barker, *San Francisco Memoirs*, 198.

23   Farnham is quoted in ibid., 205.

24   Lammot is quoted in William Beneman, *A Year of Mud and Gold: San Francisco in Letters and Diaries, 1849–1850* (Lincoln: University of Nebraska Press, 1999), 126.

25   For a succinct discussion of site and situation, see Ari Kelman, *A River and Its City: The Nature of Landscape in New Orleans* (Berkeley: University of California Press, 2003), 5–6; Vance, *Geography and Urban Evolution in the San Francisco Bay Area*, 33.

26   Barbara Berglund, *Making San Francisco American: Cultural Frontiers in the Urban West, 1846–1906* (Lawrence: University Press of Kansas, 2007), 3–5, 13. For histories of California during the Gold Rush, see Andrew C. Isenberg, *Mining California: An Ecological History* (New York: Hill and Wang, 2005); and Malcolm J. Rohrbough, *Days of Gold: The California Gold Rush and the American Nation* (Berkeley: University of California Press, 1997), among many excellent works.

27   Washington Bartlett, Ordinance of January 30, 1847, Museum of the City of San Francisco, www.sfmuseum.org; Lotchin, *San Francisco, 1846–1856*, 5–9; James D. Phelan, "Historical Sketch of San Francisco," in *Report on a Plan for San Francisco*, by Daniel H. Burnham, 193–209 (1905; reprint, Berkeley, CA: Urban Books, 1971), 193–94.

28   Barker, *San Francisco Memoirs*, 165, 184–87; Beneman, *Year of Mud and Gold*, 125.

29   Delgado, *Gold Rush Port*, 56–57.

30   Lotchin, *San Francisco, 1846–1856*, 41–42; Soulé, Gihon, and Nisbet, *Annals of San Francisco*, 291–93. McKenna is quoted in Delgado, *Gold Rush Port*, 60–62.

31   Booker, *Down by the* Bay, 47, 50.

32   Rutté is quoted in Barker, *San Francisco Memoirs*, 271.

33   For discussions of land making in other coastal cities, see Michael Rawson, *Eden on the Charles: The Making of Boston* (Cambridge, MA: Harvard University Press, 2010); Nancy S. Seasholes, *Gaining Ground: A History of Landmaking in Boston* (Cambridge, MA: MIT Press, 2003); William A. Newman, *Boston's Back Bay: The Story of America's Greatest Nineteenth-Century Landfill Project* (Boston: Northeastern University Press, 2006); and Matthew Klingle, *Emerald City: An Environmental History of Seattle* (New Haven, CT: Yale University Press, 2007).

34   Beneman, *Year of Mud and Gold*, 25.

35   Introduction in Bankoff, Lübken, and Sand, *Flammable Cities*, 8.

36   Taylor is quoted in Barker, *San Francisco Memoirs*, 275–77.

37   Charles R. Boden, "San Francisco's Cisterns," *California Historical Society Quarterly* 15, no. 4 (1936): 311–12 (311–23); Soulé, Gihon, and Nisbet, *Annals of San Francisco*, 274–76; Dreyfus, *Our Better Nature*, 101–4.

38   Martyn John Bowden, "The Dynamics of City Growth: An Historical Geography of the San Francisco Central District, 1850–1931," Ph.D. diss., University of California, Berkeley, 1967, 84–85, 161–62.

39   Soulé, Gihon, and Nisbet, *Annals of San Francisco*, 289–91; Young, *San Francisco: A History of the Pacific Coast Metropolis*, 141–42; Hittell, *History of the City of San Francisco*, 156–57.

40   "A Fourth Terrible Conflagration! San Francisco Again in Ashes!" *Alta California*, October 1, 1850; "Ports of Entry and a Mint," *Alta California*, November 30, 1850.

41   "William Kelly on San Francisco, 1851," in *The American City: A Documentary History*, ed. Charles N. Glaab, 196–99 (Homewood, IL: The Dorsey Press, Inc., 1963), 198.

42   Soulé, Gihon, and Nisbet, *Annals of San Francisco*, 329–33; Archibald MacPhail, *Of Men and Fire: A Story of Fire Insurance in the Far West* (San Francisco: Fire Underwriters Association of the Pacific, 1948), 22–23.

43   Soulé, Gihon, and Nisbet, *Annals of San Francisco*, 608–10; Albert Bernard de Russailh is quoted in Barker, *San Francisco Memoirs*, 286.

44   Bates is quoted in Barker, *San Francisco Memoirs*, 291.

45   John Bernard McGloin, *San Francisco: The Story of a City* (San Rafael, CA: Presidio Press, 1978), 57–58, 72; MacPhail, *Of Men and Fire*, 23–25.

46 Soulé, Gihon, and Nisbet, *Annals of San Francisco*, 341–43, 449–50; Young, *San Francisco: A History of the Pacific Coast Metropolis*, 166.

47 Young, *San Francisco: A History of the Pacific Coast Metropolis*, 407–8; Gray Brechin, *Imperial San Francisco: Urban Power, Earthly Ruin* (Berkeley: University of California, 1999), 76–80.

48 Only a few firefighters recognized the utility of the cistern system, with fire chief Dennis Sullivan regularly calling for the installation of new cisterns in the 1890s. Although a few old cisterns aided the battle against the flames in April 1906, most notably on the Montgomery Block, this passive defense system had been too poorly maintained to provide much assistance in the city's moment of crisis. The fire department recommended the construction of additional cisterns after the 1906 fire, and by 1915, 135 cisterns were in use, 85 of them newly constructed. Bowden, "Dynamics of City Growth," 312–18.

49 McGloin, *San Francisco: The Story of a City*, 71–72.

50 Stephen Tobriner, *Bracing for Disaster: Earthquake-Resistant Architecture and Engineering in San Francisco, 1838–1933* (Berkeley, CA: Heyday Books, 2006), 32.

51 Booker makes a similar argument in *Down by the Bay*, 55. In an article comparing urban fires in nineteenth-century cities, L. E. Frost and E. L. Jones emphasize fires as "immensely capital-destructive shocks" and suggest that fires hampered urban development as a result. Although fires certainly wiped out capital in San Francisco, the city's rapid rebuilding and growth indicate that repeated fires did not limit the city's development. Frost and Jones, "The Fire Gap and the Greater Durability of Nineteenth Century Cities," *Planning Perspectives* 4 (1989): 335 (333–47).

52 Soulé, Gihon, and Nisbet, *Annals of San Francisco*, 295.

53 Nash, "Finishing Nature," 39. See also the discussion of "second nature" in William Cronon, *Nature's Metropolis: Chicago and the Great West* (New York: W. W. Norton & Co., 1991), 55–93.

54 Quoted in Delgado, *Gold Rush Port*, 83.

55 Soulé, Gihon, and Nisbet, *Annals of San Francisco*, 358–59; Roger Olmsted, Nancy L. Olmsted, and Allen Pastron, *San Francisco Waterfront: Report on Historical Cultural Resources for the North Shore and Channel Outfalls Consolidation Projects* (San Francisco: San Francisco Wastewater Management Program, 1977), 267, 462–65; Nancy Olmsted, *Vanished Waters: A History of San Francisco's Mission Bay* (San Francisco: Mission Creek Conservancy, 1986), 12.

56 Soulé, Gihon, and Nisbet, *Annals of San Francisco*, 159–60; State Earthquake Investigation Commission, *The California Earthquake of April 18, 1906* (Washington, DC: Carnegie Institute of Washington, 1908), vol. 1, 235.

57 Olmsted, *Vanished Waters*, 12; Young, *San Francisco: A History of the Pacific Coast Metropolis*, 162; Phelan, "Historical Sketch of San Francisco," 199–200; William Crittenden Sharpsteen, "Vanished Waters of Southeastern San

Francisco," *California Historical Society Quarterly* 21, no. 2 (June 1942): 113–14 (113–26).

58 Soulé, Gihon, and Nisbet, *Annals of San Francisco*, 354.

59 Quoted in Citizens' Anti-Bulkhead Committee of San Francisco, *The Antidote for the Poison: Abstract of Speeches and Documents against the Parsons Bulkhead Bill* (San Francisco: Towne & Bacon, 1860), 17.

60 Hittell, *History of the City of San Francisco*, 433–34.

61 Soulé, Gihon, and Nisbet, *Annals of San Francisco*, 529; Young, *San Francisco: A History of the Pacific Coast Metropolis*, 144.

62 Bates is quoted in Barker, *San Francisco Memoirs*, 266–67.

63 Purkitt, "Letter on the Water Front Improvement," 16; Edgerton is quoted in *The Bulkhead Question Completely Reviewed* (Sacramento, CA: Daily Standard Office, 1860), 11; Lotchin, *San Francisco, 1846–1856*, 96, 161–62, 173; Booker, *Down by the Bay*, 53. For a broader history of shipworms, see Derek Lee Nelson, "The Ravages of Teredo: The Rise and Fall of Shipworm in U.S. History," *Environmental History* 21 (2016): 100–24.

64 Gunther Barth, *Instant Cities: Urbanization and the Rise of San Francisco and Denver* (New York: Oxford University Press, 1975), 210–11.

65 Purkitt, "Letter on the Water Front Improvement," 13.

66 "Report of the Board of Engineers upon the City Grades" (San Francisco: Commercial Advertiser Power Presses, 1854), 5–6.

67 Soulé, Gihon, and Nisbet, *Annals of San Francisco*, 160–61; emphasis in the original.

68 Ibid., 408–9; "San Francisco Earthquake History 1769–1879," Virtual Museum of the City of San Francisco, online at www.sfmuseum.org/alm /quakes1.html, accessed October 21, 2013. Any such list for years prior to the development of seismographs is obviously subject to uneven reporting. Tobriner (*Bracing for Disaster*, 15–16) believes that an earthquake did not cause this 1852 incident, although he does not give a reason for this statement.

69 Tobriner, *Bracing for Disaster*, 17–18.

70 Neville is quoted in Malcolm E. Barker, ed., *More San Francisco Memoirs, 1852–1899: The Ripening Years* (San Francisco: Londonborn, 1996), 181; Titus Fay Cronise, *The Natural Wealth of California* (San Francisco: H. H. Bancroft & Company, 1868), 648.

71 J. C. Branner, "Earthquakes and Structural Engineering," *Bulletin of the Seismological Society of America* 3 (March 1913): 2 (1–5); Bowden, "Dynamics of City Growth," 320.

72 Soulé, Gihon, and Nisbet, *Annals of San Francisco*, 165.

73 Edward S. Holden, "Earthquakes in California and Elsewhere," *Overland Monthly* 11 (January 1888): 48 (39–49); Clyde Wahrhaftig, *A Streetcar to Subduction and Other Plate Tectonic Trips by Public Transit in San Francisco*, rev. ed. (Washington, DC: American Geophysical Union, 1984), 56; Tobriner, *Bracing for Disaster*, 15–16, 35–36. An 1867 novel by Bret Harte included the spectacle

of San Francisco being "totally engulfed by an earthquake," with Oakland being spared because "there are some things the earth cannot swallow." Harte is quoted in Young, *San Francisco: A History of the Pacific Coast Metropolis*, 468.

74 Hittell, *History of the City of San Francisco*, 345; Cronise, *Natural Wealth of California*, 648–49.

75 *Alta California*, October 9, 1865, quoted in Walter L. Huber, "San Francisco Earthquakes of 1865 and 1868," *Bulletin of the Seismological Society of America* 20 (December 1930): 261–62 (261–72); Cronise, *Natural Wealth of California*, 648.

76 State Earthquake Investigation Commission, *California Earthquake of April 18, 1906*, vol. 1, 438–39. Carl-Henry Geschwind speculates that the damage estimates varied so widely because of Chamber of Commerce efforts to downplay the threat of earthquakes in San Francisco; see Geschwind, *California Earthquakes: Science, Risk, and the Politics of Hazard Mitigation* (Baltimore, MD: Johns Hopkins University Press, 2001), 17.

77 State Earthquake Investigation Commission, *California Earthquake of April 18, 1906*, vol. 1, 436–39. *Alta California* is quoted in Huber, "San Francisco Earthquakes of 1865 and 1868," 266.

78 M. G. Upton, "Earthquake Theories," *Overland Monthly* 1, no. 6 (December 1868): 519–20 (516–23).

79 *San Francisco Bulletin*, October 21, 1868, quoted in Huber, "San Francisco Earthquakes of 1865 and 1868," 269; J. D. B. Stillman, "Concerning the Late Earthquake," *Overland Monthly* 1, no. 5 (November 1868): 476–77 (474–79); Thomas Rowlandson, *A Treatise on Earthquake Dangers, Causes, and Palliatives* (San Francisco: Dewey, 1868), 89.

80 Bruce A. Bolt, *Earthquakes*, 5th ed. (New York: W. H. Freeman, 2006), 302; Huber, "San Francisco Earthquakes of 1865 and 1868," 266–70.

81 Stillman, "Concerning the Late Earthquake," 477–79.

82 Ibid., 474; emphasis in the original.

83 Andrea Sbarboro, "Life of Andrea Sbarboro: Reminiscences of an Italian-American Pioneer" (San Francisco, 1911), 59, BANC MSS G-D 5180, Bancroft; Bowden, "Dynamics of City Growth," 309–13; Gladys Hansen and Emmet Condon, *Denial of Disaster* (San Francisco: Cameron and Company, 1989), 29.

84 John F. Byrnes, "The New Mint," *South of Market Journal*, February 1934, 8.

85 Huber, "San Francisco Earthquakes of 1865 and 1868," 266–67.

86 Bosqui is quoted in Barker, *More San Francisco Memoirs*, 187–89.

87 Rowlandson, *Treatise on Earthquake Dangers, Causes, and Palliatives*, 3–5. In 1908, in the aftermath of the city's destruction, George Davidson, then eighty-three and one of the surviving members of the 1868 committee, wrote a letter to the Seismological Society claiming that San Francisco's Chamber of Commerce had silenced the committee. According to Davidson, the

committee's estimate of $1.5 million in damages particularly concerned the city's merchants since it undermined their claim that the quake had caused minimal damage. William H. Prescott, "Circumstances Surrounding the Preparation and Suppression of a Report on the 1868 California Earthquake," *Bulletin of the Seismological Society of America* 72 (December 1982): 2389–93; State Earthquake Investigation Commission, *California Earthquake of April 18, 1906*, vol. 1, 434; Tobriner, *Bracing for Disaster*, 58; Michele L. Aldrich, Bruce A. Bolt, Alan E. Leviton, and Peter U. Rodda, "The 'Report' of the 1868 Haywards Earthquake," *Bulletin of the Seismological Society of America* 76, no. 1 (February 1986): 71–76.

88   Hittell, *History of the City of San Francisco*, 371. Whitney is quoted in Ted Steinberg, *Acts of God: The Unnatural History of Natural Disaster in America* (New York: Oxford University Press, 2000), 28.

89   Rowlandson, *Treatise on Earthquake Dangers, Causes, and Palliatives*, 48, 95.

90   State Earthquake Investigation Commission, *California Earthquake of April 18, 1906*, vol. 1, 25. For the state of seismology during this time, see Deborah R. Coen, *The Earthquake Observers: Disaster Science from Lisbon to Richter* (Chicago: University of Chicago Press, 2013).

91   Samuel Bowles, *Our New West* (Hartford, CT: Hartford Publishing Co., 1869), 351; Hubert Howe Bancroft, *History of California*, vol. 6 (San Francisco: History Co. Pub., 1888), 778.

92   Tobriner, *Bracing for Disaster*, 35, 45–47, 59, 66–67.

93   Hittell, *History of the City of San Francisco*, 320–23, 369–75; Henry George, "What the Railroad Will Bring Us," *Overland Monthly* 1 (October 1868): 297–306. In keeping with the boom and bust history of the West, the completion of the transcontinental railroad did not lead to the instant profits that San Franciscans anticipated. When the arrival of the railroad did not spark the expected demand for land, speculators panicked, and many city residents worried that the railroad would ultimately hurt their city's standing. San Francisco's location on the tip of its peninsula made it an excellent site for access by water, but citizens were concerned that the railroad's major California terminus would be built elsewhere. In fact, although San Francisco was the official endpoint of the Central Pacific line, rail travel provided a substantial boost to Oakland. Richard Walker, "Industry Builds the City: The Suburbanization of Manufacturing in the San Francisco Bay Area, 1850–1940," *Journal of Historical Geography* 27, no. 1 (2001): 36–57. Barth, *Instant Cities*, 217–18.

94   Hittell, *History of the City of San Francisco*, 366, 432–33; Cronise, *Natural Wealth of California*, 647.

95   *The Bulkhead Question Completely Reviewed*, 59–60; Booker, *Down by the Bay*, 56–59.

96   Hittell, *History of the City of San Francisco*, 380; Olmsted, Olmsted, and Pastron, *San Francisco Waterfront*, 239–40.

97   Stoddard is quoted in Barker, *More San Francisco Memoirs*, 126.

98   Terence Young, *Building San Francisco's Parks, 1850–1930* (Baltimore, MD: Johns Hopkins University Press, 2004), 44–97; Raymond H. Clary, *The Making of Golden Gate Park The Early Years: 1865–1906* (San Francisco: California Living Books, 1980), 2–14; Sloan, *Geology of the San Francisco Bay Region*, 119.

99   Dreyfus, *Our Better Nature*, 47–48; Andrew Robichaud and Erik Steiner, "Trail of Blood: The Movement of San Francisco's Butchertown and the Spatial Transformation of Meat Production, 1849–1901," the Spatial History Project, Stanford University, online at www.stanford.edu/group/spatialhistory/cgi-bin/site/pub.php?id=31, accessed April 10, 2013.

100   Barker, *More San Francisco Memoirs*, 194–95; Walker, "Industry Builds the City"; Marie Bolton, "Recovery for Whom? Social Conflict after the San Francisco Earthquake and Fire, 1906–1915," Ph.D. diss., University of California, Davis, 1998, 15.

101   Peter R. Decker, *Fortunes and Failures: White-Collar Mobility in Nineteenth-Century San Francisco* (Cambridge, MA: Harvard University Press, 1978), 74–79, 235; Barth, *Instant City*, 135.

102   William Issel and Robert W. Cherney, *San Francisco, 1865–1932: Politics, Power, and Urban Development* (Berkeley: University of California Press, 1986), 55–56.

103   Andrea Rees Davies, *Saving San Francisco: Relief and Recovery after the 1906 Disaster* (Philadelphia: Temple University Press, 2012), 25. The census significantly undercounted the Chinese population, many of whom sought to avoid census workers.

104   Ibid., 11–12; Frank Soulé, "The Earthquake and Fire and Their Effects on Structural Steel and Steel-Frame Buildings," in *The San Francisco Earthquake and Fire of April 18, 1906 and Their Effects on Structures and Structural Materials*, 131–58 (Washington, DC: Government Printing Office, 1907), 141.

105   Kipling is quoted in Barker, *More San Francisco Memoirs*, 274.

106   Hansen and Condon, *Denial of Disaster*, 11.

107   Young, *San Francisco: A History of the Pacific Coast Metropolis*, 170.

108   Quoted in Tobriner, *Bracing for Disaster*, 101–2.

CHAPTER TWO: CATASTROPHE AND ITS INTERPRETATIONS

1   The National Board of Fire Underwriters is quoted in John Stephen Sewall, "The Effects of the Earthquake and Fire on Buildings, Engineering Structures, and Structural Materials," in *The San Francisco Earthquake and Fire of April 18, 1906 and Their Effects on Structures and Structural Materials*, 62–130 (Washington, DC: Government Printing Office, 1907), 64.

2   Stephen Tobriner, *Bracing for Disaster: Earthquake-Resistant Architecture and Engineering in San Francisco, 1838–1933* (Berkeley, CA: Heyday Books, 2006), 177.

3   San Francisco Board of Supervisors, "Board of Public Works Reports," *San*

Francisco Municipal Reports for the Fiscal Year 1907–1908 (San Francisco: Neal Publishing Co., 1909), 680–81. All reports by city agencies are from the Municipal Reports for a given year unless otherwise stated. The exact names of the agencies vary (i.e., the Department of Public Health is renamed the Board of Health), and report titles therefore vary slightly as well. S. Albert Reed, "The San Francisco Conflagration of April, 1906: Special Report to the National Board of Fire Underwriters, Committee of Twenty," May 1906, New York, 5; Frank Soulé, "The Earthquake and Fire and Their Effects on Structural Steel and Steel-Frame Buildings," in The San Francisco Earthquake and Fire of April 18, 1906 and Their Effects on Structures and Structural Materials, 131–58 (Washington, DC: Government Printing Office, 1907), 135–41; Richard L. Humphrey, "The Effects of the Earthquake and Fire on Various Structures and Structural Materials," in The San Francisco Earthquake and Fire of April 18, 1906 and Their Effects on Structures and Structural Materials, 14–61 (Washington, DC: Government Printing Office, 1907), 49–50.

4   Quoted in Malcolm E. Barker, ed., Three Fearful Days: San Francisco Memoirs of the 1906 Earthquake and Fire (San Francisco: Londonborn, 1998), 69–71.

5   Lucille Eaves, "Where San Francisco Was Sorest Stricken: The Mission District—Telegraph Hill—Barbary Coast—the Water Front and Other Quarters," Charities and The Commons 16, no. 5 (May 5, 1906): 161 (161–63); Barker, Three Fearful Days, 138, 97–99.

6   State Earthquake Investigation Commission (SEIC), The California Earthquake of April 18, 1906: Report of the State Earthquake Investigation Commission, vol. 1 (Washington, DC: Carnegie Institute of Washington, 1908), 382–83.

7   "History of the San Francisco Fire," South of Market Journal, May 1926, 26 (6–7, 22–23, 26–27); William Douglas Alexander, letter to his sister, Mary C. Alexander, San Francisco, May 16, 1906, BANC MSS C-Z 133, Bancroft.

8   Josephine Fearon Baxter, letter to her parents in Omaha, Nebraska, April 23, 1906, p. 2, BANC MSS 73/122 c:94, Bancroft.

9   Barker, Three Fearful Days, 37, 101–3.

10   "History of the San Francisco Fire," 27.

11   Gladys Hansen and Emmet Condon, Denial of Disaster (San Francisco: Cameron and Company, 1989), 20–24, 38.

12   Granucci is quoted in Patricia Turner, ed., 1906 Remembered: Firsthand Accounts of the 1906 Disaster (San Francisco: Friends of the San Francisco Public Library, 1981), 51.

13   Powell is quoted in Barker, Three Fearful Days, 80; Hansen and Condon, Denial of Disaster, 24–25.

14   O'Brien is quoted in Turner, 1906 Remembered, 45; Hansen and Condon, Denial of Disaster, 30–31, 142.

15   Herman Schussler, The Water Supply of San Francisco, California, before, during, and after the Earthquake of April 18th, 1906, and the Subsequent Conflagration

(New York: Martin B. Brown Press, July 23, 1906), 7. Calhan is quoted in Turner, *1906 Remembered*, 27.

16   Hansen and Condon, *Denial of Disaster*, 19, 40–41; Barker, *Three Fearful Days*, 35.

17   "The San Francisco Earthquake and Fire of April, 1906: General History," Appendix, in *San Francisco Municipal Reports for the Fiscal Year 1906–07*, 720; Soulé, "Earthquake and Fire and Their Effects on Structural Steel and Steel-Frame Buildings," 137; Reed, "San Francisco Conflagration of April, 1906," 5–7.

18   On the printing of the proclamation, see Barker, *Three Fearful Days*, 38. On the military response, see Major General Adolphus W. Greely, *Special Report on the Relief Operations Conducted by the Military Authorities* (Washington, DC: Government Printing Office, 1906), 5–6, 12; and Hansen and Condon, *Denial of Disaster*, 46–47. Greely had left San Francisco on a short leave on April 16 and learned of the disaster while, in his words, "passing through Omaha." He immediately telegraphed General Funston and turned around in Chicago, arriving back in San Francisco on April 22 to oversee the army's role in the relief.

19   John Bernard McGloin, *San Francisco: The Story of a City* (San Rafael, CA: Presidio Press, 1978), 144–45.

20   Hansen and Condon, *Denial of Disaster*, 49.

21   Barker, *Three Fearful Days*, 41, 116, 159 (Hopper quotation); Mary McD. Gordon and Cameron King, "Earthquake and Fire in San Francisco," *Huntington Library Quarterly* 48, no. 1 (1985): 69–79. For a discussion of the spectacle of disaster in Victorian and Progressive Era America, see Kevin Rozario, *The Culture of Calamity: Disaster and the Making of Modern America* (Chicago: University of Chicago Press, 2007).

22   Barker, *Three Fearful Days*, 125–28.

23   Jack London, "The Story of an Eyewitness," *Collier's*, May 5, 1906.

24   Philip Fradkin, *The Great Earthquake and Firestorms of 1906: How San Francisco Nearly Destroyed Itself* (Berkeley: University of California Press, 2005), 16–17; Hansen and Condon, *Denial of Disaster*, 144.

25   Soulé, "Earthquake and Fire and Their Effects on Structural Steel and Steel-Frame Buildings," 137.

26   Bell and Liang are quoted in Barker, *Three Fearful Days*, 144, 119–23.

27   Fradkin, *Great Earthquake and Firestorms of 1906*, 75. Hansen and Condon, *Denial of Disaster*, 73–74.

28   Report of Captain Coleman is quoted in Greely, *Special Report on the Relief Operations Conducted by the Military Authorities*, 138; Christopher Morris Douty, *The Economics of Localized Disasters: The 1906 San Francisco Catastrophe* (New York: Arno Press, 1977), 81.

29   For a description of the dawn, see London, "The Story of an Eyewitness." Hopper is quoted in Barker, *Three Fearful Days*, 161. King is quoted in Gordon and King, "Earthquake and Fire in San Francisco," 75–77.

30 Hansen and Condon, *Denial of Disaster*, 72–73; Reed, "San Francisco Conflagration of April, 1906," 9–10.

31 Hansen and Condon, *Denial of Disaster*, 82–88; Andrea Sbarboro, "Life of Andrea Sbarboro: Reminiscences of an Italian-American Pioneer" (San Francisco, 1911), 186, BANC MSS G-D 5180, Bancroft.

32 Hansen and Condon, *Denial of Disaster*, 89–94.

33 Greely, *Special Report on the Relief Operations Conducted by the Military Authorities*, 9; Reed, "San Francisco Conflagration of April, 1906," 11.

34 Douty, *Economics of Localized Disasters*, 81–82; Russell Sage Foundation, *San Francisco Relief Survey: The Organization and Methods of Relief Used after the Earthquake and Fire of April 18, 1906* (New York: Survey Associates, Inc., 1913), 4–5.

35 Leach is quoted in Barker, *Three Fearful Days*, 175–79. For the temperature of the fire, see Gladys Hansen, "Who Perished: A List of Persons Who Died As a Result of the Great Earthquake and Fire in San Francisco on April 18, 1906," (San Francisco: San Francisco Archives, 1980), 2.

36 Martyn John Bowden, "The Dynamics of City Growth: An Historical Geography of the San Francisco Central District, 1850–1931," Ph.D. diss., University of California, Berkeley, 1967, 316; Sbarboro, "Life of Andrea Sbarboro," 182–86.

37 Hansen and Condon, *Denial of Disaster*, 64–66; Soulé, "Earthquake and Fire and Their Effects on Structural Steel and Steel-Frame Buildings," 155; Sewall, "Effects of the Earthquake and Fire on Buildings, Engineering Structures, and Structural Materials," 128.

38 Schussler, *Water Supply of San Francisco*, 7, 29, 40; Charles Derleth Jr., "The Destructive Extent of the California Earthquake," in *The California Earthquake of 1906*, ed. David Starr Jordan, 81–212 (San Francisco: A. M. Robertson, 1907), 164–77.

39 John Casper Branner, "Geology and the Earthquake," in Jordan, *California Earthquake of 1906*, 72 (65–77); Derleth, "Destructive Extent of the California Earthquake," 162–64.

40 "The San Francisco Earthquake and Fire of April, 1906," 784; National Board of Fire Underwriters Committee on Fire Prevention, *Report on the City of San Francisco, Cal.* (July 1910), 13; Schussler, *Water Supply of San Francisco*, 7, 33.

41 "First Things First," *Coast Seamen's Journal*, May 23, 1906, 6.

42 Ted Steinberg, *Acts of God: The Unnatural History of Natural Disaster in America* (New York: Oxford University Press, 2000), 21–22.

43 Griswold and Sedgwick are quoted in Barker, *Three Fearful Days*, 128–29, 207. David Starr Jordan, "The Earthquake Rift of 1906," in Jordan, *California Earthquake of 1906*, 12 (1–62).

44 W. W. Campbell, "The Economic Aspects of the Earthquake," in *The Story of the California Disaster: An Authentic Account of the Earthquake of April 18,*

1906, *and The Great Fire* (Portland, OR: Pacific Monthly Publishing Co., 1906), 82 (82–84).

45   "Vanity of Brick and Mortar," and P. C. Yorke, "Father Yorke to The Leader Readers," *The Leader*, April 28, 1906; Mary Austin, "The Temblor: A Personal Narration," in Jordan, *California Earthquake of 1906*, 356, 358–59 (339–61).

46   Deborah R. Coen, *The Earthquake Observers: Disaster Science from Lisbon to Richter* (Chicago: University of Chicago Press, 2013), 215–26; Fradkin, *Great Earthquake and Firestorms of 1906*, 254–62.

47   SEIC, *California Earthquake of April 18, 1906*, vol. 2, 55.

48   Ibid., vol. 1, 227, 241, 340–41 (quotations).

49   "Report of the Board of Public Works, 1901–02," 354; "Report of the Department of Public Works, 1902–03," 382. These numbers represent the maximum subsidence found at any location along these streets. The mean subsidence throughout the entire section was less: for 1901–1902, it was 1.80 inches on Harrison and 0.60 inches on Sixth; for 1902–1903, it was 2.28 inches on Harrison and, on Sixth, 0.96 inches south of Brannan and 0.60 inches between Brannan and Howard.

50   SEIC, *California Earthquake of April 18, 1906*, vol. 1, 236.

51   Ibid., vol. 1, 233–42; Douty, *Economics of Localized Disasters*, 79. Humphrey considered the Ferry Building to have suffered significant damage, while Soulé declared it to have been "little injured." Soulé, "Earthquake and Fire and Their Effects on Structural Steel and Steel-Frame Buildings," 135; Humphrey, "Effects of the Earthquake and Fire on Various Structures and Structural Materials," 28.

52   SEIC, *California Earthquake of April 18, 1906*, vol. 1, 3, 162, 399; Grove Karl Gilbert, "The Earthquake as a Natural Phenomenon," in *The San Francisco Earthquake and Fire of 1906 and Their Effects on Structures and Structural Materials*, 7–9 (1–13); Robert Anderson, "Earthflows at the Time of the Earthquake of April 18, 1906," typescript, folder 12, box 26, Andrew C. Lawson papers, BANC MSS C-B 602, Bancroft.

53   "Account of the 1906 Earthquake and Fire by Chief Jesse B. Cook," dated March 1, 1935, 1906 Earthquake and Fire Digital Collection, Bancroft.

54   Barker, *Three Fearful Days*, 34; Schussler, *Water Supply of San Francisco*, 30, 34–36; SEIC, *California Earthquake of April 18, 1906*, vol. 1, 239; Hansen and Condon, *Denial of Disaster*, 24–25.

55   "Report of the Board of Public Works, 1910–11," 862; Hansen and Condon, *Denial of Disaster*, 20–23.

56   SEIC, *California Earthquake of April 18, 1906*, vol. 1, 236, 238.

57   Ibid., 220–35.

58   For questions of class, race, and vulnerability in floods, see Craig E. Colten, *An Unnatural Metropolis: Wresting New Orleans from Nature* (Baton Rouge: Louisiana State University Press, 2005); Steinberg, *Acts of God*; and many

works on Hurricane Katrina. The invisibility of poor, transient lodging-house residents is comparable to the invisibility of victims of environmental injustice in other contexts, but the overall lack of concern for earthquake preparedness measures in early twentieth-century San Francisco undermines the significance of this invisibility for seismic vulnerability. This parallels Andrew Hurley's argument that environmental racism in Gary, Indiana, was a product of the increased concern with environmental amenities that characterized the age of ecology; see Hurley, *Environmental Inequalities: Class, Race, and Industrial Pollution in Gary, Indiana, 1945–1980* (Chapel Hill: University of North Carolina Press, 1995).

59 Quoted in Andrea Rees Davies, *Saving San Francisco: Relief and Recovery after the 1906 Disaster* (Philadelphia: Temple University Press, 2012), 31.

60 Ibid., 275, 280–81.

61 Sedgwick is quoted in Barker, *Three Fearful Days*, 207.

62 Hansen and Condon, *Denial of Disaster*, 110–11.

63 Chamber of Commerce of San Francisco, "Report of the Special Committee of the Board of Trustees of the Chamber of Commerce of San Francisco on Insurance Settlements Incident to the San Francisco Fire," November 13, 1906, 22–55; "Report of the Committee of Five to the 'Thirty-Five Companies' on the San Francisco Conflagration," April 24, 1907, 12; Archibald MacPhail, *Of Men and Fire: A Story of Fire Insurance in the Far West* (San Francisco: Fire Underwriters Association of the Pacific, 1948), 102–10; Douty, *Economics of Localized Disasters*, 196–203.

64 Soulé, "Earthquake and Fire and Their Effects on Structural Steel and Steel-Frame Buildings," esp. 135–36; Humphrey, "Effects of the Earthquake and Fire on Various Structures and Structural Materials"; Sewall, "Effects of the Earthquake and Fire on Buildings, Engineering Structures, and Structural Materials," 66. All three articles were published in the same volume, *The San Francisco Earthquake and Fire of 1906 and Their Effects on Structures and Structural Materials*.

65 Chamber of Commerce of San Francisco, "Report," October 1906 [?], 5–6, San Francisco Earthquake and Fire Pamphlets, Bancroft; Ray Stannard Baker, "A Test of Men: The San Francisco Disaster as a Barometer of Human Nature," *The American Magazine*, November 1906, 87 (81–96).

66 SEIC, *California Earthquake of April 18, 1906*, vol. 1, 239–40.

67 Sewall, "Effects of the Earthquake and Fire on Buildings, Engineering Structures, and Structural Materials," 97–103.

68 Gilbert, "Earthquake as a Natural Phenomenon," 12; Derleth, "Destructive Extent of the California Earthquake," 105–6; Humphrey, "Effects of the Earthquake and Fire on Various Structures and Structural Materials," 20.

69 Plume is quoted in Tobriner, *Bracing for Disaster*, 173–75.

70 "Report of the Sub-Committee on Statistics to the Chairman and Committee on Reconstruction," San Francisco, April 24, 1907, 12–13; "Report of the

Special Committee on Investigation of the Demolition of the City Hall," *Organized Labor*, April 17, 1909. Sewall defended the workmanship on City Hall as "above average" and "not poor work by any means"; see Sewall, "Effects of the Earthquake and Fire on Buildings, Engineering Structures, and Structural Materials," 84.

71 J. C. Branner, "Earthquakes and Structural Engineering," *Bulletin of the Seismological Society of America* 3, no. 1 (March 1913): 1–3; Letter from Fred G. Plummer to G. K. Gilbert, October 10, 1906, folder 7, box 26, Andrew C. Lawson papers, BANC MSS C-B 602, Bancroft.

72 Derleth, "Destructive Extent of the California Earthquake," 87; Letter from Plummer to Gilbert, October 10, 1906; J. C. Branner, "Earthquakes," in *Nature and Science on the Pacific Coast*, 62–64 (San Francisco: Paul Elder and Company Publishers, 1915), 62–63. For an earlier example of this line of argument, see Edward S. Holden, "Earthquakes in California and Elsewhere," *Overland Monthly* 11 (January 1888): 48 (39–49).

73 Letter from Charles Derleth Jr., May 7, 1906, folder 14, box 4, Andrew C. Lawson papers, BANC MSS C-B 602, Bancroft. Coen, *Earthquake Observers*, makes a similar point.

74 "Report of the Sub-Committee on Statistics to the Chairman and Committee on Reconstruction," San Francisco, April 24, 1907, 3.

75 These thoughts stem in part from comments by Adam Sitze and other participants in a forum on "Terror and Catastrophe" at Amherst University, October 24, 2013.

CHAPTER THREE: BREAD LINES AND EARTHQUAKE COTTAGES

1 Mary Kelly, *Shame of the Relief: Being an Expose of the Disgraceful Methods of the Relief Committee during the Dark Days Following San Francisco's Great Disaster* (San Francisco, June 1, 1908), 3.

2 Ibid; Andrea Rees Davies, *Saving San Francisco: Relief and Recovery after the 1906 Disaster* (Philadelphia: Temple University Press, 2012), 76–78, 80.

3 Hurricane Katrina and its disproportionate impact on poor, African American communities in New Orleans highlighted the relevance of the concept of environmental injustice for the study of natural disasters, but research in the aftermath of Katrina seldom considered how this concept might relate to earlier disasters in the United States. For an example, see Glenn S. Johnson, "Environmental Justice and Katrina: A Senseless Environmental Disaster," *Western Journal of Black Studies* 32, no. 1 (2008): 42–52. Robert D. Bullard compares Katrina to other disasters in the American South; see Bullard, "Differential Vulnerabilities: Environmental and Economic Inequality and Government Response to Unnatural Disasters," *Social Research* 75, no. 3 (Fall 2008): 753–84.

4 For examples of urban environmental protests, see Andrew Hurley,

Environmental Inequalities: Class, Race, and Industrial Pollution in Gary, Indiana,
1945–1980 (Chapel Hill: University of North Carolina Press, 1995), 111, 168–69;
Sylvia Hood Washington, *Packing Them In: An Archaeology of Environmental*
Racism in Chicago, 1865–1954 (Lanham, MD: Lexington Books, 2005); Julie
Sze, *Noxious New York: The Racial Politics of Urban Health and Environmental*
Justice (Cambridge, MA: MIT Press, 2007); and Dawn Day Biehler, *Pests in*
the City: Flies, Bedbugs, Cockroaches, and Rats (Seattle: University of Wash-
ington Press, 2013).

5   Scholars who have emphasized community mobilizations after disasters,
particularly Hurricane Katrina, include Rachel Luft, "Beyond Disaster
Exceptionalism: Social Movement Developments in New Orleans after
Hurricane Katrina," *American Quarterly* 61, no. 3 (2009): 499–527; and Kevin
Fox Gotham and Miriam Greenberg, *Crisis Cities: Disaster and Redevelop-*
ment in New York and New Orleans (New York: Oxford University Press,
2014).

6   James Forbes, "After the Deluge: The Varied Outcroppings of Charitable
Impulse after a Great Calamity—The 'Yegg' and the Bogus Solicitor," *Chari-*
ties and the Commons, May 5, 1906, 168 (168–71).

7   Edward T. Devine, "The Housing Problem in San Francisco," *Political Science*
Quarterly 21, no. 4 (December 1906): 597–99 (596–608).

8   "A Financial Review of the Relief Work in San Francisco," Appendix, in *San*
Francisco Municipal Reports for the Fiscal Year 1907–1908 (San Francisco: Neal
Publishing Co., 1909), 1312 (1312–32); Charles J. O'Connor, "Organizing the
Force and Emergency Methods," in *San Francisco Relief Survey*, ed. Russell
Sage Foundation, 3–106 (New York: Survey Associates, 1913), 35.

9   "Report of the Los Angeles Chamber of Commerce Citizens' Relief Committee of Receipts and Disbursements of Funds," January 1908, 7–9;
O'Connor, "Organizing the Force and Emergency Methods," 30–33; Adolphus W. Greely, *Special Report on the Relief Operations Conducted by the Mili-*
tary Authorities (Washington, DC: Government Printing Office, 1906), 28.

10   Archibald A. Hill, "San Francisco and the Relief Work Ahead," *Charities*
and the Commons, April 28, 1906, 136–38 (135–38); O'Connor, "Organizing the
Force and Emergency Methods," 32, 97, 101–2; Greely, *Special Report on the*
Relief Operations Conducted by the Military Authorities, 21–22.

11   Andrea Sbarboro, "Life of Andrea Sbarboro: Reminiscences of an Italian-
American Pioneer" (San Francisco, 1911), 186, BANC MSS G-D 5180, Ban-
croft, 186–87; Dominic Ghio with Tony Ghio, "Fisherman By Trade: Sixty
Years on San Francisco Bay," oral history conducted in 1986 by Judith K.
Dunning, Regional Oral History Office, Bancroft, 1990, 15–16.

12   *San Francisco Chronicle*, April 26, 1906; *Napa Valley Packing Company v. San*
Francisco Relief and Red Cross Funds (California Supreme Court 1909),
45–46; O'Connor, "Organizing the Force and Emergency Methods," 101–2;
Schmitt is quoted in Malcolm E. Barker, ed., *Three Fearful Days: San*

Francisco Memoirs of the 1906 Earthquake and Fire (San Francisco: London-born, 1998), 225.

13   Davies, *Saving San Francisco*, 75–76; Kelly, *Shame of the Relief*, 5–7; "Irate Women Mob the Keepers of Relief Stores," *San Francisco Chronicle*, July 7, 1906; J. W. Loomis, "Best Flour $2.25 per bbl," *Socialist Voice*, June 9, 1906; and Jane Cryan, "Hope Chest: The True Story of San Francisco's 1906 Earthquake Refugee Shacks" (1998), box 2, folder 5, Society for the Preservation and Appreciation of San Francisco Refugee Shacks Archive, SFH 9, San Francisco History Center (SFHC), San Francisco Public Library (SFPL), 25.

14   Greely, *Special Report on the Relief Operations Conducted by the Military Authorities*, 27; *San Francisco Chronicle*, April 27, 1906; *Somers & Co. v. General Relief Committee et al.* (California District Court of Appeal, 1910), 30–40, 49–54. For the difficulty of obtaining both horses and forage, see Frank C. Jewell, Report of Supply Officer, April 23, 1906, Folder: Inspection Reports of Captain H. H. Rutherford; Dr. W. A. Mackenzie, Harbor View Sanitorium, Report for May 3, 1906, Folder: Inspection Reports for Harbor View Contagious Hospital; Telegrams between G. W. McIver, Maj. Devol, and G. H. Torney, May 2 and 3, 1906, Folder 3, RG 112, Entry 363, Box 1, NASF.

15   Greely, *Special Report on the Relief Operations Conducted by the Military Authorities*, 15. For an example of a neighborhood patrol, see Notice Citizen's Committee, "All Citizens will observe the following. . . " (San Francisco: Pacific Heights Printery, 1906), 1906 San Francisco Earthquake and Fire Digital Collection, Bancroft. On the looting of Chinatown, see Joseph Leung, "The Fury and Fire That Shocked Chinatown," trans. Danny Lone, in *The Unshakable—Rebirth of S.F. Chinatown in 1906*, 6–13 (Sing Tao Newspapers, 2006), 11. For the mayor's response, see "The San Francisco Earthquake and Fire of April, 1906: General History," 765–66. Greely's official report (*Special Report on the Relief Operations Conducted by the Military Authorities*) put the number of violent deaths at nine, but one researcher has estimated 490—a number that seems much too high. Philip Fradkin estimates a maximum of fifty or seventy-five murders, a number that may also be inflated; see Fradkin, *The Great Earthquake and Firestorms of 1906: How San Francisco Nearly Destroyed Itself* (Berkeley: University of California Press, 2005), 67–69, 140–43, 292–93.

16   Fear of looters is a common phenomenon after disasters, a manifestation of "elite panic." Rebecca Solnit discusses the case of San Francisco, among other examples, in *A Paradise Built in Hell: The Extraordinary Communities That Arise in Disaster* (New York: Viking, 2009). For other examples, see Carl Smith, *Urban Disorder and the Shape of Belief: The Great Chicago Fire, the Haymarket Bomb, and the Model Town of Pullman*, 2nd ed. (Chicago: University of Chicago Press, 2007); and Kathleen Tierney, Christine Bevc, and Erica Kuligowski, "Metaphors Matter: Disaster Myths, Media Frames, and Their Consequences in Hurricane Katrina," *Annals of the American Academy of Political and Social Science* 604, no. 1 (March 2006): 57–81.

17 Kevin L. Rozario, "Nature's Evil Dreams: Disaster and America, 1871–1906," Ph.D. diss., Yale University, 1996, 218–19; O'Connor, "Organizing the Force and Emergency Methods," 9; *San Francisco Chronicle*, April 26, 1906 (quotation).

18 O'Connor, "Organizing the Force and Emergency Methods," 14–15; Hill, "San Francisco and the Relief Work Ahead," 136; Davies, *Saving San Francisco*, 53–55.

19 Rozario, "Nature's Evil Dreams," 251–52.

20 Karen Sawislak, "Relief, Aid, and Order: Class, Gender, and the Definition of Community in the Aftermath of Chicago's Great Fire," *Journal of Urban History* 20, no. 1 (November 1993): 15 (3–18).

21 Bernard Cornelius Cronin, *Father Yorke and the Labor Movement in San Francisco, 1900–1910* (Washington, DC: Catholic University of America Press, 1943), 218; Sbarboro, "Life of Andrea Sbarboro," 188–89; O'Connor, "Organizing the Force and Emergency Methods," 94–95; Yong Chen, *Chinese San Francisco, 1850–1943: A Trans-Pacific Community* (Stanford, CA: Stanford University Press, 2000), 164–65.

22 *Socialist Voice*, May 19, 1906; *Organized Labor*, May 5, 1906, and May 12, 1906; "Report of the General Masonic Relief Fund Incident to Earthquake and Fire of April 18, 1906" (Los Angeles: Grand Lodge of California, October 1, 1906), 14.

23 Josephine Fearon Baxter, letter to her parents in Omaha, Nebraska, April 23, 1906, BANC MSS 73/122 c:94, Bancroft; "Progress of Relief Work," *Charities and The Commons* 16, no. 5 (May 5, 1906): 147 (147–48); *The Refugees' Cook Book, Compiled by One of Them* (San Francisco, 1906), Bancroft; Notice Citizen's Committee, "All Citizens will observe the following. . ."

24 O'Connor, "Organizing the Force and Emergency Methods," 40.

25 Baxter, letter to her parents, April 23, 1906.

26 Greely, *Special Report on the Relief Operations Conducted by the Military Authorities*, 41–42; O'Connor, "Organizing the Force and Emergency Methods," 37; Christopher Morris Douty, *The Economics of Localized Disasters: The 1906 San Francisco Catastrophe* (New York: Arno Press, 1977), 109–12.

27 Coxe is quoted in Barker, *Three Fearful Days*, 147; "Stores Will Resume Business," *San Francisco Chronicle*, April 27, 1906.

28 Edward Livingston Sr., "A Personal History of the San Francisco Earthquake and Fire in 1906" (San Francisco, 1941), 14, Edward Livingston Papers, BANC MSS 2010/921, Bancroft; "Labor in San Francisco," *Coast Seamen's Journal*, May 2, 1906, 1. Although I agree with Solnit that such feelings were widespread in San Francisco in the immediate aftermath of the fire, I find them to be short-lived and limited by persistent criticism of poorer classes. My analysis emphasizes the disaster's medium- and long-term effect of increasing inequality rather than the brief interlude of unity. Solnit, *Paradise Built in Hell*.

29   Southern Pacific Company, "San Francisco Imperishable," June 1906 (?), San Francisco earthquake and fire pamphlets collection, Bancroft; *San Francisco Chronicle*, April 30, 1906; Ray Stannard Baker, "A Test of Men: The San Francisco Disaster as a Barometer of Human Nature," *The American Magazine*, November 1906, 86–87 (81–96).

30   A special diet of "meat, fresh milk, butter and eggs, vegetables, and fruit" was available only for "the sick, the aged, and for mothers and infants." O'Connor, "Organizing the Force and Emergency Methods," 37–40, 44–52. Greely, *Special Report on the Relief Operations Conducted by the Military Authorities*, 24, 40–50, 61, 70, 154–55, 164.

31   Bine, ledger entry, August 7, 1906, folder 15, MS 3640 Dr. René Bine Papers, CHS.

32   *Socialist Voice*, June 23, 1906 (quotation), and July 7, 1906; Jane Cryan, "From Tents to Shacks: A Guide to San Francisco's 1906 Earthquake Refugee Camps," unfinished manuscript (1999) box 2, folder 6, Society for the Preservation and Appreciation of San Francisco Refugee Shacks Archive, SFH 9, SFPL, 27–29.

33   Committee of Friends of Refugees, "Refugees Attention," poster, San Francisco earthquake and fire pamphlets collection, Bancroft; Kelly, *Shame of the Relief*, 7–8. See *Socialist Voice* issues throughout the summer of 1906, particularly May 19, June 30, July 21, July 28, and August 4.

34   Cryan, "From Tents to Shacks," 29.

35   Davies, *Saving San Francisco*, 86–87.

36   Wall is quoted in Barker, *Three Fearful Days*, 201–2; Greely, *Special Report on the Relief Operations Conducted by the Military Authorities*, 32–33, 164; "A Financial Review of the Relief Work in San Francisco," 1316; Douty, *Economics of Localized Disasters*, 128–29; O'Connor, "Organizing the Force and Emergency Methods," 79, 84. The barracks in Golden Gate Park were constructed under the auspices of the Committee for Housing the Homeless, a subcommittee created on the second day of the fire. Committee for Housing the Homeless, "A Resume of the Work Performed" (May 9, 1906), BANC MSS 95/194c, 1–15, Bancroft.

37   Ghio, "Fisherman By Trade." Granucci is quoted in Patricia Turner, ed., *1906 Remembered: Firsthand Accounts of the 1906 Disaster* (San Francisco: Friends of the San Francisco Public Library, 1981), 52.

38   Leung, "The Fury and Fire That Shocked Chinatown," 6–13; Harris Bishop, ed., *Souvenir and Resume of Oakland Relief Work to San Francisco Refugees* (Oakland, CA: Press of the Oakland Tribune, 1906); Erica Y. Z. Pan, *The Impact of the 1906 Earthquake on San Francisco's Chinatown* (New York: Peter Lang, 1995), 35–49, 105; Committee for Housing the Homeless, "Resume of the Work Performed," 14; Greely, *Special Report on the Relief Operations Conducted by the Military Authorities*, 46. The Chinese population was reported at 13,954 at the time of the earthquake, but the Chinese themselves believed the number to be closer to 25,000.

39   The mean temperature for San Francisco in April and May was in the low
      50s, according to 1907 records. US Department of Agriculture, *Annual Sum-
      mary, 1907, California Section of the Climatological Service of the Weather Bureau*
      (San Francisco: Weather Bureau Office, March 16, 1908), 153; O'Connor,
      "Organizing the Force and Emergency Methods," 69 (quotation about tem-
      perate weather); "The Health of the City," *San Francisco Chronicle*, April 27,
      1906; Greely, *Special Report on the Relief Operations Conducted by the Military
      Authorities*, 26, 34, 96; Claire Leeds, "Women Proved Courage in Quake,"
      San Francisco Examiner, April 15, 1956.

40   Kelly, *Shame of the Relief*, 4.

41   William Douglas Alexander, letter to his sister, Mary C. Alexander, San
      Francisco, May 16, 1906, 1, BANC MSS C-Z 133, Bancroft; Amelia Woodward
      Truesdell, *Francisca Reina* (Boston: Garham Press, 1908), 38; Kelly, *Shame of
      the Relief*, 4.

42   McCarron is quoted in Daughters of Charity, *Steel Frames: Eyewitness
      Accounts of the 1906 San Francisco Earthquake and Fire* (Los Altos, CA: Año
      Nuevo Island Press, 2005), 39–40. For the "back to nature" impulse, see Peter
      J. Schmitt, *Back to Nature: The Arcadian Myth in Urban America* (New York:
      Oxford University Press, 1969); and David E. Shi, *The Simple Life: Plain Living
      and High Thinking in American Culture* (New York: Oxford University Press,
      1985).

43   O'Connor, "Organizing the Force and Emergency Methods," 7; "First Things
      First," *Coast Seamen's Journal*, May 23, 1906, 6; Kelly, *Shame of the Relief*, 3–5.
      Refugee advocates appear to have been correct in seeing exposure as a health
      threat; the San Francisco Board of Health reported that a record number of
      patients had been treated at the City and County Hospital during October
      and November. "Board of Health Report, 1906–07," 558.

44   Cryan, "Hope Chest," 29.

45   C. D. Burk to Chief Sanitary Officer, May 10, 1906, Folder 8; M. Harrison to
      Chief Sanitary Officer, May 22, 1906, Folder: Inspection Reports, General
      Inspections, Report of Special Inspections, RG 112, Entry 363, Box 1, NASF.

46   Joel A. Tarr, *The Search for the Ultimate Sink* (Akron, OH: University of Akron
      Press, 1996), 323.

47   Robert E. Noble to Chief Sanitary Officer, May 12, 1906, and Chief Sanitary
      Officer to Military Secretary, May 15, 1906, Folder: Camp No. 6 Speedway;
      Sgt. H. R. Richmond to Captain Wright, May 30, 1906, Folder: Earthquake
      and Fire—1906, RG 112, Entry 363, Box 2, NASF; Mary Roberts Coolidge,
      "The Residuum of Relief," *San Francisco Relief Survey*, ed. Russell Sage Foun-
      dation, 321–68 (New York: Survey Associates, 1913), 321.

48   Charles Clark, Report of the Third Sanitary District, May 10–21, 1906 (first
      quotation from May 16), Folder: Inspection Reports, General Inspections,
      Reports of Special Inspections; W. C. Chidester, Camp Four (Tennesse
      Camp) Report, May 4, 1906, Folder: Inspection Reports of Captain H. H.

Rutherford; W. T. Davidson to George H. Torney, Chief Sanitary Officer, May 6, 1906, Folder: Inspection Reports Camps 8 and 9 Lobos Square and Harbor View Camp; Correspondence, Inspector Sanitary District No. 3 to Torney, May 21, 1906, Folder 12; Consolidated Sanitary Report, Presidio of San Francisco, May 12, 1906, Folder 1, RG 112, Entry 363, Box 1, NASF.

49   Chief Sanitary Officer George H. Torney to Lt. Col. Robert K. Evans, May 8 and May 10, 1906, RG 112, Entry 363, Box 1, Folder 11, NASF. In the first days after the disaster, cavalry horses refused to drink the water in the area, probably because of pollution. Frank C. Jewell, Captain, Reports of Supply Officer, April 25, 1906, RG 112, Entry 363, Box 1, Folder: Inspection Reports of Capt. H. H. Rutherford, NASF.

50   W. T. Davison, Sanitary Officer, to Lt. Col. George H. Torney, Chief Sanitary Officer, April 26, 1906, RG 112, Entry 363, Box 1, Folder: Inspection Reports Camps 8 and 9 Lobos Square and Harbor View Camp, NASF. Bine, ledger entries, August 13 and August 16, 1906, Folder 15, MS 3640, Dr. René Bine Papers, CHS.

51   "Presidio Refugees Shift Their Camp," San Francisco Examiner, July 17, 1906.

52   Bine, ledger entry, July 28, 1906, Folder 15, MS 3640, Dr. René Bine Papers, CHS; Mary Louise Bine Rodriguez, "The Earthquake of 1906," San Francisco, privately printed, 1951, 32–33, 39, 44, 67.

53   Rodriguez, "Earthquake of 1906," 42–43; San Francisco Relief and Red Cross Funds, "Department Reports, as submitted to the Board of Directors at the regular monthly meeting, March 19, 1907" (San Francisco: Starkweather, Latham, & Emanuel, 1907), 19.

54   Bine to Adjutant Permanent Camps, July 27, 1906, folder 16, Dr. René Bine Papers, MS 3640, CHS.

55   René Bine, Camp 1 Report, May 6, 1906, Folder: Inspection Reports of Captain H. H. Rutherford, RG 112, Entry 363, Box 1, NASF. At this time, Bine was working at the Presidio.

56   Russell Sage Foundation, San Francisco Relief Survey, viii (quotation). Andrea Rees Davies (in Saving San Francisco) independently makes a similar argument.

57   According to one study, 14 percent of high-income white-collar workers and 7 percent of low-income white-collar workers availed themselves of the opportunity to settle temporarily in other Bay Area cities. However, only 3 percent of blue-collar workers, 1 percent of the semiskilled, and 2 out of 140 unskilled workers chose that option, suggesting the prohibitive cost. A significant number of working-class people did relocate permanently in the face of the disaster. Martyn J. Bowden et al., "Reestablishing Homes and Jobs: Cities," in Reconstruction Following Disaster, ed. Eugene J. Haas, Robert W. Kates, and Martyn J. Bowden, 69–145 (Cambridge, MA: MIT Press, 1977), 83–85.

58   Douty, Economics of Localized Disasters, 131–32, 330–31; Helen Swett Artieda,

"Business Rehabilitation," in *San Francisco Relief Survey*, 180–83 (171–214); "The Press on the Strikes," *Coast Seamen's Journal*, August 8, 1906, 1.

59 A study of South of Market residents between 1870 and 1900 found that only 21 percent remained at the same address over a five-year period. Alvin Averbach, "San Francisco's South of Market District, 1850–1950: The Emergence of a Skid Row," *California Historical Quarterly* 52, no. 3 (Fall 1973): 203 (197–223); Marie Bolton, "Recovery for Whom?: Social Conflict after the San Francisco Earthquake and Fire, 1906–1915," Ph.D. diss., University of California, Davis, 1998, 85–86.

60 Douty, *Economics of Localized Disasters*, 127; Hutchinson poem printed on card with photos and poems, San Francisco earthquake and fire pamphlets collection, Bancroft.

61 Edward T. Devine, "The Situation in San Francisco," *Charities and the Commons*, June 2, 1906, 302 (299–304).

62 Richard Dillon, *North Beach: The Italian Heart of San Francisco* (Novato, CA: Presidio Press, 1985), 156–61 (quotation 158); Telegraph Hill Neighborhood Association, "Fourth Annual Report," January 1907, 3.

63 San Francisco Housing Association, "First Report of the San Francisco Housing Association" (San Francisco, November 1911), 11–13; Dillon, *North Beach*, 160.

64 C. G. Adams, "On the Roofs of the Latin Quarter," *Overland Monthly*, March 1911, 330.

65 O'Connor, "Organizing the Force and Emergency Methods," 12–14; Rozario, "Nature's Evil Dreams," 249–50; San Francisco Relief and Red Cross Funds, "Department Reports," 23–25; "A Financial Review of the Relief Work in San Francisco," 1317.

66 John F. Moors, "A Hero of the San Francisco Relief," *Charities and the Commons* 17 (1906–1907): 424 (418–26).

67 James Marvin Motley, "Housing Rehabilitation," in *San Francisco Relief Survey*, 237–38 (215–80).

68 Ibid., 218–19.

69 Lilian Brandt, "Rehabilitation Work in San Francisco," *Charities and the Commons* 17 (October 1906): 43 (43–45).

70 Artieda, "Business Rehabilitation," 195.

71 Motley, "Housing Rehabilitation," 225. As Paul Groth notes, "in 1900, up to ninety-five percent of American rooming house keepers were women," half of them widows; see Groth, *Living Downtown: The History of Residential Hotels in the United States* (Berkeley: University of California Press, 1994), 179–80.

72 The percentage of foreign-born men and women was very high among the cottage recipients, although somewhat surprisingly not as high as among the recipients of bonuses. Motley, "Housing Rehabilitation," 224–31.

73 O'Connor, "Organizing the Force and Emergency Methods," 81.

74 Bine, ledger entries, August 3 and August 10, 1906, folder 15, and October 9,

1906, folder 17, MS 3640, Dr. René Bine Papers, CHS. A memorandum of June 25 had forbidden "the establishment of booths" and "the sale of all articles," except newspapers, in the camps. Bine, ledger entry, June 25, 1906, Dr. René Bine Papers, CHS.

75 Cryan, "From Tents to Shacks," 30, 39. Leonard is quoted in Cryan, "Hope Chest," 32–35. The cottages were built by union labor, with carpenters earning between four and five dollars per day, bricklayers receiving six to eight dollars per day, and plumbers earning six to seven dollars.

76 San Francisco Relief and Red Cross Funds "Department Reports," 19, 28–29. The San Francisco Relief and Red Cross Funds reported 5,938 cottages; O'Connor counted 5,610 (see O'Connor, "Organizing the Force and Emergency Methods," 81). Cryan, "Hope Chest," 32, 38; "The 1906 Earthquake Refugee Shack—Summary of Historic Data," box 1, folder 1, Society for the Preservation and Appreciation of San Francisco Refugee Shacks Archive, SFH 9, SFPL, 1–2.

77 Kelly, *Shame of the Relief*, 8–9.

78 Ibid., 9–13; Jane Cryan, "Re-Cap—Mary Kelly Citations," box 2, folder 3, Society for the Preservation and Appreciation of San Francisco Refugee Shacks Archive, SFH 9, SFPL, 1–2.

79 Bine, ledger entry, July 10, 1906, Folder 15, MS 3640, Dr. René Bine Papers, CHS.

80 W. D. Sohier and Jacob Furth, "Report to the Massachusetts Association for the Relief of California on the San Francisco Relief and Red Cross Funds," San Francisco, September 27, 1906, 14; Bolton, "Recovery for Whom?" 87–88.

81 Sohier and Furth, "Report of the Massachusetts Association," 7–8.

82 United Refugees Enrollment Card, Bine ledger, July 16, 1906, folder 15, and United Refugees poster, Bine ledger, October 5, 1906, folder 16, MS 3640, Dr. René Bine Papers, CHS.

83 Examples for rural parks in US history are described in Karl Jacoby, *Crimes against Nature: Squatters, Poachers, Thieves, and the Hidden History of American Conservation* (Berkeley: University of California Press, 2001); and Mark David Spence, *Dispossessing the Wilderness: Indian Removal and the Making of the National Parks* (New York: Oxford University Press, 1999). Urban examples include Ray Rosenzweig and Elizabeth Blackmar, *The Park and the People: A History of Central Park* (Ithaca, NY: Cornell University Press, 1992).

84 Committee for Housing the Homeless, "Resume of the Work Performed," 1–2; *Socialist Voice*, August 4, 1906, and September 8, 1906. Women would win the right to vote in California in 1911.

85 Kelly, *Shame of the Relief*, 15; Motley, "Housing Rehabilitation," 222; Associated Charities of San Francisco, *Annual Reports 1904–1910* (San Francisco: Blair Murdoch Company), 8. The *San Francisco Relief Survey* gives a statistic of 703 cottages moved or repaired by the Associated Charities. This discrepancy reflects different time periods covered, with the *Relief Survey* ending its

study in June 1908 and the Associated Charities report covering through October 1910. O'Connor, "Organizing the Force and Emergency Methods," 85–86.

86   Hanna Astrup Larson, "Enrichment of the Refugees," *San Francisco Call*, October 20, 1907; Cryan, "Hope Chest," 42–44, 88; Motley, "Housing Rehabilitation," 231–37.

87   M. J. Bowden, "Geographical Change in Cities Following Disaster," in *Period and Place: Research Methods in Historical Geography*, ed. Alan R. H. Baker and Mark Billinge, 114–26 (New York: Cambridge University Press, 1982), 120–23. This rate of relocation was 30 percent higher than expected without the disaster.

88   Kelly, *Shame of the Relief*, 15–16; Bolton, "Recovery for Whom?" 63–64. For a detailed discussion of the 1907 bubonic plague outbreak and the city's reaction, see chapter 6 in this book. Lobos Square, the surviving cottage camp, was a locus of the outbreak.

89   "Board of Health Report 1909–10," 267; "Report of Board of Health 1911–12," 619; Bolton, "Recovery for Whom?" 67–68, 79.

90   John J. Jordan, "Sout' O' Market," *South of Market Journal*, October 1925, 16.

91   Davies, *Saving San Francisco*, 122–24; Bowden et al., "Reestablishing Homes and Jobs: Cities," 96.

92   San Francisco Housing Association, "First Report," 11.

93   Mary Edith Griswold, "San Francisco's Ocean Beaches," *Western World*, October 5, 1907, 17–20. Davies has described the expansion of Bay Area suburbs after 1906 as "disaster suburbanization" (see *Saving San Francisco*, 134–38).

94   Simon Winchester, *A Crack in the Edge of the World: America and the Great California Earthquake of 1906* (New York: HarperCollins, 2005), 179; City of Daly City, History of Daly City, online at www.dalycity.org/About_Daly_City /History_of_Daly_City.htm, accessed January 8, 2017.

95   Griswold, "San Francisco's Ocean Beaches," 18; Edgemar Realty Syndicate, *Edgemar: The Nearest Seaside Suburb* (San Francisco: Bolte & Braden Co., 1907[?]). Exclusionary zoning to keep Chinese out of white neighborhoods dated back to the 1880s in San Francisco. Richard Walker, "Landscape and City Life: Four Ecologies of Residence in the San Francisco Bay Area," *Ecumene* 2 (1995): 44 (33–64).

96   J. C. Smith, "The Bay Shore Cut-Off and Peninsular Development," *Western World*, October 19, 1907, 13–15 (13–18).

97   Ethelbert D. Burrows, "San Francisco—Yesterday, Today and Tomorrow," *New San Francisco Magazine*, May 1906, 5 (1–22).

98   "An Appeal for the Shack Dwellers," *Organized Labor*, April 3, 1909.

99   Adam Rome, *The Bulldozer in the Countryside: Suburban Sprawl and the Rise of American Environmentalism* (New York: Cambridge University Press, 2001), discusses the sanitary challenges facing post–World War II suburban

residents. See also Hurley, *Environmental Inequalities*; and Christopher C. Sellers, *Crabgrass Crucible: Suburban Nature and the Rise of Environmentalism in Twentieth-Century America* (Chapel Hill: University of North Carolina Press, 2012).

100　Motley, "Housing Rehabilitation," 228–37. For statistics on commutes, see Bowden, "Geographical Change in Cities Following Disaster," 120–23.

101　Kelly, *Shame of the Relief*, 7.

102　John McPhee, *Assembling California* (New York: Farrar, Straus and Giroux, 1993), 4.

103　Similarly, many of the towns south of San Francisco on the peninsula rested on the unstable ground of alluvial valleys and, later, fill. Doris Sloan, *Geology of the San Francisco Bay Region* (Berkeley: University of California Press, 2006), 163–66; Barbara VanderWerf, *Granada, A Synonum for Paradise: The Ocean Shore Railroad Years* (El Granada, CA: Gum Tree Lane Books, 1992), 39–40, 193–99; San Francisco Trains, "A Brief History of the Ocean Shore Railroad," online at http://sanfranciscotrains.org/ocean-shore.html, accessed June 18, 2012.

CHAPTER FOUR: REBUILDING AND THE POLITICS OF PLACE

1　"Chinese Consul Pleads for Freedom," *San Francisco Examiner*, May 3, 1906; "Want Chinese on the Front," *San Francisco Examiner*, May 4, 1906.

2　Many historians have discussed Burnham's *Report on a Plan for San Francisco* and the debates over its implementation in the wake of the earthquake, but to my knowledge none has explicitly analyzed the environmental vision in the *Report*. The best work on the political debates over implementation remains Judd Kahn, *Imperial San Francisco: Politics and Planning in an American City, 1897–1906* (Lincoln: University of Nebraska Press, 1979).

3　California State Board of Trade, "The Rebuilding of San Francisco," in *The Story of the California Disaster: An Authentic Account of the Earthquake of April 18, 1906 and The Great Fire*, 37–38 (Portland, OR: Pacific Monthly Pub. Co., 1906), 38. For general discussion of cities' resilience after disaster, see Lawrence J. Vale and Thomas J. Campanella, "Conclusion: Axioms of Resilience," in *The Resilient City: How Modern Cities Recover from Disaster*, ed. Vale and Campanella, 335–55 (New York: Oxford University Press, 2005); J. Eugene Haas et al., "Reconstruction Issues in Perspective," in *Reconstruction Following Disaster*, ed. J. Eugene Haas, Robert W. Kates, and Martyn J. Bowden, 25–68 (Cambridge, MA: MIT Press, 1977); Robert W. Kates and David Pijawka, "From Rubble to Monument: The Pace of Reconstruction," in *Reconstruction Following Disaster*, 1–23. Kates and Pijawka note that the "last significant urban place that failed to rebuild was St. Pierre in Martinique, destroyed by the eruption of Mt. Pelee in 1902" (20). In the years since the publication of their research in 1967, nuclear crises in Chernobyl and Fukushima have suggested possible exceptions to this trend.

4   Sylvia Hood Washington, *Packing Them In: An Archaeology of Environmental Racism in Chicago, 1865–1954* (Lanham, MD: Lexington Books, 2005).

5   Laura Pulido, "Rethinking Environmental Racism: White Privilege and Urban Development in Southern California," *Annals of the Association of American Geographers* 90, no. 1 (March 2000): 13 (12–40). Harvey is quoted in Kevin Fox Gotham and Miriam Greenberg, *Crisis Cities: Disaster and Redevelopment in New York and New Orleans* (New York: Oxford University Press, 2014), 62–64. For historical connections between discriminatory restraints on racial minorities and environmental policies, particularly during the Progressive Era, see Jeff Romm, "The Coincidental Order of Environmental Injustice," in *Justice and Natural Resources: Concepts, Strategies, and Applications*, ed. Kathryn M. Mutz, Gary C. Bryner, and Douglas S. Kenney, 117–37 (Washington, DC: Island Press, 2002).

6   James D. Phelan, "Historical Sketch of San Francisco," in *Report on a Plan for San Francisco*, by Daniel H. Burnham, 193–209 (1905; Berkeley, CA: Urban Books, 1971), 208.

7   James D. Phelan, "The New San Francisco," address at the opening of the Mechanics' Institute Fair (California, September 1, 1896), 6–7.

8   William H. Wilson, "The Ideology, Aesthetics, and Politics of the City Beautiful Movement," in *The Rise of Modern Urban Planning, 1800–1914*, ed. Anthony Sutcliffe, 165–98 (New York: St. Martin's Press, 1980).

9   M. Christine Boyer, *Dreaming the Rational City: The Myth of American City Planning* (Cambridge, MA: MIT Press, 1983), 59. For a history of the City Beautiful movement, see William H. Wilson, *The City Beautiful Movement* (Baltimore, MD: Johns Hopkins University Press, 1989).

10 Association for the Improvement and Adornment of San Francisco (AIASF), "Second Annual Report," March 15, 1906, 17, San Francisco History Center, San Francisco Public Library (SFPL); James R. McCarthy, "Introduction," to reprint of Daniel H. Burnham, *Report on a Plan for San Francisco* (Berkeley, CA: Urban Books, 1971).

11 Kahn, *Imperial San Francisco*, 95–97; Burnham, *Report on a Plan for San Francisco*, 79, 145, 168.

12 Burnham, *Report on a Plan for San Francisco*, 111–14, 145.

13 Of course, as discussed in chapter 1, the area that became San Francisco was in fact densely settled by Native peoples for thousands of years before the arrival of the Spanish. The same was true of places like Yellowstone and Yosemite that were set aside as parks during this period and subsequently labeled "wilderness." See, among other works, Mark David Spence, *Dispossessing the Wilderness: Indian Removal and the Making of the National Parks* (New York: Oxford University Press, 1999).

14 Burnham, *Report on a Plan for San Francisco*, 114, 157, 180.

15 Ibid., 35–36, 39–41, 53–55, 67, 132; Kahn, *Imperial San Francisco*, 90–92; AIASF, "Second Annual Report," 7.

16 Burnham, *Report on a Plan for San Francisco*, 35.

17 Quoted in "Burnham Plans," Appendix, in *San Francisco Municipal Reports for the Fiscal Year 1904–1905*, 609–10.

18 Kahn, *Imperial San Francisco*, 87, 108–9; AIASF, "Second Annual Report," 5–6, 12.

19 James D. Phelan, "Cosmo Oct. 6," 3, James D. Phelan papers, Carton 18, BANC MSS C-B 800, Bancroft.

20 S. E. Moffett and C. F. Gould, "An Ideal San Francisco," *Collier's*, May 12, 1906, 13–14.

21 Committee on Extending, Widening, and Grading Streets and Committee on Burnham Plans, "Plan of Proposed Street Changes in the Burned District and Other Sections of San Francisco" (San Francisco: Hicks-Judd Co., May 1906); Kahn, *Imperial San Francisco*, 171–76.

22 Kahn, *Imperial San Francisco*, 159–60; Southern Pacific Company, "San Francisco Imperishable," June 1906 (?), San Francisco earthquake and fire pamphlets collection, Bancroft; James D. Phelan, "The Present Situation," in *The Story of the California Disaster*, 25–30; Kevin Rozario discusses the Burnham Plan in *The Culture of Calamity: Disaster and the Making of Modern America* (Chicago: University of Chicago Press, 2007), 88–94.

23 "Pressing Needs of the Hour," *Coast Seamen's Journal*, May 23, 1906, 1. See also H. B. Salisbury, "How Socialism Would Meet the Calamity," *Socialist Voice*, May 26, 1906.

24 *San Francisco Chronicle*, April 30, 1906; Kahn, *Imperial San Francisco*, 170, 181–82.

25 Kahn, *Imperial San Francisco*, 191–93; Mulligan is quoted in Stephen Tobriner, *Bracing for Disaster: Earthquake-Resistant Architecture and Engineering in San Francisco, 1838–1933* (Berkeley, CA: Heyday Books, 2006), 202–03.

26 B. J. S. Cahill, "The Bond Issue and the Burnham Plan—A Study in 'Panhandling,'" *The Architect and Engineer* (June 1909): 63 (63–72).

27 "Report of the Board of Public Works, 1908–09," 497.

28 Kahn, *Imperial San Francisco*, 177–78.

29 Marsden Manson, *Report of Marsden Manson to the Mayor and Committee on Reconstruction on Those Portions of the Burnham Plans Which Meet Our Commercial Necessities and an Estimate of the Cost of the Same* (San Francisco: s.n., October 1906), 5–6. Chapter 7 discusses the Hetch Hetchy debates in more detail. For Manson's role, see Robert W. Righter, *The Battle over Hetch Hetchy: America's Most Controversial Dam and the Birth of Modern Environmentalism* (New York: Oxford University Press, 2005).

30 Manson, *Report of Marsden Manson*, 3–13.

31 Burnham, *Report on a Plan for San Francisco*, 86, 168, 181.

32 San Francisco Real Estate Board, "Views of the San Francisco Real Estate

Board upon the Plan Submitted by Mr. Marsden Manson for the Reconstruction of San Francisco," in *Report of Marsden Manson*, 28–34 (October 26, 1906), 28–29. Galloway is quoted in Tobriner, *Bracing for Disaster*, 208.

33 Phelan, "Cosmo Oct. 6," 2; Kahn, *Imperial San Francisco*, 195–98. In San Francisco the vote was 4,128 yes to 7,940 no (only one-third of voters cast a ballot on this issue). Statewide, 35,649 people voted yes to 58,042 no votes.

34 For example, Sarah J. Moore has referred to "the hope for redemption out of the rubble with Burnham's ideal plan as its enlightened guide"; see Moore, *Empire on Display: San Francisco's Panama-Pacific International Exposition of 1915* (Norman: University of Oklahoma Press, 2013), 82.

35 Erica Y. Z. Pan, *The Impact of the 1906 Earthquake on San Francisco's Chinatown* (New York: Peter Lang, 1995), 51–55; Philip Fradkin, *The Great Earthquake and Firestorms of 1906: How San Francisco Nearly Destroyed Itself* (Berkeley: University of California Press, 2005), 292–93; Major William P. Humphreys to Assistant Adjutant General, April 28, 1906, Virtual Museum of the City of San Francisco, online at www.sfmuseum.org/1906.2/ngc.html, accessed July 1, 2014. On looting after disasters, see Kathleen Tierney, Christine Bevc, and Erica Kuligowski, "Metaphors Matter: Disaster Myths, Media Frames, and Their Consequences in Hurricane Katrina," *Annals of the American Academy of Political and Social Science* 604, no. 1 (March 2006): 57–81; and Rebecca Solnit, *A Paradise Built in Hell: The Extraordinary Communities That Arise in Disaster* (New York: Viking, 2009).

36 Pan, *Impact of the 1906 Earthquake on San Francisco's Chinatown*, 98–99, 105–9.

37 Ibid., 6–8, 20–22; Anthony W. Lee, *Picturing Chinatown: Art and Orientalism in San Francisco* (Berkeley: University of California Press, 2001), 14–26. Whiteness was a complicated category in the nineteenth-century United States, and racial formations in California and the West differed from those in the East. In the West the category of "white" was generally more inclusive of a variety of peoples of European descent, in large part because "whiteness" was defined in opposition to Native Americans, Chinese, and Mexican Americans. See Alexander Saxton, *The Indispensable Enemy: Labor and the Anti-Chinese Movement in California* (Berkeley: University of California Press, 1971); Tomás Almaguer, *Racial Fault Lines: The Historical Origins of White Supremacy in California* (Berkeley: University of California Press, 1994); Barbara Berglund, *Making San Francisco American: Cultural Frontiers in the Urban West, 1846–1906* (Lawrence: University Press of Kansas, 2007); Linda Gordon, *The Great Arizona Orphan Abduction* (Cambridge, MA: Harvard University Press, 1999); and Carlos A. Schwantes, "Protest in a Promised Land: Unemployment, Disinheritance, and the Origin of Labor Militancy in the Pacific Northwest, 1885–1886," *Western Historical Quarterly* 13 (1982): 373–90.

38 Quoted in Joan B. Trauner, "The Chinese as Medical Scapegoats in San Francisco, 1870–1905," *California History* 57 (Spring 1978): 73 (70–87).

39   For histories of disease in San Francisco, see Nayan Shah, *Contagious Divides: Epidemics and Race in San Francisco's Chinatown* (Berkeley: University of California Press, 2001); Susan Craddock, *City of Plagues: Disease, Poverty, and Deviance in San Francisco* (Minneapolis: University of Minnesota Press, 2000); and Trauner, "Chinese as Medical Scapegoats in San Francisco, 1870–1905." For histories of similar phenomena in other cities, see Natalia Molina, *Fit To Be Citizens?: Public Health and Race in Los Angeles, 1879–1939* (Berkeley: University of California Press, 2006); Alan M. Kraut, *Silent Travelers: Germs, Genes, and the "Immigrant Menace"* (New York: BasicBooks, 1994); and Tera W. Hunter, *To 'Joy My Freedom: Southern Black Women's Lives and Labors after the Civil War* (Boston: Harvard University Press, 1998).

40   K. Animashaun Ducre, "Racialized Spaces and the Emergence of Environmental Injustice," in *Echoes from the Poisoned Well: Global Memories of Environmental Injustice*, ed. Sylvia Hood Washington, Paul C. Rosier, and Heather Goodall, 109–24 (Lantham, MD: Lexington Books, 2006); and Romm, "Coincidental Order of Environmental Injustice."

41   Shah, *Contagious Divides*, 18–38. See also Craddock, *City of Plagues*. Molina identifies similar processes in Los Angeles; see Molina, *Fit To Be Citizens?*.

42   Curt Abel-Musgrave, "The Cholera in San Francisco: A Contribution to a History of Corruption in California" (San Francisco: San Francisco News Company, 1885), 5, 12.

43   The same report, however, recognized that San Francisco's Chinese population did not entirely fit stereotypes of a racial underclass, noting that they were well fed and well clothed. *Report of the Commission Appointed by the Secretary of the Treasury for the Investigation of Plague in San Francisco* (Washington, DC: Government Printing Office, 1901), 8–9.

44   For historical examples of these processes, see Washington, *Packing Them In*; and Ellen Stroud, "Troubled Waters in Ecotopia," *Radical History Review* 74 (1999): 65–95. A 2007 study found that racial and socioeconomic disparities in exposure to hazardous waste facilities not only persist but may have increased in the past twenty years. Robert D. Bullard, Paul Mohai, Robin Saha, and Beverly Wright, *Toxic Wastes and Race at Twenty, 1987–2007* (Cleveland, OH: United Church of Christ, 2007).

45   Craddock, *City of Plagues*, 61–81; Shah, *Contagious Divides*, 57, 61.

46   Trauner, "Chinese as Medical Scapegoats in San Francisco, 1870–1905," 74; Pan, *Impact of the 1906 Earthquake on San Francisco's Chinatown*, 25–27; Shah, *Contagious Divides*, 36–37, 71–72.

47   The plague was most likely present among San Francisco's rodents, if not its people, before Wong Chut King's death. Chapter 6 provides more detailed context on the plague outbreaks of the early twentieth century. "Report of the Board of Health, 1899–1900," 532–33; Marilyn Chase, *The Barbary Plague: The Black Death in Victorian San Francisco* (New York: Random House, 2003), 18–44.

48 "Report of the Board of Health, 1899–1900," 521–23; Chase, *Barbary Plague*, 18–30; Craddock, *City of Plagues*, 128–34.

49 State Board of Health, "The Disinfecting, Cleaning, and Fumigating of Chinatown, in the City and County of San Francisco, State of California," August 27, 1901, published with the Report of the Special Health Commissioners (Sacramento, CA: A. J. Johnson, Superintendent State Printing, 1901), 37–40.

50 The disease did overwhelmingly claim Chinese victims from 1900 to 1904, at least among the confirmed cases. In those years San Francisco had 121 known cases of bubonic plague and 113 deaths. Of those deaths, 107 were Chinese, 4 were Japanese, and 2 were white. Plague diagnoses were highly controversial in these years, and similar cases among whites may have been less likely to be characterized as plague. The processes of quarantine and containment probably also shaped the racial makeup of victims. The Asian origins of the disease and the habits of its vector species of rats—which tend to remain within limited territories unless disturbed—undoubtedly contributed to the outbreak's focus on Chinatown. As detailed in chapter 6, victims of the 1907–1908 outbreak had a very different racial profile, with nearly all victims identified as white. Shah, *Contagious Divides*, 150–51.

51 Kraut, *Silent Travelers*, 93. The burning of Honolulu's Chinatown had been accidental, occurring when a small fire to destroy a cluster of plague-infected shacks got out of control, but Chinese communities throughout the Pacific world feared similar fates. For a full account of the events in Honolulu, see James C. Mohr, *Plague and Fire: Battling Black Death and the 1900 Burning of Honolulu's Chinatown* (New York: Oxford University Press, 2005). William Deverell describes similar attempts to quarantine and disinfect Mexican neighborhoods, as well as the destruction of Mexican neighborhoods in the name of eradicating plague and rats, during an outbreak in Los Angeles in 1924; see Deverell, *Whitewashed Adobe: The Rise of Los Angeles and the Remaking of Its Mexican Past* (Berkeley: University of California Press, 2004).

52 "Mayor Schmitz on Chinese Exclusion," *Labor Clarion*, March 28, 1902, 1.

53 Minutes of the State Board of Health and the California Public Health Association, May 11, 1903, Department of Public Health, State Board of Health, Executive Secretary, F3676:1 C1810-C1811, CSA; *San Francisco News Letter*, August 30, 1902; Kahn, *Imperial San Francisco*, 203.

54 Craddock, *City of Plagues*, 96.

55 "Report of the Board of Health, 1899–1900," 546–47.

56 For example, Chinese people were right to question the safety and efficacy of the vaccines of the time. Vaccination campaigns and other public health measures such as autopsies also violated Chinese cultural mores. Chase, *Barbary Plague*.

57 Connie Young Yu, "The End and the Beginning," in *The Unshakable—Rebirth*

of *S.F. Chinatown in 1906*, 14–16 (Brisbane, CA: Sing Tao Newspapers, 2006), 15; "The San Francisco Earthquake and Fire of April, 1906," 764.

58 "Plan to Build an Oriental City," *San Francisco Chronicle*, April 27, 1906; Yong Chen, *Chinese San Francisco, 1850–1943: A Trans-Pacific Community* (Stanford, CA: Stanford University Press, 2000), 165–66; Chase, *Barbary Plague*, 48; *Organized Labor*, May 26, 1906.

59 "New Chinatown Near Fort Point," *San Francisco Chronicle*, April 28, 1906.

60 Andrew Robichaud and Erik Steiner, "Trail of Blood: The Movement of San Francisco's Butchertown and the Spatial Transformation of Meat Production, 1849–1901," the Spatial History Project, Stanford University, online at www.stanford.edu/group/spatialhistory/cgi-bin/site/pub.php?id=31, accessed April 10, 2013; Major Wm. W. Harts Report to Brigadier Gen. A. Mackenzie, April 25, 1907, RG 77, Box 23, folder Islais Creek, NASF; Shah, *Contagious Divides*, 71–72.

61 Arthur E. Hippler, *Hunter's Point: A Black Ghetto* (New York: Basic Books, 1974), 13–17; Richard A. Walker, *The Country in the City: The Greening of the San Francisco Bay Area* (Seattle: University of Washington Press, 2007), 212–18, 235–36.

62 Chen, *Chinese San Francisco*, 152–61. The 1906 earthquake may have played an important role in ending the boycott by creating a crisis among the Chinese in San Francisco that preempted concerns about boycotting American goods. Pan, *Impact of the 1906 Earthquake on San Francisco's Chinatown*, 119.

63 *Coast Seamen's Journal*, May 16, 1906; Fradkin, *Great Earthquake and Firestorms of 1906*, 299.

64 Roger Daniels, *Asian America: Chinese and Japanese in the United States since 1850* (Seattle: University of Washington Press, 1988), 118–33; Gray Brechin, *Imperial San Francisco: Urban Power, Earthly Ruin* (Berkeley: University of California Press, 1999), 157–60; Fradkin, *Great Earthquake and Firestorms of 1906*, 296–304.

65 Pan estimates there were roughly 39 Chinese owners of property in Chinatown of 550 landowners in the district in 1906. Estimates vary, however. Pan, *Impact of the 1906 Earthquake on San Francisco's Chinatown*, 8, 69–75. Marie Bolton gives a figure of 82 percent in "Recovery for Whom?: Social Conflict after the San Francisco Earthquake and Fire, 1906–1915," Ph.D. diss., University of California, Davis, 1998, 57–58. Mary Roberts Coolidge reported that, in 1904, 25 pieces of property in Chinatown (of 316) were Chinese-owned; see Coolidge, *Chinese Immigration* (New York: Henry Holt and Company, 1909), 411. See also Shah, *Contagious Divides*, 152; Fradkin, *Great Earthquake and Firestorms of 1906*, 293–96; Anna Naruta, "Relocation," in *Earthquake: The Chinatown Story*, Chinese Historical Society of America Museum Exhibit, online at http://chsa.org/exhibits/online-exhibits/earthquake-the-chinatown-story, accessed March 16, 2016.

66 "New Chinatown Near Fort Point," *San Francisco Chronicle*, April 28, 1906; "Chinese Make Strong Protest," *San Francisco Chronicle*, April 30, 1906; "Chinese Consul Pleads for Freedom," *San Francisco Examiner*, May 3, 1906; "Want Chinese on the Front," *San Francisco Examiner*, May 4, 1906.

67 Daniels, *Asian America*, 90; Lee, *Picturing Chinatown*, 124–25.

68 "Chinese Colony at Foot of Van Ness," *San Francisco Chronicle*, April 27, 1906; "Now Fear That Chinese May Abandon City," *San Francisco Chronicle*, May 2, 1906; "Want Chinese on the Front," *San Francisco Examiner*, May 4, 1906.

69 Pan, *Impact of the 1906 Earthquake on San Francisco's Chinatown*, 15–17, 71, 79–82.

70 "Will Fight for Greater New Chinatown," *San Francisco Examiner*, May 20, 1906.

71 "Residents of Telegraph Hill Want No Chinese," *San Francisco Examiner*, May 28, 1906.

72 Frank J. Sullivan, "Widen Grant Avenue and the Chinese Will Leave," *San Francisco Examiner*, May 17, 1906.

73 Such architectural elements drew on traditions from Beijing, not Guangdong Province, from which most San Francisco Chinese immigrated. Raymond W. Rast, "Chinatown, San Francisco, California," in *American Tourism: Constructing a National Tradition*, ed. J. Mark Souther and Nicholas Dagen Bloom, 45–52 (Chicago: Center for American Places at Columbia College Chicago, 2012), 49; Shah, *Contagious Divides*, 153; Pan, *Impact of the Earthquake on San Francisco's Chinatown*, 66, 95–98; Look Tin Eli, "Our New Oriental City—Veritable Fairy Palaces Filled with the Choicest Treasures of the Orient," in *San Francisco, the Metropolis of the West* (San Francisco: Western Press Association, 1910).

74 *San Francisco's Chinatown: An Aid to Tourists and Others in Visiting China-town* (San Francisco, 1909), 2.

75 Raymond W. Rast, "The Cultural Politics of Tourism in San Francisco's Chinatown, 1882–1917," *Pacific Historical Review* 76, no. 1 (2007): 33–34 (29–60); John Kuo Wei Tchen, ed., *Genthe's Photographs of San Francisco's Old Chinatown* (New York: Dover Publications, Inc., 1984), 13–15, 122–23.

76 Stellman is quoted in Lee, *Picturing Chinatown*, 149, 173–74. See also Chen, *Chinese San Francisco*, 179–82; Pan, *Impact of the 1906 Earthquake on San Francisco's Chinatown*, 113–23.

77 Rast, "Cultural Politics of Tourism in San Francisco's Chinatown, 1882–1917," 59–60.

CHAPTER FIVE: DISASTER CAPITALISM IN THE STREETS

1 Bion J. Arnold, *Report on the Improvement and Development of the Transportation Facilities of San Francisco* (San Francisco: Hicks-Judd Co., March 1913), 316, 331.

2 The geographer Don Mitchell has written: "The two landscapes—the broad, perspectival, aesthetic view from atop the hill, and the ugly, violent, dirty

landscape of workers' everyday lives—are intimately linked." Mitchell, *The Lie of the Land: Migrant Workers and the California Landscape* (Minneapolis: University of Minnesota Press, 1996), 16.

3   For a discussion of labor and transportation in a different context, see Kathryn Morse, *The Nature of Gold: An Environmental History of the Klondike Gold Rush* (Seattle: University of Washington Press, 2003). Although environmental historians increasingly acknowledge the importance of work as a means of knowing and influencing nature, connections between environmental history and labor history seldom extend beyond studies of the involvement of union members in environmental organizing. When historians and environmentalists do discuss work and nature, they often focus on premodern work or its simulacrum—work that takes place in rural settings and employs minimal technology to mediate the relationship between human labor and nature. Such conceptions reinforce the separation of nature and culture and the exclusion of the city from nature. Richard White, "Are You an Environmentalist or Do You Work for a Living?: Work and Nature," in *Uncommon Ground: Rethinking the Human Place in Nature*, ed. William Cronon, 171–85 (New York: W. W. Norton & Co., 1996); Gunther Peck, "The Nature of Labor: Fault Lines and Common Ground in Environmental and Labor History," *Environmental History* 11 (April 2006): 212–38.

4   Naomi Klein, *The Shock Doctrine: The Rise of Disaster Capitalism* (New York: Henry Holt and Company, 2007); Kevin Rozario, *The Culture of Calamity: Disaster and the Making of Modern America* (Chicago: University of Chicago Press, 2007), 75–100; Kevin Fox Gotham and Miriam Greenberg, *Crisis Cities: Disaster and Redevelopment in New York and New Orleans* (New York: Oxford University Press, 2014).

5   See Michael Rawson, *Eden on the Charles: The Making of Boston* (Cambridge, MA: Harvard University Press, 2010), for a discussion of urban infrastructure connecting humans and the natural world.

6   Kerry Odell and Marc D. Weidenmier, "Real Shock, Monetary Aftershocks: The San Francisco Earthquake and the Panic of 1907," *Journal of Economic History* 64, no. 4 (2004): 1002–27; James K. Mitchell, "Natural Disasters in the Context of Mega-cities," in *Crucibles of Hazard: Mega-cities and Disasters in Transition*, ed. James K. Mitchell, 15–55 (New York: United Nations University Press, 1999), 32, 39.

7   J. C. Smith, "San Francisco's New Street Cars," *Western World: New San Francisco Magazine* (April 1907): 54 (51–55).

8   Garvey is quoted in Daughters of Charity, *Steel Frames: Eyewitness Accounts of the 1906 San Francisco Earthquake and Fire* (Los Altos, CA: Año Nuevo Island Press, 2005), 117; "The Future of Van Ness Avenue," *Western World* (July 7, 1907): 10 (9–10). Verdier's shop on Van Ness Avenue was not even located in the burned district.

9   *Western World*, September 14, 1907, 32; "What Our City Needs," *Western World*, September 28, 1907, 5.

10 The chaos of San Francisco's streets in this era can be viewed firsthand in a video recording of a trip down Market Street in 1905. It is available at "A Trip Down Market Street before the Fire," www.sfmuseum.org/loc/trip.html, accessed July 10, 2012. See also David O. Stowell, *Streets, Railroads, and the Great Strike of 1877* (Chicago: University of Chicago Press, 1999), 20–25. Jessica Ellen Sewell discusses women's presence in the streets of San Francisco during this era. Sewell, *Women and the Everyday City: Public Space in San Francisco, 1890–1915* (Minneapolis: University of Minnesota Press, 2011).

11 "Public Walks; Carmen Win!," *Coast Seamen's Journal*, May 22, 1907, 1.

12 Arnold, *Report on the Improvement and Development of the Transportation Facilities of San Francisco*, xiii, 6, 16, 35 (quotation).

13 Thomas G. Andrews, *Killing for Coal: America's Deadliest Labor War* (Cambridge, MA: Harvard University Press, 2008), 123–25.

14 Arnold, *Report on the Improvement and Development of the Transportation Facilities of San Francisco*, 32, 333.

15 Ibid., 422; John P. Young, *San Francisco: A History of the Pacific Coast Metropolis* (San Francisco: S. J. Clarke Publishing Company, 1912), 275, 413.

16 Andrew S. Hallidie, *A Brief History of the Cable Railway System, Its Origins and Progress, and Papers in Connection Therewith* (San Francisco, 1891), 4, 17.

17 Paul C. Trimble, *The Platform Men* (San Francisco, 1984), 26; Arnold, *Report on the Improvement and Development of the Transportation Facilities of San Francisco*, 423.

18 Wayne Bonnet, *San Francisco by Land & Sea: A Transportation Album* (Sausalito, CA: Windgate Press, 1997), 27; Arnold, *Report on the Improvement and Development of the Transportation Facilities of San Francisco*, 33–34.

19 J. J. O'Neill, "The Street Carmen's Union: A Review of What It Has Accomplished during a Few Years," in *Fourth Annual Outing Carmen's Union Division Number 205 and Street Railway Employees Hospital Association, 44–46* (San Francisco, 1905), 44; Robert Emery Bionaz, "Death of a Union: The 1907 San Francisco Streetcar Strike," online at http://userwww.sfsu.edu/~epf/1996/street.html, accessed April 14, 2010, 4–5; Judd Kahn, *Imperial San Francisco: Politics and Planning in an American City, 1897–1906* (Lincoln: University of Nebraska Press, 1979), 112.

20 Michael Kazin, *Barons of Labor: The San Francisco Building Trades and Union Power in the Progressive Era* (Chicago: University of Illinois Press, 1987), 51–59; Kahn, *Imperial San Francisco*, 30–31.

21 Robert Edward Lee Knight, *Industrial Relations in the San Francisco Bay Area, 1900–1918* (Berkeley: University of California Press, 1960), 60–95; Jules Tygiel, *Workingmen in San Francisco, 1880–1901* (New York: Garland Publishing, 1992), 355–78; Kahn, *Imperial San Francisco*, 39–41; *Coast Seamen's Journal*, October 10, 1901.

22   Bionaz, "Death of a Union," 3. Kahn notes that San Francisco's unions were relatively conservative, and their leaders generally pursued policies of "caution and gradualism"; see Kahn, *Imperial San Francisco*, 32–33.

23   "A Fair Day's Pay for a Fair Day's Work," argument of Tirey L. Ford, General Counsel, United Railroads of San Francisco, in the matter of the Arbitration of Certain Differences between the Amalgamated Association of Street Railway Employees of America, Division No. 205, and United Railroads of San Francisco, 1903?, 6–7, 21–25, 38–39, 44–45 (quotation), ephemera: street electric rail, LARC; Herbert V. Ready, "The Labor Problem," self-published pamphlet, 1904, 26, ephemera: streetcars, LARC. Ready ran an employment bureau and testified on behalf of the United Railroads at the arbitration hearing.

24   "Report of the General Strike Committee of San Francisco, California, on Strikes By Carmen, Telephone Operators, Laundry Workers and Iron Trades Workers," June 10, 1907, to December 30, 1907, 1. For a more detailed discussion of the economic conditions of widespread seasonal unemployment in San Francisco during these decades, see Joanna Leslie Dyl, "Urban Disaster: An Environmental History of San Francisco after the 1906 Earthquake," Ph.D. diss., Princeton University, 2006, chapter 3.

25   Kahn, *Imperial San Francisco*, 42, 112–13.

26   O'Neill, "Street Carmen's Union," 46; Bionaz, "Death of a Union," 6.

27   Kahn, *Imperial San Francisco*, 29, 54–56.

28   Smith, "San Francisco's New Street Cars," 54–55; "United Railroads' Great Work," *San Francisco Newsletter*, July 21, 1906.

29   Kahn, *Imperial San Francisco*, 111–14. The question of self interest versus civic interest is a complicated one in this dispute. Prominent supporters of beautification, such as Spreckels and Phelan, were also property owners along the streets in question.

30   Bionaz, "Death of a Union," 6; Francis J. Heney, "What They Are Doing to San Francisco," *Western World*, July 20, 1907, 9. Ruef had been receiving five hundred dollars per month to serve as an adviser to the United Railroads since 1902, a sum that increased to one thousand dollars per month in November 1905. In April 1906 the company paid him two hundred thousand dollars, some of which he passed on to elected Union Labor officials. Kahn, *Imperial San Francisco*, 43–44, 52–53, 118–22.

31   Klein, *Shock Doctrine*.

32   Patrick Calhoun, "The United Railroads and San Francisco," *Western World*, July 13, 1907, 15. Haskell is quoted in Sewell, *Women and the Everyday City*, 1.

33   *Western World*, September 14, 1907, 6; Michael H. Newman, "Our Coming Auto Bus Lines," *Western World*, October 5, 1907, 24. The strike affected the company's service by the fall of 1907 as well, and Newman specifically complained about the "incompetent men" operating the cars during the strike.

34   Arnold, *Report on the Improvement and Development of the Transportation Facilities of San Francisco*, 332.

35   Ibid., 8.

36   Edward P. E. Troy, "Municipal Ownership," *Organized Labor*, December 18, 1909.

37   Stowell, *Streets, Railroads, and the Great Strike of 1877*, 7 (quotation). See also Clay McShane and Joel A. Tarr, *The Horse in the City: Living Machines in the Nineteenth Century* (Baltimore, MD: Johns Hopkins University Press, 2007), 70–72; Lynn Kirby, *Parallel Tracks: The Railroad and Silent Cinema* (Durham, NC: Duke University Press, 1997), 21–32.

38   "The Municipal Service Muddle," *Organized Labor*, June 27, 1908; Edward P. E. Troy, "The Municipal Bond Elections," *Organized Labor*, December 25, 1909.

39   Merchants' Association of San Francisco, "Report on the Operation of the Street Railroad Lines of San Francisco" (February 1, 1909), 24–27, 32; Merchants' Association of San Francisco, "The Street Cleaning Problem in San Francisco" (September 1, 1909), 21–22, pamphlets, SFPL. See also Thomas A Maloney, "Recollections," *South of Market Journal*, December 1932, 10.

40   Leigh H. Irvine, "Fundamentals of Street-car Control" (San Francisco, Calkins Newspaper Syndicate, 1907), 3–6, pamphlet, ephemera: streetcars, LARC; Calhoun, "United Railroads and San Francisco," 28.

41   Kahn, *Imperial San Francisco*, 116–17, 124–26.

42   "Carmen Demand Calhoun's Arrest," *Organized Labor*, May 11, 1907; Kahn, *Imperial San Francisco*, 123.

43   W. D. Wood, "San Francisco's Optimism and Reasons for It," in *The Story of the California Disaster: An Authentic Account of the Earthquake of April 18, 1906 and the Great Fire*, 53–55 (Portland, OR: Pacific Monthly Publishing Co., 1906), 55; Rozario, *Culture of Calamity*, discusses this thinking as widespread, distinctly American, and central to modern thinking about "progress."

44   W. V. Holloway, "Nothing but Big Capital Goes in San Francisco Today," *Socialist Voice*, May 5, 1906.

45   "Labor in San Francisco," *Coast Seamen's Journal*, May 2, 1906, 1; "The Power of Labor," *Coast Seamen's Journal*, October 10, 1906, 1.

46   Yorke is quoted in Bernard Cornelius Cronin, *Father Yorke and the Labor Movement in San Francisco, 1900–1910* (Washington, DC: Catholic University of America Press, 1943), 187.

47   *Coast Seamen's Journal*, April 25, 1906, 2; "The Problem of Wages," *Coast Seamen's Journal*, May 9, 1906, 1.

48   Rufus Steele, *The City That Is: The Story of the Rebuilding of San Francisco in Three Years* (San Francisco: A. M. Robertson, 1909), 38, 42–43; Alvin Averbach, "San Francisco's South of Market District, 1850–1950: The Emergence of a Skid Row," *California Historical Quarterly* 52, no. 3 (Fall 1973): 204 (197–223).

49 "Stricken and Sold," *Coast Seamen's Journal*, May 30, 1906, 1.

50 *Coast Seamen's Journal*, June 1906; Paul S. Taylor, *The Sailors' Union of the Pacific* (New York: Ronald Press Company, 1923), 104–7; *Socialist Voice*, June 9, 1906, and August 4, 1906; Knight, *Industrial Relations in the San Francisco Bay Area*, 169–73.

51 "Events of Three Months," *Coast Seamen's Journal*, September 5, 1906, 1.

52 *Coast Seamen's Journal*, September 26, 1906, 7; "The Strenuous Work of a Year—The Future," *Labor Clarion*, April 21, 1907, 1.

53 Stowell makes a similar argument for the Great Railroad Strike of 1877 in *Streets, Railroads, and the Great Strike of 1877*.

54 "The Street Carmen's Strike," *Coast Seamen's Journal*, August 29, 1906; Richard Cornelius, "Strike As Seen by the Carmen," *Labor Clarion*, August 16, 1907, 18; Bionaz, "Death of a Union," 6–8.

55 Christopher Morris Douty, *The Economics of Localized Disasters: The 1906 San Francisco Catastrophe* (New York: Arno Press, 1977), 253–54. The telephone operators sought recognition of their union while other trades sought the eight-hour day.

56 "The Industrial Crisis," *Labor Clarion*, May 10, 1907, 1, 8.

57 Bionaz, "Death of a Union," 9–10; Douty, *Economics of Localized Disasters*, 255. Stowell notes a similar phenomenon of "crowds" during the Great Strike of 1877 that combined striking workers with neighborhood residents expressing more nebulous grievances by joining in the conflict. Stowell, *Streets, Railroads, and the Great Strike of 1877*, 117–19. By Kazin's count, at least twenty-five people were killed and over two thousand injured as a result of either gunfire or streetcar accidents during the strike; see Kazin, *Barons of Labor*, 135.

58 Proclamation reprinted in *Organized Labor*, May 11, 1907; "Maintain Law and Order," *Organized Labor*, May 11, 1907.

59 "Report of the General Strike Committee of San Francisco," 7.

60 Bionaz, "Death of a Union," 10–12; Jane Cryan, "From Tents to Shacks: A Guide to San Francisco's 1906 Earthquake Refugee Camps," unfinished manuscript (1999) box 2, folder 6, Society for the Preservation and Appreciation of San Francisco Refugee Shacks Archive, SFH 9, SFPL, 45.

61 Bionaz, "Death of a Union," 12; John Bernard McGloin, *San Francisco: The Story of a City* (San Rafael, CA: Presidio Press, 1978), 280; Arnold, *Report on the Improvement and Development of the Transportation Facilities of San Francisco*, 331.

62 J. K. Turner, "The Lesson of San Francisco," pamphlet, November 1906, SFPL, 12–13; "Report of the General Strike Committee of San Francisco," 1, 7. Lack of patronage eventually caused the strike wagons to lose money. Knight, *Industrial Relations in the San Francisco Bay Area*, 195.

63 *Union Picket*, San Francisco, August 17, 1907, CSL. The library possesses a single, damaged issue of this publication, which appears to be the only surviving issue.

64   "Public Walks; Carmen Win!," *Coast Seamen's Journal*, May 22, 1907, 1.

65   Knight suggests that sabotage such as greasing the tracks played a role in the high accident rate; see Knight, *Industrial Relations in the San Francisco Bay Area*, 193–96. See also *Labor Clarion*, October 11, 1907, 1, 8.

66   "What the Unions Forgot," *Western World*, July 13, 1907, 7.

67   "Maintain Law and Order" and "Carmen Demand Calhoun's Arrest," *Organized Labor*, May 11, 1907.

68   Young, *San Francisco: A History of the Pacific Coast Metropolis*, 880–83; Cronin, *Father Yorke and the Labor Movement in San Francisco*, 180–81; George E. Mowry, *The California Progressives* (Berkeley: University of California Press, 1951), 26–27.

69   Bionaz, "Death of a Union," 8–9, 12–13.

70   "'Union Labor's Disgrace," *Coast Seamen's Journal*, March 27, 1907, 1; Kahn, *Imperial San Francisco*, 38–56 (quotation 56).

71   Cronin, *Father Yorke and the Labor Movement in San Francisco*, 169–73.

72   Bionaz, "Death of a Union," 13–15.

73   Clarence E. Edwords, "San Francisco's Reconstruction," *San Francisco Phoenix*, November 30, 1906, 1.

74   Douty, *Economics of Localized Disasters*, 229–31, 236–37, 264–71, 276–77, 292–94, 300. By 1910 union membership had dropped to only 10 percent above predisaster levels.

75   Bionaz, "Death of a Union," 6, 16. Bionaz notes the splits within the labor movement but does not discuss the potential impact of the earthquake and fire in exacerbating those divisions.

76   William Issel and Robert W. Cherney, *San Francisco, 1865–1932: Politics, Power, and Urban Development* (Berkeley: University of California Press, 1986), 158–59.

77   Young, *San Francisco: A History of the Pacific Coast Metropolis*, 880–83; James P. Walsh, "Machine Politics, Reform, and San Francisco," in *The San Francisco Irish, 1850–1976*, ed. James P. Walsh, 59–72 (San Francisco: The Irish Literary and Historical Society, 1978), 70; Mowry, *California Progressives*, 33–37.

78   Knight, *Industrial Relations in the San Francisco Bay Area*, 195–97; Bionaz, "Death of a Union," 14–15; *Western World*, September 14, 1907, 6.

79   "What It All Means: There Is a Conspiracy to Reduce the Standard of Living in San Francisco," *Socialist Voice*, May 18, 1907. Cost-of-living numbers are obviously difficult to calculate. Douty estimates a 9 to 10 percent increase in the cost of living in San Francisco after the disaster; see Douty, *Economics of Localized Disasters*, 296–98.

80   "San Francisco Is All Right," *Coast Seamen's Journal*, June 26, 1907, 1.

81   Odell and Weidenmier, "Real Shock, Monetary Aftershocks," 1011; "Catastrophe Markets," *New York Times*, April 23, 1906. Stock prices as a whole recovered almost immediately.

82   Odell and Weidenmier, "Real Shock, Monetary Aftershocks," 1010–17 (quotation 1017).

83   Ibid., 1002 (quotation), 1017–24. The Panic of 1907 was an impetus for the founding of the Federal Reserve in 1913.

84   "The Industrial Depression," *Labor Clarion*, January 24, 1908, 1; "The Municipal Service Muddle," *Organized Labor*, June 27, 1908; Jessica Peixotto, "Relief Work of the Associated Charities," in *San Francisco Relief Survey*, ed. Russell Sage Foundation, 281–320 (New York: Survey Associates, 1913), 304–5; Carleton H. Parker, *The Casual Laborer and Other Essays* (New York: Harcourt, Brace and Howe, 1920), 119.

85   "Who Are the Real Friends of San Francisco?" *Organized Labor*, September 26, 1908; "Invoke the Recall," *Organized Labor*, March 20, 1909; "Extend the Time Limit," *The Leader*, December 4, 1909.

86   "Fifty Cents a Day on Public Work," *Organized Labor*, April 10, 1909.

87   "Unemployed in San Francisco," *Coast Seamen's Journal*, April 10, 1912, 7; "California Warns Labor," *Coast Seamen's Journal*, March 20, 1912, 2.

88   Mowry, *California Progressives*, 23–24; Anthony Perles, *The People's Railway: The History of the Municipal Railway of San Francisco* (Glendale, CA: Interuban Press, 1981), 16.

89   Martin S. Vilas, *Municipal Railway of San Francisco* (Burlington, VT: Free Press Association, September 1, 1915).

90   Edward P. E. Troy, "The Municipal Bond Elections," *Organized Labor*, December 25, 1909.

91   "Public Service for the People," *Organized Labor*, June 12, 1909; "Vote for the Geary Street Bonds," *Organized Labor*, June 5, 1909; Vilas, *Municipal Railway of San Francisco*.

92   Perles, *People's Railway*, 27; McGloin, *San Francisco*, 208–12.

CHAPTER SIX: PLAGUE, RATS, AND UNDESIRABLE NATURE

1   Marguerite Brindley, "Account of the San Francisco Earthquake and Fire, April 20 and 21, 1906," Eli T. Sheppard papers and related family material, BANC MSS 71/253 cz, Bancroft, accessed online February 1, 2013; William Bronson, *The Earth Shook, the Sky Burned; 100th Anniversary Edition: A Photographic Record of the 1906 San Francisco Earthquake and Fire* (San Francisco: Chronicle Books, 2006), 76.

2   Charles Rosenberg, *The Cholera Years: The United States in 1832, 1849, and 1866* (Chicago: University of Chicago Press, 1987); Ari Kelman, *A River and Its City: The Nature of Landscape in New Orleans* (Berkeley: University of California Press, 2003), 87–118; J. R. McNeill, *Mosquito Empires: Ecology and War in the Greater Caribbean, 1620–1914* (New York: Cambridge University Press, 2010); Martin V. Melosi, *The Sanitary City: Urban Infrastructure in America from*

Colonial Times to the Present (Baltimore, MD: Johns Hopkins University Press, 2000).

3   Ted Steinberg, *Down to Earth: Nature's Role in American History*, 3rd ed. (New York: Oxford University Press, 2013), 155–69.

4   Rupert Blue, "The Underlying Principles of Anti-Plague Measures," reprinted in Frank Morton Todd and Citizens' Health Committee, *Eradicating Plague from San Francisco: Report of the Citizens' Health Committee and an Account of Its Work*, 215–24 (San Francisco: Press of C. A. Murdock & Co., March 31, 1909), 218.

5   Michael McCormick, "Rats, Communications, and Plague: Toward an Ecological History," *Journal of Interdisciplinary History* 34, no. 1 (Summer 2003): 2–5 (1–25); Myron Echenberg, *Plague Ports: The Global Urban Impact of Bubonic Plague, 1894–1901* (New York: New York University Press, 2007); John W. Kerr, "The Rat in Relation to International Sanitation," in *The Rat and Its Relation to Public Health*, 227–54 (Washington, DC: Government Printing Office, 1910), 227; Mike Davis, *Ecology of Fear: Los Angeles and the Imagination of Disaster* (New York: Vintage Books, 1998), 251–52.

6   "Report of the Board of Health, 1899–1900," 521–24; "Report of the Special Health Commissioners Appointed by the Governor to Confer with the Federal Authorities at Washington Respecting the Alleged Existence of Bubonic Plague in California" (Sacramento, CA: A. J. Johnson, Superintendent State Printing, 1901), 15–19; W. H. Kellogg, "Present Status of Plague, with Historical Review," *American Journal of Public Health* 10, no. 11 (November 1920): 840–42 (835–44).

7   Sylvio J. Onesti Jr., "Plague, Press, and Politics," *Stanford Medical Bulletin* 13, no. 1 (February 1955): 4 (1–10). John P. Young continued to deny that the bubonic plague had existed in San Francisco in 1901 in the text of his 1912 history; see Young, *San Francisco: A History of the Pacific Coast Metropolis* (San Francisco: S. J. Clarke Publishing Company, 1912), 784. Even some recent histories have perpetuated the uncertainty. For example, Natalia Molina writes: "It is unclear from the sources whether there really was an epidemic or whether officials simply feared one." Molina, *Fit to Be Citizens? Public Health and Race in Los Angeles, 1879–1939* (Berkeley: University of California Press, 2006), 28. There is, however, a clear consensus among historians that the outbreak was real, and in fact, most scholars suspect that its extent probably exceeded the official reports. The most thorough account is Marilyn Chase, *The Barbary Plague: The Black Death in Victorian San Francisco* (New York: Random House, 2003).

8   "Report of Department of Public Health, 1902–03," 659.

9   W. H. Kellogg, "Rodent Plague in California," *Journal of the American Medical Association* 105 (September 14, 1935): 856 (856–59).

10   Albert Lawrence Burroughs, "Sylvatic Plague Studies: The Vector Efficiency of Nine Species of Flea Compared to *Xenopsylla cheopis*," *Journal of Hygiene*

45, no. 3 (August 1947): 372–74 (371–96). Wyman is quoted in Chase, *Barbary Plague*, 105–6.

11   Rupert Blue, "Rodents in Relation to the Transmission of Bubonic Plague," in *The Rat and Its Relation to the Public Health*, 145–52 (Washington, DC: Government Printing Office, 1910), 146. This describes the transmission of the most common form of the plague, the bubonic form. The more deadly pneumonic variation can spread from human to human via bacilli located in the sputum.

12   Citizens' Health Committee, "Insanitary Conditions Along the San Francisco Water Front: A Report to the Citizens Health Committee of San Francisco by Its Water Front Committee" (San Francisco: Citizens' Health Committee of San Francisco, 1908), 5; Frank Morton Todd and Citizens' Health Committee, *Eradicating Plague from San Francisco: Report of the Citizens' Health Committee and an Account of Its Work* (San Francisco: Press of C. A. Murdock & Co., 1909), 12.

13   Chase, *Barbary Plague*, 190–91; Charles T. Gregg, *Plague: An Ancient Disease in the Twentieth Century* (Albuquerque: University of New Mexico Press, 1985), 76–78; Burroughs, "Sylvatic Plague Studies," 376–94. One study found that 68 percent of fleas were *N. fasciatus* and only 21 percent were *X. cheopis* (three other species made up the remainder). Vernon B. Link, *A History of Plague in the United States of America* (Washington, DC: Government Printing Office, 1955), 20–21; R. W. Doane, "Notes on Fleas Collected on Rat and Human Hosts in San Francisco and Elsewhere," *Canadian Entomologist* 40 (1908): 303–4.

14   Chase, *Barbary Plague*, 32–35, 88–141.

15   Minutes of the State Board of Health and the California Public Health Association, April 18, 1904, 26, Department of Public Health, State Board of Health, Executive Secretary, F3676:1 C1810-C1811, CSA. The writings of the State Board of Health from 1904 show an awareness of the role of rats in spreading the disease, but they also contain statements blaming the Chinese and implying connections between their racial background and the likelihood that they would spread the plague. See Minutes of the State Board of Health, January 5, 1904, 18–19, and April 18, 1904, 22–23.

16   Todd and Citizens' Health Committee, *Eradicating Plague from San Francisco*, 31–32.

17   On the lack of preparation for a return of the disease, see "Board of Health Report, 1907–1908," 588. On conditions in the city, see Todd and Citizens' Health Committee, *Eradicating Plague from San Francisco*, 35–36; and Walter M. Dickie, "Plague in California 1900–1925," in *Proceedings of the Conference of the State and Provincial Health Authorities of America* (1926): 36 (30–67). Blue is quoted in Chase, *Barbary Plague*, 156–57.

18   S. A. Barnett, *The Rat: A Study in Behavior*, rev. ed. (Chicago: University of Chicago Press, 1975), 3–4, 52–60; James M. Clinton, "Rats in Urban America,"

Public Health Reports 84, no. 1 (January 1969): 4–6 (1–7); McCormick, "Rats, Communications, and Plague," 14–18.

19   McCormick, "Rats, Communications, and Plague," 19.

20   David E. Davis, "The Characteristics of Rat Populations," *Quarterly Review of Biology* 28, no. 4 (December 1953): 391–92 (373–401). One study found that rats did not even cross from one block to colonize an adjacent one, which remained rat-free for two and a half years. David P. Durham and Elizabeth A. Casman, "Threshold Conditions for the Persistence of Plague Transmission in Urban Rats," *Risk Analysis* 29, no. 12 (2009): 1656 (1655–63); L. C. Gardner-Santana et al., "Commensal Ecology, Urban Landscapes, and Their Influence on the Genetic Characteristics of City-Dwelling Norway Rats (*Rattus norvegicus*)," *Molecular Ecology* 18 (2009): 2774–75 (2766–78).

21   Dickie, "Plague in California," 30–32; Todd and Citizens' Health Committee, *Eradicating Plague from San Francisco*, 38–40, 183.

22   Blue, "Rodents in Relation to the Transmission of Bubonic Plague," 262; "Report of the Committee of the Society of Sigma Xi on the Plague Conditions in Berkeley, San Francisco, and Oakland" (Stockton, CA: Lithomount Pamphlet Binder, March 4, 1908), 3–4.

23   Richard H. Creel, "Rat Proofing as an Antiplague Measure," in *The Rat and Its Relation to Public Health*, 171–78 (Washington, DC: Government Printing Office, 1910), 172; Rupert Blue, "The Campaign against Plague in San Francisco, California," in Todd and Citizens' Health Committee, *Eradicating Plague from San Francisco*, 293.

24   Susan Craddock, *City of Plagues: Disease, Poverty, and Deviance in San Francisco* (Minneapolis: University of Minnesota Press, 2000), 149; Blue, "Campaign against Plague in San Francisco," 291; Creel, "Rat Proofing as an Antiplague Measure," 172; Telegram from William C. Hobdy to Surgeon-General, August 13, 1907, vol. 33, RG 90, NASF.

25   "Board of Health Report, 1907–1908," 632–33.

26   Ibid., 493.

27   Blue, "Rodents in Relation to the Transmission of Bubonic Plague," 147.

28   Todd and Citizens' Health Committee, *Eradicating Plague from San Francisco*, 9, 141; Augustin C. Keane, "San Francisco's Plague War," *American Review of Books* 38, no. 5 (November 1908): 568–69 (561–71).

29   Nancy Tomes discusses how immigrant and working-class families became the targets of "intensive popular health education about domestic sanitation in the early 1900s." Epidemics often sparked educational crusades; see Tomes, "The Private Side of Public Health: Sanitary Science, Domestic Hygiene, and the Germ Theory, 1870–1900," *Bulletin of the History of Medicine* 64, no. 4 (Winter 1990): 509–39.

30   William Colby Rucker, "Rodent Extermination," in *The Rat and Its Relation to the Public Health*, 153–62 (Washington, DC: Government Printing Office, 1910), 153; Creel, "Rat Proofing as an Antiplague Measure," 173.

31 "Board of Health Report, 1907–1908," 481–83; Chase, *Barbary Plague*, 140–41, 154–58.

32 "Board of Health Report, 1907–1908," 482–83; Todd and Citizens' Health Committee, *Eradicating Plague from San Francisco*, 39, 153 (quotation).

33 Blue, "Campaign against Plague in San Francisco, California," 289; Chase, *Barbary Plague*, 183.

34 Link, *History of Plague*, 17–18; Guenter P. Risse, "'A Long Pull, a Strong Pull, and All Together': San Francisco and Bubonic Plague, 1907–1908," *Bulletin of the History of Medicine* 66 (1992): 281 (260–86). For resistance to cleanup efforts, see Keane, "San Francisco's Plague War," 566–69. Keane mentions the proprietors of hog pens, bakeries, rag dens, and stables as objecting to orders to clean up their premises.

35 Risse, "'A Long Pull, a Strong Pull, and All Together,'" 280–82. By mid-May of 1908, as enthusiasm for the campaign and evidence of infection waned, judges began to dismiss cases against alleged violators of sanitary laws, helping bring the most intense phase of the war on rats to a close.

36 "Board of Health Report, 1907–1908," 481–88; Chase, *Barbary Plague*, 152–53; Craddock, *City of Plagues*, 152.

37 "Board of Health Report, 1907–1908," 481, 486 (first quotation), 588 (second quotation).

38 "Board of Health Report, 1907–1908," 486–88, 588; Blue, "Campaign against Plague in San Francisco," 286–87; "Board of Public Works Report, 1907–1908," 799; "Board of Health Report, 1908–1909," 679–80. Ironically, in the previous year's report, the warden of the City and County Hospital urged that the hospital be torn down and rebuilt on the existing site. In an unfortunate choice of language, he urged that the enthusiasm for rebuilding "be kept burning until next November, when it should burst into a flame." He was not far off in his prediction of flames consuming the City and County Hospital. "Board of Health Report, 1906–1907," 565.

39 Quoted in "Board of Health Report, 1907–1908," 588.

40 Letter from William C. Hobdy to Surgeon General, February 28, 1908, vol. 34, RG 90, NASF; Gregg, *Plague: An Ancient Disease in the Twentieth Century*, 87.

41 Todd and Citizens' Health Committee, *Eradicating Plague from San Francisco*, 42–44.

42 Ibid., 7–10.

43 Ibid., 164.

44 "Report of the Committee of the Society of Sigma Xi," 6–7.

45 Todd and Citizens' Health Committee, *Eradicating Plague from San Francisco*, 50–51, 59–70, 86–88. The committee ultimately did not need all of its funds and returned a dividend of 19 percent to all subscribers. Todd described "the saving of the City from quarantine" and the dividend as the two main accomplishments of the Committee (154).

46 Documents reprinted in Todd and Citizens' Health Committee, *Eradicating Plague from San Francisco*, 211 (first quotation), 199 (second quotation).

47 *Labor Clarion*, February 14, 1908, 8.

48 "The Elks' Letter on Plague Conditions," reprinted in Todd and Citizens' Health Committee, *Eradicating Plague from San Francisco*, 246–55.

49 Todd and Citizens' Health Committee, *Eradicating Plague from San Francisco*, 42–48, 81, 121, 207; Link, *History of Plague*, 14–15.

50 Todd and Citizens' Health Committee, *Eradicating Plague from San Francisco*, 91–107, 161. Although the circulars were produced in three languages, 270,000 circulars were published in English and only 10,000 each in Italian and Greek (199).

51 Keane, "San Francisco's Plague War," 571.

52 Todd and Citizens' Health Committee, *Eradicating Plague from San Francisco*, 72, 110–17.

53 Ibid., 72–75.

54 "Board of Health Report, 1907–1908," 598–99. Calculated from reports of the Board of Health from 1906 to 1915. Alfred W. Crosby has written that "lethal epidemics were not as unexpected and therefore not as impressive in 1918 as they would be today." This would be even more applicable to 1907–1908; see Crosby, *America's Forgotten Pandemic: The Influenza of 1918* (New York: Cambridge University Press, 1989), 319.

55 Veiller is quoted in M. Christine Boyer, *Dreaming the Rational City: The Myth of American City Planning* (Cambridge, MA: MIT Press, 1983), 98; "San Francisco Labor Losses," *Coast Seamen's Journal*, May 23, 1906, 2; Dino Cinel, "Italians in San Francisco: Patterns of Settlement," in *European Immigrants in the American West: Community Histories*, ed. Frederick C. Luebke, 65–74 (Albuquerque: University of New Mexico Press, 1998), 71–73. Cinel does note the relative predominance in San Francisco of immigrants from northern Italy, who were more likely to have been exposed to an urban industrial setting such as Genoa. He also describes a strong "preservation of old-world customs" among Italians in comparison to other immigrant groups in the city.

56 Todd and Citizens' Health Committee, *Eradicating Plague from San Francisco*, 141.

57 Rucker, "Rodent Extermination," 154; Todd and Citizens' Health Committee, *Eradicating Plague from San Francisco*, 158–59; Chase, *Barbary Plague*, 194–95.

58 Blue, "Campaign against Plague in San Francisco," 287–88; Blue, "The Conduct of a Plague Campaign," in Todd and Citizens' Health Committee, *Eradicating Plague from San Francisco*, 239–40 (235–45); "Board of Health Report, 1907–1908," 483.

59 Creel, "Rat Proofing as an Antiplague Measure," 171–72.

60 Chase, *Barbary Plague*, 201–4, 209; Risse, "'A Long Pull, a Strong Pull, and All Together,'" 260.

61 Todd and Citizens' Health Committee, *Eradicating Plague from San Francisco*, 141–42, 188–98.

62 Creel, "Rat Proofing as an Antiplague Measure," 174–75.

63 "Board of Health Report, 1907–1908," 485.

64 Todd and Citizens' Health Committee, *Eradicating Plague from San Francisco*, 165–66.

65 Ibid., 141, 183.

66 "Board of Health Report, 1907–1908," 484–85.

67 Blue, "Campaign against Plague in San Francisco," 291.

68 "The Tenement House Question in California," *Transactions of the Commonwealth Club of California* 2, no. 2 (October 1906): 71 (69–103). An editorial in the *San Francisco Examiner* just before the earthquake refered to "foolish, out-of-date 'household pets,'" implying that at least some observers believed that not even pets belonged in the modern city. The piece focused on the need to eliminate disease-carrying animals such as rats, mosquitos, mice, and flies. "We Must Kill the Little Monsters," *San Francisco Examiner*, April 10, 1906.

69 These totals may not include houses with stables under them, which were condemned and destroyed. Todd and Citizens' Health Committee, *Eradicating Plague from San Francisco*, 73, 131–34; Keane, "San Francisco's Plague War," 567–69. The quality of stables, like the quality of human housing, had declined in some areas after the fire, with horses being stabled in woodsheds and other small quarters. *San Francisco Daily News*, October 27, 1906. Nationally, urban stables were increasingly perceived as sources of disease and fire in this period. Clay McShane and Joel A. Tarr note that "urban horses experienced mortality patterns roughly consistent with those of urban humans" and "suffer from roughly 200 of the 250 diseases affecting their fellow mammals." This suggests that improving stables could have improved the health of horses as well as humans. Horses do not, however, seem to contract the bubonic plague. McShane and Tarr, *The Horse in the City: Living Machines in the Nineteenth Century* (Baltimore, MD: Johns Hopkins University Press, 2007), 149, 168–69; Center for Food Security and Public Health, "Plague," Iowa State University, October 2009, 5, online at www.cfsph.edu/Factsheets/pdfs/plague.pdf, accessed March 26, 2013.

70 "Board of Health Report, 1907–1908," 485.

71 Todd and Citizens' Health Committee, *Eradicating Plague from San Francisco*, 139–40; Creel, "Rat Proofing as an Antiplague Measure," 175–76. For the price of eggs, see California Promotion Committee, "Poultry Raising in California," pamphlet (San Francisco, 1905), Bancroft. For the prevalence of eggs in contemporary recipes, see *The Refugees' Cook Book, Compiled by One of Them* (San Francisco, 1906), Bancroft.

72 Todd and Citizens' Health Committee, *Eradicating Plague from San Francisco*, 139; "Report of the Board of Health, 1911–1912," 621.

73 Petaluma Incubator Co., "Petaluma Incubator" catalog, Petaluma, CA, 1895,

1–2, 16–17, Bancroft; "The Mammoth Chicken Coop of the Fairmont, St. Francis, and Palace Hotels," pamphlet, San Francisco, 1912, Bancroft.

74   "Report of the Department of Public Health, 1901–1902," 564; "Report of the Board of Health, 1908–1909," 685–86; "Report of the Board of Health, 1910–1911," 181; "Report of the Board of Health, 1911–1912," 657–58. On the ethnic composition of the dairy industry, see "San Francisco Labor Losses," *Coast Seamen's Journal*, May 23, 1906, 2.

75   Joel A. Tarr, "From City to Farm: Urban Wastes and the American Farmer," *Agricultural History* 49 (1975): 605 (598–612); Richard Dillon, *North Beach: The Italian Heart of San Francisco* (Novato, CA: Presidio Press, 1985), 70–73; David Igler, *Industrial Cowboys: Miller and Lux and the Transformation of the Far West, 1850–1920* (Berkeley: University of California, 2001), 133–34.

76   Todd and Citizens' Health Committee *Eradicating Plague from San Francisco*, 131–34; "Report of the Department of Public Works, 1907–1908," 709. For a discussion of the shifting perception of manure produced by urban horses from valuable resource to nuisance, see McShane and Tarr, *Horse in the City*, 25–27, 124–25.

77   Stewart Perry, *San Francisco Scavengers: Dirty Work and the Pride of Ownership* (Berkeley: University of California Press, 1978), 15, 218. On the prominence of recent immigrants in the waste trades, see Carl Zimring, "Dirty Work: How Hygiene and Xenophobia Marginalized the American Waste Trades, 1870–1930," *Environmental History* 9, no. 1 (January 2004): 80–101.

78   "Report of the Department of Public Health, 1902–1903," 658, 664; "Report of the Board of Health, 1907–1908," 484; "Report of the Board of Public Works, 1907–1908," 709; Sanitary Inspector Williamson to Chief Sanitary Officer, May 12, 1906, RG 112, Entry 363, Box 1, Folder: Inspection Reports from Golden Gate Park, NASF.

79   Rucker, "Rodent Extermination," 160; Todd and Citizens' Health Committee, *Eradicating Plague from San Francisco*, 110–12, 123–25, 187–88. Todd estimates 100,000 new garbage cans while Link says it was 49,046 (still "practically one for every home"); see Link, *History of Plague*, 18.

80   Todd and Citizens' Health Committee, *Eradicating Plague from San Francisco*, 144–45; Susan Strasser, *Waste and Want: A Social History of Trash* (New York: Henry Holt and Company, 1999).

81   Melosi, *Sanitary City*, 194–96.

82   "Report of the Board of Public Works, 1907–1908," 709–11, 716–19; "Report of the Board of Public Works, 1909–1910," 546; "Report of the Board of Public Works, 1912–1913," 495–96. For evidence regarding nuisance problems with the Sanitary Reduction Works even before the earthquake, see "Report of the Board of Public Works, 1904–1905," 346.

83   "Report of the Board of Public Works, 1913–1914," 404–5; "Report of the Board of Public Works, 1914–1915," 360–63; Marsden Manson, "Garbage Disposal

System, Contract No. 1 for the Construction of Two Incinerating Plants" (San Francisco: Department of Public Works, June 1910), 21; Perry, *San Francisco Scavengers*, 18.

84 "Report of the Board of Public Works, 1899–1900," 490, 502; "Report of the Board of Public Works, 1903–1904," 336–37; "Report of the Board of Public Works, 1907–1908," 683.

85 Link, *History of Plague*, 18; Blue, "Underlying Principles of Anti-Plague Measures," 217. Craddock suggests that "the sewer became both the real and symbolic reminder to the upper classes that they could not completely disassociate themselves from the poor and their filth. The sewers transected and thus linked each section of a city whose topographical distinction by this point was a relative degree of class segregation." Craddock, *City of Plagues*, 99–100.

86 Quoted in Roger Olmsted, Nancy Olmsted, and Allen Pastron, *San Francisco Waterfront: Report on Historical Cultural Resources for the North Shore and Channel Outfalls Consolidation Projects* (San Francisco, 1977), 127. Citizens' Health Committee, "Insanitary Conditions along the San Francisco Water Front," 9–10.

87 "Report of the Board of Health, 1910–1911," 180.

88 Melosi, *Sanitary City*, 153, 162–63.

89 "Report of the Board of Health, 1909–1910," 269. Quoted in Chase, *Barbary Plague*, 172.

90 "Report of the Board of Health, 1908–1909," 681–82.

91 Citizens' Health Committee, "Insanitary Conditions along the San Francisco Water Front," 8–13; "Report of the Board of Public Works, 1913–1914," 393; Matthew Morse Booker, *Down by the Bay: San Francisco's History Between the Tides* (Berkeley: University of California Press, 2013), 139–45.

92 "Report of the Board of Public Works, 1907–1908," 684; Todd and Citizens' Health Committee, *Eradicating Plague from San Francisco*, 144.

93 Citizens' Health Committee, "Insanitary Conditions along the San Francisco Water Front," 6–8.

94 Ibid., 6–7, 12; "Report of the Board of Health, 1907–1908," 486.

95 William C. Hobdy, "The Rat in Relation to Shipping," in *The Rat and Its Relation to Public Health*, 207–13 (Washington, DC: Government Printing Office, 1910), 209–13.

96 Letters from William C. Hobdy to Surgeon General, especially September 17, 1907, January 2, 1908 (quotation), February 28, 1908, vols. 33 and 34, RG 90, NASF.

97 Link, *History of Plague*, 18.

98 "Report of the Board of Health, 1911–1912," 621–24; San Francisco Housing Association, "Second Report of the San Francisco Housing Association" (San Francisco, June 1913), 27; San Francisco Department of Public Health, "Mimeographed list of violations, 1916–1920," folder 10, carton 50, California

Department of Industrial Relations, Division of Immigration and Housing Records, BANC MSS C-A 194, Bancroft.

99 Link, *History of Plague*, 23; "Report of the Committee of the Society of Sigma Xi," 3; Blue, "Rodents in Relation to the Transmission of Bubonic Plague," 151.

100 Burroughs, "Sylvatic Plague Studies," 372–73; Doane, "Notes on Fleas," 304; and Virgil I. Miles, Alva R. Kinney, and Harold E. Stark, "Flea-Host Relationships of Associated *Rattus* and Native Wild Rodents in the San Francisco Bay Area of California, with Special Reference to Plague," *American Journal of Tropical Medicine and Hygiene* 6, no. 4 (1957): 752–60.

101 "Report of the Board of Health, 1908–1909," 674; Kellogg, "Rodent Plague in California," 1–2; Dickie, "Plague in California," 58; Onesti, "Plague, Press, and Politics," 5.

102 Kellogg, "Rodent Plague in California," 2–3; Link, *History of Plague*, 30–35; Gregg, *Plague: An Ancient Disease in the Twentieth Century*, 99.

103 In another example of an unprepared medical community, the disease was not diagnosed as plague until after six people had died. Dickie, "Plague in California," 32–35; W. H. Kellogg, "The Plague Situation," *American Journal of Public Health* 25, no. 3 (March 1935): 320–21 (319–22); Link, *History of Plague*, 23, 35–36.

104 Dickie, "Plague in California," 35–66; Davis, *Ecology of Fear*, 255–58. For a detailed discussion of the Los Angeles outbreak, see William Deverall, "Plague in Los Angeles, 1924: Ethnicity and Typicality," in *Over the Edge: Remapping the American West*, ed. Valerie J. Matsumoto and Blake Allmendinger, 172–200 (Berkeley: University of California Press, 1999).

105 Miles et al., "Flea-Host Relationships of Associated *Rattus* and Native Wild Rodents," 757–58.

106 Gregg, *Plague: An Ancient Disease in the Twentieth Century*, 5, 233–58; Chase, *Barbary Plague*, 210; Veronica Rocha, "Second Person Contracts Plague after Visiting Yosemite National Park," *Los Angeles Times*, August 19, 2015. Modern antibiotics have made the plague far less deadly than in the early twentieth century, but the bubonic form is still fatal in 13 percent of cases. Centers for Disease Control and Prevention, "Plague: Maps and Statistics," online at www.cdc.gov/plague/maps/index.html, accessed March 11, 2013.

107 Keane, "San Francisco's Plague War," 561.

108 Chase, *Barbary Plague*, 195–97. Craddock has suggested that disease benefited the population of San Francisco by encouraging the creation of more efficient public services and the construction of new infrastructure in the city, with the plague outbreaks representing one example; see Craddock, *City of Plagues*, 246.

109 Adam Rome, "Nature Wars, Culture Wars: Immigration and Environmental Reform in the Progressive Era," *Environmental History* 13, no. 3 (July 2008): 433 (432–53).

1 State Earthquake Investigation Commission (SEIC), *The California Earthquake of April 18, 1906*, vol. 1 (Washington, DC: Carnegie Institute of Washington, 1908), 232; Gladys Hansen and Emmet Condon, *Denial of Disaster* (San Francisco: Cameron and Company, 1989), 31.

2 Bine to Adjutant Permanent Camps, November 12, 1906, ledger entry, folder 17, MS 3640, Dr. René Bine Papers, CHS.

3 Many scholars have noted the connections between the Panama Pacific International Exposition and the 1906 earthquake and fire as well as the exposition's status as a symbol of the city's recovery from the disaster. However, the detailed process of constructing the exposition and its implications for the mind-set of San Franciscans regarding seismic risk remains largely unexplored. The role of contradictory ideas about nature has also been undertheorized. Scholarship on the exposition has focused primarily on the aesthetics and content of exhibits. Such works include Burton Benedict, ed., *The Anthropology of World's Fairs: San Francisco's Panama Pacific International Exposition of 1915* (London and Berkeley: The Lowie Museum of Anthropology and Scolar Press, 1983); Sarah J. Moore, *Empire on Display: San Francisco's Panama-Pacific International Exposition of 1915* (Norman: University of Oklahoma Press, 2013); Laura Ackley, *San Francisco's Jewel City: The Panama-Pacific International Exposition of 1915* (Berkeley, CA: Heyday, 2015). A recent book that places the exposition in social and political context is Abigail M. Markwyn, *Empress San Francisco: The Pacific Rim, the Great West, and California at the Panama-Pacific International Exposition* (Lincoln: University of Nebraska Press, 2014).

4 Quote from Frank Morton Todd, *The Story of the Exposition: Being the Official History of the International Celebration Held at San Francisco in 1915 to Commemorate the Discovery of the Pacific Ocean and the Construction of the Panama Canal* (New York: Knickerbocker Press, 1921), vol. 3, 309.

5 Lawrence J. Vale and Thomas J. Campanella, "Introduction: The Cities Rise Again" and "Conclusion: Axioms of Resilience," in *The Resilient City: How Modern Cities Recover from Disaster*, ed. Vale and Campanella, 3–23 and 335–55 (New York: Oxford University Press, 2005), 16–17, 344; Robert W. Kates and David Pijawka, "From Rubble to Monument: The Pace of Reconstruction," in *Reconstruction Following Disaster*, ed. Eugene J. Haas, Robert W. Kates, and Martyn J. Bowden, 1–23 (Cambridge, MA: MIT Press, 1977), 3.

6 Panama-Pacific International Exposition Company, "The Panama Pacific International Exposition Celebrating the Opening of the Panama Canal at San Francisco in 1915," (1913), carton 72, folder 3, Panama-Pacific International Exposition Records, BANC MSS C-A 190, Bancroft. Unless otherwise stated, archival sources cited in this chapter are from this collection and abbreviated as PPIE Records, Bancroft.

7   Todd, *Story of the Exposition*, vol. 1, 158.

8   Gunther Barth applied the term *instant city* to San Francisco (and Denver) in his classic *Instant Cities: Urbanization and the Rise of San Francisco and Denver* (New York: Oxford University Press, 1975).

9   "Reconstruction Plans," *Organized Labor*, May 12, 1906; Judd Kahn, *Imperial San Francisco: Politics and Planning in an American City, 1897–1906* (Lincoln: University of Nebraska Press, 1979), 205–7.

10   John P. Young, *San Francisco: A History of the Pacific Coast Metropolis* (San Francisco: S. J. Clarke Publishing Company, 1912), 862, 906.

11   Ibid., 927–28; Roger Olmsted, Nancy L. Olmsted, and Allen Pastron, *San Francisco Waterfront: Report on Historical Cultural Resources for the North Shore and Channel Outfalls Consolidation Projects* (San Francisco: December 1977), 128, 350–71.

12   On the use of earthquake debris to fill Mission Bay and lands to the south of burned district, see Christopher Morris Douty, *The Economics of Localized Disasters: The 1906 San Francisco Catastrophe* (New York: Arno Press, 1977), 225; and Peter Cohen, "Transformation in Industrial Landscape: San Francisco's Northeast Mission," M.A. thesis, San Francisco State University, 1998, 72. On Islais Creek, see Major William W. Harts Report to Brigadier General A. Mackenzie, April 25, 1907, RG 77, Box 23, folder 3, NASF. On the dumping of debris in Marina Cove as more myth than fact, see Stephen Tobriner, *Bracing for Disaster: Earthquake-Resistant Architecture and Engineering in San Francisco, 1838–1933* (Berkeley, CA: Heyday Books, 2006), 264–66.

13   Richard L. Humphrey, "The Effects of the Earthquake and Fire on Various Structures and Structural Materials," in *The San Francisco Earthquake and Fire of April 18, 1906 and Their Effects on Structures and Structural Materials*, 14-61 (Washington, DC: Government Printing Office, 1907), 59.

14   Fitzpatrick is quoted in Tobriner, *Bracing for Disaster*, 188. Andrea Rees Davies, *Saving San Francisco: Relief and Recovery after the 1906 Disaster* (Philadelphia: Temple University Press, 2012), 117. In 1911–1912 the Board of Public Works worried about the large numbers of "temporary" structures still in use within the fire limits. "Report of the Board of Public Works, 1911–1912," 971.

15   Tobriner, *Bracing for Disaster*, 207–20, 236–40. Tobriner maintains that San Francisco architects and engineers implemented changes after the disaster, but even his evidence seems to indicate the limited scope of improvements. Hansen and Condon, *Denial of Disaster*, 137; Ted Steinberg, *Acts of God: The Unnatural History of Natural Disaster in America* (New York: Oxford University Press, 2000), 36; Marilyn Chase, *The Barbary Plague: The Black Death in Victorian San Francisco* (New York: Random House, 2003), 195.

16   "Report of the Board of Public Works, 1907–1908," 676–80; National Board of Fire Underwriters, *Report on the City of San Francisco, California* (July 1910), 18.

17   "Report of the Board of Public Works, 1913–1914," 395–97.

18 "Fire Commissioners' Report, 1907–1908," 328; "Fire Commissioners' Report, 1909–1910," 791–93; "Chief Engineers' Report, Fire Commissioners' Report, 1910–1911," 753–54; "Fire Commissioners' Report, 1911–1912," 336–38; "Chief Engineers' Report, Board of Fire Commissioners, 1912–1913," 361; "Chief Engineers' Report, Fire Commissioners' Report, 1913–1914," 493–95. All are from the *San Francisco Municipal Reports*.

19 Robert W. Righter notes that public power was a major issue as well, with proponents of municipal control fearing that private power companies would gain control over Hetch Hetchy and Lake Eleanor; see Righter, *The Battle over Hetch Hetchy: America's Most Controversial Dam and the Birth of Modern Environmentalism* (New York: Oxford University Press, 2005), 6, 37–44.

20 "Report of the Department of Public Works, 1902–1903," 405–70. For a detailed recounting of the political debates over Hetch Hetchy, see Righter, *Battle over Hetch Hetchy*.

21 "Report of the Department of Public Works, 1902–1903," 404; "San Francisco Water Supply Investigation," *Appendix to the San Francisco Municipal Reports for the Fiscal Year 1902–1903*, 1074–78; "Report of the Department of Public Works, 1903–1904," 391; National Board of Fire Underwriters, *Report on the City of San Francisco, California*, 10–11.

22 Herman Schussler, *The Water Supply of San Francisco, California, before, during and after the Earthquake of April 18th, 1906, and the Subsequent Conflagration* (New York: Martin B. Brown Press, July 23, 1906), 19, 42. Derleth's piece was from *Engineering News*, May 17, 1906.

23 *Coast Seamen's Journal*, January 19, 1910, 6; Gray Brechin, *Imperial San Francisco: Urban Power, Earthly Ruin* (Berkeley: University of California, 1999), 109–10. Righter notes that San Francisco found it difficult to sell the bonds to finance the project; see Righter, *Battle over Hetch Hetchy*, 135.

24 Brechin, *Imperial San Francisco*, 113–16.

25 Todd, *Story of the Exposition*, vol. 1, 300. The reference to 70 acres referred specifically to the area of the cove. An additional 114 acres were reclaimed in the Presidio.

26 Ibid., vol. 1, 34–41; Young, *San Francisco: A History of the Pacific Coast Metropolis*, 927–31.

27 Harbor View Improvement Association, "Success of Exposition Depends on Location," pamphlet in scrapbook of Willard E. Worden, *The Exposition Site, San Francisco 1915*, n.p., Bancroft.

28 Flyer in Worden, *Exposition Site;* Tunnel Committee of the Civic League of Improvement Clubs of San Francisco, *Tunnels: Gateways to the Greater San Francisco* (n.d., 1913?), 12, carton 155, folder 32, PPIE Records, Bancroft; Marjorie M. Dobkin, "A Twenty-Five-Million-Dollar Mirage," in Benedict, *Anthropology of World's Fairs*, 84 (63–93).

29 Quoted in Todd, *Story of the Exposition*, 129–30; Markwyn, *Empress San Francisco*, 63–74.

30 A. H. Markwart, "The Organization and Description of the Panama-Pacific International Exposition, San Francisco" (July 30, 1913), 25–26, carton 60, folder 17; "Annual Report of the Law Department," March, 1, 1913, carton 170, folder 29; Legal Department, "Sixth Semi-monthly Report," October 8, 1912, carton 170, folder 29; and "President's Office Report of Activities," September 5, 1912, 4–5, carton 66, folder 14, PPIE Records, Bancroft. See also Todd, *Story of the Exposition*, vol. 1, 283.

31 Telegram from James D. Phelan to Mrs. Oelrichs and Mrs. W. K. Vanderbilt, December 29, 1911; Telegram from William H. Crocker to Ogden Mills, January 2, 1912; and Telegram from Charles C. Moore to McNab, January 4, 1912, carton 61, folder 36. Panama-Pacific International Exposition Division of Works, "Notes on Site Restoration with Particular Reference to the Properties of Virginia Vanderbilt and Theresa A. Oelrichs of New York" (January 1916): 1, carton 61, folder 38. "Indenture of Lease Between Virginia Vanderbilt and Panama Pacific International Exposition" (January 1912); Letter from Director of Works to Tobin, April 13, 1912, carton 61, folder 35, PPIE Records, Bancroft.

32 President's Office Report, September 5, 1912; Director of Works to Comptroller, January 13, 1913, carton 66, folder 22; F. S. Brittain to Buildings and Grounds Committee, January 13, 1913, carton 61, folder 32; and Land Department notes, February 15, 1913, carton 67, folder 7, PPIE Records, Bancroft. See also Ackley, *San Francisco's Jewel City*, 18–19.

33 Letter from Mrs. Mary E. Suters to Board of Commissioners, April 19, 1912, carton 61, folder 32, PPIE Records, Bancroft.

34 Letter from G. H. Umbsen & Co. to PPIE Co., April 11, 1912, carton 156, folder 6; and Land Department notes, February 15, 1913, April 23, 1913, PPIE Records, Bancroft.

35 R. G. Brodrick to Harris Connick, September 27, 1912, carton 61, folder 34, PPIE Records, Bancroft; Markwart, "Organization and Description of the Panama-Pacific International Exposition," 25–26.

36 Land Department, "The Official Area of the Entire Exposition Site," n.d., 1–2, carton 62, folder 2, PPIE Records, Bancroft. Some sources state the area of the exposition as 625 acres. Todd, *Story of the Exposition*, vol. 1, 299–300.

37 The final composition of the fill averaged 72 percent sand. Charles L. Reynolds, "Report on Hydraulic Fill at Harbor View," typescript, San Francisco, October 14, 1912, 1–3, 6–7, 9–13, 85–112, BANC MSS 98/89 c, Bancroft.

38 "Engineering and Construction Features of the Panama-Pacific International Exposition," pamphlet, San Francisco Association of Members of the American Society of Civil Engineers, February 19, 1915, carton 60, folder 8, PPIE Records, Bancroft.

39 Tunnel Committee of the Civic League of Improvement Clubs of San Francisco, *Tunnels: Gateways to the Greater San Francisco*; "Hand of Destiny Points

to Harbor View," unidentified newspaper clipping, July 13, 1913, carton 155, folder 31, PPIE Records, Bancroft.

40 Letter from Mrs. W. Smith, September 10, 1913, carton 155, folder 28; and "Who Wants the Fillmore Street Tunnel and Why" (1913), carton 155, folder 29, PPIE Records, Bancroft.

41 Resolution No. 10392 (New Series), San Francisco Board of Supervisors, September 22, 1913. Ackley states that the Exposition Company joined the opposition to the tunnel after realizing that it would become responsible for paying any extra assessments on land that it had leased; see Ackley, *San Francisco's Jewel City*, 46.

42 In building the Twin Peaks tunnel, contractors had to install a system of piles and braces where the excavation cut through an old fill near 18th and Hattie Streets. Anthony Perles, *The People's Railway: The History of the Municipal Railway of San Francisco* (Glendale, CA: Interuban Press, 1981), 42, 63–70.

43 "Engineering and Construction Features of the Panama-Pacific International Exposition."

44 Moore, *Empire on Display*, 95.

45 Letter from Alexander G. McAdie to Chairman and Members of the Architectural Board, February 20, 1912, carton 64, folder 51, PPIE Records, Bancroft.

46 Markwart, "Organization and Description of the Panama-Pacific International Exposition," 63, 68; "Draft Indenture of Lease between Hartland Law and Anglo-American Securities Company with Panama Pacific International Exposition Company" (1911), 7, carton 61, folder 35, PPIE Records, Bancroft.

47 Tobriner, *Bracing for Disaster*, 267–68.

48 PPIE Company Division of Works, "Memorandum of Activities in Connection with the Construction of the Panama Pacific International Exposition Company," June 10, 1913, 4–5, carton 60, folder 32; Progress Report from E. E. Carpenter to Connick, March 29, 1913, 6, carton 67, folder 24, PPIE Records, Bancroft. Markwart, "Organization and Description of the Panama-Pacific International Exposition," 25, 67–68; San Francisco Association of Members of the American Society of Civil Engineers, "Engineering and Construction Features of the Panama-Pacific International Exposition"; L. F. Leurey, "Soft-Ground Foundations, Panama-Pacific International Exposition," *Engineering News* 72, no. 5 (July 30, 1914): 250–54; Todd, *Story of the Exposition*, vol. 4, 160–61.

49 Todd, *Story of the Exposition*, vol. 1, 339.

50 Letter from Director of Works to Park Commissioners, Golden Gate Park, April 28, 1915, carton 64, folder 65; and Letter from F. W. Krogh to Guy L. Bayley, November 8, 1915, carton 64, folder 65, PPIE Records, Bancroft.

51 PPIE Company Division of Works, "Memorandum of Activities in Connection with the Construction of the Panama Pacific International Exposition Company," 5–6; Todd, *Story of the Exposition*, vol. 2, 8.

52   Markwart, "Organization and Description of the Panama-Pacific International Exposition," 88–90; "Chief Engineer's Report, Fire Commissioners' Report, 1913–1914," 492–93.

53   Letter from Vice-Chairman, Buildings and Grounds Committee, to Board of Public Works, June 7, 1912, carton 64, folder 53; Letter from H. Connick to C. C. Moore, November 30, 1912, and Letter from Connick to Joseph Cummings, November 11, 1913, carton 64, folder 43; and PPIE Division of Works to US War Department and Treasury Department, December 8, 1913, carton 64, folder 39, PPIE Records, Bancroft.

54   Letter from A. H. Kohler to Surgeon J. D. Long, US Public Health Service, May 1, 1914, and Letter from Long to Moore, September 29, 1914, carton 64, folder 54; Letter from C. C. Pierce to Surgeon General, May 8, 1915, and Letter from Pierce to H. Connick, November 30, 1915, carton 64, folder 56, PPIE Records, Bancroft.

55   Donald McLaren, "Gardening Features of the Panama-Pacific International Exposition," *Pacific Service Magazine* 6, no. 2 (July 1914): 39 (39–45); Panama-Pacific International Exposition Company Division of Works, "Memorandum of Activities in Connection with the Construction of the Panama Pacific International Exposition Company," 22; Progress Report from E. E. Carpenter to Connick, November 27, 1912, carton 67, folder 22, PPIE Records, Bancroft; Todd, *Story of the Exposition*, vol. 1, 308–11.

56   Barbara VanderWerf, *Granada, a Synonym for Paradise: The Ocean Shore Railroad Years* (El Granada, CA: Gum Tree Lane Books, 1992), 175; Ben Macomber, *The Jewel City: Its Planning and Achievement; Its Architecture, Sculpture, Symbolism, and Music; Its Gardens, Palaces, and Exhibits* (San Francisco: John H. Williams, 1915), 41. White sand from Santa Cruz was reportedly heated to tint it pink.

57   Todd, *Story of the Exposition*, vol. 1, 161–62; Rose Virginia Stewart Berry, *The Dream City: Its Art in Story and Symbolism* (San Francisco: Walter N. Brunt, 1915), 12–13.

58   Macomber, *Jewel City*, 15; John D. Barry, *The City of Domes* (San Francisco: John J. Newbegin, 1915), 10; George Starr, "Truth Unveiled: The Panama Pacific International Exposition and Its Interpreters," in Benedict, *Anthropology of World's Fairs*, 162 (134–75).

59   Todd, *Story of the Exposition*, vol. 3, 309.

60   Ibid., vol. 4, 158; Panama Pacific International Exposition Company, *Information for Visitors* (San Francisco: Panama Pacific International Co., 1913).

61   Letter from McAdie to the Architectural Board, February 20, 1912.

62   Todd, *Story of the Exposition*, vol. 2, 247–53, 265; Ackley, *San Francisco's Jewel City*, 60. Such unusually heavy and persistent rains may have represented an El Niño year.

63   Panama Pacific International Exposition Company, *Panama Pacific International Exposition, San Francisco, 1915* (San Francisco, 1914); Markwart,

"Organization and Description of the Panama-Pacific International Exposition," 72–73; Gray Brechin, "Sailing to Byzantium: The Architecture of the Fair," in Benedict, *Anthropology of World's Fairs*, 98 (94–113).

64   Macomber, *Jewel City*, 101.

65   Moore, *Empire on Display*, 9; Ackley, *San Francisco's Jewel City*, 245–46.

66   Todd, *Story of the Exposition*, vol 2, 357; vol. 4, 106, 109–10, 113.

67   Ibid., vol. 5, 99; vol. 2, 72–78; vol. 3, 49.

68   Ibid., vol. 3, 48; Ackley, *San Francisco's Jewel City*, 316–17; Brechin, "Sailing to Byzantium," 99.

69   Todd, *Story of the Exposition*, vol. 5, 231–32.

70   Starr, "Truth Unveiled," 161.

71   Todd, *Story of the Exposition*, vol. 3, 167; Draft of argument for preserving part of exposition site (1916?), carton 156, folder 28, PPIE Records, Bancroft.

72   Todd, *Story of the Exposition*, vol. 5, 146–47, 246–47; Panama-Pacific International Exposition Division of Works Misc. document re: post-Exposition, n.d., 7, carton 57, folder 6, PPIE Records, Bancroft.

73   Panama-Pacific International Exposition Division of Works, "Notes on Site Restoration," 1–2; Panama-Pacific International Exposition Division of Works, Misc. document re: post-Exposition, 26–27; Letter from Tobin to Markwart, January 7, 1916; and Letter from Markwart to Hale, August 15, 1916, carton 61, folder 38, PPIE Records, Bancroft.

74   Panama-Pacific International Exposition Division of Works, "Notes on Site Restoration," 6–8. Lease between Hartland Law and Anglo-American Securities Company and Panama-Pacific International Exposition Company, February 15, 1912, carton 155, folder 22; and Panama-Pacific International Exposition Division of Works, Misc. report re: site restoration, n.d., 3–5, carton 57, folder 6, PPIE Records, Bancroft.

75   Letter from Assistant Director of Works to Herbert Edward Law, December 18, 1915, carton 61, folder 37; and R. C. Maclachlan, "Report on the Meeting of the Exposition Site Property Owners" (January 1916), 1–5, carton 62, folder 2, PPIE Records, Bancroft. "Great Coup Wins Marina Ground," *San Francisco Examiner*, November 14, 1916.

76   Resolution on preservation of Marina, n.d., 1, carton 156, folder 30, PPIE Records, Bancroft.

77   Todd, *Story of the Exposition*, vol. 5, 252.

78   Tobriner, *Bracing for Disaster*, 268.

79   Robert W. Rydell, *All the World's a Fair: Visions of Empire at American International Expositions, 1876–1916* (Chicago: University of Chicago Press, 1984), 209; Martyn John Bowden, "The Dynamics of City Growth: An Historical Geography of the San Francisco Central District, 1850–1931," Ph.D. diss., University of California, Berkeley, 1967, 530–37.

80   "Earthquakes," *Transactions of the Commonwealth Club of California* 16, no. 10 (December 1921): 347 (347–85).

81   A. C. Lawson, "Shifting Movements of the Earth," and Bailey Willis, "The Next Earthquake," *Transactions of the Commonwealth Club of California* 16, no. 10 (December 1921): 358, 375–79.

82   C. Derleth Jr., "Earthquake Engineering," *Transactions of the Commonwealth Club of California* 16, no. 10 (December 1921): 369–73.

83   Tobriner, *Bracing for Disaster*, 220.

84   Robert W. Kates, Neil J. Ericksen, David Pijawka, and Martyn J. Bowden, "Alternative Pasts and Futures," in *Reconstruction Following Disaster*, ed. Eugene J. Haas, Robert W. Kates, and Martyn J. Bowden, 207–60 (Cambridge, MA: MIT Press, 1977), 252; Carl-Henry Geschwind, *California Earthquakes: Science, Risk, and the Politics of Hazard Mitigation* (Baltimore: Johns Hopkins University Press, 2001), 23–32.

CONCLUSION

1   The Loma Prieta quake was originally believed to have occurred on the San Andreas, but subsequent research suggests it may have been the rupture of a nearby fault. Susan Elizabeth Hough, *Finding Fault in California: An Earthquake Tourist's Guide* (Missoula, MT: Mountain Press Publishing Company, 2004), 78–80. As with many large earthquakes, estimates of the magnitude have been adjusted. The quake was originally estimated at magnitude 7.1. In general, such statistics offer a false sense of precision as numbers vary in diferent authoritative sources. Even the number of fatalities ranges from sixty-three to sixty-seven. See, for example, "Earthquake Damage, Loma Prieta Earthquake, October 1989," US Department of Commerce, National Oceanic and Atmospheric Administration, and National Geophysical Data Center, 1990(?), part 2; National Research Council, "Overview: Lessons and Recommendations from the Committee for the Symposium on Practical Lessons from the Loma Prieta Earthquake," in *Practical Lessons from the Loma Prieta Earthquake* (Washington, DC: National Academies Press, 1994), 1.

2   The death toll from the Cypress freeway collapse would almost certainly have been much higher if traffic had not been unusually light because of the World Series. *The Quake of '89: As Seen by the News Staff of the San Francisco Chronicle* (San Francisco: Chronicle Books, 1989), 3–39; John McPhee, *Assembling California* (New York: Farrar, Strauss, and Giroux, 1993), 295–302; William P. McGowan, "Fault-Lines: Seismic Safety and the Changing Political Economy of California's Transportation System," *California History* 72, no. 2 (Summer 1993): 171 (170–93).

3   "Earthquake Damage, Loma Prieta Earthquake, October 1989."

4   McGowan, "Fault-Lines," 171–90.

5   Kevin Starr, *Golden Gate: The Life and Times of America's Greatest Bridge* (New York: Bloomsbury Press, 2010), 191–93.

6   Stephen K. Harris and John A. Egan, "Effects of Ground Conditions on the

Damage to Four-Story Corner Apartment Buildings," in *The Loma Prieta, California, Earthquake of October 17, 1989—Marina District*, US Geological Survey Professional Paper 1551-F (1992), F181–185; J. P. Bardet, M. Kapuskar, G. R. Martin, and J. Proubet, "Site-Response Analysis," in *The Loma Prieta, California, Earthquake of October 17, 1989—Marina District*, F87–F88; McPhee, *Assembling California*, 302.

7   Charles R. Scawthorn, Keith A. Porter, and Frank T. Blackburn, "Performance of Emergency-Response Services after the Earthquake," in *The Loma Prieta, California, Earthquake of October 17, 1989—Marina District*, F195–F213; Thomas D. O'Rourke, "Introduction," in *The Loma Prieta, California, Earthquake of October 17, 1989—Marina District*, F4; Thomas D. O'Rourke, Jonathan W. Pease, and Harry E. Stewart, "Lifeline Performance and Ground Deformation during the Earthquake," in *The Loma Prieta, California, Earthquake of October 17, 1989—Marina District*, F159.

8   G. Wayne Clough, James R. Martin II, and Jean Lou Chameau, "The Geotechnical Aspects," in *Practical Lessons from the Loma Prieta Earthquake*, 29–68 (Washington, DC: National Academies Press, 1994), 32. The fills in the former Mission Bay did hold up surprisingly well in 1989 (ibid., 38).

9   Scawthorn, Porter, and Blackburn, "Performance of Emergency-Response Services after the Earthquake," F214; National Research Council, "Overview: Lessons and Recommendations from the Committee for the Symposium on Practical Lessons from the Loma Prieta Earthquake," 5; H. T. Taylor, J. T. Cameron, S. Vahdani, and H. Yap, "Behavior of the Seawalls and Shoreline during the Earthquake," in *The Loma Prieta, California, Earthquake of October 17, 1989—Marina District*, F152; McPhee, *Assembling California*, 252.

10   National Research Council, "Overview: Lessons and Recommendations from the Committee for the Symposium on Practical Lessons from the Loma Prieta Earthquake," 8, 13; Clough, Martin, and Chameau, "Geotechnical Aspects," 41.

11   Scawthorn, Porter, and Blackburn, "Performance of Emergency-Response Services after the Earthquake," F201-202, F206, F214.

12   For a discussion of the 1994 Northridge earthquake and seismic hazards in Los Angeles, see Mike Davis, *Ecology of Fear: Los Angeles and the Imagination of Disaster* (New York: Vintage Books, 1998).

13   Robert B. Olshansky, "Land Use Planning for Seismic Safety: The Los Angeles County Experience, 1971–1994," *Journal of the American Planning Association* 67, no. 2 (Spring 2001): 173–85; Carl-Henry Geschwind, *California Earthquakes: Science, Risk, and the Politics of Hazard Mitigation* (Baltimore, MD: Johns Hopkins University Press, 2001).

14   N. A. Toké, C. G. Boone, and J. R. Arrowsmith, "Fault Zone Regulation, Seismic Hazard, and Social Vulnerability in Los Angeles, California: Hazard or Urban Amenity?" *Earth's Future* 2 (2014): 440–57.

15   City of Colton, *Hazard Mitigation Plan* (July 2011), 45–49; Hough, *Finding*

Fault in California, 27–32; Rong-Gong Lin II, "Two Active Southern California Faults May Cause a Big One by Rupturing Together," *Los Angeles Times*, March 17, 2016.

16 City and County of San Francisco, *Hazard Mitigation Plan* (November 2014), 31, 110.

17 Thomas Fuller, "In San Francisco, a Sinking Skyscraper and a Deepening Dispute," *New York Times*, September 22, 2016; Lauren Smiley and Joe Eskenazi, "The Big Sink," *San Francisco Magazine*, October 21, 2016.

MANUSCRIPT COLLECTIONS

I consulted material from the following archives and collections in researching this book. Abbreviations used for archives are noted in parentheses.

Bancroft Library, University of California, Berkeley (Bancroft)
    1906 San Francisco Earthquake and Fire Digital Collection
    Andrea Sbarboro Papers, BANC MSS G-D 5180
    Andrew C. Lawson Papers, BANC MSS C-B 602
    California Department of Industrial Relations, Division of Immigration
        and Housing Records, BANC MSS C-A 194
    Charles L. Reynolds, "Report on Hydraulic Fill at Harbor View," BANC
        MSS 98/89 c
    Committee for Housing the Homeless, BANC MSS 95/194c
    Edward Livingston Papers, BANC MSS 2010/921
    Eli T. Sheppard papers and related family material, BANC MSS 71/253 cz
    James D. Phelan Papers, BANC MSS C-B 800
    Josephine Fearon Baxter, letter to her parents in Omaha, Nebraska, BANC
        MSS 73/122 c:94
    Panama-Pacific International Exposition Records, BANC MSS C-A 190
    San Francisco earthquake and fire pamphlets
    William Douglas Alexander, letter to his sister, Mary C. Alexander, San
        Francisco, BANC MSS C-Z 133
California Historical Society, North Baker Research Library, San Francisco
    (CHS)
    Dr. René Bine Papers, MS 3640
California State Archives, Office of the Secretary of State, Sacramento (CSA)
    Department of Public Health, State Board of Health, Executive Secretary,
        F3676:1 C1810-C1811
California State Library, Sacramento (CSL)
Labor Archives and Research Center, San Francisco State University, San
    Francisco (LARC)
National Archives at San Francisco, San Bruno (NASF)
    US District Court, RG 21

Office of the Chief of Engineers, RG 77
Public Health Service, RG 90
Office of the Surgeon General, RG 112
San Francisco History Center, San Francisco Public Library (SFPL)
Society for the Preservation and Appreciation of San Francisco Refugee
Shacks Archive, SFH 9

INDEX

Note: San Francisco is abbreviated "SF" in subentries.

culture of risk, 6–7, 8, 31, 50–51, 83, 273–74.
   See also hazards, human agency in; risk,
   reduction of
Cushing, William, 4
Cypress Freeway collapse, 271–72, 340n2

Daly, John, 123
Daly City, 123, 126
Dana, Richard Henry, 23
D'Ancona, A. A., 136
Davies, Andrea Rees, 76, 97, 285n32,
   308n93
Davis, Mike, 19
Derleth, Charles, Jr., 79–80, 81, 82, 245,
   268–69
Devine, Edward T., 16, 87, 91, 96, 97
disaster capitalism: after 1860s earthquakes,
   43; concept of, xii, 12, 166, 285n29; Panama
   Pacific International Exposition, 247–48;
   and public control, 166–67, 179–80, 196–
   97; in rebuilding efforts, 180–84, 197;
   United Railroads, 175–76, 319n30. *See
   also* streetcar strike of 1907
"disaster suburbanization," 122–25, 308n93
disaster tourism, 146*fig.*, 159–61
discrimination. *See* race, class, and ethnic
   tensions
disease, 147, 196, 199, 217, 236. *See also*
   epidemics
donations for relief, 87–88, 91–92
dynamite, use of in firefighting, 62–63

earthquake cottages, 108, 113–16, 120, 124,
   278, 306n72, 307n75
earthquake country, 6–7, 8, 16, 43, 51, 81, 83,
   276
earthquake denial, 76–81, 82
"earthquake love," 94–95, 182
earthquakes: attitudes toward, 30–31, 44–
   45, 68–70, 81–83, 267–70; characteristics,
   7, 70–71, 73–75, 82; in the 1800s, 39, 40–
   44, 42*fig.*, 290n68, 291n76; preparedness,
   275, 298n58. *See also* liquefaction; Loma
   Prieta earthquake; natural disasters; San
   Francisco earthquake of 1906; seismic
   risk in San Francisco area; seismology
Eaves, Lucile, 111
economic crisis of 1907–1908, 167, 192–96,
   197, 322n79
economic growth, 77, 80–81, 139–44, 156–
   57, 173, 192. *See also* recessions; urban
   development

Edgemar, 122, 123, 126, 308n95
Edgerton, Henry, 38
elastic rebound theory, 77
Elks' response to plague, 214
environmental equity, 14, 15–16; during the
   earthquake and fire, 75–76; in relief process, xi, 98, 108, 116, 125, 127, 278; tunnel
   development, 253. *See also* race, class, and
   ethnic tensions; vulnerability
environmental history, 8–10, 165, 283nn17–
   18, 317n3
environmental justice and injustice, xii–
   xiii, 86, 87, 96–98, 127, 131–32, 150–51,
   298n58, 299n3
environmental racism, 131, 132, 149, 154, 162,
   298n58, 313n44. *See also* Chinatown; race,
   class, and ethnic tensions; vulnerability
epidemics, 199, 202–3, 206, 213, 233, 325n11,
   326n29, 328n54. *See also* bubonic plague;
   Chinatown; disease; war on rats
Erikson, Kai, 8
Exposition Preservation League, 264

Fair, James G., 237, 248–49
Fairbanks, Harold W., 21
Farnham, Eliza W., 25
Federal Reserve, 323n83
Felton, Katherine C., 91, 97, 111
Ferry Building, 70, 71, 297n51
fill. *See* made land; subsidence
Fillmore Street tunnel, 253–54
Finance Committee, 91
fire department, x, 34, 58, 242–43, 273
firefighting, 30, 33, 34, 62–63, 64, 289n48
fire ordinances, 30, 34, 240
fire protection, 30, 31, 43, 45, 52, 66, 256.
   See also risk, reduction of
fires: after 1906 earthquake, 59–64, 65, 65*fig.*
   (*See also* San Francisco earthquake of
   1906); Great Fire of 1851, 31–32, 32*fig.*; as
   known hazard, 5, 29–34, 52, 240, 241–42,
   279, 334n14. *See also* San Francisco, early
   development of
firestorms, 62
Fisk, Henry A., 222
Fitzpatrick, F. W., 241–42
fleas, 199, 203–4, 232, 325n13
flour scandal, 89
food supply, 84, 88–89, 93–94, 95, 303n30
Ford, Tirey L., 174
forgetting past history, xiii, 53, 240, 241–42,
   255, 270, 279, 334n14

sanitation; streets and transportation infrastructure; technology; urban ecosystems

insurance, 78, 193–94, 195, 262–63

Irish immigrants, 14, 48, 64, 82, 92, 99. *See also* Mission district; South of Market district; Yorke, Peter C.

Irvine, Leigh H., 179

Islais Creek district, 47, 135, 228, 230, 241

Italian immigrants: in camps, 99, 104, 105*fig.*, 107; districts of residence, 14, 48, 328n55; livelihoods, 88, 222, 225, 226, 227; and plague, 207; rebuilding efforts, 110; relief efforts, 92; resistance to sanitary regulations, 217–18, 233. *See also* Lobos Square camp; North Beach; Telegraph Hill

Jacobs, James Madison, 56

James, William and Susan, 118, 124

Jefferson Square camp, 84–85, 96, 103*fig.* *See also* refugee camps

Jewish immigrants, 14

Jordan, David Starr, 21, 68

Kahn, Judd, 190

Kates, Robert W., 309n3

Keane, Augustin C., 209, 216, 222, 235–36, 327n34

Kearney, Denis, 146

Kearney, Stephen Watts, 24

Kellner, Andrew, 183

Kellogg, Wilfred H., 202

Kelly, Mary: as activist, 86, 89, 96, 108–9, 115*fig.*, 117, 125–26, 127; camp conditions, 100, 101, 102, 103*fig.*; experience after earthquake, 84–85; housing and relocation, 114–16, 118, 120. *See also* women's activism

Kelman, Ari, 10

King, Cameron, 63

Kinyoun, Joseph J., 149, 202

Kipling, Rudyard, 49

Klebingat, Fred, 229, 241

Klein, Naomi, 176, 285n29

labor disputes, 80, 166, 172–75, 183–84. *See also* organized labor; streetcar strike of 1907

laborers, 181, 182, 191–92, 193, 194, 195. *See also* organized labor

Lammot, Robert Smith, 25

Latin Quarter, 6, 99, 110, 207

Law, Hartland, 265–66

Lawson, Andrew C., 69, 268

Leach, Frank A., 66

legislation, 22–23, 24, 245, 274–75

Leonard, George L., 113

Liang, Hugh Kwong, 62

lifelines, disruption of, 85, 87, 127

liquefaction, 73, 272, 273, 276. *See also* earthquakes; made land

Livingston, Edward, Sr., 94

Lobos Square camp, 99, 118, 120, 207, 209, 221, 257, 308n88. *See also* Italian immigrants; refugee camps

Loma Prieta earthquake (1989), 271–74, 277, 340nn1–2. *See also* earthquakes

London, Jack, 4, 61–62

Look Tin Eli, 159

looting, 90, 145, 146*fig.*, 301nn15–16

Lotchin, Roger W., 28

Macomber, Ben, 261

made land: building on piles, 28–29, 34, 35, 37, 38, 71, 79, 255–56, 265; earthquake damage, 59, 73–74; Manson's rebuilding plan, 142; Mission district, 46, 341n8; Panama Pacific International Exposition, 239, 241, 246, 249, 251–52, 254–56, 258, 265–66, 270, 336n37; population on, in 1906, 49; risks of, 37, 41–42, 82–83, 279; waterfront development, 34–39. *See also* liquefaction; mud flats and salt marshes; San Francisco, early development of; San Francisco, geology of; seismic risk in San Francisco area; subsidence; urban construction

Maloney, Thomas A., 178

Manson, Marsden, 141, 161

Manson's plan to rebuild San Francisco, 141–44. *See also* rebuilding San Francisco

man traps, 38

Marina district, 266, 270, 272–73, 276

maritime commerce, 22–23

Markwart, Arthur H., 255

Marshall, James, ix, 27

Martinez, Maria Antonio, 22

McAdie, Alexander G., 3, 255, 260

McArthur, Walter, 96

McCarron, Louise, 102

McCarthy, Patrick H., 191

McKenna, Benjamín Vicuña, 28

Pardee, George C. (governor), 69, 91, 156
parks, 47, 85, 103–4, 117, 134–35, 142–43, 310n13. *See also* Golden Gate Park; national parks; refugee camps
Petersen, John A., 192
Phelan, James D.: Chinese relocation, 152–53; disputes with United Railroads, 175–76, 319n29; municipal authority, 143; recovery efforts, 91, 130; relationship with labor, 173, 190; vision for SF, 27, 132–33, 138, 139, 162. *See also* Progressivism
Pijawka, David, 309n3
plague. *See* bubonic plague
Plume, E. J., 80
Plummer, Fred G., 81
pneumonic plague, 234, 332n103. *See also* bubonic plague
"politicized domesticity," 97
politics of place, 13, 158, 161–63, 285n30. *See also* Chinatown; rebuilding San Francisco
Porter, Robert Langley, 230
Potrero Hill district, 47, 48, 100, 129, 229
poverty and disease, 207, 208, 209, 221
Powell, Henry N., 57
power and resistance. *See* immigrant populations; refugee activism; women's activism; working-class activism
Presidio district, 99–100, 103, 104, 252, 257, 335n25
Progressivism, x, 12–13, 16, 111, 133–34, 141, 236. *See also* Burnham plan; City Beautiful movement; Panama Pacific International Exposition; Phelan, James D.
public health education, 209, 214–18, 326n29
public transportation. *See* streets and transportation infrastructure
Purkitt, J. H., 18, 38

quarantines, 149–50, 202, 212, 314n50

race, class, and ethnic tensions: class stratification, 74–75, 85, 121; in grant giving, 111–12; history of discrimination, 156, 284n28; housing practices, 13–14, 117–26, 151–52, 306n72; as policy, 155; in providing relief, 95, 99, 100, 116, 145; resilience affected by, 127; scapegoating, 147–49; in SF neighborhoods, 48–49; and social unity, 94; suburban locales, 123, 124–25. *See also* Chinatown: calls to relocate;

environmental equity; environmental racism; relief efforts; social control; vulnerability
racial integration, 129–30, 161
racialized space, 144–52, 162
racial violence, 146, 154–55, 156
Rafferty, John, 64
railroads, 46, 79, 88, 146, 178, 292n93, 321n57; specific companies, 123, 126, 182, 196–97, 214. *See also* United Railroads
Raker Act (1913), 245
Ralston, William, 43
rats: habitat and behavior, 198, 205, 206, 208*fig.*, 326n20; in Panama Pacific International Exposition site, 257, 262; spread of disease, 202, 203, 206. *See also* animals in the city; war on rats
rebuilding San Francisco: after 1868 earthquake, 43–44; as creative destruction, 131; disaster capitalism in, 180–84, 320n43; and politics of place, 161–63; question of, 130, 309–10n3; streets, 167–72; Telegraph Hill, 110. *See also* Burnham plan; Chinatown; Manson's plan to rebuild San Francisco; politics of place
recessions, 194–96. *See also* economic growth
reconstruction. *See* creative destruction; rebuilding San Francisco
Red Cross. *See* American Red Cross
Reed, S. Albert, 59
refugee activism, 14, 96–98, 108, 114–16, 115*fig.*, 120, 125–26, 186, 304n43. *See also* women's activism; working-class activism
refugee camps: camp restaurants, 95, 96; exhibits on, 261–62, 263; official and makeshift, 98, 101*fig.*; open land and parks for, 103–4, 117; outdoor living, 100–102, 101*fig.*, 304n39, 304n43; populations, 99–100; poverty and transience, 278; sanitation, 104–8, 305n49. *See also* Golden Gate Park; Harbor View camp; Jefferson Square camp; Lobos Square camp; Mission district; parks; relief efforts; Richmond district; San Francisco earthquake of 1906; Telegraph Hill; working-class people
refugees: attitudes toward, 95–96; economic, 109; entrepreneurial actions, 113, 307n74; escaping the fire, 60–61; relocations, 109, 117–26, 119*fig.*, 170–71,